This groundbreaking book, authored by Asians from every part of the vast continent, will be standard reading for every Asian student of theology in the evangelical tradition for years to come. But its importance will inspire Asian evangelical scholars as well, and students and scholars from other ecclesial and theological traditions. Rooted in the tradition of the wider church, it embraces Asian methods and concerns in a generous, responsible, and creative way.

Stephen B. Bevans, PhD
Louis J. Luzbetak, SVD Professor of Mission and Culture,
Catholic Theological Union, Chicago, Illinois, USA

This groundbreaking book is not vaguely Christian nor parochially Asian. It is, rather, the effort of leading Asian theologians to articulate Christian faith in terms that are biblically rooted, committed to historic orthodoxy, contextually engaged, and suffused with evangelical zeal. As we continue in the "Asian Century," the future of Christianity will be increasingly shaped by Asian Christians such as those writing in this volume. As this book shows, the future is bright because Asian Christianity is theologically rigorous and missiologically driven, something the Western churches would seriously benefit from imbibing. Well done to the editors Timoteo D. Gener and Stephen T. Pardue for assembling such a fine collection of essays by a sterling group of leading Asian theologians of Christ. This book is simply mandatory reading for anyone interested in theology from the global church, missions, cross-cultural ministry, or serving in multi-cultural settings.

Rev Michael F. Bird, PhD
Academic Dean and Lecturer in Theology,
Ridley College, Melbourne, Australia

Asian Christian Theology: Evangelical Perspectives is a groundbreaking selection of theological reflections from Asia. The sixteen authors represent a wide variety of Asian contexts and include pastors and church leaders as well as seminary professors, offering a historically informed biblical and evangelical take on Asian realities. The first section provides a competent survey of traditional theological themes in biblical and historical perspective. But it is the second section of articles on contextual topics that constitutes the special contribution of this book. Tackling key topics, often by means of compelling case studies – spirits, traditional cultures and identity, interfaith conversations, the public sphere – the authors show the exciting emergence of a truly Asian voice in theology. The editors aim to present a biblical faith for Asian believers; some of us hope and pray this solid presentation of Asian theology will also be read by North American (and European and African) believers. *Asian Christian Theology* makes an important contribution to that global conversation.

William Dyrness, PhD
Senior Professor of Theology and Culture,
Fuller Theological Seminary, Pasadena, California, USA

It is with enormous pride that I commend this book to you. We find here a much-needed compendium of contemporary evangelical thinking on many of the key theological issues that define Christianity in Asia today. It is a rare privilege to have, in one book, contributions from some of today's outstanding Asian creative and biblical thinkers. May the insights found here trickle down to the churches and contribute to helping the growing church in Asia to mature in depth, relevance and national influence.

Ajith Fernando, ThM
Teaching Director, Youth for Christ, Sri Lanka

Decentering the dominant strands of the Western theological tradition in the practice of evangelical theology is of utmost importance for its witness to the gospel among the people of every tribe and nation. This volume contributes admirably to that task by offering a rich and compelling collection of essays on a full range of theological topics and concerns from the perspectives of Asian evangelical theologians. As such, it makes a significant contribution to the formation of a global Christian faith that deserves to be widely read and contemplated, particularly by those interested in the future of evangelical theology.

John R. Franke, PhD
General Coordinator, The Gospel and Our Culture Network

With steady growth in recent decades, evangelicalism in the world's largest continent has come of age. This compendium of essays, with leading evangelical theologians from various parts of this vast continent writing on topics traditional in theology – from revelation and Trinity to Christology – and issues of contemporary concern such as culture, religious plurality, and immigration, is an amazing treasure of voices and insights. What is particularly noteworthy about the book is the presence of comparative theology throughout the discussions of various topics. Unlike most evangelicals, those from Asian soil are accustomed to reflecting on and framing their Christian theology in a sympathetic and critical dialogue with the teachings of other living faiths. This is mandatory reading not only for evangelicals in the global church but also for everyone who wishes to keep updated about the latest theological developments.

Veli-Matti Kärkkäinen, Dr Theol Habil
Professor of Systematic Theology,
Fuller Theological Seminary, Pasadena, California, USA
Docent of Ecumenics, University of Helsinki, Finland

Evangelical theology that is "biblically rooted, historically aware, and contextually relevant" has at times been considered unattainable. But this book effectively demonstrates a mode of Asian reflection and theologizing that supports classical theology and compels us to be more committed to biblical truth.

Jung-Sook Lee, PhD
President, Torch Trinity Graduate University, Seoul, South Korea

This book contains sixteen distinguished essays succinctly addressing not only the classical dogmas ranging from revelation to eschatology, but also a variety of contemporary issues on culture and mission. They speak from a shared Asian identity, with an earnest commitment to be "biblically rooted, historically aware, contextually engaged, and broadly evangelical." A "must read" for all seminary faculty, students, and alumni, whether you are of the Majority World or in the post-Christian West.

Rev Stephen Lee, PhD
President and Lam Ko Kit Tak Professor of Biblical Studies,
China Graduate School of Theology, Hong Kong

Studying and doing theology in ways appropriate and relevant to the Asian situation has been limited for the longest time by the lack of Asian resources and our dependence on systematic theology books from the West. Finally, here is a textbook on Christian theology written by Asian theologians for the Asian church! Written from an evangelical perspective, it engages the worldviews shaped by the frameworks of major Asian religions and traditional cultures, as well as addressing the contemporary challenges and issues confronting churches in Asia. An excellent resource on thinking theologically in context, I highly recommend this to be required reading in Bible colleges and seminaries as it will definitely help in equipping leaders who are not only rooted in the evangelical tradition but are also responsive to the contextual realities in Asia.

Theresa Lua, EdD
General Secretary, Asia Theological Association

This book is for anyone who cares deeply about making disciples and planting churches in Asia – the most populous and diverse continent in the world. Considering the unprecedented growth of Asian Christianity and the bewildering cultural and religious diversity of the region, we need more books like this that model for us what it looks like to be faithful to the gospel and mindful of the context in which it is delivered. Covering a wide range of topics from Christology to pneumatology to ecclesiology, this volume serves a guide to reflective practitioners who desire to be "biblically rooted, historically aware, contextually engaged, and broadly evangelical." I wish that this volume had been written sooner, and I hope that more like it will be published in the future.

Steve Murrell, DMin
Founding Pastor, Victory Manila, Philippines
Cofounder and President, Every Nation Churches & Ministries

If you are being challenged by the pressures of secular society, or by the uncertainty of the uniqueness of the gospel, or you want to know why the churches in Asia continue to grow under persecution, then this book will help you reset your mission compass. In the first eight chapters, eight well-known Asian theologians explore contemporary theological issues from their biblical foundations, through the history of the church and on to their missiological goal of effective witness to their Hindu, Buddhist and Muslim neighbours. This book marks evangelical mission theology breaking new ground. It embraces the authority of Scripture and the work of the triune God in revelation as creator, sustainer, redeemer, the church and our eschatological hope. In the second eight chapters, the writers outline how Asian churches live with suffering and persecution and have developed their own theology of mission. Practical insights into the lives of Christians across Asia in the context of the public square, poverty, religious pluralism, cultural identity and demonic power are a goldmine of information inspiration and hope.

It is essential for theological students and their teachers wanting to develop their own theology of mission to study this book.

Bruce J. Nicholls, PhD
Senior Adviser, Asia Theological Association

Here is a fantastic and timely example of incarnational theology, in which the Asian church articulates what it means to be faithful, relevant and effective in its time and place. This is a much-needed exercise in all global Christianity, and we thank our Asian sisters and brothers for providing such an excellent precedent and stimulus. This book is a "must read" not only for Asian church leaders, theologians, theological educators and theology students, but for anyone wanting to deeply understand how contemporary Asian Christianity is responding to its challenges today.

Marvin Oxenham, PhD
General Secretary, European Council for Theological Education
Director, ICETE Academy
Educationalist, London School of Theology, UK

This is an important publication not only for the Asian Church but for the global church. For too long, Western theology has set the agenda for theological discussion in the Majority World, while important contextual issues in the Majority World have not been addressed. *Asian Christian Theology: Evangelical Perspectives* begins to offer a corrective as it provides a robust engagement with some of the best insights of Western evangelical scholarship while also contextually engaging with issues, questions, and concerns within Asian contexts. The volume certainly succeeds in its goal of being "biblically rooted, historically aware, and contextually engaged, and broadly evangelical" and serves as a model for how to engage the church not just theologically but also missiologically.

Rev Andrew Prince, PhD
Director of Centre for Asian Christianity,
Brisbane School of Theology, Australia

As the church continues to grow in Asia, there is need for continued reflection on the changeless meaning of Scripture in a changing world. This book, featuring leading Asian scholars, offers fresh and relevant theological reflection on the significant issues facing the church throughout our region. Each chapter offers constructive answers to the complexities of Asian realities from an evangelical perspective. It is the best book on contextual theology to date!

Joseph Shao, PhD
President Emeritus, Biblical Seminary of the Philippines
4th General Secretary, Asia Theological Association

With the stunning rise of the Asian church in our day, we welcome this remarkable collection of essays which remind us that evangelical theology is part of a global confession which encircles the world and traces back to the apostolic faith of the earliest Christians. Nevertheless, this collection is no mere echo chamber of Western theologizing. Rather, while fully resonating with historic faith, it nevertheless speaks with clarity and fresh insight into the new shape of evangelical theology for the 21st century. The volume is distinctive in that it not only addresses traditional themes such as Christology, pneumatology and eschatology, but it also speaks seamlessly and compellingly about evangelical perspectives on emigrant communities, public theology and interfaith dialogue. This is truly a wonderful collection of essays and a timely contribution to the global church!

Timothy C. Tennent, PhD
President and Professor of World Christianity,
Asbury Theological Seminary, Wilmore, Kentucky, USA

Born in the vibrant evangelical theological culture of the Asian churches, these essays faithfully engage the gospel on issues of distinctive significance in Asia. The theology expressed here is at once deeply biblical, alert to life-giving voices of the global and historic church, engaged with Asian cultures and contexts, and above all, rooted in the gospel. What falls apart in less careful hands, coheres in these essays around common confession of the Lordship of Christ and love for where in the world the authors bear witness.

Rev Richard R. Topping, PhD
Principal and Professor of Studies in the Reformed Tradition,
Vancouver School of Theology, British Columbia, Canada

This book is a wonderful testimony to the work of representative evangelical theologians striving to balance the importance of staying focused on the text of Scripture and the traditions of its interpretation ("Christian") while simultaneously engaging the demands and complexities of their various contexts ("Asian"). The editors achieve this balance by asking half the contributors to engage biblical doctrines and the other half realities on the ground that are particularly relevant to Asian Christians. The book as a whole provides further welcome evidence of the truth of Andrew Walls's observation that each time the gospel is understood in a new context, the whole church – east, west, north, and south – benefits.

Kevin J. Vanhoozer, PhD
Research Professor of Systematic Theology,
Trinity Evangelical Divinity School, Deerfield, Illinois, USA

Asian Christian Theology: Evangelical Perspectives is not just interesting reading but is a timely publication. Over the last few decades, Christians in Asia have come to realize that good exegesis alone is not enough in the task of mission. We must also enter into dialogue with the local culture and context. That context is, by and large, dominated by two realities here in Asia – poverty and religious plurality. In this collection of essays, each of which deals with a selected tenet of the Christian faith, the author first sets out historic Christian thought but then turns to the task of relating that thinking to the context. The end product is a book that is a comprehensive theological treatise, and will certainly prove to be both informative and useful, especially to those who are concerned with the witness of the church to the grace of God manifested in Jesus Christ.

Brian C. Wintle, PhD
Former Regional Secretary, Asia Theological Association, India
Former Principal, Union Biblical Seminary, Pune, India

With this outstanding volume, the Asia Theological Association adds sparkling crown jewels to its long and expanding heritage of significant publications. The contributors amply live up to the editors' claim "to offer an approach to Christian theology that is biblically rooted, historically aware, contextually engaged, and broadly evangelical." Indeed, the book provides some very refreshing reflections on what the word "evangelical" still means, and ought to mean, in a world where the term has become so compromised and besmirched. This richly informative collection is not only a gift to Asian Christian churches and seminaries from some of their own finest theologians, it is also a most welcome gift from the Asian church to the global Christian community. And for that reason it ought to be in the libraries and syllabi of seminaries anywhere that are serious about hearing and understanding mature theological voices outside the echo chambers of the western academy. Thank you, ATA, for such a feast of living theology!

Christopher J. H. Wright, PhD
International Ministries Director, Langham Partnership

If we are honest, almost all the books used for teaching theology or Christian doctrine in our seminaries come from the West. Thus they are unable to speak with penetration and power to the felt needs and existential cries of Asia. Significantly, this present collection of papers by evangelical scholars, all of whom are native Asians and have worked in Asia, comes across with a very different feel. The essays are defined by the four parameters of being "biblically rooted, historically aware, contextually engaged, and broadly evangelical." This engagement with biblical, historical and contextual materials has resulted in some fine explorations of theology firmly rooted in the Asian soil. Hopefully, many of these essays will be given more extensive treatment and developed into full-fledged volumes in their own right. I commend this book most warmly and pray that in turn it will contribute to the wider development of truly contextual Asian Christian theologies.

Hwa Yung, PhD
Bishop Emeritus, The Methodist Church in Malaysia

Asian Christian Theology

Asian Christian Theology

Evangelical Perspectives

General Editor
Timoteo D. Gener

Associate Editor
Stephen T. Pardue

© 2019 Timoteo D. Gener and Stephen T. Pardue

Published 2019 by Langham Global Library
An imprint of Langham Publishing
www.langhampublishing.org

Langham Publishing and its imprints are a ministry of Langham Partnership

Langham Partnership
PO Box 296, Carlisle, Cumbria, CA3 9WZ, UK
www.langham.org

Published in partnership with Asia Theological Association

ATA
QCC PO Box 1454 – 1154, Manila, Philippines
www.atasia.com

ISBNs:
978-1-78368-643-8 Paperback
978-1-83973-187-7 Hardback
978-1-78368-672-8 ePub
978-1-78368-673-5 Mobi
978-1-78368-674-2 PDF

Timoteo D. Gener and Stephen T. Pardue have asserted their right to be identified as Author of the Editors' part in the Work in accordance with sections 77 and 78 of the Copyright, Designs and Patents Act 1988. The Contributors have also asserted their right to be identified as Author of their portion in the Work.

All rights reserved. No part of this publication may be reproduced, stored in a retrieval system or transmitted, in any form or by any means, electronic, mechanical, photocopying, recording or otherwise, without the prior written permission of the publisher or the Copyright Licensing Agency.

Requests to reuse content from Langham Publishing are processed through PLSclear. Please visit www.plsclear.com to complete your request.

All Scripture quotations, unless otherwise indicated, are taken from the Holy Bible, New International Version®, NIV®. Copyright ©1973, 1978, 1984, 2011 by Biblica, Inc.™ Used by permission of Zondervan.

Scripture quotations marked NRSV are from the New Revised Standard Version Bible, copyright © 1989 National Council of the Churches of Christ in the United States of America. Used by permission. All rights reserved.

Scripture quotations marked RSV are from Revised Standard Version of the Bible, copyright © 1946, 1952, and 1971 National Council of the Churches of Christ in the United States of America. Used by permission. All rights reserved.

Scripture quotations marked NKJV are from New King James Version (NKJV). Copyright © 1982 by Thomas Nelson, Inc. Used by permission. All rights reserved.

British Library Cataloguing-in-Publication Data
A catalogue record for this book is available from the British Library
ISBN: 978-1-78368-643-8

Cover & Book Design: projectluz.com

Langham Partnership actively supports theological dialogue and an author's right to publish but does not necessarily endorse the views and opinions set forth here or in works referenced within this publication, nor can we guarantee technical and grammatical correctness. Langham Partnership does not accept any responsibility or liability to persons or property as a consequence of the reading, use or interpretation of its published content.

CONTENTS

Foreword..xv

Acknowledgments xvii

Introduction...1
    Timoteo D. Gener and Stephen T. Pardue

Part I: Doctrinal Themes

1   Divine Revelation and the Practice of Asian Theology.............13
    Timoteo D. Gener

2   On the Doctrine of Scripture: An Asian Conversation............39
    Havilah Dharamraj

3   The Trinity in Asian Contexts...................................61
    George N. Capaque

4   Christology in Asia: Rooted and Responsive 83
    Ivor Poobalan

5   Creation, New Creation, and Ecological Relationships............101
    Ken Gnanakan

6   Lord and Giver of Life: The Holy Spirit among the Spirits in Asia....119
    Wonsuk Ma

7   Toward An Asian Evangelical Ecclesiology......................139
    Simon Chan

8   Eschatology and Hope in Asia 157
    Roland Chia

Part II: Contemporary Concerns

9   A Theology of Suffering and Mission for the Asian Church........181
    Kar Yong Lim

10   Cultural Identity and Theology in Asia........................199
    Lalsangkima Pachuau

11   Jesus and Other Faiths 221
    Ivan Satyavrata

12 God's *Basileia* in Asia's *Res Publica*: Situating the Sacred in
    Asia's Public Sphere. 245
    Aldrin M. Peñamora

13 Finding Home for the Unhomed: Helping Diaspora Communities
    Discover Identity and Belonging 265
    Juliet Lee Uytanlet

14 Hans Frei's Typology of Theology for Religious Encounters in
    Asian Contexts 279
    Kang-San Tan

15 Theology in a Context of Radical Cultural Shift: A Chinese
    Reflection. 297
    Carver T. Yu

16 Reconciliation and the Kingdom of God: Reflections from the
    Middle East 315
    Salim J. Munayer

Contributors. 337

Index of Names 343

Index of Subjects 347

Index of Scripture 351

Foreword

This is a very significant book for the Asian Church for two reasons. First, it emphasizes what classical Christianity is to the vast non-Christian population in Asia, where there has been much misunderstanding regarding the true identity of the faith. Second, it seeks to present biblically rooted theology against the inroads of theological trends and other popular belief systems which confuse the hearts and minds of many Asian Christians today.

What characterizes the Asian region? Asia is the largest continent, with 60 percent of the total world population of over 7.6 billion people. It is divided into five major regions: North East Asia, South East Asia, South Asia, Central Asia, and West Asia with the population of over 4.5 billion people in forty-four nations. Asia is also remarkably diverse, with multiple racial, cultural, historical, and religious backgrounds represented throughout.

All the living religions in the world today exist in Asia: Hinduism, Buddhism, Islam, Confucianism, Taoism, Shintoism, and Animism, along with Christianity. There seems to be a movement among governments in Asia to revive these traditional religions out of a desire to unify the different ethnic tribes and peoples within their jurisdictions. Moreover, since all nations in Asia except Japan and Thailand were under the Western and Japanese colonial rule for many years, these nations also seek the preservation of their indigenous cultures, particularly through traditional religions, customs, and traditions.

Christianity is a minority faith in Asia, with roughly 7 percent of the population. The Asian church has been attacked in many parts of Asia, not only physically but also ideologically by government officials, religious fanatics, traditional intellectuals, and secularists. Many Asians still believe that Christianity is a foreign religion, imported by Western missionaries through Western colonialism. At the same time, rapid church growth in a number of Asian nations in recent years, especially in South Korea, China, the Philippines, Singapore, and some Islamic nations, has attracted much attention.

In addition, globalization in the areas of world economy, mass communication, and travel has made the world into a "global village." The rapid economic development and many changes in Asian nations today create new challenges for the Asian church. They must find new ways to meet the constantly changing political, economic, social, intellectual, and religious environment.

The church thus faces enormous external challenges. Yet it also faces challenges from within, particularly through the spread and influence of theological beliefs and practices that are inconsistent with biblical teaching. The Asian evangelical church has been facing multiple theological challenges from mainline Christianity. In the name of contextualization and local theologies, many have ultimately devalued the gospel and the Bible, turning them into mere human ethical constructs and ideals. In the process, the uniqueness of Christ as Lord and Savior is denied or de-emphasized.

Notwithstanding their differences, the circumstances of Asian Christians are similar in many ways to that of the early church, which faced marginalization from the non-Christian environment as well as heretical teachings from within the church. In response, the Apologists, such as Justin Martyr and Irenaeus of Lyons, sought to defend biblical faith from enemies without and within.

The Asia Theological Association has sought to encourage the development of Asian contextual theologies that achieve a balance of being classically biblical yet contemporarily relevant. Its previous books have had significant impact already: *The Bible and Theology in Asian Contexts* (1984), *God in Asian Contexts* (1988), *Light for Our Path* (2013), and *Jesus among the Nations* (2017). In a fitting continuation of this work, *Asian Christian Theology: Evangelical Perspectives* seeks to present biblical faith for Asian believers, providing clarity amid the many confusing challenges facing the Asian church today. To God be the glory!

Rev Bong Rin Ro, ThD
AGST-Pacific President
ATA General Secretary (1970–1990)
WEA Theological Commission Moderator (1990–1996)

Acknowledgments

Assembling a book like this is far beyond the capacities that we as editors bring to the table. Thus, we wish to thank here the many individuals and organizations who helped make this volume possible. First, we wish to thank the Board of ATA Publications, especially Dr Rico Villanueva and Dr Theresa Lua, for fostering the vision for this book in the first place. We also thank Langham Publishing, especially Pieter Kwant and Vivian Doub, for recognizing the strategic value of the project and offering their capable support.

We must also thank publishers who have permitted versions of previously published works to appear in modified form here. Ken Gnanakan's "Creation, New Creation, and Ecological Relationships" is largely drawn from an essay by the same name that previously appeared in *Emerging Voices in Global Christian Theology*, ed. William Dyrness (Grand Rapids: Zondervan, 1994). Roland Chia's "Eschatology and Hope in Asia" previously appeared in his book, *Hope for the World: The Christian Vision* (Carlisle, UK: Langham Global Library, 2012). Portions of Kang-San Tan's "Hans Frei's Typology of Theology as a Heuristic Tool for Religious Encounters in Asian Contexts" appeared previously in "The Christian Challenge of Religious Encounter," *Connections: The Journal of the WEA* 5 (December 2006): 54–58. Portions of Carver T. Yu's, "Theology in a Context of Radical Cultural Shift: A Chinese Reflection," previously appeared in "Redeemer and Transformer: The Relevance of Christ for China's Cultural Renewal and Liberation," in *Diverse and Creative Voices: Theological Essays from the Majority World*, eds. Dieumeme Noelliste and Sung Wook Chung (Eugene, OR: Pickwick, 2015), 67–83.

We are also grateful to our families – Caroline, Mia, Chelsea and Emil, and Teri, Ava, Lucy, Simon, and Ivy – who have sacrificed to make space in our lives for this project over the last two years; to our churches, where we have learned to speak of and live before God in the context of Asian realities; and most of all to the authors of these essays, who labored in love to make this final product possible.

Introduction

Timoteo D. Gener and Stephen T. Pardue

The church in Asia is rising. Whereas a century ago, Asian Christians represented only a tiny fraction of the overall Christian population, roughly one out of every eight Christians worldwide now lives in Asia. This is a slightly greater fraction of the world Christian population than North America represents.[1] While Christians remain a minority in most Asian nations, the Asian church continues to grow rapidly – about 13,000 new Christians per day on average. Given this growth, experts predict that the Asian Christian population will balloon to over 500 million by 2050, by which time Christians will represent over 10 percent of the Asian population as a whole.[2]

Moreover, some of the most dramatic growth in the church worldwide is among Asian evangelical Christians in particular. For example, out of all the countries with the highest growth rates of evangelical Christians, three of the top four are in Asia – Mongolia, China, Nepal – with each nation putting up stunning growth rates of about 15 percent per year (on average) from 1970 to 2010.[3] The growth of the Asian evangelical church is also reflected in the expansion – both in numbers and in strength – of Asian evangelical seminaries and Bible colleges. The Asia Theological Association, the primary accrediting body for such institutions, now counts over three hundred member schools dedicated to training leaders for the growing evangelical church. Evangelical scholars at these institutions are increasingly influencing the global theological conversation, in addition to wielding influence in local conversations about politics and ethics.

Even so, much work remains in supporting the flourishing of evangelical theology in the Asian church. Although Christians in Asia now outnumber their

---

1. Pew Research Center, "Global Christianity: A Report on the Size and Distribution of the World's Christian Population," http://www.pewforum.org/2011/12/19/global-christianity-exec/, accessed 14 February 2019.

2. Todd M. Johnson and Gina A. Zurlo, eds., *World Christian Database* (Leiden: Brill, 2019), accessed 14 February 2019.

3. Gina A. Zurlo, "Demographics of Global Evangelicalism," in *Evangelicals around the World: A Global Handbook for the 21st Century*, ed. Brian C. Stiller et al. (Nashville: Thomas Nelson, 2015), 42.

counterparts in North America, evangelical theological resources still reflect an almost exclusively North American outlook. Very few theological resources that reflect classically evangelical commitments are deeply engaged with the issues that are of distinctive significance for the Asian church. Meanwhile, those theological resources that are deeply engaged with distinctively Asian realities have often failed to share the high view of Scripture and other commitments that evangelicals prize. In the context of an expanding and strengthening Asian church, then, this book has a simple goal: to offer an approach to Christian theology that is biblically rooted, historically aware, contextually engaged, and broadly evangelical.

These four characteristics deserve some explanation, as they help clarify the through lines connecting all the essays in this book. First, every essay in this volume is committed to the notion that Scripture is the norming norm for theology, the very Word of God spoken to and for the church. It is not merely *a* source for theology, to be tamed and formed to fit the conveniences of the moment; it is *the* source against which all other sources must ultimately be measured.

Scholars have rightly noted in recent years that it is a complex matter to discern what exactly it means for theology to be biblically rooted. To be sure, it must involve more than mere proof-texting – the listing of various verses plucked out of context in support of specific theological claims. Such a method is susceptible to the manipulation of the contemporary theologian, who can often find out-of-context support for almost any claim they wish to support. Further, this method ultimately glosses over the beautiful and wild diversity of authorship, genre, and historical provenance that we find in the Christian Scriptures.

If this is not what it means for theology to be biblically rooted, then what does it mean? In short, we can say that Christian teaching is biblically rooted inasmuch as it reflects deep study of Scripture, which is to be viewed as a unified but diverse testimony to the drama of creation, fall, redemption, and restoration in Christ. The essays in this volume achieve this in different ways – reflecting the authors' diverse denominational commitments, cultural backgrounds, and disciplinary training – but they all seek the same goal: ensuring that their treatment of their subject reflects not only professional expertise, but a deep acquaintance with the biblical text.

A second unifying characteristic of all the essays in this volume is their commitment to historical awareness. None of the essays in this book pretend to offer a theology that starts *de novo*, as if we could or should, with the aid of Scripture alone, develop a completely novel approach to Christian teaching.

Instead, the authors operate under the assumption that we can and must gain important insight from our fathers and mothers in the faith and that it is only at our great peril that we can either reject the best insights of previous Christian reflection or ignore the failures of the past.

Of course, this need not mean slavish mimicry of the creeds and theological conclusions of the past. It is true that the world of a Christian living in twenty-first-century Asia is radically different from the world in which most Western theology emerged. Today's church has concerns unanticipated by its forebears, and many teachings once considered critically important are now rightly regarded as relatively minor. Contemporary theology, then, especially in the emerging churches of the Majority World, must be free to find its own way of expressing the classical Christian faith.

But even as all of the essays in this book reflect a willingness to develop theology in new directions, none pursue this task without attention to the best insights of the past. Where the Nicene Creed speaks to the topic of an essay, for example, the essay will reference the relevant portion of the Creed and reflect on how it should inform present discussion. Similarly, essays on topics unrelated to creedal affirmations will draw from the broad sweep of Christian tradition to gain insight and traction in responding to contemporary concerns.

In addition to being biblically rooted and historically aware, all of these essays are also committed to producing theology that is contextually engaged. At a minimum, this commitment is rooted in a practical reality: theology exists to serve the church, and the church does not exist in a vacuum. If theologians are to be of any benefit to the church at all, then, they must communicate Christian teaching in understandable terms, and must address the most pressing questions of a given context or culture. This is the kind of "contextualization" that evangelicals have long vocally supported, given their desire to see the whole world fully grasp the rich beauty of the gospel.

But as you will see, the essays in this book do not merely seek to engage culture in the *delivery* of theology. If this were the goal, a mere translation of some Western theology texts might suffice. Instead of such surface-level engagement, the authors of this volume are all committed to bringing the faith into deep acquaintance with Asian cultures and contexts. As Hwa Yung argued decades ago, the goal is not "banana" theology – Asian on the outside, but Western on the inside – but "mango" theology, in which the very formation and articulation of Christian doctrine emerges out of a serious engagement with Asian cultures and realities.[4]

---

4. Hwa Yung, *Mangoes or Bananas? The Quest for an Authentic Asian Christian Theology*, 2nd ed. (Maryknoll: Orbis, 2014). Originally published in 1997.

This commitment is not rooted in political correctness or a mere passion for diversity. In fact, it is as old as Christianity itself. The New Testament – with its four gospels, each articulating the good news to a distinctive audience, for example – bears the conspicuous markings of a faith that sees strength rather than weakness in contextual engagement. Moreover, as Andrew Walls has demonstrated, the earliest Christians showed a remarkable willingness not only to translate Scripture into diverse languages immediately, but also to permit the development and articulation of Christian teaching by means of local terms.[5] Rather than seeking some supracultural articulation of the faith, they recognized that there was tremendous power in the words, concepts, and imagery furnished by their local cultures. Moreover, as the church developed into a worldwide phenomenon in the centuries after Christ, they sought – in their best moments – to make the most of their remarkably diverse constituency by holding "ecumenical" (which could be translated as "worldwide") councils. Christians have thus classically affirmed that theology must be local – in that it makes sense to, and addresses the concerns of, its immediate community – while also being catholic – taking seriously the commitments and concerns of the wider body of Christ scattered across space, culture, and time.

In these essays, then, you will see snapshots of deep engagement between the Christian faith and the realities of cultures all over Asia. You will see how the gospel challenges local beliefs and customs, but also how our understanding of the gospel and its implications is enriched and deepened through engagement with distinctively Asian realties. In addition, you will observe authors working to move between local insights and catholic (i.e. universally Christian) sensibilities, and back again, noting where there may be tension, and seeking to articulate a way forward.

Finally, in addition to being biblically rooted, historically aware, and contextually engaged, the essays in this volume are all broadly evangelical. This term is currently the source of significant dispute, but we believe it is worth continuing to use. What does it mean when we use it? One of the best answers is provided by John Stott. Fundamentally, Stott argues, to be "evangelical" is to be concerned with the trinitarian gospel: "the revealing work of God the Father, the redeeming work of God the Son, and the transforming ministry of God the Holy Spirit."[6] Yet evangelicals do not merely affirm these truths

---

5. Andrew F. Walls, "Old Athens and New Jerusalem: Some Signposts for Christian Scholarship in the Early History of Mission Studies," *International Bulletin of Missionary Research* 21, no. 4 (1997): 146–153.

6. John Stott, *Evangelical Truth: A Personal Plea for Unity, Integrity and Faithfulness*, rev. ed. (Carlisle, UK: Langham Publishing, 2013), 11.

in the abstract – confessing that the triune God has acted once and for all in order to reveal, redeem, and transform. Rather, as "gospel people," evangelicals are committed to speaking of and living before God in light of these realities. "It is because we have grasped the finality of what God has said and done in Christ," Stott explains, that we insist on the primacy of Scripture, the centrality of the atoning work of Christ, and the power of the Holy Spirit to transform us as God's people.[7]

Of course, to identify evangelicalism in terms of these commitments only tells half the story, for evangelicals are not only held together by shared belief. The other part of the story is that evangelicalism is a specific, historical movement, birthed in the midst of the church's varying responses to modernity. As church historian Timothy Larsen has noted, to be evangelical is to identify in some way with the "tradition of global Christian networks arising from the eighteenth-century revival movements associated with John Wesley and George Whitefield."[8] Specifically, then, the essays in this book seek to do theology in a manner consistent with the values and commitments of those "global networks." Here in Asia, the most prominent of these may be the Asia Theological Association, the Lausanne Movement, and the World Evangelical Alliance.

Plan of the Book

Having sketched the goals of this book fairly broadly, we are now in a position to identify the specific path by which the book seeks to achieve those goals. As readers will note, the sixteen essays of the book divide neatly into two sections: while the first eight essays offer distinctive takes on traditional topics often used in Christian theology – from revelation to Christology to eschatology – the final eight essays focus not on these traditional loci, but on topics in which Asian evangelicals will have distinctive interest. In this way, we hope that the book offers a double model for the future flourishing of Asian evangelical theology – first by reassessing traditional areas of Christian teaching in light of the Asian church's distinctive needs and resources, and second by revising the very areas of focus themselves, recognizing that while the gospel is the same, its implications must be newly realized in every generation and place.

---

7. Stott, *Evangelical Truth*, 16.

8. Timothy Larsen, "Defining and Locating Evangelicalism," in *The Cambridge Companion to Evangelical Theology*, eds. Timothy Larsen and Daniel J. Treier (Cambridge: Cambridge University Press, 2007).

The first half of the book kicks off with Timoteo D. Gener's essay on revelation, that doctrine that drives all Christian theology forward. Gener surveys recent developments in the doctrine of revelation, both in Asia and around the globe, and offers a vision for how Asian theologies can simultaneously hold onto their distinctive Asianness – which is tied up in part with allowing Asian experience to serve as a theological resource – but also to give enduring priority to the primacy of divine revelation in Christ and Scripture. Havilah Dharamraj's essay is a fitting complement, offering readers an account of the doctrine of Scripture that is exceptionally engaged in the details – both in terms of articulating the beautiful complexity of the Christian canon, and also in terms of articulating the material similarities and differences between Christian Scripture and other sacred texts in Asia.

The next four essays offer analysis of the God we worship and his primary works. George Capaque and Ivor Poobalan treat the Trinity and Christology respectively, offering first a summary of the history of the doctrines, and then providing a survey of the proposals on offer within the Asian context. In both cases, they find many of these proposals problematic, but ultimately also commend specific approaches that can provide a productive way forward. Ken Gnanakan offers a rich account of Scripture's view of creation and humanity's place within it, and on the basis of that analysis, offers a number of specific recommendations for the Asian church in particular, which is grappling at the moment with its place in contemporary conversations about climate, ecology, and creation care. Wonsuk Ma's essay fittingly follows up this treatment of creation by addressing the "Lord and giver of life," the Holy Spirit. Ma offers an insightful treatment of the history of the doctrine of the Holy Spirit in Asia, and offers several paths forward for continuing to develop this underappreciated aspect of Christian teaching.

Simon Chan and Roland Chia conclude this section of the book by focusing respectively on Christian teaching related to the church (ecclesiology) and last things (eschatology). Chan makes a compelling case that evangelicals generally, and in Asia specifically, have given far too little consideration to the church. To move forward in this area, Chan contends, we need a richer sense of what the church *is* (its ontology), rather than merely focusing on what the church *does* (its function). Chia examines the Christian teaching of "last things" through the lens of Christian hope. In a region that is often characterized by pervasive suffering and uncertainty, it is critical that Asian Christians grasp and articulate what it means to hope in the good unfolding plan of God to redeem all things through the power of Christ and the blood of his cross.

The second half of the book starts with an extended reflection on three pressing realities for Asian Christians: suffering, struggles around cultural identity, and tension with other world religions. Suffering is a reality for all Christians, but one of special import in a region where Christians are routinely marginalized and persecuted. Lim's perspective is focused especially on how suffering can and must inform a theology of mission for the Asian church, a critical topic at a moment when the Asian church is increasingly taking over the global missionary workforce. Lalsangkima Pachuau, meanwhile, focuses on the difficult and sometimes awkward questions that Asian Christians routinely face as they confront the apparent conflicts between their cultural identities (which are often also tied up with religion) and their allegiance to Christ. Readers are sure to benefit from his analysis of these issues, both in terms of clarifying their thinking about culture and theology, and also in terms of the practical challenge of transforming cultures increasingly into the image of Christ. Yet in most places in Asia, bearing witness to the triune God of the gospel creates more than just cultural tension – it ultimately sets Christians in direct conflict with at least some of the religious beliefs of their families, neighbors, and communities. Ivan Satyavrata argues that in the third millennium, Christians have no choice but to engage in such interfaith relationships with both courage and sensitivity. While it may be tempting simply to set religious differences aside in favor of a bland affirmation of all belief systems, he wisely charts a course that takes religious diversity seriously while still humbly bearing witness to the uniquely good news of Christ.

The next three essays focus less on the struggles of Asian Christians, and more on the unique opportunities before them. In many nations in the region, the evangelical church is growing, and is, for the first time, gaining the opportunity to influence public policy and debate. In this context, Aldrin Peñamora notes the absence of, and seeks to sketch out, a coherent vision for, evangelical engagement in the Asian public square. While we rightly view the consummation of God's kingdom as a future reality, we must also grapple with the imperative to seek the good of our cities and nations, and to bear witness to the Lordship of Christ over all. Meanwhile, Juliet Uytanlet contends that in our current political realities, Asian evangelicals must grapple with remarkably large and strategic populations of people in diaspora. In the migrant, we must not only see echoes of our own reality (as strangers in a strange land, with no place to lay our heads), but also a strategic mission field in need of the eternal identity, belonging, and rootedness available only in Christ. Finally, Kang-San Tan returns to the Christian's interactions with the world's religions. Whereas Satyavrata focused on addressing the tension of personal engagement with those of other faiths, Tan complements this view by outlining a theoretical framework for understanding the Christian relationship to other religions. Ultimately, he contends, the Asian context presents Christian theologians with a unique opportunity: to know their own faith more deeply even as they engage with sincere adherents of other faiths.

The book concludes with two essays that speak to the promise of Asian evangelical theology for addressing problems that are not unique to Christianity, but are recognized globally as serious threats to human flourishing: globalization and conflict. Carver Yu takes on two specific threats tied closely to globalization: the loss of local cultural identities, and the emergence of unbridled capitalism and materialism. These threats are felt in distinctive ways in twenty-first-century China, but they are also profoundly universal. Similarly, while Yu's response to these issues is rooted in part in the need to draw from the Chinese cultural tradition, his approach – drawing from the rich heritage of Christian theology while also attending to local resources – will be of interest to readers from all over the region. Finally, Salim Munayer offers hard-won expertise on the matter of reconciliation in light of the biblical-theological theme of the kingdom of God. By examining one of the most vexing instances of conflict in the world – the ongoing Palestinian-Israeli conflict – Munayer offers a Christocentric model for reconciliation that readers will be able to appreciate and apply in many contexts.

It was a joy and privilege to work with so many fine scholars from such a wide variety of denominations, cultures, and disciplinary backgrounds. We don't agree on everything, but the journey of learning to do theology together has been well worth the price of admission for us. We trust the same will be true for you.

References

Hwa Yung. *Mangoes or Bananas? The Quest for an Authentic Asian Christian Theology*. 2nd edition. Maryknoll: Orbis, 2014.

Johnson, Todd M., and Gina A. Zurlo, eds. *World Christian Database*. Leiden: Brill, 2018.

Larsen, Timothy. "Defining and Locating Evangelicalism." In *The Cambridge Companion to Evangelical Theology*, edited by Timothy Larsen and Daniel J. Treier, 1–14. Cambridge: Cambridge University Press, 2007.

Pew Research Center. "Global Christianity: A Report on the Size and Distribution of the World's Christian Population." Last modified 19 December 2011.

Stott, John R. W. *Evangelical Truth: A Personal Plea for Unity, Integrity and Faithfulness*. Revised edition. Carlisle, UK: Langham Publishing, 2013.

Walls, Andrew F. "Old Athens and New Jerusalem: Some Signposts for Christian Scholarship in the Early History of Mission Studies." *International Bulletin of Missionary Research* 21, no. 4 (1997): 146–153.

Zurlo, Gina A. "Demographics of Global Evangelicalism." In *Evangelicals around the World: A Global Handbook for the 21st Century*. Edited by Brian C. Stiller, Todd M. Johnson, Karen Stiller, and Mark Hutchinson, 34–47. Nashville: Thomas Nelson, 2015.

Part I

Doctrinal Themes

1

Divine Revelation and the Practice of Asian Theology

Timoteo D. Gener
Asian Theological Seminary

In presenting the contours of Asian evangelical theology, it is foundational to begin with the biblical teaching on revelation. Why so? Because the very identity of evangelical theology lies in giving witness to God's self-revelation in Christ, relating and applying the Word to the world.[1] It is in this sense that theology serves the purposes of God, hence its doxological and missional

---

1. John Stott, *The Contemporary Christian: Applying God's Word to Today's World* (Downers Grove: InterVarsity Press, 1992), 27–29. As such, this calls for "double listening," both to the Word and to the world (Stott, 24, 27). For an appropriation of this double listening in theological method, see Timoteo D. Gener, "Transformational Correlation: A Reformational Perspective on Cultural Theological Method in Conversation with David Tracy's and Paul Tillich's Correlational Approach," in *That the World May Believe: Essays on Mission and Unity in Honour of George Vandervelde*, eds. Michael W. Goheen and Margaret O'Gara (Lanham: University Press of America, 2006), 29–43. One could make a case for a continuum of contextual theological methods based on "double listening," stressing on the one side the historical nature of the faith, and the relevance pole on the other. On this plurality of theological methods, see Stephen Bevans, *Models of Contextual Theology* (Maryknoll: Orbis, 2002), 7, 32. See also Kang-San Tan's attempt at a typology of methods below, pp. 279–295. For this section and the rest of this book as systematic theology, the emphasis falls on the historical revealedness of the biblical message, a "theology of retrieval" as it were, but in dialogue with the realities and challenges Asians face. On theologies of retrieval, see John Webster, Kathryn Tanner, and Iain Torrance, eds., *The Oxford Handbook of Systematic Theology* (Oxford: Oxford University Press, 2007), ch. 32.

Note that Stott was the chief architect of the Lausanne Covenant (1974), "the most acceptable evangelical statement of faith of the twentieth century, uniting believers around the world" (Brian Stiller, et al., eds., *Evangelicals around the World: A Global Handbook for the 21st Century*, [Nashville: Thomas Nelson, 2015], 61). See also John Stott, *Evangelical Truth: A Plea for Unity, Integrity, and Faithfulness* (Leicester: Inter-Varsity Press, 1999), 25–62.

nature.[2] In other words, theology exists for the sake of following the God of Scripture who has revealed himself in Jesus Christ in the power of the Holy Spirit. Put more concretely, flowing from the theological nature of the writings of the apostles and prophets, theology is about thinking and living Christianly, toward authentic "discipleship-in-context."[3]

Consequently, this study aligns itself with missional and contextual theologies that further God's communal reign in Christ within and beyond Asia.[4] Particularly in Asia, a theology of revelation needs to be attentive to the plurality of cultures, churches, and religions, the contemporary realities of globalization, migration, and geopolitics, as well as the challenges of poverty and suffering in the region.[5]

---

2. Simon Chan has emphasized the rootedness of theology in doxology and prayer; see his *Liturgical Theology: The Church as Worshipping Community* (Downers Grove: InterVarsity Press, 2006), 48–52. On the mission of God and missional theology, see Christopher J. H. Wright, *The Mission of God: Unlocking the Bible's Grand Narrative* (Downers Grove: InterVarsity Press, 2006). On the practical or missiological nature of theology, see Timoteo D. Gener, "Re-visioning Local Theology: An Integral Dialogue with Practical Theology, A Filipino Evangelical Perspective," *Journal of Asian Mission* 6, no. 2 (2004): 137–154. The approach taken in this chapter also aligns with the quest for a missional or missiological hermeneutic in theology. On the latter, see George Hunsberger, "Proposals for a Missional Hermeneutic: Mapping a Conversation," *Missiology* 39, no. 3 (2011): 309–321. From a pastoral perspective combining worship and mission in global evangelical theologizing, see Stephen T. Pardue and Timoteo D. Gener, "Global Theology: Where to from Here?," in *God at the Borders: Globalization, Migration and Diaspora*, eds. Charles Ringma, Karen Hollenbeck-Wuest, and Athena Gorospe (Quezon City, Philippines: OMF Literature, 2015), 67–74.

3. Timoteo D. Gener, "Christologies in Asia: Trends and Reflections," in *Jesus without Borders: Christology in the Majority World*, eds. Gene L. Green, K. K. Yeo, and Stephen T. Pardue (Carlisle: Langham Global Library, 2015), 60, 64–69; also Timoteo D. Gener, "Every Filipino Christian, a Theologian: A Way of Advancing Local Theology for the 21st Century," in *Doing Theology in the Philippines*, ed. John Suk (Mandaluyong, Philippines: OMF Literature, 2005), 3–23. On the theological process and contextual systematics, see Gener "Doing Contextual Systematic Theology in Asia: Challenges and Prospects," *Journal of Asian Evangelical Theology* 22 (2018): 58–64.

Beyond fundamentalism and contextualism, Asian evangelicals view theology, even doctrines, as integral to Christian life and practice (see Simon Chan, "Evangelical Theology in Asian Contexts," in *The Cambridge Companion to Evangelical Theology*, eds. Timothy Larsen and Daniel J. Treier [Cambridge: Cambridge University Press, 2007], 225–240). Viewed as integral to discipleship, doctrine should not be sacrificed in favor of gaining or attracting new members or keeping old ones (see Kevin Vanhoozer, *The Drama of Doctrine: A Canonical-Linguistic Approach to Christian Theology* (Louisville: Westminster John Knox, 2005), xii.

4. Below I refer to the theological efforts of the Asia Theological Association (evangelical) and the Federation of Asian Bishops' Conference (Catholic) as examples. This study finds affinity too with the efforts of Simon Chan, *Grassroots Asian Theology* (Downers Grove: InterVarsity Press, 2014). From outside Asia, aside from the documents and occasional papers of the Lausanne Movement, I find helpful Stanley Grenz and John Franke's *Beyond Foundationalism: Shaping Theology in a Postmodern Context* (Louisville: Westminster John Knox, 2001).

5. See Gener, "Christologies in Asia," 61–78.

In dialogue with the classical understanding of theology, and mindful of the above qualification on revelation, the definition of theology as "faith seeking understanding" might better be rephrased as "faith *in the divine self-revelation in Christ* seeking understanding."[6] By "understanding" here, what is being sought does not focus just on cognitive knowing, but rather on holistic acquaintance with Christ which is relational, embodied, and lived out (in Filipino, *pangangatawan*) in diverse contexts.[7]

From a big-picture perspective, the reality of God's revelation in Christ holds together major doctrinal themes (e.g. Trinity, Christology, church) within the field of Christian dogmatics or systematic theology.[8] Not only is it foundational in terms of holding other doctrines together, it is also a threshold concept.[9] For when one deals with what is revealed, one crosses beyond the ancient Christian text and tradition into the threshold of the living Christ's teaching for God's people and the world.[10] Indeed, it is the revelation of this God in Christ which is "the means of entrance into God's eternal kingdom for the peoples of humankind to whom it is addressed."[11] No doubt, presenting such teaching is hermeneutical, but sooner or later one must reckon with what is the living Christ's teaching, and not merely wrestle with the meaning of some ancient text.[12]

This beginning chapter will highlight the centrality of biblical revelation in Christian faith and how this teaching relates to the practices of Asian theology, mission, and discipleship. Note that these evangelical convictions regarding the primacy of revelation and the authority of the Bible find their roots in

---

6. For this apt rephrasing, I am indebted to Gerald O'Collins, *Revelation: Towards a Christian Interpretation of God's Self-Revelation in Jesus Christ* (Oxford: Oxford University Press, 2016), v (emphasis mine). For a contemporary appropriation of theology as faith seeking understanding, see Stephen Bevans, *An Introduction to Theology in Global Perspective* (Maryknoll: Orbis, 2009); Kevin Vanhoozer, *Faith Speaking Understanding* (Louisville: Westminster John Knox, 2014).

7. Gener, "Re-visioning Local Theology," 133–166.

8. O'Collins, *Revelation*, v; see also Veli-Matti Kärkkäinen, *Trinity and Revelation* (Grand Rapids: Eerdmans, 2014), 18.

9. William J. Abraham, "The Church's Teaching on Sexuality," in *Staying the Course: Supporting the Church's Position on Homosexuality*, eds. Maxie Dunnam and H. Newton Malony (Nashville: Abingdon, 2003), 25–26. See also William J. Abraham, *Crossing the Threshold of Divine Revelation* (Grand Rapids: Eerdmans, 2006).

10. Note that in what follows, I use the terms "revelation," "gospel," and "the biblical message" synonymously. For a similar direction, see Grenz and Franke, *Beyond Foundationalism*, ch. 3.

11. T. D. Alexander et al., eds., *New Dictionary of Biblical Theology* (Leicester: Inter-Varsity Press, 2000), 736.

12. Abraham, "Church's Teaching on Sexuality," 25–26.

the history of the evangelical movement down through the centuries.[13] On the one hand, the finality of Christ in disclosing the fullness of God requires proper confidence and faithfulness to the gospel.[14] As such, this involves *a priori* faith commitments or convictions in the practice of theology.[15] On the other hand, such revelation calls for a process of theologizing that draws from God's presence (universal and particular) as rooted in Christ. In other words, revelation also forms the basis for doing contextual systematics such as what this book attempts to do. With this understanding, theology then is approached as both a product (results of considered faith seeking understanding expressed in teaching) and a process of correlating the biblical message and context, to render the gospel and Christian faith in Asia in meaningful ways and with cultural theological impact.[16]

To accomplish our task for this section, we will begin with an overview of the Christian doctrine of revelation, briefly looking at its history and missiological import, and then we will highlight its implications for doing theology and mission in the Asian setting.

---

13. Stott recounts this history succinctly in *Evangelical Truth*. *Historically*, the word "evangelical" came into widespread use in the early eighteenth century in relation to the evangelical revival associated with Wesley and Whitefield. Earlier, it had been applied to Puritans and Pietists in the seventeenth century as well as to the Reformers during the sixteenth century. Theologically, Stott clarifies that evangelicals differ from Fundamentalists in the sense articulated by Carl Henry in his important book, *The Uneasy Conscience of Modern Fundamentalism* (Grand Rapids: Eerdmans, 1947). Stott then identifies the evangelical essentials as focusing on the being and work of the three persons of the Godhead, with conversion, evangelism, and fellowship flowing from the Trinitarian gospel as an elaboration. In essence, then, the evangelical essentials can be reduced to three, "namely the revealing initiative of God the Father, the redeeming work of God the Son and the transforming ministry of God the Holy Spirit" (Stott, *Evangelical Truth*, 25). On the developing notion of evangelical identity in the current US scene, see the introduction in Roger Olson's *How to Be an Evangelical without Being Conservative* (Grand Rapids: Zondervan, 2008).

14. See also Gener "Every Filipino Christian."

15. More on this below, particularly the convictions of evangelical theologians/theological schools within the Asia Theological Association (ATA), along with the Lausanne Movement. For the *a priori* presupposition of revelation within Christianity, especially in relation to theology of religions, which is also applicable to theological reflection in general, see Gavin D'Costa, "Revelation and Revelations: Discerning God in Other Religions. Beyond a Static Valuation," *Modern Theology* 10, no. 2 (April 1994): 165–183. A different approach is Alister McGrath's project of scientific theology, which moves in the other direction of establishing theory on the basis of *a posteori* commitments aligned with a hermeneutic of revelation in (missional) dialogue with the natural sciences. For a good overview of McGrath's project, see his *The Order of Things: Explorations in Scientific Theology* (Oxford: Blackwell, 2006).

16. On doing theology as process and as systematic theology, see Gener, "Doing Contextual Systematic Theology in Asia." See also Clark Pinnock, *Tracking the Maze* (New York: Harper & Row, 1990), 12–13. On doctrine as theological "product" or result, Kevin Vanhoozer has referred to Christian doctrine as the "considered result of faith's search for biblical understanding," Vanhoozer, *Drama of Doctrine*, 2.

Historical, Missiological Look

The theme of revelation was not a dominant concern in the early years of the church, even if it was "in the foreground of all Christian awareness in the first three centuries."[17] It was the doctrine of the Trinity as well as christological, ecclesiological, and soteriological concerns which preoccupied the postapostolic, medieval, and Reformation periods of church history.[18] The idea of revelation did not call for immediate, focused investigation because it was neither a pressing need nor an urgent problem then. As H. D. McDonald has put it, "Questions concerning how and why and where God has revealed Himself must ever be of fundamental importance. Yet, as the student of historical theology will have observed, the problems raised by the idea of a disclosure of God were not early discussed. Centuries of theological debate, created by other needs, were to pass before attention was focused upon the subject of revelation as such. It is living issues, after all, which call for immediate investigation."[19]

In the English-speaking world, what spurred the deeper focus on the idea of God's disclosure in the Christian faith were the intellectual challenges of the Age of Reason, particularly deism and atheism in the eighteenth century.[20] "From the turn of the eighteenth century to the middle of the nineteenth century theology and philosophy of religion were grappling with the issue of special revelation. An era opened by deism and closed by Darwinism, this period was molded by the framework of Cartesian philosophy. In his search for a worldview grounded upon indisputable foundations, Descartes fused the mathematical rationalism of clear and distinct ideas with the mystical immediacy of individual consciousness."[21]

Yet even as the Age of Reason introduced new doctrinal challenges, McDonald is right to note its missiological implications. Even as the Age of Reason sowed the seeds for crisis in the wider church body, "the complex interaction of intellectual, cultural and scientific forces . . . made possible the tremendous advance of Christian missions from the end of the eighteenth

---

17. René Latourelle, *Theology of Revelation* (New York: Alba House, 1966), 142.

18. H. D. McDonald, *Theories of Revelation: An Historical Study 1700–1960* (Grand Rapids: Baker, 1979), 1–3.

19. McDonald, *Theories of Revelation*, 1.

20. McDonald, 1. For an elaboration of this historical summary, see Kärkkäinen, *Trinity and Revelation*, 12–34.

21. Denny Reiter, "Review of H. D. McDonald, *Ideas of Revelation: An Historical Study, A.D. 1700 to A.D. 1860*," *Trinity Studies* 2 (1972): 100.

century onwards."[22] The Age of Reason also "gave rise to the optimism about social progress, the belief in the superiority of western culture and values, and even the consequent advocacy of colonialism by some church leaders and missionaries, all of which underlie so much of Christian mission in the nineteenth and first half of the twentieth centuries."[23]

Admittedly, there were also gains in the Christian faith's encounter with the Enlightenment, including contributions from the postmodern turn in contemporary theologizing. At the very least, Christian theology now has to be more integrative and conversational rather than monologic in presenting the faith.[24] Alongside this integrative task, one has to theologize mindful of the global nature of the Christian movement, and proffer theologies that engage the hermeneutical spaces opened up by this new reality.[25]

In the emerging ferment in global and missional theologizing, the biblical teaching on revelation continues to be a refreshing point of departure and resource for the Christian church on the road to fulfilling God's mission. Indeed, the Catholic Church recognized the *pastoral* import of this doctrine in engaging the modern world, via its dogmatic constitution on divine revelation, *Dei Verbum* (1965).[26] This continues to be the case at the dawn of the twenty-first century. Biblical revelation addresses anew our postmodern context, a period much aware and suspicious of the valorizing perils of foundationalism in theorizing.[27] Revelation theology at its best conveys "the undeserved and wondrous event of God's grace toward us, not as a predictable occurrence the theoretical justification of which is found in a theory."[28] Such biblical teaching is also congenial to the flourishing of intercultural hermeneutics attuned to diverse and profound cultural-theological readings of the Bible with the vision

---

22. Hwa Yung, "Review of David Bosch's *Transforming Mission*," *International Review of Mission* 81, no. 322 (1992): 321.

23. Yung, "Review," 321.

24. Kärkkäinen, *Trinity and Revelation*, 27.

25. Justo L. Gonzalez, *The Story of Christianity*, vol. 2 (New York: HarperCollins, 2010), 913.

26. See Walter Abbott, ed., *The Documents of Vatican II* (Piscataway: Association Press, 1966, 1982); also Latourelle's translation and commentary of *Dei Verbum* in his *Theology of Revelation*, 453–588. Note that the term "'pastoral' does not mean lightweight, insignificant, or without doctrinal content; it refers to the pope's goal of reaching out to the modern world to help the faith to be understood better" (Ronald Witherup, *The Word of God at Vatican II: Exploring* Dei Verbum [Collegeville: Liturgical Press, 2014] 6).

27. *Dei Verbum* rightly situates revelation's centrality for the church's missionary engagement with the world.

28. Mark I. Wallace, "Theological Table-Talk: Theology without Revelation?," *Theology Today* 45, no. 2 (1988): 209.

of a God-intended, Christ-centered world.[29] "Revived interest in the doctrine of revelation can help facilitate this task in a world worn down by pessimism and despair. Indeed, in the possibility of hearing God's Word again in the play between text and reader, the building of renewed communities of faith and hope is undergirded, informed, and empowered for the future."[30]

God's Final Revelation in Christ

How, then, did God reveal himself? The living God has made himself known in Israel through historical acts of election, deliverance, and exposure to his judgment within Israel and among the nations. God's election of Israel had as its goal the creation of a light for, and the blessing of, the nations (Gen 12; Isa 49:6, 22–23). The fulness of God's universal, loving intentions are fulfilled when God himself enters human history in the person of Jesus Christ through the agency of the Holy Spirit to redeem the world from what ultimately hinders God's vision of human and cosmic wholeness: sin, evil, and death. God has spoken finally and fully in Christ, his Son (Heb 1:1–2; John 1:1–14; Matt 1:20; 3:11–12, 16–17). According to John's gospel, which speak of Jesus being sent by the Father, Jesus Christ's mission was to reveal and embody the God who is love; the God whose love for the world is expressed in the coming of Christ who is both the *logos* of the world and *kerygma* of salvation (John 1:1–14; 3:16). In and through Jesus Christ, through the power of the Holy Spirit, God's universal, even creation-wide mission is opened up and carried through to all the nations and the world through the power of the Spirit, especially through the agency of Christ's body, his followers (Matt 28:18–20; John 20:21; Rom 8:18–30; Col 1:15–20; Acts 1:1–11; 2:1–11).[31]

From a biblical perspective, then, God's project in the world is the revelation of the triune God's great love, shown in creation and providence, redemption (from sin, evil, and death) and community, and the inbreaking of God's kingdom and the new creation. It unfolds with

> the work of forming the world at creation, involving the continuing commitment to the creation, in spite of the rebellion of that part

---

29. For the missional biblical hermeneutic that this involves, see Grenz and Franke, *Beyond Foundationalism*, 64–92.

30. Wallace, "Theological Table-Talk," 213.

31. This short summary is indebted to Christopher J. H. Wright, *Mission of God*, chs. 3–4. Also helpful as summary is Alexander et al., eds., *New Dictionary of Biblical Theology*, 732–738. For an extended treatment of God's self-revelation in Christ, see O'Collins, *Revelation*, 19–38; also his *Rethinking Fundamental Theology* (Oxford: Oxford University Press, 2011), chs. 4–5.

made like God; the entrance into its history (and its physicality) of Jesus Christ to suffer from and heal its corruption; the continuing divine presence expressed through the historical body of Christ, the church, and by God's general providential work, as God through the ministry of the Holy Spirit seeks to bring creation to its created purpose as a vehicle for God's glory.[32]

God's Revelation and the Bible

At this point, one may ask: What is the role of the Bible in God's revelation of himself? Is the Bible equal to divine revelation or the actual Word of God? What is the proper way of understanding the relationship between Scripture and revelation? Put simply, evangelicals believe Scripture is inscripturated revelation, or the written Word of God.[33] This is to be distinguished from the Word of God incarnate, Jesus Christ (John 1:1–14), and the human proclamation (preaching) of the word of God.[34] Both the written word and the word proclaimed are revelation insofar as they witness to God's self-revelation in Jesus Christ through the Spirit. Note that by itself the whole Bible or the words of the Bible are nothing without the Spirit of Christ who gives them life (e.g. 2 Cor 3:6), and it is this same Spirit who is recreating the world in and through Christ, with the aid of the Scriptures being re-read and Christ's life re-enacted in the world (see Rom 8:18–25).

Word and Spirit are bound together in reading the Bible as a text for followers of Christ in all cultures and generations.[35] We must go beyond

---

32. William Dyrness, *The Earth Is God's* (Maryknoll: Orbis, 1997), 68.

33. Stanley Grenz and Roger Olson, *Who Needs Theology? An Invitation to the Study of God* (Downers Grove: InterVarsity Press, 1996), 93. Admittedly, as Grenz and Franke summarize it, the New Testament writers did not use the phrase "the word of God" to refer to the Jewish Scriptures (the Bible of the early Christians). NT writers employ "the word of God" to refer to "messages actually spoken by God to or through prophets and centering above all on the person and work of Jesus (e.g. Acts 6:7; 12:24; 19:20; 1 Pet 1:23, 25). Elsewhere this Word is an active agent before whom no creature is hidden (Heb 4:12–13)" (Grenz and Franke, *Beyond Foundationalism*, 71).

34. Karl Barth is credited for reframing it in this (arguably more biblical) way, which evangelicals have critically adopted. See Stanley Grenz, *Revisioning Evangelical Theology* (Downers Grove: InterVarsity Press, 1993), 129.

35. Grenz and Franke, *Beyond Foundationalism*, 65. On the limitations of the historical-critical method for Bible interpretation across cultures, see Ulrich Luz, *Matthew in History: Interpretation, Influence, and Effects* (Minneapolis: Fortress, 1994). For more on Scripture and hermeneutics attuned to the world Christian movement, see Grenz and Franke, *Beyond Foundationalism*, 64–92; also Kelly M. Kapic and Bruce L. McCormack, eds., *Mapping Modern Theology: A Thematic and Historical Introduction* (Grand Rapids: Baker Academic, 2012), ch. 4.

both fundamentalist as well as liberal readings toward a truly theological and missional hermeneutic of the Scripture. On the one hand, as Holy Scripture, the Bible is authoritative for Christians across the centuries because the sovereign Spirit has "bound authoritative, divine speaking to this text" (see 2 Tim 3:16).[36] On the other hand, the Bible and Spirit go together as the foundation for the church's authoritative approach and use of the Scriptures in the one church of Jesus Christ. Bernard Ramm points to this union of the biblical message and the Holy Spirit as the appropriate principle of biblical authority in the church: "The proper principle of authority within the Christian church must be . . . the Holy Spirit speaking in the Scriptures, which are the product of the Spirit's revelatory and inspiring action."[37] Indeed, "according to the New Testament community, 'the word of God' is the Holy Spirit announcing the good news about Jesus, which word the church speaks to us in the Spirit's power and by the Spirit's authority."[38] The "word of God," or God's revelation in Scripture, is ultimately "Christologically and pneumatologically focused."[39] Interestingly, the revelation and guidance of the Holy Spirit in the church embraces and engages the promise and challenges of new contexts and places, enabling the preservation of particularities, as well as the crossing of boundaries.[40]

God's Wider Presence in Creation, Conscience, and Culture

With God's universal purposes in mind, the Bible also notes "God's wider presence" through Christ and the Spirit beyond the confines of Israel and church.[41] This biblical understanding of general revelation gives us warrant to use cultural experiences and concepts as theological sources, albeit secondary (not co-equal), to God's Word.[42] Scripture testifies that God reveals himself in creation (for example, Ps 19:1–6) through conscience (for example, Rom 2:14), and through culture (for example, Agur's Sayings in Prov 30 which were

---

36. Grenz and Franke, *Beyond Foundationalism*, 65.
37. Grenz and Franke, 64.
38. Grenz, *Revisioning Evangelical Theology*, 131.
39. Grenz and Franke, *Beyond Foundationalism*, 71.
40. See Colin Gunton, *The One, the Three and the Many* (Cambridge: Cambridge University Press, 1993), 181–184.
41. Robert K. Johnston, *God's Wider Presence: Reconsidering General Revelation* (Grand Rapids: Baker, 2015), chs. 4–5.
42. This assumes that the wider presence of God not tied to salvation is equivalent to general (or universal) revelation.

Egyptian in origin; also of non-Israelite origins are King Lemuel's words in Prov 31).[43]

There are also biblical accounts of Yahweh speaking through Pharaoh Neco (2 Chr 35:20–27), God making use of Cyrus of Persia as his instrument (2 Chr 36:22–23), the foreigner Abimelech who became Abraham's teacher in acting righteously (Gen 20), the foreigner-high priest Melchizedek who blessed Abram (Gen 14:17–20), the non-Israelite diviner Balaam who delivered Yahweh's message (Num 22–24), as well as Paul's use of creational realities in engaging the Lystrans (Acts 14) and his use of Roman poetry and religion among the Athenians on Mars Hill (Acts 17).[44] Jesus himself drew gospel lessons from creational realities and human experiences (for example, Matt 6:28, 30).[45]

God's Revelation and the Religions

As the living God revealed himself as the one true God of Israel and the nations (Deut 10:14; 2 Kgs 19:15; Jer 32:27; Isa 54:5; Ps 47:7), this one God is thus the creator, not only of heaven and earth but of all peoples.[46] Hence the biblical prologue is universally oriented and directed to all humankind (Gen 1–11). This universal orientation does not stop with primeval history, however. Before and after the first covenant with God's people, non-Jewish, non-covenant individuals are lifted up as examples of faith, including Abel, Seth, Enoch, Noah, Melchizedek, and Job.[47]

Set apart for a universal purpose (Gen 12:3), Israel came to know the uniqueness and universality of Yahweh particularly through their experience of the exodus (e.g. Exod 5:22 – 6:8; Deut 4:32–35) and the return from exile (e.g. Ezek 36:22–23; Isa 45:11–13). In the process, the nations also came to know the Lord through exposure to God's judgment (Isa 43:9–12). Deliverance or salvation involves allegiance to this one God. Such allegiance means following God's ways and rejecting idolatry and rebellion, which is the way of destruction (e.g. Deut 10:14–19). Yahweh has no favorites, not even Israel (Amos 9:7; 3:2), and God can use any nation to chastise Israel. Yet God's people remain God's

---

43. Johnston, *God's Wider Presence*, 72–77.

44. Paul Louis Metzger, "Theology of Culture and General Revelation: An Interview with Professor Robert K. Johnston," *Cultural Encounters* 12, no. 1 (2016): 97–103.

45. See Alexander et al., *New Dictionary of Biblical Theology*, 732.

46. Wright, *Mission of God*, 75–104.

47. Veli-Matti Kärkkäinen, *An Introduction to the Theology of Religions* (Downers Grove: InterVarsity Press, 2004), 37.

people, even under judgment (Jer 29:1–14).[48] While "Israel was commanded to seek the Lord in unique, normative, and exclusive ways, they were especially careful, even inclusive we might say, in their treatment of foreigners," reflecting a God who is impartial and loving.[49]

Jesus himself responded to the needs of non-Jews and communicated compassion, healing, and deliverance to them. For instance, he commended the faith of a Gentile outsider, a Roman centurion, whose faith, according to Jesus, put Israel to shame (Matt 8:10). In effect, the centurion became the first member of the Gentile church.[50] Indeed, Jesus called attention to the fact that many outsiders from east and west would enter the kingdom and many Israelites would be excluded (Matt 8:11–12). In Paul, we see both strong judgment of pagans and their futile gods but also an equally "stern verdict of the Jews who live apart from faith in Christ (Rom 2–3)."[51] Being in Christ, however, did not mean "absolute denial of any value in other religious traditions," as shown in Paul's sermon in Acts 17.[52] A relationship of discontinuity and continuity can be discerned in Paul's mind between Romans 1 and Acts 17. "Discontinuity places the stress on the radical newness of Christ and his resurrection and by contrast sees the ancient world as darkness and sin. That is the viewpoint of Rom[ans] 1. The continuity, on the contrary, underlines the homogeneity of salvation unfolding according to God's plan. It is the viewpoint of Acts 17, which, where the religion of gentiles is concerned, presents a Greek world waiting for the unknown God and prepared by its poet-theologians to meet him."[53] Later, in Ephesians and Colossians as well as in Hebrews 1, we see a cosmic orientation to Christology that universalizes the work of Christ, beyond just reconciliation of Jews and Gentiles with God and each other, toward victory over all spiritual powers of this world and redemption that encompasses all creation and humanity.[54]

Kärkkäinen's summary of the biblical testimony on the theme is apt:

> While it is true that in general the Bible offers a quite consistent negative judgment of other religions and as a consequence seems

---

48. Wright, *Mission of God*, 99–100.
49. Daniel Clendenin, *Many Gods, Many Lords: Christianity Encounters World Religions* (Grand Rapids: Baker, 1995), 135, quoted in Kärkkäinen, *Introduction*, 40.
50. O'Collins, *Revelation*, 198.
51. Kärkkäinen, *Introduction*, 44.
52. Jacques Dupuis, *Toward a Christian Theology of Religious Pluralism* (Maryknoll: Orbis, 1997), 48–49, quoted in Kärkkäinen, *Introduction*, 44.
53. Dupuis, *Toward a Christian Theology*, 50, quoted in Kärkkäinen, *Introduction*, 45.
54. Kärkkäinen, *Introduction*, 46.

to support an exclusive attitude, a range of biblical passages point to the relative value of religions and to God's power in transforming religions and cultures to acknowledge the truth. It is the continuing task of Christian theology – under changed circumstances, yet in faithfulness to the tradition – to try to make sense of the church's calling on the basis of biblical teaching and theological reflection.[55]

Recently there has been an increasing awareness, brought about by the interrogations of the social sciences, that "religion" itself is a modern Euro-American academic construct which needs to be rethought from the grassroots, from the religions/religious practitioners themselves. It is not a native term from within "religions" but a theoretical construct devised by scholars or religionists.[56] Indeed, the very term "religion" has no vernacular equivalent in Filipino, and I would not be surprised if this is the case in most, if not all, Asian languages, for it is a way of life rather than a concept.[57] Perhaps a better theological framework would be to view religions as analogous to cultures: human responses to God's action in creation, and thus able to be (re-)directed to meaningful, life-giving ends reflecting God's vision of fulness of life in the new creation.[58] Yet another helpful approach is the comparative theology route as a way into actual dialogue with religions. As Kärkkäinen notes, "Comparative theology provides a challenging interdisciplinary platform as it calls for basic knowledge of not only Christian theology but also other

---

55. Kärkkäinen, 34–35.

56. As Jonathan Z. Smith reports: "Religion is not a native term; it is a term created by scholars for their intellectual purposes and therefore is theirs to define. It is a second-order generic concept that plays the same role in establishing a disciplinary horizon that a concept such as 'language' plays in linguistics or 'culture' plays in anthropology. There can be no disciplined study of religion without such a horizon" (Jonathan Z. Smith, "Religion, Religions, Religious," in *Critical Terms for Religious Studies*, ed. Mark C. Taylor [Chicago: University of Chicago Press, 1998], 281–282, as cited in Paul J. Griffiths "Religion," in *Dictionary for Theological Interpretation of the Bible*, eds. Kevin Vanhoozer et al. [Grand Rapids: Baker, 2005], 674).

57. Leonardo Mercado, *Elements of Filipino Theology* (Tacloban City: Divine Word Press, 1975), 26. Melba Maggay accounts for this reality in this way: "[The Filipino] sees himself as part of the cosmic whole... participating in and not reflecting upon the world" (Melba Maggay, *The Gospel in Filipino Context* [Manila: OMF, 1987], 15). Emerita Quito's explanation parallels Maggay's. According to Quito, in the Philippines, as in all of Asia, "religion is a way of life that is to be revered" (Quito, *The Merging Philosophy of East and West* [Manila: De Lasalle University Press, 1991], 6–7).

58. William Dyrness, *Insider Jesus: Theological Reflections on New Christian Movements* (Downers Grove: InterVarsity Press, 2016), 45–131.

faith traditions."⁵⁹ Applying genuine conversation and listening, one could look first at the other faith traditions (then beliefs and morals) and then construct a Christian proposal, or vice versa.⁶⁰

Revelation and the Practice of Theology in Asia

As was intimated above, Asian evangelical theology (henceforth AET) is both the result of a considered faith and a constructive process normed by God's revelation in Christ as witnessed to by Holy Scripture. In this, AET assumes fundamental presuppositions of what makes for a truly *Christian* theology, which is allegiance to the biblical Christ or the biblical message.⁶¹ As Vanhoozer puts it, "Non-Western Christianity does not need to become Western. Yet non-Western Christianity should strive to stay authentically Christian and one way to do that is to remain in communion with catholic theological tradition."⁶² In relation to evangelical theology's grounding in the Bible, McGrath advances that Christian community and theology is only identifiable and sustainable as distinctly *Christian* insofar as it continues to maintain its dedication to the "paradigmatic biblical narrative."⁶³

Evangelicals affirm this linkage of the Christian faith with the gospel or the biblical message. The Willowbank Report, a product of the 1978 Lausanne Consultation on Gospel and Culture, proves this point well. Here is how Section 5 of the report, on the content and the communication of the gospel, identified "the heart of the gospel":

---

59. Veli-Matti Kärkkäinen, "Response 2," in G. McDermott and H. Netland, *A Trinitarian Theology of Religions: An Evangelical Proposal* (Oxford: Oxford University Press, 2014), 301.

60. Kärkkäinen, "Response 2," in McDermott and Netland, *Trinitarian Theology*, 301.

61. Thus see Braaten, who says: "If there is a specifically Christian foundation for the study of religious phenomena, it is well to clarify the fundamental presuppositions of what makes theology Christian. These are explicitly dogmatic presuppositions," Carl E. Braaten and Robert W. Jenson, eds., *Christian Dogmatics*, vol. 1 (Philadelphia: Fortress, 2011), 33.

62. Kevin Vanhoozer, "Christology in the West: Conversations in Europe and North America," in *Jesus without Borders*, eds. Gene L. Green, K. K. Yeo, and Stephen T. Pardue (Carlisle: Langham Global Library, 2015), 33.

63. Cited in Marc Cortez, "Context and Concept: Contextual Theology and the Nature of Theological Discourse," *Westminster Theological Journal* 67, no. 1 (Spring 2005): 85–102. McGrath clarifies: doctrine "provides the conceptual framework by which the scriptural narrative is interpreted," and immediately notes that this "is not an arbitrary framework... but one which is suggested by that narrative, and intimated (however provisionally) by scripture itself" (Cortez, "Context and Concept," 96). On the notion of the Bible's "paradigmatic events," see Grenz and Franke, *Beyond Foundationalism*, 79–81.

> It is important to identify what is at the heart of the gospel. *We recognize as central the themes of God as Creator, the universality of sin, Jesus Christ as Son of God, Lord of all, and Saviour through his atoning death and risen life, the necessity of conversion, the coming of the Holy Spirit and his transforming power, the fellowship and mission of the Christian church, and the hope of Christ's return.* While these are basic elements of the gospel, it is necessary to add that no theological statement is culture-free. Therefore, all theological formulations must be judged by the Bible itself, which stands above them all. Their value must be judged by their faithfulness to it as well as by the relevance with which they apply its message to their own culture.[64]

Interestingly, the report did not come up with propositional statements on the nature of the gospel. Instead, it gave biblical theological themes or faith commitments that flow from the biblical story, from creation to new creation.[65] The statement talks about these themes as basic elements of the good news of Christ. It is the biblical story that determines the shape and content of biblical teachings, and not a presupposed doctrinal system with corresponding proof-texts or Bible references.[66] Evangelical theologians have critiqued this approach as one that treats the Bible as "a sourcebook of Christian doctrines" and tends to "overlook, suppress or deny [Scripture's] narrative character."[67] But does this mean abandoning the use of system in theological construction? In narrative-

---

64. "The Willowbank Report: Consultation on Gospel and Culture" (Lausanne Occasional Paper 2, Lausanne Committee on World Evangelization, 1978), Section 5B (italics mine).

65. Marc Cortez notes, however, that the logic of the traditional order of theological topics (cf. the theological themes noted in the Lausanne "Gospel and Culture" document) is not inimical to the shape of the gospel story ("The Insanity of Systematic Theology: A Review of Michael Bird's *Evangelical Theology*," *Southeastern Journal of Theology* 6, no. 2 [2015]: 172–174). "Beginning with the God who is Lord and Creator of all, they then talk about God's purposes for creation in general and humanity in particular. That sets the stage for appreciating the tragedy of the Fall and the amazing goodness of God's grace in Christ, the transformation of his people through the Spirit, and the final culmination of God's creative purposes in the eschaton" (Cortez, "Insanity of Systematic Theology," 173–174).

66. The constructive directions toward contextual systematic theology are offered here in the spirit of communal dialogue mindful of the limits of systematization. These limits are premised on the fact that (1) the gospel of Christ as revealed in the biblical story is a drama or story needing reenactment rather than a set of timeless propositions; and that (2) we do not possess comprehensiveness or totality in understanding. See Colin E. Gunton, "A Rose by Any Other Name? From 'Christian Doctrine' to 'Systematic Theology,'" in *Intellect and Action* (Edinburgh: T&T Clark, 2005), 38–39.

67. Alister E. McGrath, *A Passion for Truth* (Leicester: Apollos, 1997), 173–174, cited by Roger Olson, *Reformed and Always Reforming: The Postconservative Approach to Evangelical Theology* (Grand Rapids: Baker Academic, 2007), 162.

attuned theological construction, the notion of system has to move away from being a tightly bound structure to more of an orderly account. God is a God of order, not chaos (see 1 Cor 14:33), the coherence of which lies in Christ (Col 1:15). Here Gunton's words are apropos: "if God is indeed one, and if that oneness is revealed oneness, thus far is there a case for ordering what we are taught of God into, if not a system, then at least a dogmatics [confession] in which (1) who and what kind of being God is and (2) the various relations between God and the world – expressed in such terms as Christology, pneumatology, creation, the image of God, sin, salvation, justification, the church, the sacraments, eschatology – are held to be related to one another."[68]

The Lausanne Consultation cautions that "all theological formulations must be judged by the Bible itself" and its concomitant missional relevance to cultures. Moreover, in this frame, reason is not opposed to revelation but rather functions ministerially, subservient to clarifying the biblical coherence of God's action in Christ.[69] One could say the same with the role of tradition; it is not magisterial in its function, but rather ministerial in relation to Scriptural revelation.[70]

Missional Relevance, Syncretism, and Evangelical Orthodoxy

With respect to missional relevance in theological construction, one must recognize that culturally connected theological methods draw from the tools of social sciences in local theologizing, particularly in analyzing and revealing the dynamics of the encounter between Christian faith and cultures, and as such they aid in developing local theologies.[71] There is indeed value in experience as a source in theologizing, but allowing human experience to be

---

68. Gunton refers to this account in relation to the "dialectic of revealedness and hiddenness in terms of which it is expounded. God being God, there are limits . . . to what the human mind may confidently know," but the triune God has revealed himself and thus we are taught and we confess such revelation (Colin Gunton, *Intellect and Action* [Edinburgh: T&T Clark, 2005], 37).

69. Gunton contrasts the premodern with the modern understanding of the relationship between reason and revelation: "Modern thought has tended to oppose reason to revelation, but for the world of ancient philosophy reason is the medium of divine revelation, through attention and recollection. In the ancient world, accordingly, oppositions and conversations between theology and culture operated over a far wider range of features" (Gunton, *Intellect and Action*, 23).

70. See Alister McGrath, "Evangelical Theological Method: The State of the Art," in *Evangelical Futures: A Conversation on Theological Method*, ed. John G. Stackhouse (Grand Rapids: Baker, 2000), 31.

71. See also Benno van den Toren and Liz Hoare, "Evangelicals and Contextual Theology: Lessons from Missiology for Theological Reflection," *Practical Theology* 8, no. 2 (2015): 77–98.

co-equal with the biblical message makes experience to be the underlying foundation and force in theology. Such an approach inevitably tends toward anthropocentrism, bracketing off the supernatural and losing the dimension of the unrepeatable newness of life integral to the kerygma of Christ.[72] In the process, ethics becomes the gospel, rather than proclaiming the earth-shaking, life-changing good news of Christ in salvation and redemption as the foundation for the practice of theology. The result of this unbiblical synthesis is an unhealthy syncretism – a phenomenon whereby the church, acting as interpreter, "allows the content of the interpretation to be affected by any of the values or premises of his culture that are incongruent with the gospel."[73] In the process, the gospel becomes fused and even reduced to cultural values and experiences. Such fusion bounds and then domesticates the biblical message, leaving behind cultural Christianity, a mere shell of the original, vital faith.

While mindful of the inevitability of acculturation and synthesis in any theologizing, the danger of syncretism calls evangelicals to be alert to the reality that the garden of theology needs boundaries to flourish.[74] Yet the call to boundaries may not always be the best way to express global evangelicalism's commitment to orthodoxy. This was a sentiment expressed by some of the educational leaders of Asia Theological Association (ATA).[75] Given that global evangelicalism lacks a magisterium that might monitor or enforce theological boundaries, and given evangelicalism's pietist roots, which emphasize spirituality more than strict adherence to doctrines, a better approach to these issues is to focus on what binds together ("centered-set" thinking) rather than what distinguishes our edges ("bounded-set" thinking).

Mindful of the global nature of the movement, Roger Olson pushes for the centered-set approach to evangelical orthodoxy:

---

72. Here I distinguish the reality of cultural-anthropological synthesis or syncretic "blending" (acculturation, enculturation) from the missiological judgment of syncretism in the gospel and culture encounter. See Timoteo D. Gener, "Engaging Chung Hyun Kyung's Concept of Syncretism," *Journal of Asian Evangelical Theology* 19 (2015): 57–58.

73. C. René Padilla, *Mission between the Times* (Carlisle: Langham Monographs, 2010), 108–109.

74. Echoing Colin Gunton's remarks, "[J]ust as a garden is not a garden without some boundaries – or just as the created world is only what it is as a work of God because it is finite in space and time – so [the garden of] theology ceases to be Christian theology if it effectively ceases to remain true to its boundaries" (See Colin E. Gunton, "Dogma, the Church and the Task of Theology," in *The Task of Theology Today*, eds. Victor Pfitzner and Hilary Regan [Grand Rapids: Eerdmans, 1998], 2).

75. Filipino social anthropologist-theologian Dr Melba Maggay at the 2018 ATA Consultation was most vocal in challenging Gunton's notion of dogma providing boundaries to contextualization (session on Asian Evangelical Systematic Theology, Asia Theological Consultation, 19 July 2018, Pasig City, Philippines).

The question is not who is "in" and who is "out" but who is nearer the center and who is moving away from it. Authentic evangelicalism is defined by its centrifugal center of powerful gravity and not by outlying boundaries that serve as walls or fences . . . People gathered around the center or moving toward it are authentically evangelical; people or institutions moving away from it or with backs turned against it are of questionable evangelical status. But it is not a matter of being "in" or "out" as there is no evangelical magisterium to decide that.[76]

Furthermore, right belief (orthodoxy) is not enough. Evangelicals also rightly value right practice (orthopraxy) and correct affections (orthopathy).[77]

Asian Dimensions in Christian Theology: Toward a Gospel-Centered Faith, Community, and Experience

While classically biblical in its theological commitments, one might ask: "What makes this theology distinctively Asian?" On this question, Simon Chan points to the broader commitment to gospel orthodoxy as the key to understanding Asian evangelical theology. Asian evangelicals propound gospel orthodoxy while making the gospel come alive in Asia through efforts at contextualization. From a regional point of view, Chan claims that evangelicalism in Asia is not as diverse as a theological movement compared to the West. It is also not as deep in its ecclesiology. He prefers to view evangelical theology as "what orthodox Christians from the major traditions – whether Catholic, Protestant, and Orthodox – hold in common regarding the centrality of the gospel of Jesus Christ."[78]

Chan's ecumenical understanding of the doctrinal essentials of AET, with its center in the gospel of Christ, resonates with me. To deepen this, one could invoke the biblical roots of the very term "evangelical." Biblically speaking, evangelicals are people of the *euanggelion* ("good news" or "gospel"). Evangelicals point to "Christians of different times and places who seek to live lives congruent with the mission given by Christ (cf. Mark 1:14–15; Luke

---

76. Olson, *Reformed and Always Reforming*, 16, 60.

77. John G. Stackhouse, "A Generic Evangelical Response," in *Four Views on the Spectrum of Evangelicalism*, eds. Andrew David Naselli and Collin Hansen (Grand Rapids: Zondervan, 2011), 56–61.

78. See Simon Chan's chapter in this book, "Toward an Asian Evangelical Ecclesiology," 139–155.

4:14–21; John 20:21)."[79] The label "evangelical" should not be viewed merely as an establishment or institutional term linked with particular theological schools, denominations, and organizations. Rather, to be an evangelical is to be part of the world Christian movement, followers of Christ sent to fulfill Christ's own mission as his representatives or agents in the world.[80] Consequently, to be missional is to be disciples of Christ in diverse contexts, and in the process, Christian faith is re-appropriated in new situations.

The focus on commonality in gospel-centered faith is not unrelated to the communal and experiential dimensions of doing Asian Christian theology. Being in community means seeking the unity of truth in Christ. Asian evangelical churches are part of the universal body of Christ, and, as such, AET is "not only a theology for Asia but also from Asia to the universal body of Christ."[81] Put another way, it is theology about the Christian faith in Asia, and this gospel-centered faith runs through diverse Christian traditions, "holding promise for a new ecumenism that goes beyond the currently deadlocked World Council of Churches."[82]

The experiential dimension of doing Asian Christian theology lies in giving prominence to the lived experience of the church as theological source. I have referred to this ecclesial experience as ecclesial praxis-in-the-world, which is "the enactment of the presence of Christ through the Spirit or simply *Christopraxis* which flows from a theological perspective advancing a biblical/contextual claim: the *reality* of the risen Lord is known in a localizing and directional way. Or to put it another way, Christ's life can be known and 'repeated' in transformational practice through the Spirit."[83] For Chan, "ecclesial experience constitutes the primary theology (*theologia prima*) of the church." It is different from cultural experience, for its "starting point [is] the givenness of revelation finding its end in the church's supernatural life – supernatural because it is the life of the indwelling Spirit of truth."[84] When the living faith of the people of God is seen as the locus of primary theology, "[t]he task of the professional theologian is not to tell the church what is good for it, but to

---

79. Gener, "Re-visioning Local Theology," 165.

80. Gener, 165. For an intentional, gospel-focused systematic theology, see Michael F. Bird, *Evangelical Theology: A Biblical and Systematic Introduction* (Grand Rapids: Zondervan, 2013).

81. Chan, *Grassroots Asian Theology*, 7.

82. Chan, 10.

83. See Gener, "Re-visioning Local Theology," 165. Cf. Tim Dakin, "The Nature of Practical Theology, Repeating Transformation: Browning and Barth on Practical Theology," *Anvil* 13, no. 3 (1996): 218–219.

84. Chan, *Grassroots Asian Theology*, 16.

listen carefully to what the Spirit of truth who indwells the church is saying through the people of God." For example, Chan argues that the concept of God as Trinitarian family could serve as theology's organizing principle for Christian theology in Asia.[85]

Thus, Asian theologies are theologies that engage issues, questions, and concerns within Asian contexts, yet which give priority to how these theologies are embodied in ecclesial engagements and experiences. In recent years, both the Asia Theological Association (ATA) and the Federation of Asian Bishops' Conference of the Catholic Church (FABC) have developed careful theological reflections dealing with poverty, religious pluralism, cultural identity, and globalization.[86] These theological reflections are instances of theologizing borne of commitment to Christian faith and ecclesial rootedness in Asian settings. They could become the building blocks for the development of contextual systematic theology in Asia.

Looking deeper in terms of method, the theological reflections from ATA and FABC make use of the Word of God as final authority in theology, but also make use of contexts as another source, albeit in a secondary way, in the process of theologizing aimed at transformation.[87] They do not seem to suggest a one-way movement of influence in theologizing but rather a two-way movement of critical or discerning transformation involving context-relatedness in Asia as well as the commitment to make sense of non-Christian insights in terms of a Christian perspective.[88] Indeed, these theologies do not just seek cultural and societal transformation through the gospel of Christ. They also draw from the unique contributions Asia brings to the universal church. For instance,

---

85. Chan, 43.

86. This section and the succeeding ones draw from my recent article, "Doing Contextual Systematic Theology in Asia," 60–62. On related FABC documents, see Gaudencio Rosales, and C. G. Arevalo, eds., *For All the Peoples of Asia: Federation of Asian Bishops' Conferences Documents from 1970–1991* (Quezon City: Claretian, 1997), 13–17; from the ATA side, see for example, Bruce Nicholls, Theresa Lua, and Julie Belding, eds., *The Church in a Changing World: An Asian Response* (Quezon City: ATA Publications, 2010); Robert J. Schreiter, *The New Catholicity* (Maryknoll: Orbis Books, 1998).

87. Helpful here is C. René Padilla, "Hermeneutics and Culture," in *Down to Earth: Studies in Christianity and Culture*, eds. Robert T. Coote and John R. W. Stott (Grand Rapids: Eerdmans, 1980), 63–78. Arguably, though, the Roman Catholic stance in theology puts church tradition alongside Scripture as part of the living Word of God. On this, see "A Report of the International Consultation between the Catholic Church and the World Evangelical Alliance (2009–2016): 'Scripture and Tradition' and the 'Church in Salvation' – Catholics and Evangelicals Explore Challenges and Opportunities," *The Holy See*, accessed 15 January 2019, http://www.vatican.va/roman_curia/pontifical_councils/chrstuni/evangelicals-docs/rc_pc_chrstuni_doc_20171017_comm-report-2009-2016_en.html.

88. See Gener, "Transformational Correlation"; also see p. 13, fn 1.

in the theological work of the Asian Bishops (FABC), we see Asia's "gifts" of spirituality, meditative prayer, the religions, and a strong family orientation as resources that could enrich the universal body of Christ, when appropriated discerningly.[89]

With respect to theological reflections within ATA, the emphases fall on common evangelical themes, such as biblical authority, atonement, and conversionism. The Asianness of such theologizing lies in emphasizing Eastern versus Western ways of thinking, "focusing mainly on the non-dualistic, concrete ways of doing theology in Asia using stories, parables, and songs, as opposed to the Cartesian, abstract, or 'Greek' way of the West."[90] There is also the desire to make the gospel come alive in Asia, which involves addressing "religious, social, political, and economic issues peculiar to the continent."[91] Asian evangelicals emphasize holistic mission, consistent with the Lausanne 1974 declarations, but usually without the underlying Euro-American presuppositions of feminism and egalitarianism. Rapid technological change is also a continuing theological concern being addressed. There is also a healthy recognition of the ethnographic context of theologizing that nevertheless refuses to allow cultural observation to eclipse the importance of spiritual or supernatural realities.

Theology of mission is at the heart of evangelical theologies in Asia, bringing the biblical message to bear on issues of religious pluralism and salvation, as well as peace and creational wholeness.[92]

References

Abbott, Walter, ed. *The Documents of Vatican II*. Piscataway: Association Press, 1966, 1982.

Abraham, William J. "The Church's Teaching on Sexuality." In *Staying the Course: Supporting the Church's Position on Homosexuality*, edited by Maxie Dunnam and H. Newton Malony, 1–26. Nashville: Abingdon, 2013.

———. *Crossing the Threshold of Divine Revelation*. Grand Rapids: Eerdmans, 2006.

---

89. Here I follow the points listed by Francis X. Clark, *An Introduction to the Catholic Church of Asia* (Quezon City: Loyal School of Theology, Ateneo de Manila University, 1987), 26–29. Of course, it bears noting that the bishops operate within a Roman Catholic theological method, which arguably situates church tradition alongside Scripture as part of the living Word of God.

90. Chan, "Evangelical Theology in Asian Contexts," 228.

91. Chan, 229.

92. Chan, 229.

Alexander, T. D., Brian S. Rosner, D. A. Carson, and Graeme Goldsworthy, eds. *New Dictionary of Biblical Theology*. Leicester: Inter-Varsity Press, 2000.
Bevans, Stephen. *An Introduction to Theology in Global Perspective*. Maryknoll: Orbis, 2009.
———. *Models of Contextual Theology*. Maryknoll: Orbis, 2002.
Bird, Michael F. *Evangelical Theology: A Biblical and Systematic Introduction*. Grand Rapids: Zondervan, 2013.
Bosch, David. *Transforming Mission*. Maryknoll: Orbis, 1991.
Braaten, Carl E., and Robert W. Jenson, eds. *Christian Dogmatics*. Vol. 1. Philadelphia: Fortress, 2011.
Chan, Simon. "Evangelical Theology in Asian Contexts." In *The Cambridge Companion to Evangelical Theology*, edited by Timothy Larsen and Daniel J. Treier, 225–240. Cambridge: Cambridge University Press, 2007.
———. *Grassroots Asian Theology*. Downers Grove: InterVarsity Press, 2014.
———. *Liturgical Theology: The Church as Worshiping Community*. Downers Grove: InterVarsity Press, 2006.
Clark, Francis X. *An Introduction to the Catholic Church of Asia*. Quezon City: Loyola School of Theology, Ateneo de Manila University, 1987.
Clendenin, Daniel. *Many Gods, Many Lords: Christianity Encounters World Religions*. Grand Rapids: Baker Books, 1995.
Cortez, Marc. "Context and Concept: Contextual Theology and the Nature of Theological Discourse." *Westminster Theological Journal* 67, no. 1 (Spring 2005): 85–102.
———. "The Insanity of Systematic Theology: A Review of Michael Bird's *Evangelical Theology*." *Southeastern Journal of Theology* 6, no. 2 (2015): 172–174.
Dakin, Tim. "The Nature of Practical Theology, Repeating Transformation: Browning and Barth on Practical Theology." *Anvil* 13, no. 3 (1996): 203–221.
D'Costa, Gavin. "Revelation and Revelations: Discerning God in Other Religions. Beyond a Static Valuation." *Modern Theology* 10, no. 2 (April 1994): 165–183.
Dunnam, Maxie D., and H. Newton Malony, eds. *Staying the Course: Supporting the Church's Position on Homosexuality*. Nashville: Abingdon, 2003.
Dupis, Jacques. *Toward a Christian Theology of Religious Pluralism*. Maryknoll: Orbis, 1997.
Dyrness, William. *The Earth Is God's*. Maryknoll: Orbis, 1997.
———. *Insider Jesus: Theological Reflections on New Christian Movements*. Downers Grove: InterVarstiy Press, 2016.
Gener, Timoteo D. "Christologies in Asia: Trends and Reflections." In *Jesus without Borders: Christology in the Majority World*, edited by Gene L. Green, K. K. Yeo, and Stephen T. Pardue, 59–80. Carlisle: Langham Global Library, 2015.
———. "Doing Contextual Systematic Theology in Asia: Challenges and Prospects." *Journal of Asian Evangelical Theology* 22 (2018): 58–64.

———. "Engaging Chung Hyun Kyung's Concept of Syncretism." *Journal of Asian Evangelical Theology* 19 (2015): 43–68.

———. "Every Filipino Christian, a Theologian: A Way of Advancing Local Theology for the 21st Century." In *Doing Theology in the Philippines*, edited by John Suk, 3–23. Mandaluyong, Philippines: OMF Literature, 2005.

———. "Re-visioning Local Theology: An Integral Dialogue with Practical Theology, a Filipino Evangelical Perspective." *Journal of Asian Mission* 6, no. 2 (2004): 133–166.

———. "Transformational Correlation: A Reformational Persepctive on Cultural Theological Method in Conversation with David Tracy's and Pail Tillich's Correlational Approach." In *That the World May Believe: Essays on Mission and Unity in Honour of George Vandervelde*, edited by Michael W. Goheen and Margaret O'Gara, 29–43. Lanham: University Press of America, 2006.

Goheen, Michael W., and Margaret O'Gara, eds. *That the World May Believe: Essays on Mission and Unity in Honour of George Vandervelde*. Lanham: University Press of America, 2006.

Gonzalez, Justo. *The Story of Christianity*. Vol. 2. New York: HarperCollins, 2010.

Green, Gene L., K. K. Yeo, and Stephen T. Pardue, eds. *Jesus without Borders: Christology in the Majority World*. Carlisle: Langham Global Library, 2015.

Grenz, Stanley J. *Revisioning Evangelical Theology*. Downers Grove: InterVarsity Press, 1993.

Grenz, Stanley J., and John Franke. *Beyond Foundationalism: Shaping Theology in a Postmodern Context*. Louisville: Westminster John Knox, 2001.

Grenz, Stanley J., and Roger E. Olson. *Who Needs Theology? An Invitation to the Study of God*. Downers Grove: InterVarsity Press, 1996.

Gunton, Colin E. "A Rose by Any Other Name? From 'Christian Doctrine' to 'Systematic Theology.'" In *Intellect and Action*, 19–46. Edinburgh: T&T Clark, 2005.

———. "Dogma, the Church and the Task of Theology Today." In *The Task of Theology Today*, edited by Victor Pfitzner and Hilary Regan, 1–22. Grand Rapids: Eerdmans, 1998.

———. *Intellect and Action*. Edinburgh: T&T Clark, 2005.

———. *The One, the Three and the Many*. Cambridge: Cambridge University Press, 1993.

Hunsberger, George. "Proposals for a Missional Hermeneutic: Mapping a Conversation." *Missiology* 39 (2011): 309–321.

Johnston, Robert K. *God's Wider Presence: Reconsidering General Revelation*. Grand Rapids: Baker, 2014.

Kapic, Kelly M., and Bruce L. McCormack, eds. *Mapping Modern Theology: A Thematic and Historical Introduction*. Grand Rapids: Baker Academic, 2012.

Kärkkäinen, Veli-Matti. *An Introduction to the Theology of Religions*. Downers Grove: InterVarsity Press, 2004.

———. *Trinity and Revelation*. Grand Rapids: Eerdmans, 2014.

Larsen, Timothy, and Daniel J. Treier, eds. *The Cambridge Companion to Evangelical Theology.* Cambridge: Cambridge University Press, 2007.
Latourelle, René. *Theology of Revelation.* New York: Alba House, 1966.
Luz, Ulrich. *Matthew in History: Interpretation, Influence, and Effects.* Minneapolis: Fortress, 1994.
Maggay, Melba. *The Gospel in Filipino Context.* Manila: OMF Literature, 1987.
McDermott, Gerald R., and Harold A. Netland. *A Trinitarian Theology of Religions: An Evangelical Proposal.* Oxford: Oxford University Press, 2014.
McDonald, H. D. *Theories of Revelation: An Historical Study 1700–1960.* Grand Rapids: Baker Books, 1979.
McGrath, Alister E. "Evangelical Theological Method: The State of the Art." In *Evangelical Futures: A Conversation on Theological Method*, edited by John G. Stackhouse, 15–38. Grand Rapids: Baker, 2000.
———. *The Order of Things: Explorations in Scientific Theology.* Oxford: Blackwell, 2006.
———. *A Passion for Truth.* Leicester: Apollos, 1997.
Mercado, Leonardo. *Elements of Filipino Theology.* Tacloban City: Divine Word Press, 1975.
Metzger, Paul Louis. "Theology of Culture and General Revelation: An Interview with Proofessor Robert K. Johnston." *Cultural Encounters* 12, no. 1 (2016): 97–103.
Naselli, Andrew David, and Collin Hansen, eds. *Four Views on the Spectrum of Evangelicalism.* Grand Rapids: Zondervan, 2011.
Nicholls, Bruce, T. Lua, and J. Belding, eds. *The Church in a Changing World: An Asian Response.* Quezon City: ATA Publications, 2010.
O'Collins, Gerald. *Rethinking Fundamental Theology.* Oxford: Oxford University Press, 2011.
———. *Revelation: Towards A Christian Interpretation of God's Self-Revelation in Jesus Christ.* Oxford: Oxford University Press, 2016.
Olson, Roger E. *How to Be an Evangelical without Being Conservative.* Grand Rapids: Zondervan, 2008.
———. *Reformed and Always Reforming: The Postconservative Approach to Evangelical Theology.* Grand Rapids: Baker Academic, 2007.
Padilla, C. René. "Hermeneutics and Culture." In *Down to Earth: Studies in Christianity and Culture*, edited by Robert T. Coote and John R. W. Stott, 63–78. Grand Rapids: Eerdmans, 1980.
———. *Mission between the Times.* Carlisle: Langham Monographs, 2010.
Pardue, Stephen T., and Timoteo D. Gener. "Global Theology: Where to from Here?" In *God at the Borders: Globalization, Migration and Diaspora*, edited by Charles Ringma, Karen Hollenbeck-Wuest, and Athena Gorospe, 67–74. Quezon City, Philippines: OMF Literature, 2015.
Pinnock, Clark. *Tracking the Maze.* New York: Harper & Row, 1990.

Quito, Emerito. *The Merging Philosophy of East and West.* Manila: De Lasalle University Press, 1991.

Reiter, Denny. "Review of H. D. McDonald, *Ideas of Revelation: An Historical Study, A.D. 1700 to A.D. 1860.*" Trinity Studies 2 (1072):100.

Ringma, C., K. Hollenbeck-Wuest, and A. Gorospe, eds. *God at the Borders.* Mandaluyong City: OMF Literature, 2015.

Rosales, Gaudencio, and C. G. Arevalo, eds. *For All the Peoples of Asia: Federation of Asian Bishops' Conferences Documents from 1970–1991.* Quezon City: Claretian, 1997.

Schreiter, Robert J. *The New Catholicity.* Maryknoll, NY: Orbis, 1998.

Stackhouse, J. G., ed. *Evangelical Futures: A Conversation on Theological Method.* Grand Rapids: Baker, 2000.

———. "A Generic Evangelical Response." In *Four Views on the Spectrum of Evangelicalism*, edited by Andrew David Naselli and Collin Hansen. Grand Rapids: Zondervan, 2011.

Stiller, Brian, Todd M. Johnson, Karen Stiller, and Mark Hurchinson, eds. *Evangelicals around the World: A Global Handbook for the 21st Century.* Nashville: Thomas Nelson, 2015.

Stott, John. *The Contemporary Christian: Applying God's Word to Today's World.* Downers Grove: InterVarsity Press, 1992.

———. *Evangelical Truth: A Personal Plea for Unity, Integrity and Faithfulness.* Leicester: Inter-Varsity Press, 1999.

Stott, John R. W., and Robert T. Coote, eds. *Down to Earth: Studies in Christianity and Culture.* Grand Rapids: Eerdmans, 1980.

Suk, John, ed. *Doing Theology in the Philippines.* Mandaluyong City: OMF Literature, 2005.

van den Torren, Benno, and Liz Hoare. "Evangelicals and Contextual Theology: Lessons from Missiology for Theological Reflection." *Practical Theology* 8, no. 2 (2015): 77–98.

Vanhoozer, Kevin, ed. "Christology in the West: Conversations in Europe and North America." In *Jesus without Borders*, edited by Gene L. Green, K. K. Yeo, and Stephen T. Pardue, 11–36. Carlisle: Langham Global Library, 2015.

———. *The Drama of Doctrine: A Canonical-Linguistic Approach to Christian Theology.* Louisville: Westminster John Knox, 2005.

———. *Faith Speaking Understanding: Performing the Drama of Doctrine.* Louisville: Westminster John Knox Press, 2014.

Vanhoozer, Kevin, Craig G. Bartholomew, Daniel J. Treier, and N. T. Wright, eds. *Dictionary for Theological Interpretation of Scripture.* Grand Rapids: Baker, 2005.

Wallace, Mark I. "Theological Table-Talk: Theology without Revelation?" *Theology Today* 45, no. 2 (July 1988): 208–213.

Webster, John, Kathryn Tanner, and Iain Torrance. *The Oxford Handbook of Systematic Theology.* Oxford: Oxford University Press, 2007.

Witherup, Ronald. *The Word of God at Vatican II: Exploring* Dei Verbum. Collegeville: Liturgical Press, 2014.
"The Willowbank Report: Consultation on Gospel and Culture." Lausanne Occasional Paper 2, Lausanne Committee on World Evangelization, 1978.
Wright, Christopher J. H. *The Mission of God: Unlocking the Bible's Grand Narrative.* Downers Grove: InterVarsity Press, 2006.
Yung, Hwa. "Review of David Bosch's *Transforming Mission*." *International Review of Mission* 81, no. 322 (1992): 321.

2

On the Doctrine of Scripture
An Asian Conversation

Havilah Dharamraj

South Asia Institute of Advanced Christian Studies

"What is scripture?" Arguably, one of the most evocative definitions is merely a phrase: scripture is "the linguistification of the sacred."[1] Wilfred Cantwell Smith's book famously takes this question as its title,[2] and argues that scripture and the way it has been treated is so diverse that it might not be "legitimate to retain the concept at all, as a generic to cover the vast field."[3] In Asia, where religions live cheek by jowl, we well acknowledge the plurality of the noun "scripture." Hinduism has the *Vēdas* and the *Bhăgăvăd Gīta*, and Islam its *Qur'ăn*. Sikhism reveres the *Gŭrŭ Grănth*, and Zoroastrianism honors its ancient *Ăvĕsta*. In some places, these sacred texts live placidly side by side; in others, they militantly compete for privilege over their rivals. Whether working intentionally or implicitly, Asian Christians find themselves developing a doctrine of the Bible in conversation with the sacred texts of their neighbors. Perhaps, from the peculiarly Christian position in which scripture is "holy writ," it is "the mere fact of their 'writtenness' [that] invites comparison between one [faith] tradition and another."[4]

---

1. Jürgen Habermas, *The Theory of Communicative Action*, vol. 2 of *Lifeworld and System: A Critique of Functionalist Reason*, trans. Thomas McCarthy (Boston: Beacon, 1984), 77–111.

2. Wilfred Cantwell Smith, *What Is Scripture? A Comparative Approach* (Minneapolis: Fortress, 1993).

3. Smith, *What Is Scripture?*, 235.

4. Thomas B. Coburn, "'Scripture' in India: Towards a Typology of the Word in Hindu Life," *Journal of the American Academy of Religion* 52, no. 3 (1984): 435. Even Smith concludes that the term "scripture" could serve a practical purpose at this particular phase in history (Smith,

So, we ask the question again, differently: How can we talk about the Bible as a Scripture among scriptures? Borrowing from Miriam Levering and Steven Smith, we first set out the features of the term. Scripture is (1) authoritative oral or written texts; (2) often believed to be of divine origin and, therefore, considered sacred and powerful; (3) canonical and normative for a certain community of faith; (4) appropriated and perpetuated as teaching to the point that it becomes an "obligatory touchstone for religious thinking."[5]

That said, we will start with the formation of the Bible. This will lead us to consider the concept of revelation and, further, of inspiration. Wherever appropriate, we will pause to check how the Bible compares or contrasts with the sacred texts of Hinduism and Islam.

The Formation of the Old Testament Canon

Even though the word "bible" simply means "book," we are aware that the Bible is a good-sized bookshelf in itself, one that contains sixty-six books. It is basic knowledge that these sixty-six books are separated into two "testaments" or "covenants" – the Old and the New. What we don't often realize is that the Old Testament, with its thirty-nine books, is really the entire scripture of another religion, namely, Judaism. That is why it is sometimes called the Hebrew Bible. To recapitulate how the Old Testament came into formation, we must go back to the Hebrew Bible.

The books of the Hebrew Bible are organized into three sections, each added at a particular point in Israel's history.[6] We should note here that the order and the number of books are different from what we have in our Bibles. This is because our Bibles reflect the ordering of (at least one of the existing manuscripts of) the Greek translation of the Hebrew Bible, the Septuagint, which is: the Pentateuch, the histories, poetry, and the prophets.[7] In the Hebrew Bible, at the front end of the arrangement is the *Torah* (meaning "law" or "instruction"). This is the five books Genesis, Exodus, Leviticus, Numbers, and Deuteronomy. This is why it is called the "Pentateuch," from the Greek meaning "five books." The Torah is referred to in the other sections of the Hebrew Bible

---

What Is Scripture?, 237).

5. Steven G. Smith, "What Is Scripture? Pursuing Smith's Question," *Anglican Theological Review*, 90, no. 4 (2008): 753–775.

6. See Greg Goswell, "The Order of the Books in the Hebrew Bible," *Journal of the Evangelical Theological Society* 51, no. 4 (2008): 673–688.

7. Greg Goswell, "The Order of the Books in the Greek Old Testament," *Journal of the Evangelical Theological Society* 52, no. 3 (2009): 449–466.

as "the law of Moses." For example, Nehemiah 8:1 tells of Ezra ceremonially reading this "Book of the Law of Moses" to an attentive public. This was the "bible" of the Jewish people until the next two sections were added to it.

The next section is the *Prophets* (in Hebrew, *Nebi'im*) divided into the Former (or "early") Prophets and the Latter Prophets. The Former Prophets consists of four books: Joshua, Judges, and the undivided books of Samuel and Kings. Why should these books be called "prophets" when they narrate the history of Israel over the period of the conquest, the settlement, the judges, and the monarchy? The title indicates that the first readers identified the key characters of these books differently from us. They laid the emphasis, not on wonder-working judges and dazzling kings, but on the prophet, the seer, and the "man of God." Indeed, the books are thickly populated with these – Samuel, Nathan and Gad, Elijah and Elisha being just a few. Even Joshua, the military commander, came to be seen as a prophet in that his words were fulfilled at a later time (1 Kgs 16:34).

The Latter Prophets contains three books: Isaiah, Jeremiah with Lamentations attached, and "the Book of the Twelve." This last book refers to the twelve shorter prophetic oracles from Hosea to Malachi, all containable within a single standard-length scroll. These "Latter Prophets" are the "classical" prophets. They differ from the earlier prophets in that their utterances have been preserved at length in writing, making these books mostly a collection of oracles, with some narrative. And, unlike the earlier prophets, who engaged primarily with the monarch, these mostly addressed the people.

The *Prophets*, containing these seven books, were considered to be sacred writ by the time the Jews had returned from the Babylonian exile and resettled in a now-impoverished land. The value of the Prophets would be that it reminded them of a history they could take pride in at a time when they were a rather insignificant outpost of the great Persian Empire. Perhaps, also, the oracles of the prophets not only cautioned them against the sins which had resulted in the exile, but also reassured them that they could hope for a future matching their past.

The *Ketuvim* or the *Writings* (in Greek, *Hagiographa* or "Sacred Writings") is the third and last section of the Hebrew Bible. Its contents are a mixed bag of ten books: the undivided books of Chronicles and Ezra–Nehemiah, which are historical narrative; Esther, which is a historical novella; Job, Proverbs, Ecclesiastes, and Song of Songs, which are categorized as wisdom literature; Psalms (poetry); and Ezekiel and Daniel, narratives embedded within a prophetic matrix, streaked with the apocalyptic. These books were arranged variously, often with Psalms beginning the section and Chronicles ending it.

This tripartite sectioning of the Hebrew Bible explains why in the time of Jesus, Luke 24:44 refers to the Scriptures in terms of "the Law of Moses, the Prophets and the Psalms." The Psalter being the opening book of the third section, the term "the Psalms" indicates the whole of the Writings. With this background, we are now in a position to understand better Jesus's reference in Matthew 23:35: "from the blood of righteous Abel to the blood of Zechariah son of Berekiah." The Hebrew Bible's list of martyrs ranges from Abel, the first, to Zechariah, the last. This Zechariah is the priest of 2 Chronicles 24:20–22. From this range, and from Luke 24:44, we infer that Jesus was referring to the Scripture as he knew it – in a tripartite arrangement of books, from Genesis to Chronicles. On the same lines, around 132 BCE, the grandson of a certain Jesus ben Sira refers to a tripartite canon: "the law and the prophets and the other books of our ancestors" (Sirach, Prologue). Whatever the date of the formal closure of the canon, it now contains the *Torah* (Law), the *Nebi'im* (Prophets) and the *Ketubim* (Writings), giving the Hebrew Bible the acronym "Tanak."

The period on either side of the millennium, from the fourth century BCE to the first century CE, generated a slew of Jewish literature, some of which is preserved as canonical in the Catholic and Eastern Orthodox traditions as the "deuterocanon," equal in authority to the chronologically earlier "protocanonical" Tanak. Like the Writings, this is a mixed collection of books including history, historical novels, and wisdom literature, both proverbial and philosophical. The number of books in the Apocrypha varies from tradition to tradition, with the Catholic Bible including seven, not counting additions to Esther and Daniel.

The argument for considering the Apocrypha part of the Old Testament has been that this was the preference of the post-Constantinian church. One reason for this is that the Septuagint was widely used by Paul and the other apostles in the spread of the gospel in the Greek-speaking Roman Empire of their day. Early manuscripts of the New Testament have the Greek translation of the Tanak attached – that is, the Septuagint, which contains apocryphal books. This gives rise to the speculation that there may have existed, in Egyptian Jewry, a longer Old Testament canon, called the "Alexandrian canon." Be that as it may, the fact remains that at some time in the second century CE, Judaism closed its Bible without these books – a fact that directed the Protestant canon. The Apocrypha, it can be argued, has historical inaccuracies and theological inconsistencies, such as prayer for the dead (2 Macc 12:46). What is more, the New Testament never cites these "extra" books. Martin Luther therefore accorded the Apocrypha a secondary status: "books which are not held equal to the Sacred Scriptures, and yet are useful and good for reading."[8] They give us a picture of the history and developing theology of the four centuries between the Testaments. Concepts like resurrection, for example, that barely find mention in the Old Testament, are treated here, giving a helpful continuity into the New Testament.

This two-tier classification of sacred literature is also common to other Asian religions. Judaism has the Torah explained and elaborated by the sages in the collection called the Talmud (or the "oral Torah"). The Qur'an is separated in status from the Hadith, which collates the traditions of the prophet Muhammad. This similarity of categorization aside, we should note that each religion places a uniquely different value on the second tier of sacred literature. While Judaism and Islam each hold the Talmud and the Hadith as authoritative for the practice of their faith, the Apocrypha is – at least for Protestants – a body of work that is of primarily historical interest.

The scriptures of Hinduism are often (over-)simplified into a somewhat similar hierarchy of holiness.[9] The higher category consists of *shrŭti* ("heard") texts. The *Vēdas* and *Upanishads* belong to this category, with some texts (such as the *Ṛg Vēda*, which possibly dates to 1200 BCE[10]) taking primacy over the others in sanctity. These are not for public recitation, lest the sacred words fall upon the ears of the lowest of the four castes, or that of women.[11] The lower category in the Hindu canon is *smrĭti*, "remembered" texts. Containing the wisdom of the sages, they complement the *shrŭti* by unpacking, expanding, and re-stating them for a wider, popular audience. Interestingly, colonial Christianity in South Asia equated *smrĭti* with the Bible. Thus, vernacular preachers in generations past regularly referred to a biblical text as *Vēda vakya* (the words of the *Vēda*) or qualified the equivalence by referring to the Bible as the *Satya Vēda* (the "true *Vēda*").

---

8. Stephen Westerholm and Martin Westerholm, *Reading Sacred Scripture: Voices from the History of Biblical Interpretation* (Grand Rapids: Eerdmans, 2016), 216.

9. Coburn, "'Scripture' in India," 439.

10. Coburn, 439.

11. Cheever Mackenzie Brown, *God as Mother: A Feminine Theology in India* (Hartford: Claude Stark & Co, 1974), 18–19.

The Formation of the New Testament Canon[12]

In the early church period, certain writings which were considered to be scripture began to emerge.

There were mainly three criteria for their recognition as sacred text: apostolicity, catholicity, and orthodoxy. Apostolicity was the dominant criterion in the centuries before Constantine.[13] It required that the book was written either by an authoritative eyewitness of Jesus's ministry – as were the twelve disciples and, later, Paul (1 Cor 15:8) – or by someone closely connected with that eyewitness. Thus, Jesus's half-brothers James and Jude, though not disciples, were considered valid eyewitnesses. Luke's "apostolicity" comes from his having access to first-hand accounts for the writing of his Gospel (Luke 1:1–4), and from having traveled with Paul (Col 4:14; 2 Tim 4:11; Phlm 1:24). Mark, similarly, was legitimated by his proximity to both Paul and Peter (Acts 12:11–12; 12:25; 2 Tim 4:11). The criterion of apostolicity meant that all the books of the New Testament were composed within the first century CE, before the death of the longest-living of Jesus's disciples, John.

Catholicity, the second criterion, meant that the book was "catholic" in the sense of "universal." That is, the book was in use across the Christian world of that time, and considered of value for the faith and its practice. The third criterion was that of orthodoxy or non-contradiction. This was established in resistance to the heresies of the early centuries, all of which in some way challenged apostolic teaching. Orthodoxy required that the book being considered for canonical status should be faithful to this teaching, and, beyond that, be in continuity with the Old Testament, which looks toward a future restoration by an agent of God. Jesus, in his life and work, was seen as that agent, one who would complete the fulfillment of the ancient promises and prophecies at his return. In summary, by the end of the fourth century, the twenty-seven books of the New Testament were seen as authoritative and divinely inspired, because they "were composed in connection with an apostle, doctrinally sound, and widely circulated and used by the churches."[14]

---

12. I am indebted to my student Samuel Selvin for assisting with some of the research for this essay, specifically for this section.

13. Craig L. Blomberg, *Can We Still Believe the Bible? An Evangelical Engagement with Contemporary Questions* (Grand Rapids: Baker, 2014), 59.

14. Tremper Longman III, ed., *The Baker Illustrated Bible Dictionary* (Grand Rapids: Baker, 2013), 293.

If a certain text in oral or written circulation came to be considered sacred within its faith community, it was because it was seen as divine revelation. This is the concept we now turn to discuss.

Revelation

Common to sacred texts is revelation, commonly understood as the self-disclosure of deity to humans.[15] Here it is profitable to see how Christianity sits (or doesn't sit) alongside the two major religions in South and Southeast Asia – one ancient and one young – Hinduism and Islam.[16]

In Hindu sacred literature, the *shrŭti* category claims revelation by its very name. Coming from the root "to hear," *shrŭti* is the repository of "holy hearing" by those who "through extraordinary perspicacity and auditory acuity"[17] were able to penetrate the realm of the divine. What is more, *shrŭti* is open-ended in two ways – one textual, and the other experiential.

Here Smith argues that the concept of scripture was "imported" into Hinduism from the Christian West.[18] Historically, rather than having one set canon, a number of texts have played a scriptural role at various points in the life of different Hindu groups, large or small, over the last two thousand years.[19] Not all these texts are *shrŭti* texts; a good case in point is the *Bhăgăvăd Gīta*. This is a 700-line excerpt from the *Măhābhārăta*, an epic poem in the *smrĭti* category. Over time and usage, some branches of Hinduism came to recognize the *Gīta* as a summary of the *Upănishăds* and elevated it to the status of *shrŭti*. In modern times, the *Gīta* is the closest to the Western idea of what constitutes scripture and this, perhaps, has made it a free-standing text that enjoys the status of divine revelation.[20] Meanwhile, the *Măhābhārăta*, its parent text, continues with the relatively lower status of *smrĭti* literature.

A second way *shrŭti* is open-ended is through a "spiritually awake person" such as a *gŭru* ("master"). Such a one is so in tune with the supra-mundane (so much so that he may be considered divine himself) that "[i]t is from him

---

15. Robert Detweiler, "What Is a Sacred Text?," *Semeia* 31 (1985): 218–219.
16. For a quick note on the doctrine of revelation in Christian theology on both sides of modernity, see Veli-Matti Kärkkäinen, *Trinity and Revelation*, A Constructive Christian Theology for the Pluralistic World, vol. 2 (Grand Rapids: Eerdmans, 2014), 9–14.
17. Coburn, "'Scripture' in India," 442.
18. Smith, *What Is Scripture?*, 128.
19. Smith, 126.
20. Smith, 128.

that the 'Scriptures' proceed and the world receives guidance and inspiration."[21] The distinguishing distinctive to note about *shrŭti* revelation is that it exists not confined within the covers of a sacred book, but on a continuum that stretches from a time now shrouded by the mists of antiquity down to the present day. This well explains the veneration Hindus would display toward one they consider a *gŭru*, a veneration that to an Indian Christian would seem bafflingly irrational. The *gŭru* is seen as a wellspring of ongoing "revelation."

In Islam, on the contrary, revelation is directed at one single individual. In 610 AD, Muhammad had an encounter in a desert cave. He heard the angel Gabriel urging him: "Recite! Recite in the name of thy Lord!" The words that he had to recite were revealed to him, and with this began a series of revelations covering twenty-three years, disclosed to a person who was unable either to read or write.

It can be posited that the nature of the revelation indicates the nature of the deity involved, with the manner of self-disclosure being one indicator of this nature.[22] With the Qur'an there are two significant points to note. One is that the revelation is mediated by an angel. The other is that this corpus of revelation is not the self-disclosure of deity, but rather of his will. Therefore, the Qur'an does not communicate who Allah is, but only instructs the human how to live according to Allah's will. Intriguingly, this is close to the view of revelation articulated by the Jewish thinker Abraham Heschel: "It is improper to employ the term 'self-revelation' in regard to biblical prophecy. God never reveals Himself. He is above and beyond all revelation. He discloses only a word. He never unveils His essence. He communicates only His *pathos*, His will."[23] This nature of revelation in Islam – which includes an angelic intermediary and excludes self-disclosure – points to the nature of Allah as one who is utterly transcendent, one who stays entirely outside human experience.[24]

Revelation in the Old Testament was sometimes mediated by heavenly messengers.[25] More often, revelation was direct. The "word of the LORD" would directly "come" to a prophet so that he could declare, for example, "Thus says the LORD . . . " The Lord would manifest himself or his presence to human

---

21. Gopinath Kaviraj, *Aspects of Indian Thought* (Burdwan: University of Burdwan, 1967), 44.

22. See Christina Hitchcock, "A Living God, a Living Word: Christian and Muslim Revelation in Perspective," *Missiology: An International Review* 42, no. 4 (2014): 375–385.

23. Abraham J. Heschel, *The Prophets*, 2 vols in 1 (Peabody: Prince Press, 2003), 2:215, originally published 1962.

24. Hitchcock, "Living God," 376–378.

25. Angelic mediation continues into the New Testament; e.g. the Gospels, Revelation.

perception through any of a range of media: as natural phenomena (Exod 19:18); as the "angel of the Lord" (e.g. Gen 16:7; 22:11; Exod 3:2; Num 22:22; Judg 13:20; 1 Chr 21:16); as "glory" (e.g. Exod 16:10; 24:16–17; 33:22; 40:35; 2 Chr 5:14) or "fire from heaven" (1 Kgs 18:38–39); and even, as himself in person (e.g. 1 Sam 3:10; Exod 34:5–6). Beyond this, every intervention of God through his acts on behalf of Israel, at the individual level as much as at the level of the nation, constitutes divine self-disclosure.

With the New Testament, this self-disclosure reaches its fullness (Heb 1:1–3a). God is incarnated, that is, he takes on human flesh and form. He is "the image of the invisible God" (Col 1:15). Jesus subsumes into himself both message and medium and is therefore called the "Word of God." Thus, for Christianity, "[r]evelation is not a system of divine oracles only. It is primarily the system of divine deeds; one might say, revelation was the path of God in history. And the climax was reached when God entered history himself."[26] This assertion creates a head-on collision with Judaism's boast in the Talmud: "It follows from the perfection of the *Torah* that it can never be improved upon, and therefore God will never supersede it by another Revelation."[27] On the contrary, it can be argued that the evangelist John presents Jesus as the new Torah,[28] one in whom is invested all of its authority. Thus, we could say that in contrast to the sacred texts of other religions, the primary agent of divine revelation in the Christian faith is not the Bible per se, but rather Jesus Christ.[29] The function that the Old and New Testaments perform is to point to Jesus, to bear witness to him.

Here it is worth noting that the very canonical order of books itself generates and conveys meaning. The concentric ordering of the books of the Hebrew Bible points to Moses and the law. Setting aside this focus, Martin Luther in his German translation (1534) preferred the Greek Septuagint's arrangement which lumped the historical books together (Genesis to Esther) and followed them up with the prophets (Isaiah to Malachi), an order which continues into all Protestant Bibles today. This, Luther reckoned, segued the Old Testament into the New, with prophecy preparing the way for the Messiah.

---

26. Georges Florovsky, *Collected Works*, vol. 1, *Bible, Church, Tradition: An Eastern Orthodox View* (Belmont: Nordland, 1973), 18.

27. Abraham Cohen, *Everyman's Talmud: The Major Teachings of the Rabbinic Sages* (New York: Schocken Books, 1975), 131–132.

28. See Daniel Boerman, "The Self-Revelation of God in Jesus," *Calvin Theological Journal* 52, no. 1 (2017): 28–33.

29. Lydia Harder, "The Bible as Canon and as Word of God: Exploring the Mystery of Revelation," *The Conrad Grebel Review* 24, no. 1 (2006): 55.

Thus, the Christian canon's order itself mediates meaning critical to the core belief of the Christian reader: that revelation climaxes in Jesus.[30] As Veli-Matti Kärkkäinen puts it, "The incarnated, embodied nature of Christian revelation is indeed its most distinctive feature among religions."[31]

What is the purpose of revelation in sacred texts? Hinduism harnesses the *shrŭti* and *smrĭti* canons differently.[32] The *smrĭti* literature, which is generally more intentionally didactic, is often delivered to the devotee translated and interpreted, often via performance arts.[33] With the *shrŭti* literature, the impulse is quite the opposite. These sacred words, which are the eternal hum of the universe captured and frozen into human words,[34] when "duly formulated and rhythmically pronounced," become potent *măntrās* (the "formulae"). When a mantra is uttered, it is thought to set power into motion.[35] This being the case, Coburn explains that "the holiness of holy words is not a function of their intelligibility. On the contrary, sanctity often appears to be inversely related to comprehensibility."[36] Thus, the need for interpretation becomes peripheral, and for the greater part of popular practice, piety is demonstrated by hearing, memorizing, and reciting scripture[37] – a piety that the devotee hopes will bring either material or spiritual gain, or both. Thus, sacred literature has two functions, the didactic and the sacramental.

Within the Islamic community of faith, the Qur'an operates similarly.[38] On one hand, the Qur'an is "a book of guidance to the God-fearing" (Qur'an 2:1–5). Its precepts and principles are thought to provide direction on conduct, whether for the private individual or for the government of a state. On the other hand, the words themselves are considered potent. Thus, it is believed that a devotee will be rewarded on the Day of Resurrection according to the number

---

30. Stefan Alkier, "Intertextuality and the Semiotics of Biblical Texts," in *Reading the Bible Intertextually*, eds. Richard B. Hays, Stefan Alkier, and Leroy Huizenga (Waco: Baylor University Press, 2009), 12.

31. Kärkkäinen, *Trinity and Revelation*, 24.

32. Coburn rightly hesitates to make a clear demarcation between the *shrŭti* and *smrĭti* canons. See his nuanced treatment in "'Scripture' in India," 447–450.

33. Coburn, "'Scripture' in India," 450.

34. Coburn, 452.

35. J. Gonda, *The Vision of the Vedic Poets* (Berlin: De Gruyter, 1963), 63–64, 66.

36. Coburn, "'Scripture' in India," 445.

37. Coburn, 447; see also 452.

38. Daniella Talmon-Heller has two informative articles that help give perspective on the Qur'ān: "Reciting the Qur'ān and Reading the Torah: Muslim and Jewish Attitudes and Practices in a Comparative Historical Perspective," *Religion Compass* 6, no. 8 (2012): 369–380; "Scriptures as Holy Objects: Preliminary Comparative Remarks on the Qur'ān and the Torah in the Medieval Middle East," *Intellectual History of the Islamicate World* 4 (2016): 210–244.

of qur'anic verses committed to memory. Faith in its talisman-like properties motivates the inscription of its texts on buildings and vehicles.[39] Indeed, Islam's boast in the inimitability of the Qur'an (*iǧāz al-Qur'ān*) is demonstrated by the memorized recitation of the text,[40] with the correct pronunciation capable of rehearsing the original event of revelation and thereby invoking powerful benevolent effects.[41]

How is the purpose of biblical revelation different from that claimed in other religions? Biblical revelation is uniquely relational:[42] "The revelation of God is . . . a divine act of mercy throughout time and eternity directed to reconciliation" of God with humankind.[43] This act of mercy, as we have said, is consummated in the person and work of Jesus.

Besides the unique nature and purpose of biblical revelation, a third point of distinction is its involvement of all three persons of the Godhead. We have seen the work of the Father and the Son. How does the Holy Spirit participate in biblical revelation? The Spirit is regularly associated with the medium of revelation – the scripture. For example, John Stott wrote:

> The classic statement of the Holy Spirit's work in the inspiration of Scripture remains 2 Timothy 3:16: "All Scripture is given by inspiration of God" (AV), or literally is God-breathed (*theopneustos*). The word means neither that God breathed into the writers, enabling them to write his word, nor that he breathed into the writings, transforming them from human words into divine words, but rather that what they wrote was breathed out of the mouth of God. This reference to the breath of God is congruous with references elsewhere to his mouth and his words. For in speech our breath communicates our words out of our mouths. It is not literal, of course. Since God is Spirit he has no body, and since he has no body he has neither mouth nor breath. Yet human speech is a readily intelligible model of divine inspiration, since it conveys the thoughts of our minds in words out of our mouth

---

39. Mahmoud M. Ayub, "The Quran in Muslim Life and Practice," in *The Muslim Almanac*, ed. Azim Nanji (Detroit: Gale Research, 1996), 355–364.
40. Talmon-Heller, "Scriptures as Holy Objects," 239.
41. See Talmon-Heller, "Reciting the Qur'ān," 374.
42. Harder, "Bible as Canon," 56–57.
43. Harder, 57.

by our breath. It is in this sense that Scripture may accurately be described as "God-breathed."[44]

Beyond this function of actualizing the written "word," the Bible, there is the Spirit's critical function of actualizing the living "Word," Jesus. Indeed, the incarnation is mediated by "the power and energies of the Holy Spirit."[45] Thus, we see revelation as the reconciliatory work of the Father, manifested through the Son, and effected by the Spirit.

So what might we say of revelation in other religions? In an era past, the Scottish missionary to India John Nicol Farquhar famously championed the idea that Christ fulfills the best in Hinduism,[46] an idea that could be applied to other religions and their sacred texts. At the other end of the spectrum there is the view that there is no relationship between the Bible and any other sacred text. A characteristic of biblicism is that we must never expect to find a spiritual truth anywhere outside the covers of the Bible. This position would undermine the possibility of general revelation (Ps 8; Rom 1:18–20). Craig Blomberg rightly prefers a third option: "If it is wrong to expect to find salvific truth in other world religions . . . it is equally wrong to expect to be able to learn nothing, even just about the human condition, from other religions."[47] Copeland captures this sentiment in the image of dim flickering lamps with blackened globes.[48] What light they are capable of serves a purpose similar to that of the Bible, that is, of pointing to the Light of the World (John 8:12).

Here an interesting experiment undertaken in India is to read the texts of Hinduism with a Christian agenda in mind – called the *dhvani* ("resonance") reading. Brahmabandab Upadhyay (1869–1907) composed his "Ode to the Trinity" (1898) in which he described the Trinity using concepts defining the Absolute Being that can be traced back to the sacred texts called the *Upanishads* (ca. 600 BCE). The Sanskrit words and Hindu concepts maintain a degree of continuity when transposed across religions, even while the original takes on

---

44. John Stott, *Evangelical Truth: A Personal Plea for Unity, Integrity and Faithfulness* (Carlisle: Langham Global Library, 2014), 29–30.

45. Kärkkäinen, *Trinity and Revelation*, 26.

46. J. N. Farquhar, *The Crown of Hinduism* (Oxford: Oxford University Press, 1913).

47. Blomberg, *Can We Still Believe the Bible?*, 80.

48. Edwin Luther Copeland, *Christianity and World Religions* (Nashville: Convention Press, 1963).

a new application and, therefore, a new meaning. In a sort of *sensus plenior*, the Sanskrit text is made to "resonate" with biblical truth.[49]

The Word of God: Inspiration and Inscripturation

"Linguistified" sacred words eventually make their way into scrolls and books, palm leaves and paper. From the Christian perception of scripture as "holy writ," this process is "inscripturation" and is mediated by "inspiration."

Moller[50] relates revelation and inspiration like this: "Within the broader frame of the divine economy, the word (lower case) of God and then the Word (upper case) enter human history." Those who are encountered by these events of divine self-revelation are moved by the "charism of inspiration" to "preserve and transmit God's own self-communication." The sacred text, then, is "a permanent record that arises from a participation in revelation."[51] The production of this record could span years, or even centuries, and includes a complicated interweaving of oral and written transmission, proclamation and transcription, selection and compilation, editing and copying. The actors involved range from prophets and apostles to nameless redactors and scribes. Thus, Moller rightly points out that the "charism of inspiration" is more often located in the community of faith than in a single individual. The final text is then a collaborative articulation of the faith of the believing community.[52] This said, we emphasize with Stott that

---

49. See George Gispert-Sauch, "Christians in Asia Read Sacred Books of the East," in *The Oxford Handbook of Christianity in Asia*, ed. Felix Wilfred (Oxford: Oxford University Press, 2015), 487–489.

50. Here I have followed with interest the Catholic theologian Philip Moller, revisiting Vatican II's (1965) "Dogmatic Constitution on Divine Revelation" (*Dei Verbum*) in "What Should They Be Saying about Biblical Inspiration? A Note on the State of the Question," *Theological Studies* 74 (2013): 605–631.

51. Moller, "What Should They Be Saying?," 613–614.

52. Moller, 622. It is at this point that one could engage with the nature of the divine-human dual agency at work in inscripturation. The word that needs unpacking is, of course, "inspiration." Garrett boils down the debate on the nature of inspiration into six positions. See James Leo Garrett, Jr., *Systematic Theology*, vol. 1 (Grand Rapids: Eerdmans, 1990), 46–47. A subsequent round of unpacking involves more terms. In America and to those parts of the world that are influenced by American missionary efforts, *inerrancy* is generally seen as a defining element of the concept of inspiration. Other parts of the world speak of *infallibility*. Either they imply *inerrancy*, or consciously reject the term as one too narrow to apply to the Bible. (On this see, e.g. A. T. B. McGowan, *The Divine Authenticity of Scripture: Retrieving an Evangelical Heritage* [Downers Grove: InterVarsity Press, 2007], 162 and throughout; Robert C. Kurka, "Has 'Inerrancy' Outlived Its Usefulness?," *Stone-Campbell Journal* 18 [2015]: 187–204.) For those wishing to pursue the terms in detail, and the (stormy!) debates that have swirled around them, a very helpful overview, with relevant primary source materials, is Stephen J. Nichols and Eric T.

> [t]his does not mean that God somehow breathed into words which had already been written, or into the writers who wrote them, but rather that the words themselves were "God-breathed" (II Tim 3:16, literally). Of course, they were also the words of men who spoke and wrote freely. Yet these men were "moved by the Holy Spirit" (II Pet 1:21) to such an extent that it could be said of their words "the mouth of the Lord has spoken it" (Isa 40:5).[53]

With the New Testament canon, the issue of inspiration became a talking point alongside the other three criteria for canonicity. Of course, by this time, the Hebrew Bible was the sacred scripture of the church – and it is worthwhile for us to start our discussion on inspiration there. Unlike much of the New Testament, the books of each of the three sections of the Hebrew Bible nearly all had a period of oral circulation and transmission, some longer than others, before they came to be put into writing. Often, a book was constructed by assembling various literary pieces in circulation, both oral and written. The books of Kings, for example, point to sources as varied as "the Book of the Wars of the LORD" (Num 21:14) and "the annals of the kings of Judah" (14:29). More intriguingly, the Psalter contains two psalms which are identical except for minor variations: Psalms 14 and 53. Once the books were put together, how was it decided which books entered the sacred canon and which stayed out? Knowing that there are many other literary works of these times that did not find their way into the Hebrew Bible, (e.g. the book of Jashar, mentioned in Josh 10:13), we wonder what criteria were followed in attributing inspiration.

For the purposes of understanding how the Hebrew Bible views inspiration, it is helpful to visualize the three sections not as a linear sequence, but as three concentric rings. The Torah forms the core, with the Prophets and Writings laid out in encircling rings, each ring diminishing in inspiration. Judaism largely identified inspiration with the prophetic voice which gave out oracles in the name of the LORD. This being the case, the Torah claimed the status of a benchmark of inspiration, for was it not the work of one who spoke with God face to face (Exod 33:11; Num 12:8)?

The Prophets derived their authority from their oracular voices speaking in consonance with the Mosaic core. Many of these oracles had passed the test for true prophecy – fulfillment (Deut 18:21–22). Further, even the historical

---

Brandt, *Ancient Word, Changing Worlds: The Doctrine of Scripture in a Modern Age* (Wheaton: Crossway, 2009).

53. John Stott, "The Lausanne Covenant: An Exposition and Commentary by John Stott (LOP 3)," Lausanne Movement, accessed 15 January 2019, https://www.lausanne.org/content/lop/lop-3#2.

books of this second ring – Joshua, Judges, Samuel, and Kings – would have been favored because they used a fundamental Deuteronomic principle as their yardstick for the evaluation of judges and kings: that is, the principle that obedience brings reward and disobedience brings retribution (Deut 28).

In the outermost ring, the Writings, we are moving steadily into a time when the voice of prophecy is heard less and less, and then ceases altogether. Now, increasingly, tradition becomes the yardstick by which to measure inspiration. Thus, books used in the temple rituals and worship, or at the main Jewish festivals, would have eventually become part of Scripture. Examples of these are Psalms and the group called the "Five Scrolls": Ruth was read at the autumnal harvest festival of Weeks or Firstfruits; Song of Songs at Passover; Ecclesiastes at the feast of Shelters (or Tabernacles); Lamentations on the ninth of the month of Ab, the date on which both Solomon's temple and the Second Temple fell; and Esther, at Purim.

Unsurprisingly, there was debate on the sacred status of certain books in this outermost ring. We have evidence of this from rabbinic discussions as late as the second half of the first century CE on at least five books: Proverbs (because other contemporary cultures had similar non-sacred collections); Esther (because it appears to present the interventions of God as a series of coincidences); Ecclesiastes (because of its seeming pessimism); Ezekiel (because the temple-related measurements in chapter 46 do not correspond to Moses's tabernacle as did Solomon's temple); and, unsurprisingly, Song of Songs (because its embarrassing verse was considered more at home in a tavern than in a sacred canon).

All this reminds us that a doctrine of the Bible recognizes the human role in bridging the revealed sacred words and the material sacred text. Thus, inscripturation is the result of a pair of terms: revelation (by God) and inspiration (of humans). So, while it is true that Scripture is a *collection of authoritative books*, in that it is divinely inspired, it is equally true that Scripture is also an *authoritative collection of books*, in that humans discerned the authority of inspiration and submitted to it, recognizing certain books as sacred. With the Old Testament, for the most part, this recognizing must have happened gradually, with long-term community use sanctioning the sacred status of the books. For the New Testament, the first we know of a list with the twenty-seven books of our New Testament canon is from the Easter letter to the church from Athanasius, bishop of Alexandria in 367 CE. This list, on which there had been broad agreement from as early as perhaps the second century CE, was officially ratified at the Councils of Hippo (393) and Carthage (397). Blomberg nicely sums up this dispensation of discernment:

"Jews and Christians alike frequently have believed that God's Spirit testifies to his people as to which books are divinely revealed. That testimony comes to communities, not just individuals, and thus fosters international and ecumenical conversations and councils."[54] With this, we may consider the canons of the Old and New Testaments closed.

While this closed canon is, in the main, considered *norma normans non normata* (the ultimate norm above which there is no other norm), there have since been instances of alleged "revelation." Some recipients demand that their "revelations" be added to the existing canon, as was the case with Joseph Smith, leading to the (much expanded) Mormon Bible. Some recipients are more modest, but, nevertheless, vigorously claim their "revelations" to have authority on a par with that of the Bible, as do a slew of present-day high-profile charismatics.[55] Some "revelations" are relatively recent archaeological finds, like the "Gospel of Thomas." This is possibly a sectarian text, and claims to be a collection of the sayings of Jesus, discovered in 1945 in Egypt and dated to the first or second centuries CE. None of these "revelations" meet the criteria of the church councils, and, as such, will have to content themselves with camping hopefully on the steps of the permanently shut doors of the New Testament canon.

That sacred words are inscripturated and canonized by inspiration is alien to Islam. The Qur'an allows no human involvement in the recording of the revelation. Muhammad is merely a conduit for the words that are entrusted to him for passing on to the community of faith. Thus, the holy words must be untouched by human influence, and untranslated from Muhammad's Arabic rendering. Indeed, translation would evacuate the sacred text of its sanctity, rendering it no longer the Qur'an. Even though Muhammad passed on the words he heard to others, who then memorized or transcribed them, and even though the production of a standardized Qur'an took till the early tenth century CE and was achieved by reducing the dozens of variant traditions to seven canonical ones and destroying or withdrawing from circulation the rest,[56] the authority of the text lies in the claim that the divine words remain "exact

---

54. Blomberg, *Can We Still Believe the Bible?*, 63.

55. See John MacArthur, "Does God Still Give Revelation?," *Master's Seminary Journal* 14, no. 2 (2003): 217–234, for some interesting examples. For prophets and prophecy in the Old and New Testaments and today, watch Ben Witherington, "How Does Biblical Prophecy Work?," Seven Minute Seminary, *Seedbed*, published 19 November 2014, YouTube, https://www.youtube.com/watch?v=35za3lkflzE; and "What Is a Prophet: Seven Minute Seminary," Seven Minute Seminary, *Seedbed*, published 10 October 2012, YouTube, https://www.youtube.com/watch?v=VMhgaMVLHcY.

56. Talmon-Heller, "Scriptures as Holy Objects," 216–217, 228, 232.

and unadulterated" from their point of reception as divine revelation.[57] Other than this, the fact is that "the role of the written scriptural text has always been secondary to the dominant tradition of oral transmission and aural presence of the recited text."[58] Indeed, the title "Qur'an" derives from the verb "to recite."[59]

With Hinduism, it is deeply important to understand that "there has never been a happy marriage between the holy words of India, composed and transmitted orally, and the writing process."[60] The descriptors of the texts of highest sanctity are all aural – *shrŭti* ("that which is heard"), *vāc* ("word"), and *shăbda* ("sound").[61] A Vedic text describes this aural authority thus: "The Word, imperishable, is the Firstborn of Truth, mother of the *Vēda* and the hub of immortality."[62] In a late Vedic text, writing itself was held to be ritually polluting.[63] Across the millennia, orality and aurality has always been, and continues to be, a defining distinctive of Hindu sacred canon.

To an Asian Christian, an interesting (and even necessary) exercise is to see how the Bible's "writtenness" can be put into theological conversation with the aurality of the *shrŭti* canon and of the Qur'an. The starting point for that conversation could be this: revelation in Hinduism is the cosmic *shăbda* ("sound") captured into *vāc* ("word"); in Islam, as we mentioned earlier, the aurality of the Qur'an is favored to the point that even its recitation is standardized to attempt a replication of Muhammad's experience. Meanwhile, the Bible is called the "word of God." The difference between the "word" as conceived of in Hinduism and Islam, and the "word" as used in Christian scripture is captured by both the Old and New Testaments. The Old Testament uses *dabar* for the divine word that comes to the prophets, where *dabar* means both "word" and "event." Vatican II's *Dei Verbum* nicely links the two: "the deeds wrought by God in the history of salvation manifest and confirm the teaching and realities signified by the words, while the words proclaim the

---

57. Amir Dastmalchian, "Swinburne's View of the Islamic Revelation," *Journal of Shi'a Islamic Studies* 1, no. 4 (2008): 99.

58. W. A. Graham, "Orality," in *Encyclopaedia of the Qur'ān*, vol. 3, ed. Jane Dammen McAuliffe (Leiden: Brill, 2003), 584.

59. The verb is common to Judaism's scripture, since the Tanak is alternatively called *miqra*. However, here the verb is rendered "to read" rather than "to recite."

60. Coburn, "'Scripture' in India," 437.

61. John Grimes, "The Contribution of the Study of Scripture to the Study of Theology," *Religious Studies and Theology* 9, no. 2 (1989): 50.

62. *Taittirīya Brāhmaṇa*, II.8.8.5, in R. Pannikar, *The Vedic Experience* (Berkeley: University of California Press, 1977).

63. The *Aitareya Āraṇyaka*, V.5.3 requires that the *Vēda* may not be recited immediately after any one of the following: the consumption of meat; the sight of either blood or a dead body; intercourse; writing.

deeds" (#2). The New Testament continues this linking: in Jesus, the *logos* ("Word") incarnate, "[t]he gospel is something *said* about something *done... Speaking is one of God's mighty acts.*"[64]

Thus, in the Christian doctrine of Scripture, the familiar term "word of God" gets an overhaul that makes it particularly relevant to Asians. Kevin Vanhoozer holds these multiple facets together by describing the "word of God" as "divine discourse." A "discourse" (1) at once requires both "saying" and "doing"; (2) better "corresponds to the biblical depiction of God as a communicative agent"; and (3) envisages the Bible as the medium by which we converse with, and therefore relate to, God.[65] When this divine discourse is brought to fullness in Jesus, we may speak of the "Word of God" which is three things in one. The Word of God is something God says, something God is, and something God does. Perhaps in that order, it is the word "inscripturate" (the Bible), the word "incarnate" (Jesus Christ), and the word "incardiate" (taken to heart).[66] When taken "to heart," the Christian faithful find that God has indeed "given us everything we need for a godly life through our knowledge of him" (2 Pet 1:3). This is what is formulated as the sufficiency of the Bible. The assertion of "material sufficiency"[67] is that "Scripture contains everything necessary to be known and responded to for salvation and faithful discipleship."[68] The Bible, when "incardiate," transforms the one taking it to heart.

Transformation, Detweiler explains, is an important characteristic of scriptures. The scripture in question may effect it either indirectly or directly: "Indirectly [scriptures transform] by describing some extra-textual path to salvation, enlightenment, nirvana, unusual power." This extra-textual path

---

64. Kevin J. Vanhoozer, *The Drama of Doctrine: A Canonical Linguistic Approach to Christian Doctrine* (Louisville: Westminster John Knox, 2005), 46.

65. Kevin J. Vanhoozer, "Word of God," in *Dictionary of Theological Interpretation of the Bible*, eds. Kevin J. Vanhoozer et al. (Grand Rapids: Baker Academic, 2005), 853. The speech-act theory underlies this conception of Scripture, where speech (the illocutionary act) is distinguished from the act of simply uttering words (the locutionary act) in that speech has the potential to elicit the intended response in the recipient of the speech (the perlocutionary act).

66. Vanhoozer, "Word of God," 854.

67. As compared with "formal sufficiency," which sets out that Scripture is "self-interpreting" and, as such, cannot be submitted to any interpretive authority, such as, for example, a church pastor or official.

68. Timothy Ward, "Scripture, Sufficiency of," in *Dictionary of Theological Interpretation*, eds., Kevin J. Vanhoozer et al. (Grand Rapids: Baker, 2005), 730. See a reformulation of the doctrine of sufficiency using the speech-act theory in Timothy Ward, "Reconstructing the Doctrine of the Sufficiency of Scripture," *Tyndale Bulletin* 52, no. 1 (2001): 155–159. A disclaimer here is that since this is the Bible's divinely intended purpose, the concept of sufficiency does not imply that "Scripture necessarily gives exhaustive knowledge of God, the world, ourselves, history, or protological and eschatological events" (Ward, "Scripture, Sufficiency of," 731).

may take the form of "a formula to follow, a discipline to exercise, a trip to undertake, a saviour figure to recognize, emulate and obey." The text functions as the guidebook for transformation.[69] In their didactic capacity, this is how the Qur'an and the *smrĭti* canon of Hinduism work.

Besides this, as we have seen, a scripture can function directly by itself operating as the instrument of transformation. It is "as if divinity indwelt the words and caused them, through articulation of them, to bring about altered states of being." Here, scripture becomes "incantatory or sacramental."[70] Typically, this is how the *shrŭti* canon of Hinduism works, as also the Qur'an in its capacity as the very communication of Allah.

In contrast, the Bible effects transformation by pointing to Jesus as the only means by which fellowship with God becomes available to anyone, and beyond that, by calling into being that fellowship.

When the religions of Asia sit down together to answer the question "What is Scripture?," the Christian answer differentiates itself by calling attention not so much to the "text," whether oral or written, but to a triune God seeking to reconcile to himself all the peoples of the earth.

References

Alkier, Stefan. "Intertextuality and the Semiotics of Biblical Texts." In *Reading the Bible Intertextually*, edited by Richard B. Hays, Stefan Alkier, and Leroy Huizenga, 3–22. Waco: Baylor University Press, 2009.
Ayub, Mahmoud M. "The Quran in Muslim Life and Practice." In *The Muslim Almanac*, edited by Azim Nanji, 355–364. Detroit: Gale Research, 1996.
Boerman, Daniel. "The Self-Revelation of God in Jesus." *Calvin Theological Journal* 52, no. 1 (2017): 9–36.
Blomberg, Craig L. *Can We Still Believe the Bible? An Evangelical Engagement with Contemporary Questions*. Grand Rapids: Brazos, 2014.
Brown, Cheever Mackenzie. *God as Mother: A Feminine Theology in India*. Hartford: Claude Stark & Co., 1974.
Coburn, Thomas B. "'Scripture' in India: Towards a Typology of the Word in Hindu Life." *Journal of the American Academy of Religion* 52, no. 3 (1984): 435–459.
Cohen, Abraham. *Everyman's Talmud: The Major Teachings of the Rabbinic Sages*. New York: Schocken Books, 1975.
Copeland, Edwin Luther. *Christianity and World Religions*. Nashville: Convention Press, 1963.

---

69. Detweiler, "What Is a Sacred Text?," 220–221.
70. Detweiler, 221.

Dastmalchian, Amir. "Swinburne's View of the Islamic Revelation." *Journal of Shi'a Islamic Studies* 1, no. 4 (2008): 95–106.

Detweiler, Robert. "What Is a Sacred Text?" *Semeia* 31 (1985): 213–230.

Farquhar, J. N. *The Crown of Hinduism*. Oxford: Oxford University Press, 1913.

Florovsky, Georges. *Collected Works*. Vol. 1: *Bible, Church, Tradition: An Eastern Orthodox View*. Belmont: Nordland, 1973.

Garrett, Jr., James Leo. *Systematic Theology*. Vol. 1. Grand Rapids: Eerdmans, 1990.

Gispert-Sauch, George. "Christians in Asia Read Sacred Books of the East." In *The Oxford Handbook of Christianity in Asia*, edited by Felix Wilfred, 480–492. Oxford: Oxford University Press, 2015.

Gonda, J. *The Vision of the Vedic Poets*. Berlin: De Gruyter, 1963.

Goswell, Greg. "The Order of the Books in the Greek Old Testament." *Journal of the Evangelical Theological Society* 52, no. 3 (2009): 449–466.

———. "The Order of the Books in the Hebrew Bible." *Journal of the Evangelical Theological Society* 51, no. 4 (2008): 673–688.

Graham, W. A. "Orality." In *Encyclopaedia of the Qurʾān*. Vol. 3. Edited by Jane Dammen McAuliffe. Leiden: Brill, 2003.

Grimes, John. "The Contribution to the Study of Scripture to the Study of Theology." *Religious Studies and Theology* 9, no. 2 (1989): 47–54.

Habermas, Jürgen. *The Theory of Communicative Action*. Vol. 2 of *Lifeworld and System: A Critique of Functionalist Reason*. Translated by Thomas McCarthy. Boston: Beacon, 1984.

Harder, Lydia. "The Bible as Canon and as Word of God: Exploring the Mystery of Revelation." *The Conrad Grebel Review* 24, no. 1 (2006): 52–65.

Heschel, Abraham J. *The Prophets*. 2 vols. Peabody: Prince Press, 2003.

Hitchcock, Christina. "A Living God, a Living Word: Christian and Muslim Revelation in Perspective." *Missiology: An International Review* 42, no. 4 (2014): 375–385.

Kärkkäinen, Veli-Matti. *Trinity and Revelation*. A Constructive Christian Theology for the Pluralistic World. Vol. 2. Grand Rapids: Eerdmans, 2014.

Kaviraj, Gopinath. *Aspects of Indian Thought*. Burdwan: University of Burdwan, 1967.

Kurka, Robert C. "Has 'Inerrancy' Outlived Its Usefulness?" *Stone-Campbell Journal* 18 (2015): 187–204.

Longman, Tremper, ed. *The Baker Illustrated Bible Dictionary*. Grand Rapids: Baker, 2013.

MacArthur, John. "Does God Still Give Revelation?" *The Master's Seminary Journal* 14, no. 2 (2003): 217–234.

McGowan, A. T. B. *The Divine Authenticity of Scripture: Retrieving an Evangelical Heritage*. Downers Grove: InterVarsity Press, 2007.

Moller, Philip, S.J. "What Should They Be Saying about Biblical Inspiration? A Note on the State of the Question." *Theological Studies* 74 (2013): 605–631.

Nichols, Stephen J., and Eric T. Brandt. *Ancient Word, Changing Worlds: The Doctrine of Scripture in a Modern Age*. Wheaton: Crossway, 2009.

Pannikar, Raimundo. *The Vedic Experience*. Berkeley: University of California Press, 1977.

Smith, Steven G. "What Is Scripture? Pursuing Smith's Question." *Anglican Theological Review* 90, no. 4 (2008): 753–775.

Smith, Wilfred Cantwell. *What Is Scripture? A Comparative Approach*. Minneapolis: Fortress, 1993.

Stott, John. *Evangelical Truth: A Personal Plea for Unity, Integrity and Faithfulness*. Carlisle: Langham Global Library, 2014.

———. "The Lausanne Covenant: An Exposition and Commentary." *Lausanne Movement*, 1975. Accessed 15 January 2019. https://www.lausanne.org/content/lop/lop-3#2.

Talmon-Heller, Daniella. "Reciting the Qur'ān and Reading the Torah: Muslim and Jewish Attitudes and Practices in a Comparative Historical Perspective." *Religion Compass* 6, no. 8 (2012): 369–380.

———. "Scriptures as Holy Objects: Preliminary Comparative Remarks on the Qur'ān and the Torah in the Medieval Middle East." *Intellectual History of the Islamicate World* 4 (2016): 210–244.

Vanhoozer, Kevin J. *The Drama of Doctrine: A Canonical Linguistic Approach to Christian Doctrine*. Louisville: Westminster John Knox Press, 2005.

———. "Word of God." In *Dictionary of Theological Interpretation of the Bible*, edited by Kevin J. Vanhoozer, Craig C. Bartholomew, Daniel J. Treier, and N. T. Wright, 851–854. Grand Rapids: Baker Academic, 2005.

Ward, Timothy. "Reconstructing the Doctrine of the Sufficiency of Scripture." *Tyndale Bulletin* 52, no. 1 (2001): 151–159.

———. "Scripture, Sufficiency of." In *Dictionary of Theological Interpretation of the Bible*, edited by Kevin J. Vanhoozer, Craig C. Bartholomew, Daniel J. Treier, and N. T. Wright, 730–731. Grand Rapids: Baker Academic, 2005.

Westerholm, Stephen, and Martin Westerholm. *Reading Sacred Scripture: Voices from the History of Biblical Interpretation*. Grand Rapids: Eerdmans, 2016.

3

The Trinity in Asian Contexts

George N. Capaque

Asian Theological Seminary

Introduction

Christians profess that the doctrine of the Trinity stands at the center of the Christian faith. But for many, the Trinity is an abstract theological concept regarding God's nature or "God's inner life" and a mathematical puzzle ("three" and "one") that hardly relates to daily living and concerns.[1] For many Asians, the doctrine of the Trinity is understood to commit Christians to the idea that there really are three Gods for them, notwithstanding their protests to the contrary.

According to Veli-Matti Kärkkäinen, this circumstance is best understood in light of the history of the doctrine. "What happened in the history of the Christian doctrine of the Trinity," he explains, "contributed to its marginalization and its becoming both abstract and removed from liturgy, spirituality, and life in general."[2] Kärkkäinen pins the blame for this circumstance on the post-Augustinian tradition, which was prominent in the West, and which began with God's one being or essence and then moved toward an explanation of the three persons. This perspective *"implied* that the oneness of God was the

---

1. In a speech in Kidapawan City on 29 December 2018, Philippine President Rodrigo Duterte, an outspoken critic of the Roman Catholic Church, criticized the doctrine of the Trinity: "There is only one God. You cannot divide God into three. That's silly" (Christine O. Avendaño, "Duterte Rants vs. Church, Calls Belief in Holy Trinity 'Silly,'" *Philippine Daily Inquirer*, 30 December 2018, https://newsinfo.inquirer.net/1067732/rody-rants-again-vs-church-calls-belief-in-holy-trinity-silly).

2. Veli-Matti Kärkkäinen, *Trinity and Revelation*, A Constructive Christian Theology for the Pluralistic World, vol. 2 (Grand Rapids: Eerdmans, 2014), 250.

defining issue while the Trinity may or may not be integral to the doctrine."[3] Instead of the earlier approach, which would maintain prominence in Eastern Christianity and which viewed the Trinity through the lens of Christian experience of salvation as revealed in the Scriptures, Western theologians largely focused on the "inner life" of God (the "*immanent* Trinity") rather than on the "economy" of salvation (the "*economic* Trinity"), thus "making the Trinity an abstract speculation rather than reading it from the works of God."[4]

Recent developments in the doctrine, however, point to a number of "turns" that provide the atmosphere for the construction of fresh perspectives on the Trinity, not least among Asian theologians. Writing in 1994, John Thompson noted that the previous two decades had seen a genuine revival of interest in the doctrine of the Trinity that linked it with practical Christian faith.[5] If the God in the economy of salvation is God as he is in himself, might he be "not only the source of our salvation but also the ground and paradigm of true social life and liberation?"[6] Thus, "the double context of salvation and liberation in relation to the Trinity" offers a rationale for reflection on the doctrine, as well as a path forward.[7] Other factors cited by Thompson as playing a role in this renewal of interest include the ecumenical dialogue between Western tradition as represented by Barth and Rahner on the one hand and Eastern Orthodox thought on the other – an approach to the nature of God by Western theologians similar to a social view of the Trinity in the East – and the burden of suffering, poverty, and the alienation of individuals and peoples.[8]

John Franke has argued that the turn to relationality is perhaps the most significant and "the most fruitful model for understanding the doctrine of the Trinity."[9] In Franke's view, the substantialist (Western) conception of God makes him an impassible (not capable of suffering) and immutable God, leaving him quite removed from the biblical revelation of a God who enters into a loving relationship with his creation. Debates continue as to the degree to which the category of substance should be abandoned, but there is a widely

---

3. Kärkkäinen, *Trinity and Revelation*, 250.

4. Kärkkäinen, 251.

5. John Thompson, *Modern Trinitarian Perspectives* (Oxford: Oxford University Press, 1994), 3.

6. Thompson, *Modern Trinitarian Perspectives*, 3.

7. Thompson, 3.

8. Thompson, 3–4.

9. John R. Franke, "God Is Love," in *Trinitarian Theology for the Church*, eds. Daniel J. Treier and David Lauber (Downers Grove: IVP Academic, 2009), 105.

held perspective "that the primary accent should be placed on the category of relationality."[10]

In view of this, we need to revisit first the Christian understanding and experience of God as "Father, Son, and Holy Spirit" and God as "person" before we survey the Asian context and how Asian theologians have attempted to construct distinctively Asian models or categories of the Trinity. After exploring the territory as it currently stands, I will offer my own paradigm or model for understanding God as Trinity in the Asian context.

The Classical Doctrine of the Trinity

The biblical (New Testament) data states that Christians experience God in a threefold manner without attempting to explain or justify it. The Christian experience of God begins with their experience of *salvation* (forgiveness of, and freedom from, sin, and a "new possibility of existence") from *God* in *Jesus Christ* by or in the *Holy Spirit*. Salvation is also a present transformation into the image of Jesus which comes from the Holy Spirit, a transformation that will be perfected in a future glory (2 Cor 3:18). The Holy Spirit effects the salvation that God gives in Jesus Christ.[11] Christians therefore confess they know and encounter God because *he saves them in Jesus Christ by the Holy Spirit*. This is the heart of the Christian faith. Father, Son, and Holy Spirit are involved in the Christian's experience of salvation.

What is God like such that he acts this way? The Christian experience of salvation leads inevitably to the understanding of God as Trinity, that is, *one God in three persons*. God, therefore, for the Christian, is revealed as *Father, Son*, and the *Holy Spirit*. The "Trinity" is thus the normative Christian model[12] for understanding who God is: it is human reflection of the divine revelation in Jesus Christ.

The historical process involved in arriving at the particular understanding of God as Father, Son, and Spirit is complex and it is not our intention to

---

10. Franke, "God Is Love," 112.

11. God's presence among believers is experienced through the Spirit in them. The Spirit is spoken of in personal terms (1 Cor 2:10; 12:11; Rom 8:26–27). Early Christians also held him to be divine (Acts 5:3–4).

12. "Father," "Son," and "Spirit" are dominant "models" used by the Judeo-Christian tradition regarding religious language of God. See Sallie McFague, *Metaphorical Theology: Models of God in Religious Language* (Philadelphia: Fortress, 1982), 14–29; and David Tracy, *The Analogical Imagination: Christian Theology and the Culture of Pluralism* (London: SCM, 1981), who uses the term "analogical imagination."

describe it in detail here.[13] Suffice it to say that the Christian experience of God in a threefold manner can adequately be expressed only by the doctrine of the Trinity. The Christian experience of salvation ultimately finds expression in worship and prayer. The seed of the doctrine of the Trinity grew out of the first Christians' doxology. As Jürgen Moltmann notes, "There is no experience of salvation that does not find expression in praise and thanks."[14] Many of the biblical texts that are used to support the later doctrine of the Trinity were originally liturgical and creedal texts.[15] Doctrines in general developed mainly either out of the early Christians' confession and practice or in defense and clarification of the Christian proclamation in the face of heresy.[16] The former is the application of the principle *lex orandi, lex credendi* (what is prayed is what is believed), and the doctrine of the Trinity is one such example. When praying Paul addresses God through Jesus Christ (Eph 5:20; also 1 Cor 15:57; Rom 1:8; 16:27; 7:25).

The strongest Trinitarian texts are the baptismal formula in Matthew 28:19, the Pauline benediction in 2 Corinthians 13:14, and the description of Jesus's baptism in Matthew 3:16–17.[17] In addition to these, we do well to consider Galatians 4:6 and Romans 8:15; there, Christians call God "*Abba*, Father" because of the presence of the Spirit in their hearts. These are considered by many scholars to be "liturgical fragments."[18] A Trinitarian text that combines

---

13. Suffice it to say that the process leading to the Council of Constantinople's formula of three co-equal persons in one essence was complicated. For an account of the development of the doctrine, see J. N. D. Kelly, *Early Christian Doctrines*, 4th ed. (London: Black, 1968), 109–137, 252–279. For a contemporary restatement of the doctrine of the Trinity in plain terms, I have found Alister McGrath's *Understanding the Trinity* (Eastbourne: Kingsway, 1987) helpful. Veli-Matti Kärkkäinen's *The Trinity: Global Perspectives* (Louisville: Westminster John Knox, 2007) offers a comprehensive introduction to the doctrine's biblical roots, historical development, and contemporary interpretations around the world. Catherine Mowry LaCugna's "The Trinitarian Mystery of God," in *Systematic Theology: Roman Catholic Perspectives*, vol. 1, eds. Francis Schüssler Fiorenza and John P. Galvin, (Minneapolis: Fortress, 1991), 149–192, is also a good and shorter introduction. For a more technical, yet readable work, I recommend Walter Kasper, *The God of Jesus Christ* (New York: Crossroad, 1992).

14. Jürgen Moltmann, *The Trinity and the Kingdom of God*, trans. Margaret Kohl (London: SCM, 1981), 152.

15. LaCugna, "Trinitarian Mystery of God," 160.

16. The doctrine of the Trinity was forged in the course of the debate regarding the divinity and humanity of Jesus Christ.

17. The Old Testament reveals that there is only one God, Yahweh. Yet there are hints of a plurality within this oneness in the motifs of the angel of the Lord, Wisdom, and the word of God (Gen 16:7–13; Exod 3:2–6; Prov 8; Ps 33:6–9; Exod 3:4–22). See Veli-Matti Kärkkäinen, "Trinity, Triune God," in *Global Dictionary of Theology*, eds. William Dyrness et al. (Downers Grove: InterVarsity Press, 2008), 902.

18. LaCugna, "Trinitarian Mystery of God," 161, 163.

the description of the economy of salvation and doxology is Ephesians 1:3–14. Praise is rendered to "the God and Father of our Lord Jesus Christ" for the salvation he wrought in Jesus (v. 3), and this praise serves as a refrain throughout the chapter (vv. 3, 6, 12, 14). The Father "chose us in him [Christ]" (v. 4); he "predestined us for adoption to sonship through Jesus Christ" (v. 5). "In him [Christ] we have redemption through his blood, the forgiveness of sins" (v. 7). God's ultimate purpose is "to bring unity to all things in heaven and on earth under Christ" (v. 10). The Holy Spirit is then the "seal" that assures believers they are God's children and the "deposit" (guarantee) of their full redemption (vv. 13, 14).

The Christian formulation "one God, three persons" applies "person" to God. It suggests that it is in the realm of *personhood* and *personal relationship* that this threeness must be understood.[19] It has been observed, however, that the modern concept of person poses a strong objection to the church's doctrine of the Trinity, that is, the idea of three persons in one nature. In modern thinking, person is no longer understood in terms of ontology (being) but is defined more in psychological terms as a center of self-consciousness and free action and as individual personality.[20] Conceived this way, three "persons" would imply three Gods, or tritheism.

The Cappadocian fathers,[21] great defenders of the Nicene concept of *homoousius* (one essence or substance), formulated the Trinitarian formula of one *ousia* (essence or substance), three *hypostases* (persons) (*ousia* corresponds to "universal" and *hypostasis* to "particular"). Their Trinitarian doctrine begins with the three persons. *Hypostasis* is a stronger and much more appropriate word than *prosopon* (another word for "person," with a meaning rooted in "face" or "mask"),[22] which Tertullian had employed centuries earlier in the first known use of the Latin *trinitas*. Unfortunately, *prosopon*, as well as its Latin equivalent, *persona*, sometimes evoked the concept of a God hiding behind three "masks," leading to accusations of modalism.

In contrast, *hypostasis* designates the concrete existent which is noted in divine and human beings by their proper names.[23] It answers the question,

---

19. Simon Chan, *Spiritual Theology* (Downers Grove: InterVarsity Press, 1998), 41.

20. See Kasper, *God of Jesus Christ*, 285.

21. Basil the Great (d. 379), Gregory of Nazianzen (d. 390), and Gregory of Nyssa (d. 394), Basil's younger brother.

22. Latin, *persona*; originally used for "masks" worn by actors.

23. The following exposition of *hypostasis* and *ousia* comes from Thomas Hopko, "The Trinity in the Cappadocians," in *Christian Spirituality*, vol. 1, *Origins to the Twelfth Century*, eds. Bernard McGinn, John Meyendorff, and Jean Leclercq (New York: Crossroad, 1993), 268.

"Which one?" Or, for personal beings, "Who?" Every being that exists, exists hypostatically, that is, as a particular, specific, concrete existent. Yet every being that exists shares a common being with others that are of the same substance, essence, or nature. *Ousia* then designates what is common or general. It answers the question, "What?" The three persons of the Godhead share in that absolute unity and perfection of the nature of God, of which, indeed, they are, yet their particular characteristics are preserved.[24] The unity of the Godhead is not numerical unity but a unity of nature.

With their emphasis on the hypostases, the Cappadocians developed a new conception of what it is *to be*.[25] What is the relationship of the Three? In what does their oneness consist? Basil speaks of a paradoxical "united separation and separated unity." It consists in the fact that it is a communion (that is, God is a shared Being) in which the persons give to and receive from each other what they are. This giving and receiving of each other is love, for that is what God is (see 1 John 4:8). At the heart of what is given and received is their *particularity*. Social relation is not denied, but "it is in fact its basis, because reciprocity and relationship are present from the outset and not tacked on as an extra."[26] This concept of personhood is far from modern individualism or collectivism. It emphasizes uniqueness or particularity, but not at the expense of community or social relation. Personhood in this instance is freedom. "To be a person on this account is to be what one gives to and receives *freely* from the other persons with whom one is in relation."[27]

The basic concept that encompasses all we've said about the Trinity is the Trinitarian *perichoresis*,[28] the being-in-one another and mutual penetration of the divine persons. The distinct persons "inter-penetrate" each other in a "divine dance" (*peri*, "around," and *choreo*, "dance"). There is unity, symmetry, and complementarity of movement, and each dancer fulfills him/herself toward the other. In this movement there is reciprocal giving and receiving. This is how we understand Jesus's statements such as "I and the Father are one" (John 10:30) and "that all of them may be one, Father, just as you are in me and

---

24. See Gregory of Nyssa, *Letter to Ablabius*, in Edward R. Hardy and Cyril Richardson, eds., *Christology of the Later Fathers*, vol. 3 of The Library of Christian Classics (Philadelphia: Westminster Press, 1954).

25. This and the following insights are based on *The Forgotten Trinity: The Report of the BCC Study Commission on Trinitarian Doctrine Today* (London: British Council of Churches, 1989), 22.

26. *Forgotten Trinity*, 22.

27. *Forgotten Trinity*, 22 (emphasis added).

28. I owe the thoughts on *perichoresis* from a class on "Experiencing the Trinity" which I took at Regent College, Vancouver, Canada, under Drs James Houston and Edwin Hui in 1994.

I am in you" (John 17:21). The perichoretic unity in the Trinity provides a model also for the union between Jesus and believers (John 14:20; 17:23), among believers (John 17:21), and between God and humans.[29] Trinitarian perichoresis preserves each person's particularity and their unity without confusing one from the other. It also provides a model of what is ultimate reality: *persons as relations*, not some abstract philosophical substance or the modern individual personality.[30] "Person," then, as applied primarily to the Trinity, indicates "relationship, freedom, ineffability, mystery, the capacity to love and know, and the capacity to be loved and known."[31]

Asian Contexts for Trinitarian Interpretations[32]

From the foregoing we have seen that the Trinity is the Christian interpretation of or reflection upon our experience of God as revealed in Jesus Christ and Scripture. According to Simon Chan, our analogies of God depend largely on how we experience God in our lives, which varies in different places and times.[33] The existence or non-existence of God is not an issue in Asia, unlike in the West. "The question is . . . God's identity and nature . . . how to make sense of the Christian understanding of God in contexts filled with a plethora of vastly different conceptions of deity."[34] We therefore need to look, albeit briefly, at the Asian contexts, particularly how Asians experience God, in order for us to be able to construct an Asian understanding of the Trinity.

One feature of Asia is diversity or plurality. Asia is a diverse world of faiths, cultures, and races. It is the birthplace of the world's major religions: Islam, Hinduism, Buddhism, Taoism, Confucianism, Judaism, and Christianity. "Religious pluralism is at the heart of Asian empirical reality. It fills every geographic nook and cranny of her soils and waters."[35] Christianity comprises but a tiny minority except in the Philippines.

---

29. Kasper, *God of Jesus Christ*, 284.
30. Kasper, 290, 310.
31. LaCugna, "Trinitarian Mystery of God," 180.
32. On this subject generally, see also Kärkkäinen, *Trinity: Global Perspectives*, chs. 21–23.
33. Chan, *Spiritual Theology*, 42.
34. Simon Chan, *Grassroots Asian Theology* (Downers Grove: IVP Academic, 2014), 48.
35. Sathianathan Clarke, "The Task, Method, and Content of Asian Theologies," in *Asian Theology on the Way*, ed. Peniel Jesudason Rufus Rajkumar (London: SPCK, 2012), 18.

These various religious traditions represent different ways of apprehending God.[36] Islam and Judaism are monotheistic. For Muslims, the doctrine of the Trinity is *shirk* (attributing partners to God, whether they be sons, daughters, or other partners). The Qur'an says, "They do blaspheme who say Allah is one of three in a Trinity: for there is no god except one Allah" (Surah 5:73).

Hindus are pantheists. Brahman, the Ultimate Reality and Ultimate Mystery, holds the universe together and manifests itself and is worshiped in every kind of form.[37] The whole universe is conceptualized as a person, *Purusha*, the Supreme Person who fills the whole creation. Ultimate Reality is identified with the self (*atman*). Knowledge of God is attained by emptying oneself of everything including self. The *Upanishads* (part of the Hindu scriptures) "describe the Absolute in three-fold images; that is, in terms of pure existence (*sat*) (Katha Up. 6.12), consciousness (*cit*) (Mandukya Up. 2.2.11) and bliss (*ananda*) (Taittiriya Up. 2.1). In the compound form it becomes *Saccidananda*."[38] For some Christian interpreters of Hinduism, this is an appropriate appellation for the Trinity.[39]

In ancient China, the Chinese revered *Shang Di*, the Most High God. Simon Chan argues for a rough correspondence between *Shang Di* and the name Yahweh in the Old Testament, the covenantal name God used with Israel.[40] The other name for God in the ancient Chinese context was *Tian*, which Chan argues corresponds roughly to Elohim – God as he is in relation to the universe – though Chan notes that this title lacks "the personal connotation of the Old Testament names."[41]

Many consider Confucianism to be more of a social and ethical philosophy than a religion. It undergirds and embodies the ethical core of Chinese society developed through generations of human wisdom.[42] Taoism and Buddhism form the other major East Asian traditions. We will reserve our discussion of these for the next section, which focuses on Asian Trinitarian formulations.

---

36. See Chan, *Grassroots Asian Theology*, 48–61, for a survey of how Muslims, Indian, Chinese, and primal religions apprehend God.

37. Jacob Kavunkal, "The Mystery of God in and through Hinduism," in *Christian Theology in Asia*, ed. Sebastian C. H. Kim (New York: Cambridge University Press, 2008), 24.

38. Kavunkal, "Mystery of God," 26.

39. Kavunkal, 28–32.

40. Chan, *Grassroots Asian Theology*, 56.

41. Chan, 56.

42. "Confucianism," Center for Global Education, Asia Society, accessed 17 January 2019, https://asiasociety.org/education/confucianism.

Poverty is another common feature of Asia. Since Asia comprises 61 percent of the world's population, desperate poverty remains a pervasive reality. Despite the impressive economic growth of the region and significant gains in poverty reduction, 400 million, or one in 10 Asians, live in extreme poverty according to the United Nations and Asian Development Bank.[43] If wider indicators of poverty such as health, education, and living standards are included, the number of poor goes up to 931 million. Related to the issue of poverty are corruption, natural catastrophes, lack of human rights protections, and gross inequality.

Religious pluralism and poverty are, according to Aloysius Pieris, the "two inseparable realities which in their interpenetration constitute what might be designated as the Asian context and which is the matrix of any theology that is truly Asian."[44] Moreover, Pieris notes, poverty is not just economic, nor religiosity just cultural. "Both are interwoven culturally and economically to constitute the vast sociocultural reality that Asia is."[45]

Aside from the major factors of poverty and religiosity, we might also add a number of minor factors that impact the distinctively Asian context. For example, the majority of Asian countries have undergone colonial and postcolonial experiences, and Christianity was often introduced alongside colonization. As a result, Christianity is often considered a white man's or a Western religion. The aftermath of colonialism, meanwhile, has led to the introduction of different modes of production and systems of landholding, creating a new elite which owns most of the economic resources, and leaving the vast majority of the population poor. In addition to these broader trends, the Asian experience is also shaped significantly by gender. Many women in Asia regularly experience discrimination, marginalization, inequality, and violence in societies that are largely patriarchal. Although women's conditions have improved markedly in many countries, women still lag behind men in terms of status, economic opportunities, rights, and security.

Considering the above Asian contexts, how then should we name God in Asia? We shall look next at some Asian theologians' attempts to use Asian culture and thought patterns to explain the idea of the triune God.

---

43. Income of less than $1.90 per day. Thin Lei Win, "Despite Growth, One in 10 Asians Live in Extreme Poverty," *ABS-CBN News*, accessed 17 January 2019, https://news.abs-cbn.com/business/03/29/17/despite-growth-one-in-10-asians-live-in-extreme-poverty.

44. Aloysius Pieris, "Towards an Asian Theology of Liberation: Some Religio-Cultural Guidelines," in *Asia's Struggle for Full Humanity: Towards a Relevant Theology*, ed. Virginia Fabella (Maryknoll: Orbis Books, 1980), 75–76.

45. Pieris, "Towards an Asian Theology of Liberation," 75–76.

Asian Interpretations of the Trinity

Partly in reaction to the theological "imperialism" of the West and partly out of a desire to communicate the Christian faith in a culturally relevant manner, Asian theologians have attempted to reinterpret or reimagine the Christian faith, and particularly the Christian idea of God. To begin we will offer a basic survey of a number of these reinterpretations.[46]

Perhaps the most comprehensive and creative of these Asian Trinitarian theologies is that of Jung Young Lee's *The Trinity in Asian Perspective*.[47] By "Asian perspective," Lee specifically refers to the East Asian context (China, Japan, and Korea). Lee's basic assumption in his approach to the Trinity is the oneness of humanity and the world. He coined the term "cosmo-anthropology" to point out that in this worldview "human being is regarded as a microcosm of the cosmos" and "our thought process is subject to the cosmic order."[48] The cosmos operates through the *yin-yang* relationship, which symbolizes both complementary dualism and non-dualism.[49]

Lee maintains that the *yin-yang* way of thinking is ultimately the most consistent with Trinitarian thinking ("one in three and three in one"). In Western systems, which emphasize the either/or, God cannot be both one and three at the same time; but because *yin-yang* thinking is inclusive and complementary (both/and), God can be both one and three. Lee cites John 14:11 ("Don't you believe that I am in the Father and that the Father is in me?") as a support for his conception of the Trinity in these terms. "The Father and the Son are one in their 'inness,' but also at the same time, they are three because 'in' represents the Spirit, the inner connecting principle which cannot exist by itself."[50]

In Lee's reinterpretation, the Trinity begins with the Son.[51] It is through the Son that we know the Father. Moreover, the Son's dual nature (divinity and

---

46. I survey only materials I currently have access to. For other Asian reformulations which include a creative Japanese reinterpretation by Nozumu Miyahira, see Kärkkäinen, *Trinity: Global Perspectives*, ch. 22; and Natee Tanchanpongs, "Asian Reformulations of the Trinity: An Evaluation," in *The Trinity among the Nations*, eds. Gene L. Green, Stephen T. Pardue, and K. K. Yeo (Carlisle: Langham Global Library, 2015), 100–119.

47. Jung Young Lee, *The Trinity in Asian Perspective* (Nashville: Abingdon, 1996). See also Kärkkäinen, *Trinity: Global Perspectives*, ch. 22; and Tanchanpongs, "Asian Reformulations."

48. "Everything in the world has its opposite. The opposites are necessary and complementary to each other" (Lee, *Trinity in Asian Perspective*, 18).

49. Lee, 24. *Yang* is the essence of heaven, while *yin* is that of the earth. *Yang* is the masculine principle, while *yin* is the feminine principle. *Yang* is positive, *yin* is negative, etc. (25).

50. Lee, 58.

51. Lee, ch. 4.

humanity) is a key to understanding the three (Trinity). Next in the Trinitarian order is the Spirit.[52] The Spirit is not simply an attribute of being, but being itself and the power of change that originates being. With its close association with earth, the Spirit is the Trinitarian Mother[53] (*yin*), the feminine member of the Trinity who possesses maternal characteristics and complements the Father (heaven, *yang*). Lee depicts the Father as the preeminent member of the Trinity.[54] In the familial context, the father is always above the son. Preeminence is derived from the father's relation to his children.

This order of the Trinity, Lee says, "is based on historical and biblical understandings of divinity."[55] Lee also proposes five other divine orders based on life experiences, particularly using different images of family life in various religions and traditions of Asia.[56] This includes the traditional Father, Son, and Spirit. The distinctly Eastern or Asian order is Father, Spirit, and Son.

If, in the evaluation of Kärkkäinen, Lee's *yin-yang* symbolism represents a binitarian rather than a Trinitarian structure,[57] Raimundo Panikkar's Trinity is ultimately unitarian.[58] Like Lee, Panikkar employs Asian perspectives, particularly Hindu and to some extent Buddhist thoughts. Panikkar's thesis is that the Trinity should be conceived of as a model of reality. Reality is "cosmotheandric" (= Trinitarian), a term he coined by combining words for world, God, and man, the three dimensions of reality. It is also non-dualistic (*advaita*).

In Panikkar's "advaitic trinitarianism" there is only one Absolute (God). "The Father is the Absolute, the only God, *ò theos*."[59] But the Father *is not*. "In the generation of the Son he has, so to speak, given everything. In the Father the apophatism (the *kenosis* or emptying) of Being is real and total."[60] In this sense God is "Nothing." Panikkar wonders if this is where the Buddhist experience of *nirvana* and *sunyata* (emptiness) should be situated. God is Silence, absolute

---

52. Lee, 96–100.

53. Lee clarifies, however, that "'Mother' is not the name of the Spirit . . . the Spirit is the proper name" (127).

54. Lee, 124.

55. Lee, 173.

56. Lee, chapter 7. (1) The Father, the Spirit, the Son; (2) the Father, the Son, the Spirit; (3) the Spirit, the Father, the Son; (4) the Spirit, the Son, the Father; (5) the Son, the Father, the Spirit.

57. Kärkkäinen, *Trinity: Global Perspectives*, 332.

58. Raimundo Panikkar, *The Trinity and the Religious Experience of Man* (Maryknoll: Orbis, 1973).

59. Panikkar, *Trinity*, 44.

60. Panikkar, 46.

and total. "His word who completely expresses and consumes him, is the Son. The *Father has* no being, the Son is *his* being."[61] He is the *Self* of the Father.[62]

The Son was manifested in Christ, and, according to Christians, identified with Jesus of Nazareth. But Panikkar's Christ is not necessarily limited to Jesus.[63] Christ presents the fundamental characteristics of the mediator between the divine and cosmic, which are differently called in other religions. He is the symbol of the process in the world where new religions or quasi-religions are integrating the sacred and the profane and non-religious movements are becoming more sacralized.[64]

The Spirit is the revelation of God immanent, the *in-himself* of the Father.[65] Divine immanence refers first of all to God as immanent to himself. There is in God "a sort of bottomless interiority."[66] The Spirit is equally the divine immanence of the Son.[67] In relation to the Trinity, "[t]he Spirit is the communion between the Father and the Son. The Spirit is immanent to Father and Son jointly."[68] As *advaita* expresses God and man (or world) as one reality, it also can be applied to the Father and the Son. "If the Father and the Son are not *two*, they are not one either: the Spirit both unites and distinguishes them. He is the bond of unity; the *we* in between, or rather within."[69] Panikkar uses the analogy of a river to describe further the Spirit. The Father is the Source, the Son is the River who flows from the Source, and the Spirit is the End, "the limitless Ocean where the flux of divine life is completed, rests, and is consummated."[70]

To address the issue of poverty and marginalization, Indian Dalit theologian Arvind Nirmal develops "the triune nature of a Christian dalit theology." He addresses the question of God in the experience of Dalits. In his paper

---

61. Panikkar, 48.

62. Panikkar, 61. This leads Kärkkäinen to comment that "the Son is the whole focus of the deity" (Kärkkäinen, *Trinity: Global Perspectives*, 343).

63. Kärkkäinen comments that Panikkar has a "strong pluralistic bent" and his Christology is pluralistic (*Trinity: Global Perspectives*, 338). Furthermore, Panikkar "expands the Christic principle . . . beyond the figure of Jesus of Nazareth which has serious implications for the doctrine of the Trinity" (342).

64. Panikkar, *Trinity*, 53.

65. Panikkar, 58, 61.

66. Panikkar, 59.

67. Panikkar, 58, 60.

68. Panikkar, 60.

69. Panikkar, 62.

70. Panikkar, 63.

"Toward a Christian Dalit Theology,"[71] Nirmal complains that Indian Christian theology in the past has been occupied with what he calls *Brahminic* tradition. Its ecumenical involvement led to concern for dialogues with other Christian faiths. Although the questions of socio-economic justice were addressed in the 1970s with the emergence of so-called "third-world theology," the discussion has been dominated by Latin American liberation theology, and thus has failed to take into account the caste system in India, particularly the Dalits who are not even part of the caste system.

Nirmal employs what he calls a methodological exclusivism, that is, dalit theology should be done by Dalits themselves, and the term "dalit" should have primacy over "Christian"[72] in the development of his dalit theology. With the historical dalit consciousness as his primary datum, which he likens to the Deuteronomic Creed in Deuteronomy 26:5, Nirmal turns to the question of God. "A non-dalit deity cannot be the God of dalits."[73] Thus the gods the Hindus worshiped are rejected by the Dalits.

The God revealed by Jesus Christ and spoken of by the prophets of the Old Testament is a dalit God. "He is a servant-God – a God who serves."[74] Referring to an ancient Hindu religious text (*Manu Dharma Sastra*) where Svayambhu (the self-existent) created the *sudras* (the lowest caste) to do servile work, Nirmal applies this to the Dalits who are *avarnas* – lower than the *sudras*. "[T]he amazing claim of a Christian dalit theology will be that the God of the dalits, the self-existent, the Svayambhu, does not create others to do servile work but does servile work himself . . . Servitude is the *sva-dharma* [one's own right or nature] of our God."[75] As the people of this dalit God, service has been the Dalits' lot and privilege. They participate in this servant-God's ministries.

Nirmal asserts that in Jesus Christ, who the Gospel writers identified with the servant of God in Isaiah 53, the Dalits are not just Dalits but Christian Dalits. They are followers of Jesus who "was himself a dalit." Nirmal boldly maintains that Jesus's "dalitness is the key to the mystery of his divine-human

---

71. Arvind Nirmal, "Toward a Christian Dalit Theology," in *Frontiers in Asian Christian Theology: Emerging Trends*, ed. R. S. Sugirtharajah (Maryknoll: Orbis Books, 1994), 27–40. Nirmal uses lower case for "dalit." I use the upper case when referring to them as a group of people.

72. "What is Christian about dalit theology? . . . It is the dalitness which is Christian about dalit theology" (Nirmal, "Toward a Christian Dalit Theology," 32).

73. Nirmal, 35.

74. Nirmal, 35.

75. Nirmal, 35.

unity."[76] He sees the genealogy of Jesus that includes women, outcasts, and an illegitimate son as a feature of his dalitness. The "Son of Man" sayings referring to Jesus's suffering and imminent death are another feature. His rejection by the dominant religious authorities and his complete identification with the Dalits of his day (outcasts, Samaritans, aliens, etc.) are still other features of his dalitness. But it is the cross which best symbolized Jesus's dalitness. "On the cross, he was the broken, the crushed, the split, the torn, the driven-asunder man – the dalit in the fullest possible meaning of that term."[77]

Nirmal's pneumatology, he admits, is brief and sketchy. He turns to Ezekiel's vision of the valley of dry bones in Ezekiel 37. The bones represent Israel, but Israel here is under dalit conditions. The Holy Spirit gives life to these bones. "For us dalits, then, the Spirit is the life-giver, unifier, and empowerer for the liberation struggle of the Indian dalits. In our dalit experiences, the Spirit is our comforter who 'groans' along with us in our sufferings."[78]

The foregoing survey shows how cultural and contextual perspectives can provide new insights in a God talk that is related and relevant to one's life situation. But for evangelicals committed to the primacy and authority of Scripture and historic orthodoxy, these reinterpretations pose some problems.[79] Kärkkäinen[80] and Tanchanpongs[81] helpfully provide critical evaluations, with the latter suggesting an evaluative criterion of context-to-text involving movement or transformation from context to the text (Scripture).[82]

An approach that is friendlier to evangelical commitments is proposed by Simon Chan, who has suggested that with the great importance placed on the family in Asia, "the Trinity as the divine family takes on a special

---

76. Nirmal, 36. The classic doctrine of the hypostatic union states that the two natures of Jesus (divine and human) are united in the one person (hypostasis) of Jesus. Nirmal seems to identify this "person" with dalitness. Nirmal may be right in identifying Jesus as a Dalit himself (the particularity of the incarnation) but Jesus's divine nature transcends a particular race or people. Jesus Christ cannot simply be claimed exclusively by one group of people.

77. Nirmal, 39.

78. Nirmal, 39.

79. For example, Lee's process thought (God is "Change-itself") and Panikkar's and Nirmal's Christologies.

80. Kärkkäinen, *Trinity: Global Perspectives*, 329–335.

81. Tanchanpongs, "Asian Reformulations of the Trinity," 110–116.

82. This is similar to Kevin Vanhoozer's *canonic* and *christological* principle, "namely, that the Spirit speaking in Scripture about what God was/is doing in the history of Israel and climactically in Jesus Christ is the supreme rule for Christian faith, life, and understanding" (Kevin Vanhoozer, "One Rule to Rule Them All?," in *Globalizing Theology: Belif and Practice in an Era of World Christianity*, eds. Craig Ott and Harold Netland [Nottingham: Apollos, 2007], 109). We may use both criteria in evaluating these Asian reinterpretations, including my own proposal below.

significance."[83] Following this lead, it is from this paradigm or analogy of the Trinity as the divine family that my own Asian interpretation of the Trinity will take its trajectory.

The Trinity as Divine Family

The family is the basic unit of life. The ideal (human) family of father, mother, and child(ren) reflects the divine "family" of Father, Son, and Holy Spirit.[84] Because human beings are made in the image of God, the human family reflects something of that image. The structure of the human family is Trinitarian as the divine family is. Familial names (Father, Son) are also biblically sanctioned ways of conceiving and speaking of the Trinity.

Although the method I employ is analogical and "from below" – that is, using family structure and experience as a lens to reenvision the Trinity – I am well aware that the divine family is the archetype of human family (Eph 3:14–15), rather than the other way around.[85] This means that the norm for familial life is the Trinity and not vice versa. Where human experiences of the family do not conform to the Trinitarian archetype we must be prepared to revise or correct them. Yet as those who bear God's image, it remains worthwhile and meaningful to look at the family as a paradigm for the Trinity, so long as we remember that this is a second-order symbol, and that Father, Son, and Holy Spirit are primary symbols. Jung Young Lee is thus correct in arguing that "If the family as the fundamental unit of existence is manifested in the divine as the archetype of our life, we cannot dismiss the family system, which is a reflection of the divine family."[86]

My particular context is the Philippines. As in most Asian societies, family is central to Filipino life. Family-centeredness or family-orientedness is a cherished value. The value of the family is enshrined not only in the culture but also in its laws.[87]

---

83. Chan, *Grassroots Asian Theology*, 66.

84. As Jung Young Lee also states in his Asian interpretation of the Trinity, *Trinity in Asian Perspective*, 189–197.

85. *Patria* can be translated both as "fatherhood" and "family," as the NIV does.

86. Lee, *Trinity in Asian Perspective*, 191.

87. Thus, consider Article 149 of the Family Code of the Philippines: "The family, being the foundation of a nation, is a basic social institution which public policy cherishes and protects. Consequently, family relations are governed by law and no custom, practice or agreement destructive of the family shall be recognized or given effect."

Recently, the country's largest television network came up with the Christmastime slogan "Family is Love,"[88] reflecting the Filipino's orientation to, and love for, family. Christmas is reunion time for Filipino families, many of whom have members spread abroad for overseas work. Part of the station's jingle was the following:

> *Pag-ibig, pag-asa at saya* (Love, hope, and joy)
> *Yan ang laging mong dala* (Those are what you always bring)
> *Sa pamilya mo ang tunay na pasko* (In your family is real Christmas)
> *Family is love, family is love.*

What is unique about the Philippine context is that it is a majority Catholic country. The cultural influence of Latin Catholicism is something that needs to be factored in when we consider the context. This makes the Philippines different from the rest of Asia.[89]

The traditional Filipino nuclear family comprises father, mother, and child(ren) with the father as head. The family is not considered complete unless there are children. Family members and society in general pressure newly-wed couples to have children immediately; if you don't have children there must be something wrong with you. So family is three (father, mother, and children), with each member distinguishable from each other but also one (one family).

If the divine family is the archetype of the human family, what do we make of the notion that associates the Holy Spirit with the feminine gender? I agree with those who conceive of the Holy Spirit as something akin to a mother. This does not mean that the Holy Spirit's name is Mother or that the Spirit is female, any more than the Father is male. Christians have, after all, consistently expressed a commitment to the reality that God is beyond gender.[90] It only means we are employing the metaphor of mother to the Holy Spirit. The Holy Spirit acts or functions like a mother. In the Bible, generating, nurturing, and

---

88. The composer(s) may not have had 1 John 4:16 ("God is love") in mind, but the similarity is intriguing.

89. Pieris argues that in the process of becoming Christian under Spanish colonial rule, the Philippines was forced to cut off its Asian roots ("Towards an Asian Theology of Liberation," 80).

90. For further reading on this line of reasoning, see David Gelpi, *The Divine Mother: A Trinitarian Theology of the Holy Spirit* (Lanham: University Press of America, 1984); and Johannes van Oort, "The Holy Spirit as Feminine: Early Christian Testimonies and Their Interpretation," *HTS Theological Studies* 72, no. 1 (2016), accessed 24 January 2019, https://hts.org.za/index.php/hts/article/view/3225. Some indigenous Filipino religions found in Mt Banahaw (considered by some as a "New Jerusalem") have a notion of the Trinity as God the Father, God the Son, and God the Mother with God the Mother incarnated in the religion's female head.

enlightening functions are attributed to the Holy Spirit (Matt 1:20; Luke 1:35; John 3:5–8; Eph 1:18).

In Filipino culture, we call our mothers *ilaw ng tahanan* ("light of the home or family"). They are so designated because not only do they give birth to children, they also care for them and guide them. Filipino mothers usually hold the family together. If the family income is not enough, many mothers make the sacrifice to work and even go overseas (usually as domestic helpers) to sustain the family and meet its needs. This reflects the role of the Holy Spirit in the Trinity. The Holy Spirit is the bond between the Father and the Son: it is the Holy Spirit that unites the divine family together.

In the Filipino (Catholic) context, the Holy Spirit as mother should be brought to bear on the question of God. Many believe that Filipino society is matriarchal. Women hold sway over families, businesses, and politics.[91] This is manifested in a strong religious devotion to Mary, who is often elevated to the status of divinity. "To Christ through Mary" is a common refrain; Jesus Christ, it is reasoned, would be more inclined to hear our prayers if prayed through Mary, just as any son would be more inclined to grant the request of anyone who channeled it through the mother. If the Holy Spirit were recognized as filling this maternal space, it is possible that there would be no felt need to elevate Mary to the status of co-divinity with Christ.[92]

Although *pamilya* has become part of the local vocabulary, the Filipino word for "family" is *mag-anak*. It is composed of two words: *mag* (a prefix used to verbalize nouns) and the noun *anak* (child), literally, "to bear children." It denotes the whole family. Filipino families are centered on children. This reflects the Trinitarian revelation of God in the Son, Jesus Christ. It is in and through the Son that we know God and become members of his family. This is reinforced by the local word used for relatives: *kamag-anak*. *Ka* is another prefix to denote relationship. The Filipino family is not just nuclear but an extended family of relatives from both husband and wife's side.[93]

From this terminology we can see again that it is through the child(ren) that people, who might otherwise be unrelated or strangers, are brought

---

91. See Wilson Lee Flores, "Is the Philippines a Matriarchal Nation Pretending to Be a Macho Nation?," *PhilStar Global*, 29 September 2002, https://www.philstar.com/lifestyle/sunday-life/2002/09/29/177872/philippines-matriarchal-society-pretending-be-macho-nation.

92. Jung Young Lee makes a similar observation. "When the church failed to recognize the feminine element in God or to recognize the Spirit as God the Mother, the church had to elevate Mary as God the Mother" (Lee, *Trinity in Asian Perspective*, 106).

93. See Belen T. G. Medina, *The Filipino Family* (Quezon City: University of the Philippines Press, 2001), 14–21. The Filipino family is also of bilateral or bilineal descent whereas most other Asian cultures are patri-lineal.

together to form a wider family. As we noted earlier, Scripture declares that believers are chosen in the Son and redeemed through the Son (Eph 1:4–5). It is also through union with Jesus that we are included in God's family, becoming "co-heirs with Christ" (Rom 8:17). In this connection, what Gerald O'Collins says regarding Jesus as our eldest brother rings true: "Jesus' resurrection (with the outpouring of the Holy Spirit) made him the eldest Son of the Father's new, eschatological family (Rom. 8:29), a family now empowered to share intimately in Jesus' relationship to the Father in the Spirit."[94]

There is also in the Filipino family a strong filial bond between parents and children.[95] This is similar to Confucian filial piety although not as binding or obligatory. Parents are loving, caring, and protective. Children reciprocate with love, respect, and obedience. Such mutuality is demonstrated with parents willing to make the necessary sacrifices to provide for their children, especially to help them finish their education. Children, in return, when they have finished their studies, care and provide for their parents. Some, especially the eldest, would even forego marriage just so they can look after their parents in their old age. This is a reflection, albeit a pale one, of the Trinitarian *perichoresis*, the mutual giving and receiving between the persons of the Godhead. Furthermore, the Son loved the Father, obeyed him, and sacrificed his life to fulfill the Father's purpose.

Mutuality or *perichoresis*, as we saw above, involves a conception of persons not just as individuals but as persons-in-relation. In Filipino ontology I do not just exist for myself; I exist for others, especially my family. "I" is "we." The personal pronoun *ako* ("I") is used interchangeably with *kami* ("we") or *sila* ("they").[96] *Kapwa* (shared identity) is a core value. It recognizes that others are part of oneself and we become who we are in relation to others.

Conclusion

Discussion of the Trinity rightly brings us to discussion of the inner life of God or the nature of God; but it also brings us to an understanding of God's action and relation to the world. Moreover, the Trinity is about our faith and our life. As Colin Gunton rightly notes, "The Trinity is about life, life before God, with

---

94. Gerald O'Collins, *The Tripersonal God*, 2nd ed. (New York: Paulist Press, 2014), 185.
95. Medina, *Filipino Family*, 17–18.
96. This is also true in East Asian perspective. See Lee, *Trinity in Asian Perspective*, 64–65.

one another, and in the world."[97] Our understanding of God determines what kind of people we are and how we should live before him and in this world. Far from being an abstract teaching with little import for Christian life, the doctrine of the Trinity is both theological and practical.[98]

We examined in this study attempts by Asian Christians to reinterpret/reimagine the biblical revelation of God through Jesus Christ and in the Holy Spirit from the perspectives of Asian cultural traditions and thought patterns. We also offered our own reimagination by looking at the human (Filipino) family as a reflection of the divine family, reflecting on how local cultural patterns echo and deepen our understanding of the Trinity. Despite criticisms from (Western) theologians about using human, religious, moral, or cultural experiences as models for understanding God,[99] it is a theological task worth pursuing, as it links the Trinity to life in general and Christian living in particular. Moreover, it addresses the necessary, practical task of naming God in different cultural contexts – an inescapable and important task for Christian theology, especially in a region where Christianity is relatively recent. This approach is premised on the belief that God made human beings in his own image, and that he is present in all cultures, which all reflect to some degree the working out of his purposes. Father, Son, and Holy Spirit remain the primary symbols of naming the Trinity, but, as O'Collins puts it, "This does not mean that such formal Trinitarian language is the only way of speaking about and addressing God."[100]

References

Avendaño, Christine O. "Duterte Rants vs. Church, Calls Belief in Holy Trinity 'Silly.'" *Philippine Daily Inquirer*, Dec 30, 2018. https://newsinfo.inquirer.net/1067732/rody-rants-again-vs-church-calls-belief-in-holy-trinity-silly.

Chan, Simon. *Grassroots Asian Theology*. Downers Grove: IVP Academic, 2014.

———. *Spiritual Theology*. Downers Grove: InterVarsity Press, 1998.

---

97. Colin Gunton, *Father, Son, and Holy Spirit: Toward a Fully Trinitarian Theology* (London: T&T Clark, 2003), 11.

98. For an excellent reflection on the practical and theological import of the Trinity, see Fred Sanders, *The Deep Things of God* (Wheaton: Crossway, 2010).

99. For example, see Garrett Green, "The Gender of God and the Theology of Metaphor," in *Speaking the Christian God*, ed. Alvin Kimel (Grand Rapids: Eerdmans, 1992), 57; Mark Husbands, "The Trinity Is Not Our Social Program," in *Trinitarian Theology for the Church*, eds. Daniel J. Treier and David Lauber (Downers Grove: IVP Academic, 2009), 141.

100. O'Collins, *Tripersonal God*, 190.

Clarke, Sathianathan. "The Task, Method, and Content of Asian Theologies." In *Asian Theology on the Way*, edited by Peniel Jesudason Rufus Rajkumar, 3–13. London: SPCK, 2012.

"Confucianism." Center for Global Education, Asia Society. https://asiasociety.org/education/confucianism.

Dyrness, William, and Veli-Matti Kärkkäinen, eds. *Global Dictionary of Theology*. Downers Grove: IVP Academic, 2008.

Fabella, Virginia, ed. *Asia's Struggle for Full Humanity: Towards a Relevant Theology*. Maryknoll: Orbis, 1980.

Fiorenza, Francis Schüssler, and John P. Galvin, eds. *Systematic Theology: Roman Catholic Perspectives*. Vol. 1. Minneapolis: Fortress, 1991.

Flores, Wilson Lee. "Is the Philippines a Matriarchal Society Pretending to Be a Macho Nation?" *PhilStar Global*, 29 September 2002. https://www.philstar.com/lifestyle/sunday-life/2002/09/29/177872/philippines-matriarchal-society-pretending-be-macho-nation.

The Forgotten Trinity: The Report of the BCC Study Commission on Trinitarian Doctrine Today. London: British Council of Churches, 1989.

Franke, John R. "God Is Love." In *Trinitarian Theology for the Church*, edited by Daniel J. Treier and David Lauber, 105–119. Downers Grove: IVP Academic, 2009.

Gelpi, David. *The Divine Mother: A Trinitarian Theology of the Holy Spirit*. Lanham: University Press of America, 1984.

Green, Garrett. "The Gender of God and the Theology of Metaphor." In *Speaking the Christian God*, edited by Alvin Kimel, 45–64. Grand Rapids: Eerdmans, 1992.

Green, Gene L., Stephen T. Pardue, and K. K. Yeo, eds. *The Trinity among the Nations*. Carlisle: Langham Global Library, 2015.

Gunton, Colin. *Father, Son, and Holy Spirit: Toward a Fully Trinitarian Theology*. London: T&T Cark, 2003.

Hardy, Edward R., and Cyril Richardson, eds. *Christology of the Later Fathers*. Vol. 3 of The Library of Christian Classics. Philadelphia: Westminster, 1954.

Husbands, Mark. "The Trinity Is Not Our Social Program." In *Trinitarian Theology for the Church*, edited by Daniel J. Treier and David Lauber, 120–141. Downers Grove: IVP Academic, 2009.

Kärkkäinen, Veli-Matti, *The Trinity: Global Perspectives*. Louisville: Westminster John Knox, 2007.

———. *Trinity and Revelation*. A Constructive Christian Theology for the Pluralistic World. Vol. 2. Grand Rapids: Eerdmans, 2014.

Kasper, Walter. *The God of Jesus Christ*. New York: Crossroad, 1992.

Kavunkal, Jacob. "The Mystery of God in and through Hinduism." In *Christian Theology in Asia*, edited by Sebastian C. H. Kim, 22–40. New York: Cambridge University Press, 2008.

Kelly, J. N. D. *Early Christian Doctrines*. 4th ed. London: Black, 1968.

Kim, Sebastian C. H., ed. *Christian Theology in Asia*. New York: Cambridge University Press, 2008.
Kimel, Alvin Jr., ed. *Speaking the Christian God*. Grand Rapids: Eerdmans, 1992.
LaCunga, Catherine Mowry. "The Trinitarian Mystery of God." In *Systematic Theology: Roman Catholic Perspectives*, vol. 1, edited by Francis Schussler Fiorenza and John P. Galvin, 149–192. Minneapolis: Fortress, 1991.
Lee, Jung Young. *The Trinity in Asian Perspective*. Nashville: Abingdon, 1996.
McFague, Sallie. *Metaphorical Theology: Models of God in Religious Language*. Philadelphia: Fortress, 1982.
McGinn, Bernard, John Meyendorff, and Jean Leclercq, eds. *Christian Spirituality*. Vol. 1, *Origins to the Twelfth Century*. World Spirituality. New York: Crossroad, 1993.
McGrath, Alister E. *Understanding the Trinity*. Eastbourne: Kingsway, 1987.
Medina, Belen, T. G. *The Filipino Family*. Quezon City: University of the Philippines Press, 2001.
Moltmann, Jürgen. *The Trinity and the Kingdom of God*. Translated by Margaret Kohl. London: SCM, 1981.
Nirmal, Arvind. "Toward a Christian Dalit Theology." In *Frontiers in Asian Christian Theology:Emerging Trends*, edited by R. S. Sugirtharajah, 27–40. Maryknoll: Orbis Books, 1994.
O'Collins, Gerald, *The Tripersonal God*. 2nd ed. New York: Paulist Press, 2014.
Ott, Craig, and Harold A. Netland, eds. *Globalizing Theology*. Nottingham: Apollos, 2007.
Panikkar, Raimundo. *Trinity and Religious Experience of Man*. Maryknoll: Orbis Books, 1973.
Pieris, Aloysius. "Towards an Asian Theology of Liberation: Some Religio-Cultural Guidelines." In *Asia's Struggle for Full Humanity: Towards a Relevant Theology*, edited by Virginia Fabella, 75–95. Maryknoll: Orbis Books, 1980.
Rajkumar, Peniel Jesudason Rufus, ed. *Asian Theology on the Way*. London: SPCK, 2012.
Sugirtharajah, R. S., ed. *Frontiers in Asian Christian Theology: Emerging Trends*. Maryknoll: Orbis Books, 1994.
Thompson, John. *Modern Trinitarian Perspectives*. Oxford: Oxford University Press, 1994.
Torrance, James B., and Costa Carras, eds. *The Forgotten Trinity: The Report of the BCC Study Commission on Trinitarian Doctrine Today*. London: British Council of Churches, 1989.
Tracy, David. *The Analogical Imagination: Christian Theology and the Culture of Pluralism*. London: SCM, 1981.
Tanchanpongs, Natee. "Asian Reformulations of the Trinity: An Evaluation." In *The Trinity among the Nations*, edited by Gene L. Green, Stephen T. Pardue, and K. K. Yeo, 100–119. Carlisle: Langham Global Library, 2015.

Treier, Daniel J., and David Lauber, eds. *Trinitarian Theology for the Church*. Downers Grove: IVP Academic, 2009.

Vanhoozer, Kevin J. "One Rule to Rule Them All?" In *Globalizing Theology: Belief and Practice in an Era of World Christianity*, edited by Craig Ott and Harold Netland, 85–126. Nottingham: Apollos, 2007.

van Oort, Johannes. "The Holy Spirit as Feminine: Early Christian Testimonies and Their Interpretation." *HTS Theological Studies* 72, no. 1 (2016). https://hts.org.za/index.php/hts/article/view/3225.

Win, Thin Lei. "Despite Growth, One in 10 Asians Live in Extreme Poverty." ABS-CBN News, 29 March 2017. https://news.abs-cbn.com/business/03/29/17/despite-growth-one-in-10-asians-live-in-extreme-poverty.

4

Christology in Asia
Rooted and Responsive

Ivor Poobalan
Colombo Theological Seminary

Introduction

Christology takes us to the very heart of Christian theology.[1] It refers to the systematic reflection on the person and actions of Jesus of Nazareth, who lived within the period of roughly 5 BC to AD 30 in Roman Palestine.[2] Taken literally, "Christology" refers to any discussion that centers on how Jesus came to be invested with the Jewish title of *Christ* and what may be meant by this.[3]

The matter is more complex, however, than mere historical concerns. Our abiding fascination with Christology arises from the fact of our present experience of Jesus. Today, nearly a third of humanity confesses belief in Jesus and claims to interact with him as a real person who uniquely restores human beings to a relationship with God. This saving experience of Jesus, both historically and in contemporary contexts, has commonly led to spontaneous expressions of adoration and worship of Jesus as divine, with his followers addressing him as the Son of God, and even as God the Son.

Yet in what way can Jesus be divine? How are we to understand a deity who is also human at the same time? What of Jesus's relationship to God, whom

---

1. Veli-Matti Kärkkäinen, *Christology: A Global Introduction* (Grand Rapids: Baker Academic, 2003), 9–10.

2. Gerald O'Collins, *Christology* (Oxford: Oxford University Press, 1995), 1.

3. Raymond Brown, *An Introduction to New Testament Christology* (New York: Paulist Press, 1994), 3.

he uniquely called "*My* Father," and with whom he identified and from whom he distinguished himself at one and the same time? Going further, how can the Jesus narrative of the New Testament have any relevance to life today? On what basis can people claim to have a "relationship" with Jesus, who lived over two millennia ago? Is the latter an appeal to the enormous moral influence that the inspirational Jesus radiates to generations that have followed him? Or is the claim to have a relationship with him an actual spiritual experience?

For Christians in Asia there are additional concerns. How are we to speak about Jesus Christ in a context where all the major world religions vie for prominence? Are we to do so in exclusive or inclusive terms? How does our Christ-talk relate to the Asian realities of stark social inequality, abject poverty, oppressive societal structures, and postcolonial reactiveness? How is our Christology relevant to the reimagining of Asia as the theater of urbanization, technological advancement, and wealth-creation in the twenty-first century? And what difference does Christ make to the next generation of Asians adapting to the radically different demands of living in cyberspace?

Christology, like all theological reflection, must be both rooted and responsive. The Judeo-Christian tradition is rooted in the conviction that theological truth is first and foremost a matter of *revelation*. That is to say that since God is mystery, humanity may sufficiently know him not by searching for him, but only by his voluntary self-disclosure. This self-disclosure, while somewhat discernible through the material cosmos (see Ps 19:1; Rom 1:20), is supremely expressed in the written record of inspired Scripture.

Christology, too, begins with the revelation of the meaning of Jesus as unfolded in the Bible. Historically, we may know that Jesus of Nazareth lived and died in Palestine in the first century AD, but we can only know that he is Savior and Lord because of the faith and witness of the earliest Christian communities. It is the latter that we find in the New Testament, in which all the books are organized around the subject of "Jesus as the Christ": who he is, what he did, and what the Christ-event means for human existence, and, indeed, the future of the cosmos.

Christology, however, also takes its shape by *responsiveness*: the working out of the implications of the message of Jesus Christ to the lived experience of the communities to which it comes. This is what we find in the underlying narrative of the documents that eventually formed the New Testament. Initially Jesus was proclaimed among Jews in and around Palestine, and in doing so the apostles were compelled to express *their* Christology. They had to explain how Jesus fulfilled Jewish aspirations of the Messiah: how he fulfilled prophecy, and how his life, death, and resurrection certified him as God's anointed.

As the Christian gospel then moved from its original Palestinian Jewish setting, westward into the wider Mediterranean world, south to the African continent, and east as far as southern India, it encountered vastly different worldviews and sociopolitical contexts. How could the story of a Jewish itinerant preacher and miracle-worker matter to these unnumbered people groups that had so little in common with the Jewish-Christian worldview? Again, through the faithful witness to the revealed truth about the person and work of Jesus, now robustly applied to a universal longing for peace with God, and using the thought-forms and languages of the audiences addressed, the Christology of the apostles developed and took shape. It is this creative tension, between rootedness and responsiveness, revelation and relevance, which characterizes the shaping of Christology through the centuries to the present day.

Christological Development in the New Testament Period

The documents that later formed the New Testament were all written in the first century AD, during a period of no more than sixty years. Among these twenty-seven books, the letters of Paul are the oldest and give us the earliest insights into the Christ-talk of Christian communities of the time. While it is clear that Paul was aware of the stories circulating about the historical Jesus, his letters assume that his readers, too, share these same assumptions. The main thrust of his writings is to argue for Christians to live out the implications of believing and relating to Jesus Christ. What, then, did Paul want the churches to essentially believe about Jesus?

An answer to this question is found in 1 Corinthians 15:3–8:

> For what I received I passed on to you as of first importance: that Christ died for our sins according to the Scriptures, that he was buried, that he was raised on the third day according to the Scriptures, and that he appeared to Cephas, and then to the Twelve. After that, he appeared to more than five hundred of the brothers and sisters at the same time, most of whom are still living, though some have fallen asleep. Then he appeared to James, then to all the apostles, and last of all he appeared to me also, as to one abnormally born.

Paul calls this summary statement in essence "the gospel" that he had preached to the Corinthians, and reminds them that it is their conviction about this that forms the basis of their salvation (see 15:1–2). He refers to it as a sacred tradition ("what I received I passed on to you") and fundamental to the Christian faith ("of first importance"). In an earlier comment, he had said: "I resolved to know nothing while I was with you *except Jesus Christ and him crucified*" (1 Cor 2:2).[4] It is vital, therefore, to note the focus of Paul's thought: for Paul, the core of the gospel was oriented toward the death and resurrection of Jesus, which alone was sufficient to bring individuals to the experience of salvation through faith.

This early apostolic preaching (*kerygma*), which centered on the death and resurrection of Jesus as the expression and proof of his messiahship, determined the shape of the unique writings that came to be called "Gospels." Thus, we find that despite the biographical feel of the Gospel of Mark, it veers sharply away from a typical biography because of its overt focus on the passion and death of Jesus to the exclusion of typical elements of biography such as genealogy, early life and influences, and personal characteristics and habits of the subject.[5] Having begun abruptly with the baptism of Jesus, Mark displays an impatience to get his readers to the death and resurrection of Jesus (introducing the theme as early as in 8:31), and dedicates six chapters (11–16) of sixteen to just the last few days of Jesus's life and their climactic events.

How then was this core Christology explained to the diverse cultures of the first-century world? Did the apostles and evangelists deliver a stock, creedal statement such as 1 Corinthians 15:3–8 wherever they went?

What we find in the New Testament is quite the opposite. Every book – whether Gospel, Acts, letter, or Revelation – shows evidence of how the good news of Christ's death and resurrection was creatively adapted and couched to fit the thought-forms and cultural categories of the particular audience. Dean Flemming calls this "the *activity* of expressing and embodying the gospel in context-sensitive ways."[6] He explains that this may be seen in at least two ways in the New Testament. First, the Gospels and Acts are replete with examples of how both Jesus and the apostles "tailor the gospel message to address different groups of people"; and second, the writings of the New Testament are themselves models of contextualization. Each author painstakingly shapes

---

4. All emphasis in Scripture quotes has been added.

5. Vinoth Ramachandra, *Recovery of Mission* (Carlisle: Paternoster, 1996), 185: "The Gospel writers are not biographers but evangelists: the events surrounding the death and public ministry of Jesus of Nazareth are seen now, in the faith-perspective of the resurrection, as conveying a divine purpose."

6. Dean Flemming, *Contextualization in the New Testament* (Leicester: Apollos, 2005), 15.

his writings in order to "present the Christian message in a way that is targeted for a particular audience within a given sociocultural environment."[7]

New Testament scholars are in general agreement today that Matthew and Luke wrote their Gospels using Mark as a base or template, and so the adjustments and expansions of each author point to an early form of christological development.[8] The immediately noticeable feature is the addition of narratives about the birth of Jesus. Although Matthew and Luke differ considerably in the stories they present, they are both keen to inform the reader about Jesus's *birth* as a means of establishing who he is and where his special status originates.

Early church history shows us that two opposing heretical ideas challenged Christian belief during the apostolic period. The first was Ebionitism, a movement among Jews who believed in Jesus as the Messiah, but wished to safeguard the monotheism of the Hebrew Bible without any redefinition. For them, Jesus was an ordinary human being whom God set apart in an extraordinary way. Baptism was the most significant event in the life of Jesus, because it was then that the "Christ" descended in the form of a dove to act "more as the presence of God's power and influence within the man Jesus than as a personal, metaphysical reality."[9]

Ebionitism may explain the christological reshaping we find in Matthew and Luke. By including the birth narratives, both authors are able to weaken the Ebionite argument by showing that Jesus's divine origin antedates his baptism. Matthew is able to convey this primarily through Joseph's encounter with the angel, who says: "Joseph son of David, do not be afraid to take Mary home as your wife, because *what is conceived in her is from the Holy Spirit*" (Matt 1:20). In the case of Luke, we reach the same conclusion by means of Mary's experience of the angel Gabriel: "*The Holy Spirit will come on you*, and the power of the Most High will overshadow you. So the holy one to be born will be called the *Son of God*" (Luke 1:35).

A second heresy that the church faced during the apostolic period was Docetism (from the Greek word *dokeō*, which means "to seem" or "appear to be"), which argued that although Jesus appeared to be a human being, he

---

7. See Flemming, *Contextualization*, 15.

8. On this, see Flemming, 234–265.

9. Millard Erickson, *Introduction to Christian Doctrine* (Grand Rapids: Baker, 1992), 212. The Ebionite view of Jesus's baptism also lies at the heart of Dynamic Monarchianism of the second and third centuries, which attempts to preserve the "sole sovereignty of the Father" by the argument that "God was dynamically present in Jesus, thus making him higher than any other human being but not yet a God"; see Kärkkäinen, *Christology*, 67.

was in reality fully and only divine, because God could not have corrupted himself by becoming genuinely incarnate. This dispelled all notions that the Christ suffered in any real way. Docetism was welcome relief to many who thought within Greek philosophical categories. Since some held that matter was intrinsically evil and the divine could never participate in the material world, they argued that Jesus could not have assumed human flesh.

The apostle John represents those who had to contend for the faith against the heresy of Docetism. He wrote his Gospel to Greek-speaking Jews influenced by the arguments of Greek philosophy. This is the reason why he begins by speaking about Jesus as "the *Logos*" (John 1:1), which was a well-known Greek idea about impersonal "reason" (*logos*) that underlies nature. Using this lofty Greek concept as a parallel, John is able to introduce Jesus Christ, albeit as a person, and accord him the highest status possible, while simultaneously asserting his utter humanity. After introducing the *Logos* as a being *with* God and *the same as* God (1:1), John goes on to make the staggering assertion: "The Word [*logos*] became flesh [*sarx*] and made his dwelling among us" (1:14).

Here too we see the "context-sensitive" christological method of this New Testament writer.

The Christological Creeds of Nicea and Chalcedon

Given the occasional nature of all the New Testament documents, it is readily obvious that despite the affirmations they make about the person and work of Jesus Christ, there is much that they do not explicitly clarify. Bradley Hanson suggests that the authors of the New Testament left two important questions unresolved: "First, since the Son of God has an ambiguous status as divine yet subordinate to God, can we say more precisely what the relation is between the Son of God and God? Second, what is the relation between the pre-existent Son or Word and the Jesus who lived about thirty years in Palestine?"[10]

The first question became more urgent because of the teachings of an Alexandrian presbyter named Arius (AD 260–336), who made much of the subordination of the Son. He argued that the Father alone was eternal, and that the Son was created by the Father before the beginning of the world, and, thereafter, became the agent of the creation of everything else: a Logos that acted as a unique intermediary between the Father and the created universe.

A generation before Arius, Sabellius had insisted that Father, Son, and Holy Spirit were simply three modes of manifestation of one divine person.

---

10. Bradley Hanson, *Introduction to Christian Theology* (Minneapolis: Fortress, 1997), 144.

Arius distinguished the Father and the Son (he had nothing to say about the Holy Spirit), but held strictly to the inferiority of the Son, famously declaring: "There was a time when he was not."

The Arian controversy dominated the proceedings of the Council of Nicea (AD 325), and resulted in the Nicene Creed, which counterargues both Sabellianism and Arianism. Nicea definitively established that the Son is at one and the same time a distinct being, co-eternal with the Father and of the same nature (*homoousios*) as the Father. This formula was further ratified in terms of the Trinity by the First Council of Constantinople in AD 381.[11]

The second unresolved issue – how the eternal, pre-existent Logos relates to the historical Jesus – would become the focus of the church for the next several decades. The debate was between Christianity centered in Alexandria and that of Antioch. The former majored on John 1:14 and argued that it was the *divine, eternal Logos* that was born of Mary, lived and taught about the kingdom of God and eventually died and was raised. The reason for this insistence was their conviction that only God can save humanity from its predicament of sin. Their overt emphasis on the divinity of Christ, however, subsumed and even undermined his genuine humanity, and tended in the direction of early Docetism: that the Word only "seemed" to become human.

The opposing christological camp was the Antiochene Christians, whose theologians were convinced that a robust belief in the full humanity of the divine Son was essential to explain how Jesus saves. As Hanson puts it, their view was that "we humans can only be helped by a Savior who, through his own genuine moral development, brings into existence a new sinless person."[12] In his famous words, Gregory of Nazianzus asserted: "That which he has not assumed he has not healed!" The Antiochene view, however, was also fraught with danger: it could lead to the notion that Jesus Christ was constituted of two distinct beings – a good man and God – in close cooperation.

This debate was settled at the Council of Chalcedon (AD 451), although it actually took the church a total of six councils between the fourth and seventh centuries to arrive at a general consensus about these pressing concerns.[13] Thereafter, "Christology" was more or less a settled matter – deriving from

---

11. For a complete discussion of how Christology developed from Ignatius of Antioch (AD 107) to the First Council of Constantinople, see O'Collins, *Christology*, 153–183.

12. Hanson, *Christian Theology*, 145.

13. Kevin Vanhoozer, "Christology in the West: Conversations in Europe and North America," in Jesus without Borders, eds. Gene L. Green, K. K. Yeo, and Stephen T. Pardue (Carlisle: Langham Glboal Library, 2015), 15.

the teachings of the New Testament and interpreted through the various formulations of the church councils – until the dawn of the Enlightenment.

We must pause to note at this point, however, that despite the considerable time and energy spent by the church fathers in developing their christological formulations, there was an enormous amount from the New Testament presentation of Christ that had been sidelined. It is readily evident that the burden of the Gospel authors is to present Jesus through his words and his works, with their climax occurring in the events of Passion Week. Yet the actual "life of Jesus" is almost completely ignored in the creedal statements of the later church.

Christology in the Asian Context: A Critique

In examining the directions Christology has taken in the vast Asian region during the last century or more, one theme emerges as a constant driving force: how *relevant* is Jesus Christ to the lived experiences of Asia's teeming millions? As Kosuke Koyama, a Japanese theologian who worked in Thailand for many years, has put it, "There is a quiet determination among Asian Christians that their commitment to Jesus Christ and their words about Jesus Christ must be responsible to the life they live in Asia today. Such theology is called a living theology . . . Asian theology seeks to take the encounter between life in Asia and the Word of God seriously."[14]

Unlike the European and North American contexts, Christians are a distinct minority in every Asian country except the Philippines. In addition, the Asian reality displays two outstanding characteristics across the board: religious-cultural pluralism and poverty.[15] Addressing these realities has thus become the urgent task of Asian theologians. R. S. Sugirtharajah refers to Aloysius Pieris to explain this double beat in Asian christological reflection: "While conceding that poverty is a common factor between Asia and other third-world countries, Pieris contends that what distinguishes Asia is its multiple religious traditions. Hence, for him, *religious pluralism and poverty are inseparable as the reality which constitutes the one source of any theologizing*

---

14. Kosuke Koyama, "Foreword by an Asian Theologian," in *Asian Christian Theology: Emerging Themes*, ed. Douglas J. Elwood (Philadelphia: Westminster, 1980), 13.

15. See Timoteo D. Gener, "Christologies in Asia: Trends and Reflections," in *Jesus without Borders: Christology in the Majority World*, eds. Gene L. Green, K. K. Yeo, and Stephen T. Pardue (Carlisle: Langham Global Library, 2015), 61.

in Asia. In his view, Asian Christian theology must address both these issues together – *religiousness and poverty*."[16]

Asian theology has had its centers of development including Korea, Japan, Thailand, China, Taiwan, Indonesia, Philippines, India, and Sri Lanka, each providing a distinctive flavor based on its socioreligious context.[17] In several of these settings, theological development was assisted by a reactive mindset: the need within national churches to reject their embarrassing associations with colonialism and prove a new loyalty to the predominantly non-Christian local context. Vinay Samuel and Chris Sugden describe the phenomenon in this way: "The younger churches in the Two Thirds world found themselves as independent entities in newly emergent nations. Due to their origins in western missions and links with the colonial rulers, they had to demonstrate their loyalty to the new nation and to the process of nation-building. They took this to mean that the church had to be deeply involved in the quest for social justice . . . This task required common action by followers of all religions."[18]

Sugirtharajah is more explicit in his explanation for the radically creative turn of Asian Christology. Jesus was original to Asia, and in the early period there was a strong eastward thrust of the Jesus movement through Persia and Afghanistan which disintegrated and virtually disappeared until the period of Western colonial expansion in the fifteenth century. He continues:

> When Jesus made his belated second visit to the eastern part of Asia, he did not come as a Galilean sage showing solidarity with its seers and wisdom teachers. Rather he came as an alien in his own home territory, and more tellingly, as a clannish god . . . sanctioning the subjugation of the peoples of Asia and their cultures . . . *Since then there have been a number of attempts by Asian Christians to counteract this imperial, supremacist and absolutist understanding of Jesus.*[19]

---

16. R. S. Sugirtharajah, ed., *Asian Faces of Jesus* (New York: Orbis Books, 2001), 127 (emphasis added). So also Kärkkäinen: "What is distinctive about the Asian context is the continuous correlation between Christian theology and the pluralism of Asian religiosity" (Kärkkäinen, *Christology*, 265).

17. See the note in Kärkkäinen: "Theologically, perhaps the most fertile soil has been India and Sri Lanka, with their strong Hindu influence. Because of the strong tradition of English-speaking education, these countries have contributed significantly to emerging international discussions" (Kärkkäinen, *Christology*, 266).

18. Vinay Samuel and Chris Sugden, eds., *Sharing Jesus in the Two Thirds World* (Bangalore: Partnership in Mission-Asia, 1983), 180.

19. Sugirtharajah, *Asian Faces*, viii–ix (emphasis added).

At times, this overriding impulse to counteract the "imperialist, supremacist and absolutist" Christology of some Western missions has resulted in distorted christologies of our own. As we have seen, the Christology of the New Testament and the early centuries asserted the uniqueness of Jesus as the pre-existent Son of God who enters human history in order to restore humanity to a right and necessary relationship with its Creator and establish the rule of God. Jesus's nature as the eternal Son of God and the fraternal Son of Man, and his unique, historic action of defeating the power and consequences of human sin through his sacrificial death and resurrection are not Western imperialist constructs; they form the heart of the apostolic message.[20] These claims about Jesus Christ as unique Savior demand a response from all peoples in the world, whether Jew or Gentile, as expressed by Luke: "Salvation is found in no one else, for there is no other name under heaven given to mankind by which we must be saved" (Acts 4:12; see also 2 Cor 5:17).

At times this christological essential of the unique role of Jesus Christ in salvation became diluted in some Asian theologies. The tendency was either to limit his soteriological value as mediator with God as valid only for Christians, or to attempt to redefine his message purely in terms of sociopolitical liberation.

The question remained, though, where exactly these theologians might "find" the Jesus they would then so articulately explain. Was there a given understanding about the person and work of Jesus that they could use to explain his relevance to the struggles of Asia? Or did they have to christologize at both ends: fabricate their ideal Christ on the one hand, and then make him fit comfortably into the contemporary Asian mood, on the other?[21]

Arguably, this is what has sometimes taken place. The Jesus Christ of some Asian christologies is a caricature of the person who is proclaimed by the testimony of the New Testament writers. For example, to some Asian thinkers he is a God-man no different from what Krishna is to Hinduism, or a mere teacher of wisdom as Gautama the Buddha is to Buddhism.[22] Stanley Samartha suggests that in the context of Indian Christology, there is no way to avoid comparing Jesus "with the savior figures of Hinduism and other religions of the area" and so includes Buddha, Rama, and Krishna as equal saviors with Jesus.[23] To others, Jesus offers nothing more than the inspiration to continue

---

20. Aside from the New Testament passages previously cited, see also the extensive argument of Hebrews 1–2.

21. For a recent discussion on christological reflection in Asia, see Simon Chan, *Grassroots Asian Theology* (Downers Grove: InterVarsity Press, 2014), 91–127.

22. See, e.g. Sugirtharajah, *Asian Faces*, 9–45.

23. Kärkkäinen, *Christology*, 284.

the struggle against unjust and oppressive social structures since he epitomizes humanity sacrificially lived for the other.[24]

This reading of Jesus as liberator is at the heart of the Christology of Aloysius Pieris, who famously spoke of Jesus's "double baptism" in "the Jordan of Asian religions and the Calvary of Asian poverty."[25] Vinoth Ramachandra rightly critiques Pieris's approach as "reductionist" and "dubious":

> He [Pieris] describes Jesus' voluntary baptism at the hands of John the Baptizer as an identification with "the stream of an ancient spirituality," and draws from this the implication that "the first and the last word about the local church's mission to the poor in Asia is total identification . . . with monks and peasants who have conserved for us, in their *religious socialism*, the seeds of liberation that *religion* and *poverty* have combined to produce." But this is reading into the text what Pieris wants to say anyway![26]

The question that arises about this remarkably creative theologizing – which either assimilates Jesus Christ into existing religious metanarratives or reduces him to a mere example of inspirational human leadership – is with regard to its hermeneutical basis. Does the argument that Jesus was originally Asian legitimize the creation of a Christ in the image of contemporary Asian aspirations of religious co-existence and social justice?

To understand the methodology of these prominent Asian theologians of the latter period of the twentieth century, we must briefly consider the intellectual climate in which Christian truth claims were presented during the last two hundred years. Christianity in South and East Asia from the early nineteenth century was largely the extension of European missionary movements that had, in turn, been subject to the challenges of theological liberalism, which had gradually become the dominating discourse in Europe. The end of the Thirty Years' War (1648) marked the beginning of the Age of Reason in which "the *philosophe* replaced the theologian as the fount of all wisdom, and 'enlightenment' became the order of the day."[27] Human reason, and not a sacred text nor institutional tradition, had final authority in determining what was "true." Naturally, this mood eventually led to an assault on the Bible's authoritative status in the theological task: "Biblical criticism was

---

24. See Kärkkäinen, 273–278.
25. Aloysius Pieris, *An Asian Theology of Liberation* (Maryknoll: Orbis Books, 1988), 48.
26. Vinoth Ramachandra, *Gods That Fail* (Carlisle: Paternoster, 1996), 208–209.
27. Gerald Bray, *Biblical Interpretation: Past and Present* (Downers Grove: InterVarsity Press, 1996), 225.

a natural result of this new openness to the independent use of human reason. Whereas in the past the biblical text had been taken as a trustworthy historical account, now it faced mounting doubts and denials . . . it was not left to the Holy Spirit but to the human spirit and human reason to judge whether the text was convincing."[28]

This modern dogmatism not only dominated christological debates of the nineteenth and early twentieth centuries, but it also informed the curricula of theological institutions in Asia long after its heyday in Europe had ended in the 1920s. One of the later scholars to have a profound influence on Asian Christology in the last quarter of the twentieth century was John Hick, whose most famous work is *The Myth of God Incarnate*,[29] which appeared in 1977 after his extensive teaching stints in India and Sri Lanka between 1974 and 1976.[30] With no *a priori* commitment to the authority of the Bible, and confronted by the pervasive reality of religious pluralism in South Asia, Hick and his colleagues found no insuperable difficulty in affirming that all religions are equal pathways to salvation. Thereafter, all that was necessary was to fabricate a Christology that did away with any claims to Jesus's uniqueness as Savior. In Hick's words: "Once it is granted that salvation is in fact taking place not only within Christianity but also within the other great traditions, it seems arbitrary and unrealistic to go on insisting that the Christ-event is the sole and exclusive source of human salvation."[31]

This trend, however, has not gone unchallenged. One of the most thorough critiques is marshalled by Vinoth Ramachandra's *Recovery of Mission*, in which he first responds to the christological thought of three major Asian theologians – Stanley Samartha, Aloysius Pieris, and Raimundo Panikkar – before providing a compelling christological picture that is as much *rooted* in the biblical witness as it is *relevant* as a "Gospel for the World":

> The controversy over Jesus concerns who he is. For the historic Christian claim regarding Jesus of Nazareth is that no human category, whether that of "charismatic prophet," "religious genius,"

---

28. Kärkkäinen, *Christology*, 87.

29. John Hick, ed., *The Myth of God Incarnate* (London: SCM, 1977). A sequel was published a few years later: John Hick and Paul F. Knitter, eds., *The Myth of Christian Uniqueness: Toward a Pluralistic Theology of Religions* (Maryknoll: Orbis Books, 1987).

30. Kärkkäinen, *Christology*, 179–185; Karl-Josef Kuschel, "Christology and Interfaith Dialogue: The Problem of Uniqueness," in *Christology in Dialogue*, eds. Robert F. Berkey and Sarah Edwards, (Cleveland: Pilgrim, 1993), 370–372.

31. John Hick, "The Non-Absoluteness of Christianity," in *The Myth of Christian Uniqueness: Toward a Pluralistic Theology of Religions*, eds. John Hick and Paul F. Knitter (Maryknoll: Orbis Books, 1987), 22.

"moral exemplar" or "apocalyptic visionary" can do justice to the evidence of his words and actions. No category short of deity is sufficient. It is this traditional claim – that in the human person of Jesus, God has come amongst us in a decisive and unrepeatable way – that constitutes an offence to pluralist society. It is this that invites the scorn of the secular humanist, the puzzlement of the Hindu and the indignant hostility of the Muslim. The same range of responses were encountered in the Greco-Roman world that the earliest followers of Jesus inhabited.[32]

Another hopeful response by an Asian theologian to the minimalism and generalization of Jesus Christ is Ajith Fernando's *The Supremacy of Christ*.[33] Here, too, the high Christology of the New Testament with its claims to uniqueness is shown to be compatible with, and necessary for, relevant and compassionate Christian witness in a pluralistic world. Fernando's theologizing, like Ramachandra's, comes out of a committed engagement to life in Asia, facing constantly the challenge of presenting the good news of Jesus to societies shaped by multiple religions and burdened by unjust social structures.

Christology in the Asian Context: A Way Forward

What is commendable about theological developments in Asia is their emphasis on relevance in context. Asian Christians recognize the ineffectiveness of communicating Christology in terms of abstract concepts of Western philosophy, and search for presentations of Jesus that resonate with Asian categories of thought and address the most immediate challenges to witness and mission.

Over a hundred years ago the Indian itinerant evangelist Sadhu Sundar Singh famously asserted that the good news of Christ must be served in an Eastern bowl. But how can this be done? Sundar Singh was himself a model of this struggle, adopting the demeanor and dress of the Indian guru (*sadhu*) as he traveled extensively proclaiming the Jesus of the Gospels in the languages and cultural codes of South Asian peoples.

Theologies of liberation have positively reset the way Asian Christians *picture* Jesus: one who is fully at home in the context of abject poverty, social oppression, and political marginalization. Korean theologians, for example, have articulated Jesus as a "Messiah of the *minjung* [the people] because he

---

32. Ramachandra, *Recovery of Mission*, 181.
33. Ajith Fernando, *The Supremacy of Christ* (Wheaton: Crossway, 1995).

shares their suffering," and Indian theologians have endeavored to show how, through his incarnation, Jesus has overcome the curse of caste-ism.[34]

In India, 300 million people are identified as Dalits (caste-less untouchables), which means that in a society that is already hierarchically ordered by caste, these teeming millions become virtual non-persons. Dalit theology therefore represents Jesus as the Dalit "prototype because he has taken their *dalitness* upon himself, endured their humiliation and pain, and laid down his life as a 'ransom for many' (Mk 10:45)."[35]

Another example of how the message of Jesus may be conveyed in an effectively contextual manner is found in Tissa Weerasingha, *The Cross and the Bo Tree*, which presents a methodological framework for communication with Sinhalese Buddhist audiences.[36] Weerasingha argues that, similar to all forms of Buddhism in Asia, Sinhalese Buddhism also emerges from an amalgamation of Buddhist philosophy and indigenous religious beliefs and practices. Although it is a composite of seemingly contradictory beliefs – the Buddhist philosophy of *non-theism* and the radical *animism* of Sinhalese religion – Sinhalese Buddhists hold these poles in tension with little difficulty.[37] How does such a context shape our christological presentation?

The Western emphasis in evangelistic proclamation is on the *work* of Christ as Savior, and this meets the audience's overriding concern with feelings of guilt. Within animistic belief systems, however, it is more effective to emphasize the *person* of Christ as "Lord over all other powers," thus meeting the audience's overriding concern with feelings of fear: "It is the proclamation and assertion of the Lordship of Christ, rather than his Saviourhood, in the first instance, that strikes the heart of the individual held in bondage and fear to demonic powers."[38]

With regard to the work of Christ in salvation, Weerasingha articulates the atonement in terms of the Buddhist concept of *pattidāna*, "merit transference."

---

34. See J. Levison and P. Pope Levison, "Christology," in *Global Dictionary of Theology*, eds. William Dyrness, Veli-Matti Kärkkäinen, Juan Francisco Martinez, and Simon Chan (Downers Grove: InterVarsity Press, 2008), 184.

35. Levison and Levison, "Christology," 184.

36. Tissa Weerasingha, *The Cross and the Bo Tree* (Taiwan: Asia Theological Association, 1989).

37. Weerasingha, *Cross and the Bo Tree*, 53: "Although outside researchers have been baffled by the apparent paradox within the Sinhalese religious system, it is clear that no such intellectual dilemma exists in the ordinary worshippers' minds."

38. Weerasingha, *Cross and the Bo Tree*, 63; on this, also see Chan, *Grassroots*, 121: "In many primal religious contexts of Asia, conversion is more frequently the experience of freedom from bondage to fear, evil powers or the caste system. The patristic experience of *Christus Victor* is perhaps the more dominant paradigm."

This arises from the schema of *karma* that regulates all the living: the accumulation of merits (*kusala*) and demerits (*akusala*). Most Buddhists would admit that, despite their efforts at accumulating *kusala*, their *akusala* are far in excess to be counterbalanced by their merits. This leads to the practice of *dāna* (almsgiving) in memory of a deceased relative, with the hope that the living may transfer their acquired merit to the dead. Weerasingha proposes that this opens the way for a contextual presentation of how Jesus saves:

> This is the point at which the power and work of the Lord Jesus Christ is introduced. Christ was perfect. Therefore, He generated an infinite quantity of *kusala*, to negate all the *akusala* of all humanity for all time. And, because Christ was God incarnate, He not only could generate sufficient *kusala*, but He could also TRANSFER its merits onto man . . . Moreover, on the cross, man's guilt was transferred to Christ. Only God could transfer guilt. So a double transference took place wherein man's guilt was transferred to Christ and His grace was transferred to man.[39]

Another significant example of creative christologizing is found in Simon Chan, *Grassroots Asian Theology*, particularly in his proposal for seeing "Jesus as mediator-ancestor."[40] Asian societies, as in Africa, give enormous significance to ancestors.[41] In East Asian societies especially, we find the prevalence of ancestral veneration. This can range from a "supernaturalistic" religious practice to a "purely cultural expression of filial piety."[42] This reality is "one of the greatest challenges facing the church in Asia for much of its history."[43] Chan suggests that the doctrine of Christ as the ancestor-priest and the doctrine of the church as the communion of saints carry huge potential for showing the relevance of the Christian faith within the grassroots Asian context.

With regard to the doctrine of Christ, he begins with the suggestion that we might use "the doctrine of the triune God as the divine family" as a center for Asian theologizing. Since the first two persons of the triune God are revealed as Father and Son, this resonates within the Asian context: "In much of Asia a person's foremost identity is defined in relation to his or her family, and not just the immediate family but also the extended family, which may include

---

39. Weerasingha, *Cross and the Bo Tree*, 73–74.
40. Chan, *Grassroots*, 113–117.
41. For a helpful summary of how African theologians have articulated the notion of "Jesus as ancestor," see Levison and Levison, "Christology," 182–183.
42. Chan, *Grassroots*, 188.
43. Chan, 188.

the entire clan, and the linear family, which includes dead ancestors. Given its importance, the concept of God as the trinitarian family could serve as theology's organizing principle."[44]

He then argues that, in reference to Christ's "triple office," Asian theologians only proclaimed Jesus as prophet and king, and neglected his role as priest.[45] The latter is most evident within the Protestant tradition, which has overemphasized the priesthood of all believers, and ironically therefore downplayed "the post-ascension priestly ministry of Jesus."[46] But the book of Hebrews explains how Jesus is the perfect high priest, both by virtue of his total identification with humanity and by his simultaneous status as absolute divinity. Since ancestral veneration is predicated on the belief that the dead ancestor persists as a benevolent presence in the lives of the living, "Jesus can be considered our greatest ancestor." This "christological grounding" then opens the way to discuss the corporate, filial nature of the church, including "both the saints on earth and saints in heaven" in a vital communion between the living and the "dead."[47]

Conclusion

We began by recognizing the tension between rootedness and responsiveness in the theological task, and how this has played out in the history of Christology. If the church in the West was found wanting for holding too rigidly to formulations about the person of Christ based on a commitment to scriptural revelation, the church in Asia may be criticized for playing too loose with the message and mission of Christ for the sake of contextual relevance.

In this light we can be encouraged by contemporary trends in the Asian church, where examples abound of exciting ways by which the biblical revelation about Jesus is being communicated to diverse audiences in a relevant manner. As we noted at the start, Christology takes us to the very heart of Christian theology and praxis. The christological faith of the apostle Paul can inspire Christians in Asia to courageously pursue mission today. It was his Christology that transformed the ethnocentric Paul into a radical Christian in service to the world, since "God was reconciling the world to himself in

---

44. Chan, 42–43.

45. Chan, 43: "Yet both in Africa and Asia, the priestly office might be a far more significant way of conceptualizing the essential character of theology and ministry."

46. Chan, 114.

47. Chan, 115–117.

Christ, not counting people's sins against them. And he has committed to us the message of reconciliation" (2 Cor 5:19).

References

Berkey, Robert. F., and Sarah Edwards, eds. *Christology in Dialogue*. Cleveland: Pilgrim, 1993.
Bray, G. *Biblical Interpretation: Past and Present*. Downers Grove: InterVarsity Press, 1996.
Brown, Raymond. *An Introduction to New Testament Christology*. New York: Paulist Press, 1994.
Chan, Simon. *Grassroots Asian Theology*. Downers Grove: InterVarsity Press, 2014.
Dyrness, William, Veli-Matti Kärkkäinen, Juan Francisco Martinez, and Simon Chan, eds. *Global Dictionary of Theology*. Downers Grove: InterVarsity Press, 2008.
Elwood, Douglas J., ed. *Asian Christian Theology: Emerging Themes*. Philadelphia: Westminster, 1980.
Erickson, Millard. *Introduction to Christian Doctrine*. Grand Rapids: Baker, 1992.
Fernando, Ajith. *The Supremacy of Christ*. Wheaton: Crossway, 1995.
Flemming, Dean. *Contextualization in the New Testament*. Leicester: Apollos, 2005.
Gener, Timoeteo D. "Christologies in Asia: Trends and Reflections." In *Jesus without Borders: Christology in the Majority World*, edited by Gene L. Green, K. K. Yeo, and Stephen T. Pardue, 59–79. Carlilse: Langham Global Library, 2015.
Green, Gene L., K. K. Yeo, and Stephen T. Pardue, eds. *Jesus without Borders: Christianity in the Majority World*. Carlisle: Langham Global Library, 2015.
Hanson, Bradley. *Introduction to Christian Theology*. Minneapolis: Fortress, 1997.
Hick, John, ed. *The Myth of God Incarnate*. London: SCM, 1977.
———. "The Non-Absoluteness of Christianity." In *The Myth of Uniqueness: Toward a Pluralistic Theology of Religions*, edited by John Hick and Paul F. Knitter, 16–36. Maryknoll: Orbis Books, 1987.
Hick, John, and Paul F. Knitter, eds. *The Myth of Christian Uniqueness: Toward a Pluralistic Theology of Religions*. Maryknoll: Orbis Books, 1987.
Kärkkäinen, Veli-Matti. *Christology: A Global Introduction*. Grand Rapids: Baker Academic, 2003.
Koyama, Kosuke. "Foreword by an Asian Theologian." In *Asian Christian Theology: Emerging Themes*, edited by Douglas J. Elwood, 11–22. Philadelphia: Westminster, 1980.
Kuschel, Karl-Josef. "Christology and Interfaith Dialogue: The Problem of Uniqueness." In *Christology in Dialogue*, edited by Robert F. Berkey and Sarah Edwards, 368–385. Clevalnd: Pilgrim, 1993.
O'Collins, Gerald. *Christology*. Oxford: Oxford University Press, 1995.
Pieris, Aloysius. *An Asian Theology of Liberation*. Maryknoll: Orbis, 1988.
Ramachandra, Vinoth. *Gods That Fail*. Carlisle: Paternoster, 1996.

———. *Recovery of Mission*. Carlisle: Paternoster, 1996.
Samuel, Vinay, and Chris Sugden, eds. *Sharing Jesus in the Two Thirds World*. Bangalore: Partnership in Mission-Asia, 1983.
Sugirtharajah, R. S. *Asian Faces of Jesus*. New York: Orbis Books, 2002.
Vanhoozer, Kevin. "Christology in the West: Conversations in Europe and North America." In *Jesus without Borders*, edited by Gene L. Green, K. K. Yeo, and Stephen T. Pardue, 11–36. Carlisle: Langham Global Library, 2015.
Weerasingha, Tissa. *The Cross and the Bo Tree*. Taiwan: Asia Theological Association, 1989.

5

Creation, New Creation, and Ecological Relationships

Ken Gnanakan[1]
ACTS Group

In a scathing attack on the "Christian doctrine of creation" Lynn White, Jr, dealing with "man's unnatural treatment of nature and its sad results," blamed Christians for the devastation of the earth and its resources.[2] He traced the historical roots of the ecological problem to the "victory of Christianity over paganism," claiming that that was the greatest psychic revolution in the history of Western culture.[3]

White alleged that the climax of the biblical account of creation was the teaching that man and woman had "dominion" over everything. "God planned all this explicitly for man's benefit and rule. No item in the physical creation had any purpose save to serve man's purposes."[4] Therefore, for him, "especially in its western form, Christianity is the most anthropocentric religion the world has seen," encouraging one to believe that it is "God's will that man exploit nature for his proper ends."[5]

---

1. This chapter is largely drawn from an essay by the same name that previously appeared in *Emerging Voices in Global Christian Theology*, ed. William Dyrness (Grand Rapids: Zondervan, 1994).

2. Lynn White's lecture was delivered in Washington on 26 December 1966 and was reproduced by Francis Schaeffer as an appendix in his book *Pollution and the Death of Man: The Christian View of Ecology* (London: Hodder & Stoughton, 1970), 70–85 (here, 78). Schaeffer deals with Lynn White's criticisms.

3. White, in Schaeffer, *Pollution*, 78.

4. White, in Schaeffer, 78–79.

5. White, in Schaeffer, 79.

While Bible-believing Christians, shocked by such accusations, have busied themselves by pointing out what is mistaken in attacks such as these, the ecological crisis has taken such global proportions that it is impossible for anyone to stand unconcerned and indifferent. The depletion of the earth's resources, the pollution of our environment, and their alarming consequences pose a worldwide threat that is far too real to be dismissed as merely the agenda of "environmentalists."

Undoubtedly, we will need to refute White's accusations, as well as the flood of others since his paper in 1966, but what we hear is not invitation to a debate, but a call for concerned action. The ecological crisis demands our attention as well as our involvement, and such reminders have brought us to realize the enormous Christian responsibility. As a theologian, I see the urgent need for us to search for a biblical theology of creation that will relevantly address this situation, as well as clearly remind us of our responsibility.

Many attempts have been made to develop relevant theologies of creation. We need to heed these reminders, but we must also address some of the pressing present issues. We need to reiterate, or even correct, what has been said and dig deeper into the Bible in order to explore all that God has already revealed for his people and for his world. However, in doing so it is imperative that we move forward with constructive attitudes, not merely defending ourselves nor making affirmations that will have no relevance to the real issues that we face.

God and Creation

At the root of the environmental issue is the confused relationship between humankind and the rest of creation. In order to discover this relationship within its right context, it is useful for us to go back to an even more fundamental relationship: the relationship of God to his creation. Here is the underlying factor for any theology that will address the ecological issue and hence give some clear biblical direction. On the one hand, we will need to avoid any extreme dualism that separates God from his creation with no vital link of any kind. Yet, on the other hand, we will need to avoid a monism or pantheism that will confuse the Creator with his creation.

An assertion of God's lordship over his creation will imply God's continuing relation to the world. However, the Bible not only speaks of the glorious creation of God, but also graphically depicts the sad rebellion of humankind resulting in a "fallenness" of creation. Yet the fact remains that God does not abandon his creation. He continues to be concerned and reveals his redemptive purposes, desiring to bring about a "new creation," as the prophets of the Old Testament so frequently declare.

The fact of God's lordship, however, implies a distinction between God and his handiwork. The initiation that comes from God, who declares his will in the words "Let there be . . . ," is of primary significance for our theology today. Creation is no accident but the result of God's deliberate and purposeful word demonstrated in the completion of the heavens and the earth "in all their vast array" (Gen 2:1).

Gerhard von Rad points out that the idea of creation by the "word" preserves "first of all the most radical essential distinction between creator and creature."[6] What he tries to preserve is the distinction between creation accounts that make creation an emanation from God or even include God in the realm of nature, and the biblical implication of creation being "a product of his personal will."[7]

Interestingly, the Sanskrit word *sristi* which is commonly used as the equivalent of "creation" literally means "emanation." Creation is seen as an emanation of God. This monistic understanding of God has found acceptance among environmentalists who advocate respect, even reverence, for creation. The popular Hindu monistic teaching maintains the idea of a Supreme Person (*Purusa*) who pervades the whole universe to the extent that all created objects are part of that one person. The Bible allows no room for such a confusion of the Creator and the created.

However, in underlining a distinction, we must not imply that God is not involved with his creation. Here von Rad points out that "the idea of creation by the word expresses the knowledge that the whole belongs to God. It is his creation, he is Lord."[8] This kind of corrective is needed to remedy totally immanentist ideas of God and creation that sublimate God into some impersonal power behind creation. If he is Lord, God stands apart from creation and continues to give it the direction toward the new creation he has personally purposed.

The ongoing relationship of God to creation is demonstrated powerfully through his ongoing involvement with his creation as its creator and redeemer. Very clearly the Bible depicts creation, both in the Old and New Testaments, in terms of God's redemptive activity within history, moving toward a newness

---

6. Gerhard von Rad, *Genesis: A Commentary* (London: SCM, 1961), 50.
7. von Rad, *Genesis*, 50.
8. von Rad, 50.

he has purposed. On the basis of his covenant with his people he continues a relationship toward fulfilling his revealed purposes.

Almost every religion has references to some kind of a relationship between its god and creation. Israel's God is not to be made out as distinctive because of his ongoing relationship with creation. "What is distinctive of Israel's faith is the belief that God revealed his character in his activity, and that there was a moral purpose governing it."[9] God's creative activity has a purpose behind it, a redemptive mission which is unfolded through his covenant.

The Old Testament displays a very clear link between the doctrine of creation and the covenant. We will need to develop this link so that our theology will possess a firm foundation, on the one hand, and yet is able to explore the fullest implications of creation for all that is outside the covenant, on the other hand. This will also help free us from limits we impose on creation when we see it primarily as a religious affirmation of faith, purely for the believer and without any historical significance.

The covenant link is further clarified in the New Testament in its ultimate connection with Jesus Christ. This is consistent with the Old Testament. Jesus Christ clearly shows himself to be the fulfillment of all the promises of God in history and the one who ushers in the new covenant in continuity with the old. Even creation now takes on a newness as Jesus Christ fulfills his promised relationship within the reality of the new creation.

Jesus Christ and Creation

Although there are not as many references to creation in the New Testament as there are in the Old, we are not to conclude that it is an unimportant doctrine for the Christian. Some may suggest that because of sin the doctrine of creation is abandoned in favor of the new creation that is anticipated. However, scanty reference to the doctrine of creation should be taken only to imply that the early church was a Jewish congregation, and these fundamental facts were accepted without question. Timothy declares, "Everything God created is good" (1 Tim 4:4).

Also, the New Testament writers were far more concerned with spelling out the ministry of redemption and reconciliation that was anticipated by the Old Testament believers. Their Creator God was now made available in Jesus Christ. This redemption is seen in terms of its all-inclusive reconciling ministry of bringing together everything under God's control and thereby to

---

9. H. H. Rowley, *The Faith of Israel* (London: SCM, 1956), 59.

the originally intended purpose. "For God was pleased to have all his fullness dwell in him [Jesus Christ], and through him to reconcile to himself all things, whether things on earth or things in heaven, by making peace through his blood, shed on the cross" (Col 1:19–20).

Standing within the new covenant instituted by Jesus Christ, we will inevitably have to see our theology in terms of Jesus Christ and his relationship to creation. A biblical theology of ecology will have to be christological. If Jesus Christ is the Lord of history, and the one through whom all things are to be made new and are to be actualized in the new heaven and the new earth, he must undoubtedly have a crucial part to play in creation even now. It is by Jesus Christ that all things "hold together" (Col 1:17), and it is through him that "all things in heaven and on earth" will be united (Eph 1:10). He is the one who "upholds" the universe (Heb 1:3 KJV).

Moreover, it is not just for the present that the lordship of Jesus Christ over creation is to be seen. His role has to be recognized in the initial creative process itself. John ascribes to Jesus the very creative power itself: "Through him all things were made" (John 1:3). The same idea is found in Colossians 1:16, 1 Corinthians 8:6, and Hebrews 1:2. Jesus was always with God, and everything that God did, he did through Jesus Christ.

Such a christological foundation to creation is essential, or else our understanding of creation could be abandoned to abstract philosophizing or accidental evolutionary acts in the name of God. It is through Jesus that the Creator and Redeemer is revealed. Our theology must inevitably be founded firmly upon a Christology that considers Jesus Christ to be the one through whom we know our Creator God, the Lord of heaven and earth.

Moreover, creation is also seen in the New Testament from the future perspective of being under Christ's ultimate lordship. The picture of the Creator enthroned in majesty and splendor, as painted by John in his depiction of the new creation, clearly captures the total sovereignty of God over all creation and over all history. He is not merely Lord at that moment but "the Lord God Almighty, who was, and is, and is to come" (Rev 4:8).

For the New Testament, underlying the theme of creation is a strong christological emphasis. The doctrine that underlines and validates the truth is that all of history is under the sovereign purpose of God as revealed in Jesus Christ. He is the "Alpha and the Omega," "the First and the Last," "the

Beginning and the End" (Rev 1:17; 22:13; cf. 3:14). "The whole sweep of history, from creation to the new heaven and the new earth, has its fulcrum in him."[10]

Jesus and the "World"

Apart from dealing with Jesus's role in creation, we need to spell out some aspects of his attitude to the "world" – the realm of God's creation. We have asserted that the solution to the ecological crisis is to restore a right relationship between humanity and the created order, one that will be based on the fundamental relationship between God and human beings on the one hand, and God and creation on the other. What kind of attitude did the earthly Jesus display?

This could be an important aspect for us. Some Christians display negative attitudes to the world, on the grounds that Jesus wanted us to withdraw from it. Derogatory references are made to "worldliness," and consequently the ecological issue itself seems outside the scope of biblical spirituality. Some reminders are necessary to restore a more biblical concern.

We pick up some aspects of Jesus's relationship to the "world" particularly in John's Gospel. There the term "world" is used in the sense of the orderliness of the universe, as in John 1:10: "The world was made through him." The basic meaning of the word *cosmos* is an ornament, something beautifully built and artistically arranged; hence the English word "cosmetic." Jesus uses this meaning of "world" when he prays in 17:5, "Glorify me in your presence with the glory I had with you before the world began." For Jesus, there is a glory and a creative significance to the entire universe – not merely the earth – in all its orderliness.

In Johannine usage, the "world" can also refer to the human inhabitants in the sense of humankind, the human race. It is this "world" that John refers to as being the object of God's love (3:16). God loved humankind, and the environment within which he had placed them, so much that he sent his Son to live amongst them in that same environment. In all our attempts to reemphasize the importance of creation, we must not forget that there is clearly a centrality of men and women in God's plans and purposes. It is not in keeping with God's redemptive purposes if we concentrate on ecological issues without reference to people in God's world. God's redemption is directed primarily at humanity, and his salvific blessings are first for "whoever believes on him."

---

10. George Arthur Buttrick, ed., *Interpreter's Dictionary of the Bible* (New York: Abingdon, 1962), 731.

Moreover, it is through the salvation of men and women that everything else will receive God's redemptive benefits. Neither the one-sided emphasis on salvation purely for humanity nor the emphasis on a concern dealing abstractly with creation can be biblically justified. The biblical emphasis is on the concreteness of God's concern for a people within a particular world, all of which needs to be redeemed.

Having emphasized the positive sense of "world," we must not neglect the clear negative references to it as the realm of evil and at enmity with God. In Johannine writings this aspect receives emphatic treatment (7:7; 8:23; 12:31; 14:30; 15:18; 17:9, 14; 1 John 2:15). This is the new meaning that the term acquires in the New Testament and which brings out the sharp contrast between the beauty of God's creation and the ugliness of human sin. Sinful humans, and consequently a decaying creation around us, confront the perfection of Christ.

There is also another important fact we need to underline, and that is the reality of the influence of Satan on creation. John makes it clear that the "whole world is under the control of the evil one" (1 John 5:19). While this could be meant primarily in terms of Satan's influence on people, the biblical fact of the curse on creation will need to be reckoned with in all our discussions about God's relationship to the world he has created.

In fact, it is only through a proper understanding of sin and the curse that we will be able to explain some of the ecological problems that confront us. For one thing, we are able to understand the fact of greed and selfishness of humans only in terms of our fallenness. Moreover, we are confronted by pests and decay, factors within creation itself that bring about devastation of the earth and its resources. Did God create these? If he did, and creation is supposed to be "good," why does this form of evil exist? We can explain these only from the perspective of sin, the curse, and fallenness.

The Earth and Our Responsibility

However, despite creation's fallenness, God's continued dealings with humankind are clearly depicted in the Old Testament. He is still Lord of creation. If the earth and all that is in it belongs to God, there ought to be some way in which we who are God's people must be responsible for this earth. What should be our attitude?

Leviticus 25:1–17 gives us some insights into our relationship to the earth. The selfish human tendency is to think that the earth and all its resources are our possession to use as we wish. It is this kind of misuse that is behind ecological disaster. Instead, God's command points toward a more responsible utilization. Natural resources themselves have a claim to dignity, and we are accountable to God for the use to which we put them.

The endless plundering of the earth to reap maximum benefits is wrong. Even the earth has been shown to need its rest. We have no problems accepting that the Sabbath was a divine institution for human beings, but, interestingly, the Year of Jubilee extends the privilege of the Sabbath rest even to the land: "The land is to have a year of rest" (Lev 25:5). The whole network of relationships depicted, perhaps even idealized, in the Jubilee Year are the restored relationships that foreshadow ultimate new-creation relationships. Men and women must take care to recognize that even the created order, which they could so easily exploit for their own ends, has some claims of its own. God commands us to take note. While God wants the best for humankind and therefore has placed them in charge of his creation, he also desires that his nonhuman creation be treated with care.

God has created the heavens and earth in a harmonious network of interlinked elements. Economic interests must be pursued with ecological concern. That is why Moses reminds the people, "Do not take advantage of each other, but fear your God. I am the LORD your God" (Lev 25:17). Undoubtedly, this prohibition of "taking advantage of" also applies to humanity's dealings with the earth. Righteous relationships are demanded of the redeemed community, and these relationships are to be demonstrated not only within the community but with regard to all that is God's.

Israel's history sounds a warning to us today. "The story begins in a land flowing with milk and honey; it ends in barrenness."[11] Here are the consequences of disobedience: "The people refused to obey God, and the price to be paid involved not only political ruin but also a despoiled environment."[12] Israel knew God's command and yet rebelled. If they had truly been the witness God had wanted them to be, perhaps the world would have heeded God's Word more responsively. Similarly today, we refuse to obey God, setting up our own gods, our idols. Science and technology, the idols of today that have taken control of everything we say or do, must be restored to their right place. They need to be under our control, and not control us. "The danger sets in when science and technology replace the ultimate ground of our hope and their white-coated practitioners become the priests of the present age. In the specific context

---

11. Ron Elsdon, *Green House Theology: Biblical Perspectives on Creation* (Tunbridge Wells: Monarch, 1992), 113.

12. Elsdon, *Green House Theology*, 113.

of environmental issues, idolatry is then our expectation that science and technology alone can solve our problems," as Ron Elsdon puts it.[13]

Idolatry is disobedience. Today's ecological devastation is a consequence of human disobedience, the unwillingness of human beings to give heed to the Creator God and his commands. God reminded his people throughout their history that it was through his grace that they had been chosen. If that is so, then "his grace [will have] the last word, and the fundamental goodness of creation [will be] gloriously reaffirmed."[14] Because of his grace, God does not abandon his creation even though his people refuse to care for it. He will renew it.

Restoration of Creation

Whatever relationships we strive to build on earth are only shadows of the perfect relationships to come in the future. The powerful Bible theme of restoration of all creation to its original perfection is a clear reminder of the ultimate purposes of God. Beginning with creation and ending with the new creation, the Bible reveals the compassionate heart of God who continues to reveal his concern for creation despite the rebellion of humankind.

Whether it is through prophetic voices or apocalyptic visions, the Old Testament clearly directs our attention toward the fulfillment of God's purposes in and through the created order. Evil will not prevail for ever, and the righteousness of God will reign over all heaven and earth. Sin has broken God-intended relationships, but God's righteousness will restore them to ultimate harmony.

An outline of God's plans is made explicit in the unfolding of his covenant with his people in the Old Testament. Of particular interest to us in connection with an ecologically oriented theology of creation is God's covenant with Noah. In fact, it is in God's dealings with Noah that the covenant is first mentioned. When in Genesis 6:18 God says, "I will establish my covenant with you," it is the first of the biblical covenants in which God's promise for his people is unfolded.

This covenant is an everlasting covenant between God and all flesh upon the earth. Genesis 9:11–12, 16 notes the universal implications of this covenant which is made between God and "the earth" (v. 13). The rainbow is to be "the sign of the covenant between [God] and the earth" (v. 13); God says that whenever the rainbow appears, "I will remember my covenant between me

---

13. Elsdon, 125.
14. Elsdon, 125.

and you and all living creatures of every kind" (v. 15). It is a "covenant between God and all living creatures of every kind on the earth" (v. 16).

The reference here to all creation within God's redemptive and reconciliatory purposes is emphatic. As a divine covenant, it has eternal significance, and every part of God's creation has a part within this covenantal significance. We have often restricted ourselves to the personalized and individualized implications of God's redemptive purposes, seeing them only in terms of their effects on men and women. This is not wrong, but they must be placed in the context of God's covenantal concern for all of his creation.

However, it is only in God's call of Abraham that we begin to see the dramatic unfolding of the long-term purposes of God for his world. The blessings of the covenant are to be extended to all of God's creation. God clearly tells Abraham, "all peoples on earth will be blessed through you" (Gen 12:3). Once God has established his relationship with Abraham on the right basis, the potential extends to all peoples of the earth for similar relationships. God's reconciliatory program has been set in motion and the impact will be universal.

Lest we once again confine ourselves to human salvation, one of the promises specifically given to Abraham related to a land that God had ordained for his people. That which was intended in Eden would in a limited way now be made available on earth before its ultimate availability in the new creation. Canaan was not the end in itself; it was only a very earthly picture of the ultimate promised land – the new heaven and the new earth.

Bede Griffiths reminds us of the three aspects of the call issued to Abraham. The first was the call to follow God. The second was that he would become a great nation and be a blessing to all the earth. The third was that he was promised a place to dwell. Griffiths comments: "These three callings represent the call of humanity to return to its origin and to rediscover its ultimate destiny. Humanity is to be reconciled with God by going out from its present state of civilization and venturing into the unknown. To bring this about it has to be formed into a new people [who] will be reconciled with the earth, with the world of nature by being given a land in which to dwell."[15]

Clearly, then, God is concerned for the ultimate restoration of right relationships in the broadest sense. Whether it be the various emerging forces that are threatening to disintegrate humanity from within, or the ecological disaster that threatens the survival of the whole created order, remedial measures cannot be brought about by power or wealth, nor by the many manifestations

---

15. Bede Griffiths, *A New Vision of Reality: Western Science, Eastern Mysticism and Christian Faith* (London: Collins, 1989), 84.

of these cravings of humanity. The very roots of broken relationship must be remedied. "Human liberation is always seen as reconciliation with God and with nature in a renewed humanity."[16]

Resurrection and the Future

We obtain the clearest glimpse of renewed humanity in the resurrection of the Lord Jesus Christ. Creation, rather than being sublimated by other New Testament doctrines, is powerfully juxtaposed with the doctrine of resurrection. The new life of the new-creation community has its rationale in the resurrection. As Moltmann reminds us, "the New Testament testimony about creation is to be found in the resurrection kerygma and in the experience of the Holy Spirit, who is the energy of the new creation."[17]

Paul is explicit about the implications of the resurrection for the ultimate blessing of humanity in 1 Corinthians 15. Jesus Christ is the "firstfruits" of the new creation, of which we are all to be part in the *eschaton*. Our bodies are to be raised "imperishable," "in glory," and in "power" (1 Cor 15:42–43). It is the resurrection that will provide for us the perspective of the new creation in the eschatological sense.

Theologians have underlined the priority of the resurrection within the new creation. Wolfhart Pannenberg, consistent with his theology written from the eschatological perspective, proposes that the creation of all things as mediated through Jesus Christ should not be thought of in terms of a temporal beginning of the world, but rather in terms of the *eschaton* (or end event):

> It is rather to be understood in terms of the whole of the world process that receives its unity and meaning in the light of its end that has appeared in advance in the history of Jesus, so that the essence of every individual occurrence, whose meaning is relative to the whole to which it belongs, is first decided in the light of this end. To be sure, the cosmos with which we are familiar can be supposed to have had a temporal beginning, but to speak of

---

16. Griffiths, *New Vision of Reality*, 85.

17. Jürgen Moltmann, *God in Creation: An Ecological Doctrine of Creation* (London: SCM, 1985), 65. We must not minimize the role of the Holy Spirit in all of God's plans for creation and new creation. The Spirit is depicted both in his activity at creation and in the inauguration of the new-creation community, the church. However, I choose to emphasize the christological aspect solely to underline the reconciliatory work that is so vital in bringing about the right relationships urgently called for. But it is the Holy Spirit who actualizes all the influence of Jesus Christ both for the new-creation community and the creation community, as well as for the whole created order.

the creation of the world does not refer just to this beginning but to the world process as a whole. This is conceivable, because the creation must be understood as an act of God's eternity, even though what is created by this eternal act has a temporal beginning and a temporal becoming. However, God's eternal act of creation will be entirely unfolded in time first in the *eschaton*. Only at the *eschaton* will what is created out of God's eternity be consummated in the accomplishment of its own temporal becoming.[18]

Pannenberg is right to remind us that the temporal acts of creation can only be properly understood from the perspective of their eschatological fulfillment and not from the perspective of the beginning. But in reality this becomes more a matter of an abstract theology than a factual foundation on which theological considerations can be founded. There is no doubt that the eschatological dimension gives meaning and significance to creation. But to insist that even Jesus Christ's role in creation is only "in retrospect" could make Jesus Christ an afterthought, or merely a matter of perspective rather than a reality. History must have continuity, and Jesus Christ's role in creation history must not be stripped of this continuity.

There is no doubt that with the resurrection, a future has been ushered in, a future that has an overwhelming influence on creation even in the present. That is why creation is seen to "groan" in anticipation (Rom 8:22). It is only in this sense that we can look back on the entire creation process and see God's hand in it all along, despite the obvious decay and degradation of God's handiwork. The ecological crisis is only temporal and is to be expected if the biblical definition of sin is accepted as fact. With creation placed in the exploitative and manipulative hands of sinful humankind, it is not surprising that such should be its fate. Marred relationships will foster greed, selfishness, and callous nonconcern, and will bring about devastating consequences.

However, in the cross and resurrection God's eternal work has been revealed in the temporal realm. The vision of the new creation that was revealed to the prophets Isaiah and Ezekiel has been demonstrated before us in its firstfruits in Jesus Christ. This gives the new-creation community the courage to move forward in hope and confidence. Temporality is inescapable, but God's future is certain.

---

18. Wolfhart Pannenberg, *Jesus – God and Man* (London: SCM, 1968), 391.

Creation and the New Creation

The more we consider the implications of the revelation of God within history, the more we come to realize that God's purposes are demonstrated to his creation in its entirety. Any theology that abandons God's desires for the present creation will diminish the significance of God's activity in the present, which points to the fulfillment of his ultimate purposes.

Fallenness and disobedience must not be glossed over. But in affirming this, the fundamental relationship between the old fallen creation and the new creation must not be minimized. All that we set within the goodness of creation and its longings for perfection is an anticipation of all it will experience in the *eschaton*. This means that it is not possible to speak of creation except in the eschatological sense of where it is headed.

Is there a connection between the present fallen creation and the future new creation? Some biblical insights can be noted. The Old Testament prophets imply a newness in the new creation which does not totally obliterate the old (Isa 66:22). The fact of God's lordship of history is emphasized along with a constant reminder of his power and wisdom in relation to this creation, and it is upon this that the assurance of the future is built. Isaiah's eschatological depictions of the end times are painted in terms of pictures of the first things. "Creation anticipates the consummation, and the consummation is the fulfillment of the beginning."[19]

The truth that emerges is of God's creative involvement in the world. If the present creation is such a glorious act of his handiwork, planned and purposed by him, the question arises as to whether God will abandon it altogether. Despite creation at present not being what it was intended to be, Isaiah does not allow for God's withdrawal. The new creation returns to God's original perfect and purposeful designs.

Redemption primarily is about reconciliation, the restoring of new-creation relationships. The fundamental relationship between God and humankind is set right, and from there all other relationships are seen to be restored to a justice and righteousness that will anticipate the perfect relationships of the new creation.

Justice has become a very common theme in spelling out the implications of God's mission for the world. The call for justice is issued whether it be for social action or even for ecological consciousness: "justice is actualized in just relationships. Unequal partnerships and patterns of dominations are unjust.

---

19. Buttrick, *Interpreter's Dictionary of the Bible*, 731.

It is obvious that today human relationship with nature is not that of equal partners, but of domination and exploitation. Unjust treatment of the planet by humans is one of the principal causes of the ecological crisis."[20] It is on these grounds that "eco-justice" is demanded.

"Justice" is an appropriate word. It is a strong Pauline image and has been much in use in recent times. "Justice, Peace, and the Integrity of Creation" is the title of a long-running program of the World Council of Churches which is aimed at arousing an ecological consciousness regarding concerns related to human life itself, and it aptly sums up some of the crucial issues. However, the word "justice" has strong legal overtones and does not have the best of connotations within the context of relationships.

Interestingly, the word "ecology" carries with it the prefix "eco-," which is derived from the Greek *oikos*, or "home." To "legalize" such a familial relationship can deprive the whole family of God of relationships built on love, grace, compassion, and concern. One is not to discard the whole image of "justification" which so clearly describes the work of Christ that brings about reconciliation. But to stop at "justice" and not move on to the wonder of reconciliation is not to see the entire work of God for his family. We are "God's people and . . . members of his household" (Eph 2:19).

The New Testament abounds with illustrations of this familial relationship that comes from God's ultimate reconciliatory purposes. John's apocalyptic vision in the book of Revelation beautifully illustrates this fulfillment of God's familial relationships: God and his people will enjoy a perfect relationship. A continuity is definitely implied. In other words, the kinds of God-intended relationships include those between people and their God, among people, as well as between people and the rest of creation. Whatever the new creation is, it will be marked by a community characterized by new relationships.

Not only does the environmental question need urgent attention today, but there is also a growing threat from religious fundamentalism. This, too, is a matter of relationships. If we recognize that beyond our differences there is a wider community of human beings where transcultural and trans-religious relationships are possible, we will face our common future in a much more mature manner. The widening chasm that threatens humanity with fears of ultimate fragmentation will disintegrate society into narrow fundamental units which will eventually become a threat to our corporate human existence. The threat of fundamentalism does not stop with the forming of one homogeneous

---

20. K. C. Abraham, *Eco-Justice: A New Agenda for Church's Mission* (Bombay: Build Publications, [1992?]), 7.

unit. It naturally degenerates into the narrowest form of individualism that eventually threatens its existence.

The New-Creation Community

What is urgently needed alongside the call to relationships is basically a call to accepting one another's *creation-ness* – a humanness that is God-given – to build relationships on purely a creational and human level. Set within the whole ecological framework, this is a call to discovering and demonstrating our *creationality*. I use the word "creationality" instead of "creatureliness" as it refers to the privilege we are given, rather than to subservience within the environment of God's creation.

But how do we distinguish this level of relationship from the level made possible through the reconciliatory work of Jesus Christ? It is here that we speak of the community of those reconciled by Jesus Christ to God, living within the community of those composing the wider circle of God's creation. The relationship between the new and the old creation brings to light this important connection between the people of God and the people within the creation of God.

Jürgen Moltmann speaks of the "eucharistic community of creation." "In perceiving the world as creation," he writes, "the human being discerns and enters into a community of creation."[21] Moreover, Moltmann notes that "this community becomes a dialogue before the common Creator. Knowledge of the world as creation is in its primal form thanksgiving for the gift of creation and for the community found in it, and adoring praise of the Creator."[22] There ought to be a very real "dialogue before the common Creator," on a level that is not related to salvation, redemption, or reconciliation. This kind of creational relatedness could certainly resolve a number of tensions the world community faces today.

Moltmann prefers to call the human a "eucharistic being," one who is able to "discern the world in full awareness as God's creation, to understand it as God's hidden presence, and to apprehend it as a communication of God's fellowship."[23] The proposition is a bit too idealistic. It does not take into account the fact of human fallenness. We would refer to a "creation" community and a "new-creation" community. The new-creation community consists of those

---

21. Moltmann, *God in Creation*, 70.
22. Moltmann, 70.
23. Moltmann, 70.

who are able to express a genuine creational relationship with each other within the realm of God's creation, without diminishing the distinctiveness of the redeemed community of Jesus Christ. The creation community is one which has access to all the gifts of creation but is still under the bondage of sin, which restricts it from fully knowing the Creator and thereby from enjoying its full creationality.

We will need to underline the reality of sin and the ongoing influence of Satan if we want to fully understand all that is happening in God's creation over against the desires of humankind. In fact, it is Satan's blinding and our bondage to sin that hinders human beings from looking beyond creation to the Creator God. Blessed with the image of God that gives men and women a desire for God, but blinded by Satan, they direct their worship to creation as the solution to the ecological crisis. Creation itself stands in need of reconciliation, and no amount of worship will satisfy its longings for ultimate redemption.

However, within this wider creation community is the new-creation community, those in Jesus Christ who discover real creationality (2 Cor 5:17). They are able to experience the "firstfruits" of ultimate reconciliation here and now. Men and women in Christ are not transported into another realm distant from the creation community. They discover their complete creationality even more as they dwell alongside those who are still outside the reconciliatory work of Jesus Christ.

What are the distinctives of this community? First, the new-creation community that God creates is a community that cares. This is a key word for the *oikos* of God that enjoys and needs to demonstrate the privileges of the family relationship of God. The bondage of sin has diminished the joys of caring within the widest network of all that God has created. The ecological crisis is intensified because of the selfishness and greed that characterize the creation community. The community of the new creation begins to see its need to transcend such limitations and moves toward caring as a tangible expression of their new creationality. Caring for one another and caring for God's earth are essential elements that bring us closer to solutions within the ecological tensions that have assumed worldwide proportions.

There is also a sense of responsibility. The new-creation community conducts itself within the creation community with a renewed sense of responsibility as stewards of all that God has entrusted to us. Exploitation is sin. Responsible relationships are characteristic of God's new-creation community and such relationships are to be established at every level in God's creation.

Further, the community of the new creation, the body of Christ, begins to experience the joy of createdness once again. What was lost through human rebellion soon after creation and what is missing in fallen creation becomes possible. Human beings made in the image of God are created with an individuality within community. This individuality was characterized by dignity and freedom to "be" all that God intended us to be. God's work in redeeming his creation must be seen in restoring "worth" and value – re-"deeming" – so we can all be restored to relationships of dignity within the network of creational relationships. Joy is the outcome of good relationships.

Freedom within creation does not mean the liberty to do what one desires. Freedom within relationships has its boundaries at the best interests of all concerned. It is the wrong understanding of freedom that has resulted in chaos. True freedom is that which is set alongside responsibility, and therefore it is conducted within the context and function of fulfillment.

The creation community is crippled under the bondage of sin, and this is clearly manifested before our eyes in all kinds of seen and unseen shackles. The dehumanization of men and women by exploiters and oppressors, the alienation of humans by other humans through racist discrimination, the devastation of the earth's resources by those in power, and many other ills are all too obvious. But the new-creation community will demonstrate to the world the care, responsibility, dignity, and freedom which characterize the joyful relationships that Christ restores.

References

Abraham, K. C. *Eco-Justice: A New Agenda for Church's Mission.* Bombay: Build Publications [1992?].

Buttrick, George Arthur, ed. *Interpreter's Dictionary of the Bible.* New York: Abingdon, 1962.

Elsdon, Ron. *Green House Theology: Biblical Perspectives on Creation.* Tunbridge Wells: Monarch, 1992.

Griffiths, Bede. *A New Vision of Reality: Western Science, Eastern Mysticism and Christian Faith.* London: Collins, 1989.

Moltmann, Jürgen. *God in Creation: An Ecological Doctrine of Creation.* London: SCM, 1985.

Pannenberg, Wolfhart. *Jesus – God and Man.* London: SCM, 1968.

Rowley, H. H. *The Faith of Israel.* London: SCM, 1956.

Schaeffer, Francis. *Pollution and the Death of Man: The Christian View of Ecology.* London: Hodder & Stoughton, 1970.

von Rad, Gerhard. *Genesis: A Commentary.* London: SCM, 1961.

6

Lord and Giver of Life
The Holy Spirit among the Spirits in Asia

Wonsuk Ma
Oral Roberts University

Asia is the cradle of all the major religions of the world. Interaction among diverse religions is part of the daily life for its 4.55 billion people. All cultures in Asia have deep religious roots, making the separation between culture and religion difficult. The Christian presence in the continent has a varied history. Some countries have had a Christian presence since the early centuries (e.g. Georgia and India), and others for only several decades (Mongolia), while most are somewhere in between. Even though Christianity was born in Asia, many parts of the region still view it as a "foreign" and "Western" religion.

However, this "Western" face of Christianity has been engaging with Asian religions and cultures to influence the theological shaping of the church. The frontline of engagement is the realm of the S/spirit(s). It is here that Christianity and existing beliefs interact, adapt, challenge, and come to a compromise with each other. This active engagement takes place everywhere: at family gatherings, markets, and schools. This grassroots spirituality and theology confronts the established theological structures of Western missionaries, who have often fashioned Asian churches in the image of historic churches. The gap is particularly wide between Western churches with a "sensitized" theology motivated by Enlightenment thinking and their counterpart churches in Asia.[1]

---
1. Hwa Yung, *Mangoes or Bananas? The Quest for an Authentic Asian Christian Theology*, 2nd ed. (Oxford: Regnum, 2014), 2–3.

The resurgence of pneumatology in the global church in recent decades is warmly welcomed by churches in the southern continents (or "global South"). Veli-Matti Kärkkäinen attributes this growing pneumatological interest in part to the birth and exponential growth of Pentecostal Christianity, as well as to the radical southward shift of the global Christian balance both in number and theologization.[2]

This study plans to analyze the current state of pneumatology among Asian evangelical churches and then to look forward to the healthy development of pneumatology, both in theology and in praxis. For the first mapping exercise, two categories will be used to identify the vastly diverse expressions of belief in the Holy Spirit: (1) contextual range and (2) experiential range. The second section will be a modest attempt to integrate various sources, both ancient and contemporary, to imagine the future shaping of Asian pneumatology. The end result will, I hope, be a reflection toward the construction of pneumatology deeply rooted in Scripture, faithful to Christian orthodoxy through each confessional tradition, and relevant to the religious and sociocultural context of Asia.

In undertaking this task, it becomes immediately apparent that pure literary research is not viable. In addition to the scarcity of published material by Asians or on evangelical pneumatology, discernment is called for to hear the voices that are authentic but hidden. This challenge is acute particularly among "younger" churches, as their theologization is grassroots in nature or a bottom-up process. Also, pneumatology, more than any branch of theology, is shaped and practiced in pastoral and mission settings. For this reason, resources for understanding it must include sermons, songs, and prayers,[3] which can be read in frequent conversation with established theological documents.

Pneumatology in Asia Today: Two Continua

At the risk of overgeneralization, the current state of pneumatology in Asia will be presented by using two continua. There are other conceptual categories which can be fruitfully explored in delineating the varying shapes, emphases, and nuances of theological beliefs about the Holy Spirit. Nonetheless, these two seem to be the most evident and useful categories for capturing this diversity in Asia.

---

2. Veli-Matti Karkkainen, *Pneumatology: The Holy Spirit in Ecumenical, International, and Contextual Perspective*, 2nd ed. (Grand Rapids: Baker Academic, 2018), 2–3.

3. Simon Chan, *Grassroots Asian Theology: Thinking the Faith from the Ground Up* (Downers Grove: InterVarsity Press, 2014), 8.

1. The Extent of the Spirit's Presence and Work

The first continuum relates to the extent to which the Holy Spirit is present and at work in creation. When I, as an Asian Pentecostal, began an ecumenical theological dialogue with the Reformed tradition, one question repeatedly appeared in the annual week-long gatherings: "Is the Holy Spirit at work outside of the church?" This theological question probes if and just how active the presence and work of the Holy Spirit is throughout his creation. The answer reflects a complex theological understanding of creation, fall, pneumatology, religions, and mission. Some of the theological questions may include the role of the Spirit of God in creation and his continuing care, and the effect of the fall on the Spirit's presence and work in creation. They also include the potential work of the Holy Spirit in cultures and religions as a part of God's creation and God's overall missional plan for people of alternative faiths. The range of answers from the pews would span from an absolute "no" to an "of course, yes," although theological responses may be more nuanced. Given the multi-religious context of Asia, this is an important question, as most Christians in this region have at some point made a change in religious affiliation and allegiance.

One may be tempted to place this inquiry somewhere in the conservative/progressive theological polemic. Those churches maintaining conservative theological tendencies would tend toward narrowly defining the extent of the presence and work of the Holy Spirit to the church and God's people exclusively. The churches rooted in more liberal or progressive theological positions would be open to the presence and work of the Spirit in cultures and other religions as well. Although this may serve as a useful perspective, especially at the pew level, it fails to do justice to the complex process of theological formation that culminates in an answer. In Asia, established Christianity's attitude toward culture had been greatly affected by how early missionaries demonstrated and taught their views and attitudes toward culture.

For example, the sixteenth-century Chinese Catholics who came into contact with Matteo Ricci and his missionaries, who affirmed many elements and practices of Chinese culture and religion, would be perceived to have had a positive, open understanding of local culture. The Catholic missionaries who were active in nineteenth-century *Chosun* (Korea), by contrast, strictly prohibited followers from participating in ancestor rites. They also encouraged Christian men to cut their culturally customary long hair.

At the exclusive end of the continuum are found those churches which have totally severed Christian experience from traditional religious (and even cultural) practices. For example, many churches in Korea are highly sensitive to any suggested link between Korean Christianity and Shamanism. Harvey Cox, in his widely acclaimed book on Pentecostalism, insisted that David Yonggi Cho had incorporated roles and concepts of old Shamanism in his theology. This was intended as an endorsing commendation, as Cox argued that Korean Pentecostalism had wisely adapted Shamanistic rituals for healing, exorcism, childbearing, and blessing.[4] However, the church immediately rejected Cox's praise. The theologians of Yoido Full Gospel Church began to produce critical responses adamantly refuting Cox's thesis. The Korean church invited Cox several times to experience Korean Pentecostalism and its practices and get a sense of what it truly was. Although his appreciation for the vibrancy and openness of the church increased, it is not clear whether he withdrew his conclusion or not. Regardless of how one evaluates this dispute, it likely functioned as a catalyst for deeper theological engagement on the role of the Holy Spirit in religion.

Nonetheless, the absolute denial of any linkage between Korean Pentecostal practices and the old religions in the land, despite practical and functional similarities, indicates an extremely narrow view of culture and traditional religions. It was a Malaysian theologian, Hwa Yung, who suggested that Cho had assumed traditional religious functions in response to the needs of the people and religious expectations. Yet according to him, this was only a case of functional substitution, denying any continuity between Shamanism and Korean Pentecostalism in substance.[5] Although the Holy Spirit's "pre-evangelistic" work before regeneration, especially on the individual level, is generally accepted as valid, the denial of any other activity in this realm implies an attitude toward all non-Christian religions in which they are outside the Spirit's present activity. This attitude is widely held among evangelicals in Asia.

At the opposite end of this continuum is an inclusive attitude toward the presence and work of the Holy Spirit in cultures and religions. An extreme example may be the controversial ritual dance by a Korean woman theologian at the general assembly of the World Council of Churches in 1991 in Canberra, Australia. Joined by Aborigines in the dance, she summoned the spirits of the victims of injustice and the spirit of the abused earth and rainforests. Finally, calling "the spirit of the Liberator, Jesus Christ," she declared that

---

4. Harvey Cox, *Fire from Heaven: The Rise of Pentecostal Spirituality and the Reshaping of Religion in the Twenty-First Century* (Reading: Addison-Wesley, 1995), 219.

5. Hwa, *Mangoes or Bananas?*, 166.

through these spirits, we could experience the Holy Spirit.[6] Even among the delegates of the general assembly of the largely liberal World Council of Churches, the pneumatology implied in her performance drew heated reactions and controversy. Among Asian evangelicals, though there is still caution, a steady flow of reflections and suggestions has emerged, especially among academics, signaling an increasing openness to the role of the Holy Spirit in non-Christian religions. This trend may be part of the worldwide openness to, and re-evaluation of, the presence and work of the Holy Spirit in cultures. Such growing attention is a stark contrast to the extreme view initially taken by earlier evangelical missionaries to consider indigenous cultures as "pagan" or even demonic.

2. The Nature of Christian Experience of the Holy Spirit

The second continuum relates to religious experience, which is extremely subjective and difficult (or impossible) to measure in its intensity. In spite of this subjectivity, such experiences do seem to occur with varying degrees of intensity and extent of personal impact. For example, some claims of supernatural healing can be verified by medical professionals, and declarations of "radical" heart transformation can be observed by a changed lifestyle. Furthermore, how a Christian community understands, believes, anticipates, and claims the person and work of the Holy Spirit differs markedly as one crosses denominational lines. At the one end are the churches claiming that their belief and experience of the Holy Spirit is marked by immediacy and supernatural gifts. At the other end are those maintaining a cessationist stance, contending that the use of supernatural gifts is no longer necessary or valid.

Churches focused on the immediacy of the Spirit's presence and work, particularly in healing and miracles, are on the "charismatic" side of the spectrum. The most affirmative Christian groups today are Pentecostal and charismatic churches, as well as indigenous Christian communities. In studying the development of Chinese Christianity since the 1980s, Luke Wesley used the simple criterion that charismatics are "those Christians who believe that all of the gifts listed in 1 Cor 12:8–10, including prophecy, tongues, and healing, are available to the church today." According to the same categorization, "Pentecostals" add belief in the Spirit's baptism for empowered service, while

---

6. See, for example, Peter Steinfels, "Beliefs," *New York Times*, 16 March 1991, accessed 24 September 2018, https://www.nytimes.com/1991/03/16/us/beliefs-385491.html.

"Classical Pentecostals" would further believe that speaking in tongues is the "accompanying sign" of this baptism.[7]

Wesley concluded that four of the five major house church networks he studied fell into the Pentecostal-charismatic category.[8] Their commonalities in belief and practice were expressed in an unprecedented formal Statement of Faith adopted by four house church networks in November 1998, "On the Holy Spirit":

> The Holy Spirit bestows upon believers all kinds of power, and witnesses the powerful deeds of God with signs and wonders . . . In Christ, God grants a diversity of gifts of the Holy Spirit to the church to manifest the glory of Christ. With faith and desire, Christians can experience the pouring down of the Holy Spirit on them and be filled with the Holy Spirit. We deny any doctrine that teaches the cessation of signs and wonders or the termination of the gifts of the Holy Spirit after the age of the apostles.[9]

In another study on Chinese Christianity, Chambon argues that healing rituals and engaged (dynamic and emotional) worship are the characterizations of Pentecostalism in China.[10] He points out that the popular reception of Pentecostal-type spirituality and worship is attributed to three factors: (1) the propensity and ability of Chinese popular religion to incorporate elements of other religions; (2) the enduring interest of Chinese religion in healing and good health; and (3) the increasing openness of Chinese society to Christianity.[11] But the same appeal, according to Chambon, has backfired, as the similarities in Pentecostal beliefs and practices to the traditional Chinese religions are an important reason why some churches have been reluctant to embrace Pentecostalism. The visible effect of such spirituality is the growth of the churches and dynamic and lively worship. Pentecostal members tend to be zealous and eager evangelists, often with testimonies of miracles and healing.

---

7. Luke Wesley, *The Church in China: Persecuted, Pentecostal and Powerful* (Baguio: AJPS Books, 2004), 37.

8. Wesley, *Church in China*, 60.

9. China for Jesus, "Statement of Faith of Chinese House Churches," 1998, accessed 11 April 2018, http://www.chinaforjesus.com/StatementOfFaith.htm.

10. Michel Chambon, "Are Chinese Christians Pentecostal? A Catholic Reading of Pentecostal Influence on Chinese Christians," in *Global Chinese Pentecostal and Charismatic Christianity*, eds. Fenggang Yang, Joy K. C. Tong, and Allan H. Anderson (Leiden: Brill, 2017), 181.

11. Chambon, "Are Chinese Christians Pentecostal?," 183.

At the other end of the continuum are the churches which maintain that the primary work of the Holy Spirit is in the area of regeneration and enlightenment. The Holy Spirit convicts people of their sinfulness, leads people to repentance, and enables them to experience redemption. For such believers, the focus of the Spirit's role, drawn primarily from Johannine and Pauline pneumatology, is providing believers with "staying power" or perseverance. In this camp, the supernatural manifestation of the Spirit is either ignored or even theologically denied. This partly explains the traditional neglect of the Holy Spirit among many theologians and church traditions. Although the Reformers' description of the Third Person as the "shy member of the Trinity" refers to his ministry's pointing to the Father and the Son, limiting the Spirit's work to a behind-the-scenes, "quiet realm" is also a historical reality. Perhaps the most avid "cessationism" (of the supernatural gifts of the Holy Spirit today) may be the extreme dispensational stance, limiting the gifts to the apostolic era. According to this position, the Scripture has replaced the supernatural manifestations which were the norm during the apostolic dispensation. Some are even hostile to those who advocate the supernatural gifts of the Holy Spirit being in operation today.

However, not all the churches which are not open to the immediate and supernatural work of the Holy Spirit adhere to a strict cessationist theology. It is the long theological development in the West based on a rationalistic and cerebral approach that has resulted in a "demythologized" attitude, downplaying or even denying the historicity of the records of supernatural events, especially in the Gospels and Acts. The "quiet" work of the Holy Spirit, however, is no less vital in the life of believers. In this sense, "shy" may not be the best expression for today's mind. The Spirit indeed points us to Christ and fills us with bold faith to proclaim him.[12] The point is, however, that the "supernatural" camp also recognizes the illuminating and sustaining presence of the Holy Spirit, although they tend to give more weight to demonstrable and dramatic experience over the "mundane" work of the Spirit.

Tomorrow's Pneumatology in Asia

Having briefly surveyed the Asian landscape of pneumatology in belief and practice, our attention can now be directed to future theological possibilities. The diversity found in Asian Christianity is increasing as new forms of the

---

12. Fredrick Dale Bruner and William Horden, *The Holy Spirit: Shy Member of the Trinity* (Eugene: Wipf & Stock, 2001).

church are rising. Moreover, growing theological maturity is an encouraging sign as more theologians are reassessing the received forms of theologies and their suitability for Asian sociocultural contexts. As we can observe in Chinese Christianity in recent decades, rapid social change has contributed to this complexity. The diverse beliefs in the person and work of the Holy Spirit in our region are likely at least in part the result of the relative underdevelopment of pneumatology in church history, and the rich and pervasive notion of the spirits in most Asian religions. The church in Asia is now on something of a quest to find paths forward in pneumatology that are (1) faithful to the Scriptures, (2) informed by Christian tradition (notwithstanding the unwarranted silence in some Western theological traditions), and (3) capable of speaking to key cultural-religious as well as social realities in Asia.

With these challenges in mind, I would like to list several areas of pneumatology and priorities which may facilitate the Asian church in its theological exploration, both in thinking and in action. This theological exploration cannot be a purely intellectual exercise: it has to be informed and inspired by pastoral and missional realities in Asia, along with the historical development of the doctrine. Before turning to specific regional topics and their accompanying challenges, I begin with a global task to which Asian theological communities are called to contribute.

1. Pneumatology "Under Construction"

In a sense, pneumatology is still in the making. When reading the ancient creeds, it is immediately apparent that Christology received the primary attention of the early church. The description of the person and work of the Son in the Nicene Creed (AD 325), for example, was proportionately elaborate, whereas the person of the Holy Spirit received only a mention: "And [we believe] in the Holy Spirit." The Nicene-Constantinopolitan Creed (AD 381) added the first descriptive elaboration: "And [we believe] in the Holy Ghost, the Lord and Giver of life, who proceeds from the Father, who with the Father and the Son together is worshiped and glorified, who spoke by the prophets." At the same time, Christology was even further expanded in the same creed. When Christology was fully explored, finally the church's attention was directed to pneumatology. This expansion affirmed the Holy Spirit as the "Giver of life" and his being the third person of the Trinity, and the life-giving work of the Spirit is amply attested in the Old Testament. The logical step for the next development would have been the dynamic presence and empowering work of the Holy Spirit found in the New Testament canon.

However, the church was immediately caught in the heated debate about the relational nature of the Holy Spirit in the Trinity. This debate has divided the church into two theological factions, starting in the sixth century: the Eastern Church upholding the position that the Holy Spirit proceeded only from the Father, and the Western Church insisting on the double proceeding of the Holy Spirit from both the Father and the Son (a position known as the *filioque*, the Latin term meaning "and the Son").

This division marked the end of the era of truly ecumenical (worldwide) theological affirmation, and pneumatology, in the end, became the casualty of a divided church. The implications of this "underdeveloped" and divided nature of pneumatology may explain much of the fragmented beliefs which different church traditions hold today. The Asian church, therefore, is called to join in the global theological effort to continually explore pneumatology. This theological participation is a rare opportunity to develop a truly global and ecumenical pneumatology in the post-Christendom setting. Moreover, the development of regional (or even local) pneumatologies should have a direct bearing on global concerns.

2. The Spirit in Creation, Culture, and Religions

As observed above, the continuity and discontinuity between the Holy Spirit and spirits in traditional religions and beliefs is at the core of the debate around the question "Does the Holy Spirit work in other religions?" Koo Dong Yun, along with other theologians, has perceptively pointed out the root of this debate in the identity of the Holy Spirit as the Spirit of God vs. the Spirit of Christ. On this view, the Spirit of God, as the creator and sustainer of life, is universally present in all of his creation, even if that creation is corrupted and marred due to human fallenness. The Spirit of Christ, by contrast, is the redemptive Spirit present in the church, the body of Christ.[13] The Orthodox Church, according to this argument, upholds the single proceeding of the Holy Spirit from the Father. Thus, it is sensitive to the presence of the Holy Spirit in nature, resulting in a focus on God's presence through the Spirit in creation and creation care. When it comes to the question of the Spirit's presence and work in other religions, there is a clear division. Mainline Protestantism, often represented in the World Council of Churches, recently produced a new mission statement, called "Together Towards Life." It acknowledges the

---

13. Koo Dong Yun, *The Holy Spirit and Ch'i (Qi): A Chiological Approach to Pneumatology* (Eugene: Pickwick, 2012), 131.

Spirit's work in the religions, pointing to the Truth: "We believe that the Spirit of Life brings joy and fullness of life. God's Spirit, therefore, can be found in all cultures that affirm life. The Holy Spirit works in mysterious ways, and we do not fully understand the workings of the Spirit in other faith traditions."[14]

The prevailing evangelical and Pentecostal attitude toward the religions, in contrast, stems from their narrow view of the extent of the Spirit's presence, often restricting his work to the believer's life. Even the universal outpouring of the Spirit promised in Joel (2:28) is considered to be universal only upon believers. Of course, it is biblical to say the Holy Spirit is active outside of the church at least insofar as he convicts sinners, causing them to become open to the saving work of Christ.

In Asia, the church must wrestle not only with traditional theological divisions within its confines, but also contextually rooted concerns. In particular, prevailing animistic beliefs, having deeply penetrated some of the major religions in Asia, include the presence of the spirits in animate and inanimate objects. Considering this reality, how should Christians theologically differentiate between God's Spirit as the Creator and the animistic understanding of spirits' ubiquitous presence? An extreme form of Christian theology simply denies or ignores the immanent presence and work of the S/spirits altogether, limiting the Spirit's work to illumination and guidance among God's people. The other extreme is the belief, represented by some Pentecostals, in the widespread presence and work of the Spirit, angels, and evil spirits today. The similarities between the Pentecostal and tribal (that is, animistic) worldviews can pose a significant challenge of confusion, but open up opportunities as well. Julie Ma, studying a tribal group in the northern Philippines, argues that the similarities in Pentecostal and tribal worldviews provide a ready audience for Pentecostal evangelism. At the same time, she contends that the supernatural manifestation of God's power in healing and miracles can function to prevent any confusion between the Holy Spirit and the spirits.[15]

Despite these hopeful signs, Christian theology of the S/spirits remains somewhat splintered. This challenge calls the Asian church to overcome its historically bifurcated approach to the issue. It is essential for each church and theological tradition to approach the claims of other traditions in a spirit of openness, humility, and genuine inquiry. Such theological exchange

---

14. World Council of Churches, *Together Towards Life: New Affirmation on Mission and Evangelism* (Geneva: WCC, 2013), 34 (no. 93).

15. Julie C. Ma, *When the Spirit Meets the Spirits: Pentecostal Ministry among the Kankanaey Tribe in the Philippines* (New York: Lang, 2001), 222–225.

and conversations lead to mutual understanding, respect, and appreciation, and help us to recognize the distinctiveness as well as the limitations of our traditions. A global cross-denominational dialogue, therefore, has a distinct role to play.[16] At the same time, a careful examination of the role of the Holy Spirit in creation, including diverse cultures (which bear the marks of God's common grace in spite of their corruption), is called for.

An expanded pneumatology may ultimately enable Christians to engage their faith more actively with cultural and social issues, including creation care. A recent statement arising from a dialogue between Reformed and Pentecostal churches is quite balanced: "(20) We agree that the Holy Spirit is present and active ... in human history and in various cultures. The work of the Spirit is broader than we think. Nevertheless, we believe that every culture ... is in need of being reshaped by the Holy Spirit in accordance with the revelation in Jesus Christ as witnessed to in Scripture."[17]

3. The Spirit and Life

From the ancient creeds to more recent days, the life-giving, sustaining, and restoring work of the Holy Spirit has been prominently featured. As we have already noted, the Nicene-Constantinople Creed (AD 381) describes the Holy Spirit as "the Lord and Giver of life." Similarly, the third major document of the Lausanne Movement, the "Cape Town Commitment" (2010), affirms Christian work toward the flourishing of life as an integral part of evangelical mission.[18] The recent publication of the mission document of the World Council of Churches, *Together Towards Life*, is highly pneumatological, and, as the title suggests, emphasizes that the work of the Holy Spirit in allowing life to flourish is at the core of Christian mission. It is important not to simply dismiss the document as a "liberal" understanding of mission. This pneumatological feature is prominent in the Scriptures. In the midst of human suffering, for example, the full restoration of God's people would be ushered in by the coming of the

---

16. For example, a recent Reformed–Pentecostal dialogue extensively dealt with the pneumatological foci of each tradition. See Statements 68–73 in Wolfgang Vondey, "Word and Spirit, Church and World: The Final Report of the International Dialogue between Representatives of the World Alliance of Reformed Churches and Some Classical Pentecostal Churches and Leaders 1996–2000," *Asian Journal of Pentecostal Studies* 4, no. 1 (2001): 41–72.

17. Vondey, "Word and Spirit, Church and World," 49.

18. Lausanne Movement, "The Cape Town Commitment," 2011, accessed 23 September 2018, https://www.lausanne.org/content/ctc/ctcommitment. The fifth section of the Confession of Faith is on the Holy Spirit, and its first paragraph (A) reads, "In the Old Testament we see the Spirit of God active in creation, in works of liberation and justice."

Spirit (Isa 32:15). And the effect is the holistic and comprehensive flourishing of individual and communal life, until the perfect state of shalom is achieved. This life-giving work of the Holy Spirit is emphasized in the New Testament through regeneration (e.g. John 3:5). Paul climaxes his description of the Spirit's life-giving work with the glorious resurrection of Jesus and our corrupt bodies which are subject to death (Rom 8:11). Evangelicals and Pentecostals were brought into the process, and their voices have exerted substantial influence; regardless of theological or ecclesial tradition, this is an excellent starting point for pneumatology.

This consensus on the Holy Spirit's work in life is expressed in various theological and missional emphases. For Pentecostals, the priority in mission has historically been evangelism. Yet their commitment to the well-being of life becomes evident upon further observation. Although frequently motivated by their evangelistic goal, they have nonetheless been quick in responding to human suffering.[19] The Orthodox focus has historically been on meditative spirituality and care for creation as the practical expressions of its pneumatology, which contends that "the Spirit is present everywhere and fills everything."[20] Various types of liberation theology anchor their theological roots in the life-flourishing work of the Holy Spirit. The struggle for social justice of the oppressed has had a diversity of manifestations, including the Minjung movement among Korean Protestants and armed resistance by select Catholic clergy against the Marcos dictatorship in the Philippines. Evangelicals and Pentecostals, meanwhile, have generally tended to provide care for the needy, but have stopped short of seeking complete social justice or structural changes.

Regardless of their response, churches often do not see their reaction to issues such as poverty and suffering from the pneumatological perspective. In truth, whenever Asian churches seek to mitigate the effects of poverty, assist the marginalized, and offer comfort for the suffering, it is the life-giving and -flourishing work of the Holy Spirit that is introduced. For this reason, a careful pneumatological exploration is a theological and missional priority.

---

19. For example, see Ivan Satyavrata, *Pentecostals and the Poor: Reflections from the Indian Context* (Baguio: APTS Press, 2017). Perhaps the best field-based study is Donald E. Miller and Tetsunao Yamamori, *Global Pentecostalism: The New Face of Christian Social Engagement* (Berkeley: University of California Press, 2007).

20. Georges Khodr, "Christianity in the Pluralist World: The Economy of the Holy Spirit," in *Orthodox Perspectives on Mission*, ed. Petros Vassiliadis, Regnum Edinburgh Centenary Series 17 (Oxford: Regnum, 2013), 120.

4. Evangelization

Asia is the least evangelized continent in the world. Less than one in ten in the vast population of Asia are Christians, while the world average is around one-third (or 33.3 percent).[21] For global Christianity to continue its growth trend, the Asian church's engagement in evangelism is crucial. Any theological study that takes to the continent the call to witness to the saving grace of Christ will find pneumatology at its center. There are at least two theological and two practical bases for the central role of the Holy Spirit in Christian witness.

The first theological basis is the very nature of the Holy Spirit's work: to lead the world to the redemptive work of Christ. This includes convicting the world of its sin (John 16:8), birthing and forming the church (Acts 2:1–41), and sending God's people as witnesses (Matt 28:19–20). The growth of Christianity, therefore, is the work of the Holy Spirit, and Asia, along with other parts of the world, is called to develop a theological and missiological understanding of the Holy Spirit.

The second theological basis is the Spirit's work of empowering believers to be effective witnesses (e.g. Acts 1:8). This dimension of pneumatology is the rediscovery of the modern Pentecostal movement. Beyond the Spirit's regenerative ministry, he equips, enables, and empowers believers. This missional gift assumes the divine calling and commissioning to spread the good news of Christ's redemption to the ends of the earth. Empowering results not only in the giving of various gifts, including the supernatural manifestation of God's power,[22] but also in the resolute commitment to fulfill God's call in the face of adversity (e.g. Isa 42:1–4; Acts 4:29–31). In addition to healing and miracles, the book of Acts records the empowering work of the Spirit in the circumstances of imprisonment, persecution, shipwreck, mobs, and trials. It is Stephen, second only to Paul, who has the most references to the presence and work of the Holy Spirit in his life (Acts 6:5; 7:55).

The third theological basis is the role of the Holy Spirit in revivals. From the early church to present times, revivals have been the space in which the fresh work of the Holy Spirit is experienced, resulting in repentance, radical

---

21. The Pew Research Center's Forum on Religion and Public Life indicates that only 7.0 percent of Asia Pacific were Christian in 2011. "Global Christianity: A Report on the Size and Distribution of the World's Christian Population," 19 December 2011, http://www.pewforum.org/2011/12/19/global-christianity-exec/.

22. Claudia Währisch-Oblau, a German evangelical Lutheran, observes the validity of power evangelism in her "Power Evangelism in a Protestant Context? Reflections after a Workshop in Samosir/Indonesia," *International Review of Mission* 107, no. 1 (June 2018): 142–158.

encounters with God's presence, experience of God's grace (especially through the supernatural work of the Spirit), renewed zeal for evangelism, and a resultant surge in the missionary spirit. For example, in East Malaysia in the 1970s, the Bario Revival began among the youth. The youth quickly organized evangelistic teams to travel to nearby villages. As a result, the revival, along with stories of healing and miracles, quickly spread throughout Borneo Island and beyond. This revival added thousands to local churches and gave birth to the vibrant indigenous church, Sidang Injil Borneo, the largest Protestant denomination in the country.[23]

The fourth basis is the supernatural work of the Holy Spirit and its role in evangelism. The effect of supernatural healing or miracles in drawing people to the message of God's kingdom is well attested in Jesus's ministry (in the Gospels) and the early church (in Acts). Earlier research done in this area concluded that a large proportion of Christian conversions in the house churches in China were motivated by experience or testimonies of healing (of themselves or a known person).[24] Miracles serve as a powerful draw for people to accept the Christian message. Indeed, Christianity, which claims to serve the supreme deity, is expected to offer a greater possibility of healing than other religions. The phenomenal growth of David Yonggi Cho's Yoido Full Gospel Church is attributed to experiences of divine healing and the spread of such stories.[25] For the church to fulfill the urgent task of evangelizing Asia, it is essential for it to recognize the role of the Holy Spirit in empowering believers and preparing the minds of unbelievers.

5. Issues Surrounding Supernatural and Spiritual Warfare

The deep cognition of the spirit world in Asia has been almost ignored by cerebral Western (evangelical) Christianity as superstition or simple heathenism. This dissonance, scholars argue, has resulted in so-called "split-

---

23. Jin Huat Tan, *Planting an Indigenous Church: The Case of the Borneo Evangelical Mission* (Oxford: Regnum, 2011).

24. Claudia Währisch-Oblau, "Church Growth in Anhui," *China Study Journal* 9 (August 1994): 2; also Caroline Fielder argues that in Anhui, more than 50 percent of rural believers are reported to have been attracted by healing experiences. Caroline Fielder, "The Growth of the Protestant Church in Rural China," *China Study Journal* 23 (Spring/Summer 2008): 49, accessed online 2 January 2019, https://chinaonlinecentre.org/downloads/caroline_fielder_growth_of_the_rural_protestant_church.pdf.

25. Myung Soo Park, "Korean Pentecostal Spirituality as Manifested in the Testimonies of Members of Yoido Full Gospel Church," in *David Yonggi Cho: A Close Look at His Theology and Ministry*, eds. Wonsuk Ma, Hyeon-sung Bae, and William W. Menzies (Baguio: APTS Press, 2004), 43–67.

level" Christianity, where many Christians seek ultimate spiritual answers to sin and eternal life from Christianity while seeking answers to immediate daily matters, such as sickness, misfortune, childbearing, and success in business, from the traditional religions.[26] It was the theologians and Christian workers from the Majority World who first voiced the need for thorough theological work on the spirit world.[27] Even before the introduction of Pentecostalism, revivals in Africa, Asia, and Latin America included encounters with the spirit world and manifestations of power. The spread of charismatic Christianity has brought together these two concerns in Christian theology and practice. Its theology has opened up discussions on the practices of prayer for healing and exorcism. Scholars contend that this partly explains the success of Pentecostalism in many tribal communities in Asia.[28] Every religion in Asia features supernatural manifestations. Islam, for example, regards dreams and visions as a prominent means of supernatural revelation. Its Sufi branches advocate more supernatural experiences, such as miracles and healing. Encountering evil power is an integral and practical part of religious life in Asia. Therefore, Asian Christianity has a unique opportunity, along with African and Latin American counterparts, to develop a robust theology and practice of the supernatural work of the Holy Spirit. They have already been drawing parallels to Scripture in the formation of their theology and ministry. In the process, the power of the Holy Spirit over the spirits is a primary theological and pastoral building block. Openness to the Holy Spirit in encounters with evil powers is widespread among Christians across denominational boundaries.

At the same time, Asian Christians are aware that this is tricky ground, where Christian theology and popular religiosity can easily cross over. The teachings of the Third Wave movement, a charismatic expression of evangelical Christianity from the 1980s, has influenced certain sectors of the Christian population in Asia. On the one hand, they have helped Christians understand the reality of the spirit world and how to confront evil (spiritual) powers. Popular authors of the movement, such as Charles Kraft and C. Peter Wagner, spread awareness of the spiritual world and its reality through their writings.

On the other hand, some Third Wave teachings straddle the border between biblical and traditional Asian beliefs. Consider, for example, the idea

---

26. Jaime Bulatao, *Split-Level Christianity: Christian Renewal of Filipino Values* (Manila: Ateneo de Manila University, 1966).

27. For example, a consultation was organized by the Lausanne Movement on the issue: Scott Moreau, ed., *Deliver Us from Evil: An Uneasy Frontier in Christian Mission* (Monrovia: World Vision International, 2002).

28. Ma, *When the Spirit Meets the Spirits*.

of territorial spirits, which argues that each geographic area has a spirit in charge of it and that any Christian work should be preceded by the "binding of the strong man of the territory." The similarity between this view and the Asian animistic belief that the spirits animate objects and territories explains why it gained an enthusiastic reception among some Christian sectors; but thin biblical support for this argument has posed a missiological and pastoral challenge. Identifying the "strong man" and its "stronghold(s)" led to the concept of spiritual mapping, which later led to the development of the practice of prayer walks and commanding prayers.[29]

Similarly, the teaching of the intergenerational curse and the related practice of inner healing has fascinated some Christians, but has been the cause for serious doubt in many churches. Reports of prayer meetings to "cancel" the curse originating in an ancestor have at times been sensationalized in the Asian church. The so-called inner healing practice contains several controversial components, including the notion of an inner child, which has no biblical support whatsoever.[30] Also, the age-old question has resurfaced in the process: Can a believer be demon-possessed or -influenced?[31] This short list of controversial and yet important theological and pastoral topics illustrates the urgent need for continuing development of pneumatology and related subjects (such as angelology and demonology) within Asian contexts.[32]

A Way Forward

The above-discussed five themes serve only as a representation of the plethora of pneumatological issues which the Asian church faces in its missional engagements. The evangelical church in Asia faces a critical choice: to stay away or to engage. Although it is easy to make a quick vote for engagement, it will take much courage, for example, for persecuted believers to shed the defensive or survival approach to Christian life. In many parts of Asia, the contextual forces are overwhelming, and Christian (or theological) resources are not adequate. Certainly a Western-imported theology would ultimately

---

29. See, for example, Neil T. Anderson, *Victory over the Darkness: Realize the Power of Your Identity in Christ*, 2nd ed. (Bloomington: Bethany House, 2000).

30. For a Pentecostal assessment of Third Wave teaching, see Wonsuk Ma, "A 'First Wave's Look at the 'Third Wave': A Pentecostal Reflection on Charles Kraft's Power Encounter Terminology," *Pneuma* 19 (1997): 189–206.

31. Helpful biblical studies on this question can be found in William K. Kay and Robin Parry, eds., *Exorcism and Deliverance: Multi-Disciplinary Studies* (Milton Keynes: Paternoster, 2011).

32. The Lausanne Movement took this as an important theological and missiological agenda and organized consultations. The final outcome is Moreau, *Deliver Us from Evil*.

prove to be handicapped in properly responding to the Asian contextual issues. This challenging circumstance calls for a concerted effort to collaborate in theological construction.

The complexities of theology (or more specifically pneumatology) and contemporary issues, as well as abundant theological opportunities, should compel Asian evangelicals to explore several levels of collaboration. The first level of working together is across the church and theological traditions. Asian evangelicals have long been served by the Asia Theological Association through its publications, including its two journals: *Journal of Asian Mission* and *Journal of Asian Evangelical Theology*. Its monographs (like this one) and the Asia Bible Commentary Series have the potential to creatively engage with Asian pneumatological issues.[33] In addition, select evangelical institutions have been active in the process of theological construction within the Asian context.[34]

The older mainline churches in Asia likewise operate various networks and publishing arms, and have a longer history of cultural and social engagement in Asia. Journals such as the *Asian Journal of Theology* have extensively published reflections of such engagements. Just as many topics, such as ancestor worship and spiritual realities, are common to Asian churches regardless of theological leanings, so the spread of Pentecostal-like experience across denominational divides demonstrates the supra-denominational character of such experiences.[35] Again, the widespread beliefs in and practices of healing, for example, among Chinese Christians, are more evidence of the universal nature of the Spirit's

---

33. See Asia Theological Association, "ATA Publications," http://www.ataasia.com/atapublications/.

34. Asian Theological Seminary (Manila, Philippines) has explored contemporary issues in Asia in its annual theological forum, including one particularly relevant to our discussion, focused on "Principalities and Powers" (see "ATS Theological Forum Books," https://www.ats.ph/ats-theological-forum-books/). Asia Pacific Theological Seminary (Baguio, Philippines), a Pentecostal institution, has been at the forefront of Pentecostal theological publications through its *Asian Journal of Pentecostal Studies* and monographs published by its APTS Press.

35. It is notable, however, that the relationship between Pentecostal theology and mainline trends is often the subject of dispute. For example, a Korean theologian from a liberation-theology-leaning Presbyterian church, Boo-Woong Yoo, has contended that *Minjung* theology, a Korean version of liberation theology, is essentially equivalent to Korean Pentecostal theology (*Korean Pentecostalism: Its History and Theology* [Frankfurt: Peter Lang, 1988]). This equation was uncritically followed and even expanded by several key Western theologians, such as Walter J. Hollenweger. An otherwise authoritative voice on the subject of global Pentecostalism, Hollenweger wrongly pegs *Minjung* theology as the core of Korean Pentecostalism, while at the same time giving hardly any attention to David Yonggi Cho, the founder and pastor of the most influential Pentecostal church in Korea. See Walter J. Hollenweger, *Pentecostalism: Origins and Developments Worldwide* (Peabody: Hendrickson, 1997), 99–105.

operation.³⁶ For these reasons, working with other theological traditions like the mainline churches may be equally important, and there is much for evangelicals to gain through such collaborations.

The second level of working together is the interregional, especially the south-to-south, collaboration. There are several important reasons why such cooperation should be actively pursued. First, the southern continents, particularly Asia and Africa, share similar worldviews. They are closer to the Hebrew and Jewish worldviews than they are to the Western worldview shaped by Enlightenment rationalism. In this worldview, demythologization is not a rule when reading the Bible. Second, many common theological issues (from poverty to healing to ancestor veneration), born of their sociocultural and religious contexts, are commonly shared. Common interests can bring diverse groups to the same theological ground.

Today's world Christianity is no longer a "western" or northern religion. Close to two-thirds of the world's Christians now live in the south, while the churches in the north are constantly declining. The churches in the south are called to rise and take leadership of theology-making today. Interregional collaborations will bring together theological reflection undertaken in their unique contexts for mutual learning and enrichment. A steady stream of theological work from Africa, Asia, and Latin America should interact robustly with the strong Western theological tradition. Pneumatology would particularly benefit from such a global theological enterprise, precisely due to its status as doctrine still "under construction."

The Asian church is called to bring its experiences and reflections to contribute to this global undertaking as well as benefiting from it. After all, it is the Holy Spirit who gives life to God's creation and the church of Christ, including the church in Asia!

References

Anderson, Neil T. *Victory over the Darkness: Realize the Power of Your Identity in Christ.* 2nd ed. Bloomington: Bethany House, 2000.

Brunner, Fredrick Dale, and William Horden. *The Holy Spirit: Shy Member of the Trinity.* Eugene: Wipf & Stock, 2001.

---

36. For example, see Yi Liu, "The 'Galilee of China': Pentecostals without Pentecostalism"; and Rachel Xiaohong Zhu, "The Catholic Charismatic Renewal in Mainland China," in *Global Chinese Pentecostal and Charismatic Christianity*, eds. Fenggang Yang, Joy K. C. Tong, and Allan H. Anderson (Leiden: Brill, 2017), 200–215 and 264–285, respectively.

Bulatao, Jaime. *Split-Level Christianity: Christian Renewal of Filipino Values*. Manila: Ateneo de Manila University, 1966.

Chambon, Michael. "Are Chinese Christians Pentecostal? A Catholic Reading of Pentecostal Influence on Chinese Christians." In *Global Chinese Pentecostal and Charismatic Christianity*, edited by Fenggang Yang, Joy K. C. Tong, and Allan H. Anderson, 181–199. Leiden: Brill, 2017.

Chan, Simon. *Grassroots Asian Theology: Thinking the Faith from the Ground Up*. Downers Grove: InterVarsity Press, 2014.

China for Jesus. "Statement of Faith of Chinese House Churches." 1998. Accessed 11 April 2018. http://www.chinaforjesus.com/StatementOfFaith.htm.

Cox, Harvey. *Fire from Heaven: The Rise of Pentecostal Spirituality and the Reshaping of Religion in the Twenty-First Century*. Reading: Addison-Wesley, 1995.

Fielder, Caroline. "The Growth of the Protestant Church in Rural China." *China Study Journal* (Spring/Summer 2008). Accessed 2 January 2019. https://chinaonlinecentre.org/downloads/caroline_fielder_growth_of_the_rural_protestant_church.pdf.

Hollenweger, Walter J. *Pentecostalism: Origins and Developments Worldwide*. Peabody: Hendrickson, 1997.

Hwa Yung. *Mangoes or Bananas? The Quest for an Authentic Asian Christian Theology*. 2nd ed. Oxford: Regnum, 2014.

Kärkkäinen, Veli-Matti. *Pneumatology: The Holy Spirit in Ecumenical, International, and Contextual Perspective*. 2nd ed. Grand Rapids: Baker Academic, 2018.

Kay, William K., and Robin Parry, eds. *Excorcism and Deliverance: Multi-Disciplinary Studies*. Milton Keynes: Paternoster, 2011.

Khodr, Georges. "Christianity in a Pluralist World: The Economy of the Holy Spirit." In *Orthodox Perspectives on Mission*, edited by Petros Vassiliadis, 114–122. Regnum Edinburgh Centenary Series 17. Oxford: Regnum, 2013.

Lausanne Movement. "The Cape Town Commitment." Accessed 23 September 2018. https://www.lausanne.org/content/ctc/ctcommitment.

Liu, Yi. "The 'Galilee of China': Pentecostals without Pentecostalism." In *Global Chinese Pentecostal and Charismatic Christianity*, edited by Fenggang Yang, Joy K. C. Tong, and Allan H. Anderson, 200–215. Leiden: Brill, 2017.

Ma, Julie C. *When the Spirit Meets the Spirits: Pentecostal Ministry among the Kankana-ey Tribe in the Philippines*. New York: Lang, 2001.

Ma, Wonsuk. "A 'First Wave's Look at the 'Third Wave': A Pentecostal Reflection on Charles Kraft's Power Encounter Terminology." *Pneuma* 19 (1997): 189–206.

Miller, Donald E., and Tetsunao Yamamori. *Global Pentecostalism: The New Face of Christian Social Engagement*. Berkley: University of California Pres, 2007.

Moreau, Scott, ed. *Deliver Us from Evil: An Uneasy Frontier in Christian Mission*. Monrovia: World Vision International, 2002.

Park, Myung Soo. "Korean Pentecostal Spirituality as Manifested in the Testimonies of Members of Yoido Full Gospel Church." In *David Yonggi Cho: A Close Look at*

His Theology and Ministry, edited by Wonsuk Ma, Hyeon-sung Bae, and William W. Menzies, 43–67. Baguio: APTS Press, 2004.

Pew Research Center. "Global Christianity: A Report on the Size and Distribution of the World's Christian Population." 19 December 2011, http://www.pewforum.org/2011/12/19/global-christianity-exec/.

Satyavrata, Ivan. *Pentecostals and the Poor: Reflections from the Indian Context*. Baguio: APTS Press, 2017.

Steinfels, Peter. "Beliefs." *New York Times*, 16 March 1991. Accessed 24 September 2018. https://www.nytimes.com/1991/03/16/us/beliefs-385491.html.

Tan, Jin Huat. *Planting an Indigenous Church: The Case of the Borneo Evangelical Mission*. Oxford: Regnum, 2011.

Vondey, Wolfgang. "Word and Spirit, Church and World: The Final Report of the International Dialogue between Representatives of the World Alliance of Reformed Churches and Some Classical Pentecostal Churches and Leaders 1996–2000." *Asian Journal of Pentecostal Studies* 4, no. 1 (2001): 41–72.

Währisch-Oblau, Claudia. "Power Evangelism in a Protestant Context? Reflections after a Workshop in Samosir/Indonesia." *International Review of Mission* 107, no. 1 (June 2018): 142–158.

———. "Church Growth in Anhui." *China Study Jounal* 9 (August 1994): n.p.

Wesley, Luke. *The Church in China: Persecuted, Pentecostal and Powerful*. Baguio: APTS Press, 2004.

World Council of Churches. *Together Towards Life: New Affirmation on Mission and Evangelism*. Geneva: WCC, 2013.

Yang, Fenggang, Joy K. C. Tong, and Allan H. Anderson, eds. *Global Chinese Pentecostal and Charismatic Christianity*. Leiden: Brill, 2017.

Yoo, Boo-Woong. *Korean Pentecostalism: Its History and Theology*. Frankfut: Lang, 1998.

Yun, Koo Dong. *The Holy Spirit and Ch'i (Qi): A Chiological Approach to Pneumatology*. Eugene: Pickwick, 2012.

Zhu, Rachel Xiaohong. "The Catholic Charismatic Renewal in Mainland China." In *Global Chinese Pentecostal and Charismatic Christianity*, edited by Fenggang Yang, Joy K. C. Tong, and Allan H. Anderson, 264–285. Leiden: Brill, 2017.

7

Toward An Asian Evangelical Ecclesiology

Simon Chan

Trinity Theological College

Introduction

An Asian evangelical theology of the church needs to consider a number of contexts, both theological and cultural. First, if it is to be Asian *and* evangelical, it needs to be juxtaposed to other Asian ecclesiological traditions. Second, if it is to be *evangelical*, it needs to be compared with other evangelical ecclesiologies. Third, if it is to be *Asian*, it must be resonant with specifically Asian concerns. To do all these, this essay proposes a broad-based theological definition of being evangelical drawn from the larger Christian traditions with special reference to the church. From this understanding, we believe that a robust evangelical ecclesiology can be developed to address some of Asia's perennial concerns.

Locating Asian Evangelicalism in Its Wider Contexts

Any attempt to develop an Asian evangelical ecclesiology must at least consider other ecclesiastical traditions in Asia, namely the Catholic and Orthodox Churches. The Catholic Church in Asia has undergone many changes since Vatican II. While in theory it continues to uphold the documents of Vatican II, especially its two documents on the church (*Lumen Gentium* and *Gaudium et Spes*), in practice, the greater emphasis is placed on its function summed up in the "triple dialogue" with religions, culture, and the poor. This is evident in various documents produced by the Federation of Asian Bishops' Conferences.[1]

Outside of India, Orthodoxy in most of East Asia is a relative newcomer. So any Asian Orthodox ecclesiology will have to consider Thomas Christianity in India.[2] Today Thomas Christianity is fragmented into at least fifteen churches. Some have joined the Catholic Church and adopted the Western rites while others have kept the Eastern rites. Still others have become Anglican. But if we take the Malankara Orthodox Church as exemplifying Asian Orthodoxy, since it remains faithful to Thomas Christianity, we notice that its ecclesiology does not differ significantly from that of most other Orthodox Churches. In contrast to the modern Catholic emphasis on the sociological and functional aspects of the church, the Asian Orthodox Churches continue to stress their ontological reality: the church is "the abode of Christ," the place in which "the life-giving power of the Spirit is at work." It "is not simply the community [of] believers gathered together. It is a reality which spans heaven and earth." It reiterates the catholicity of the local congregation: "The local Church is not a mere part of this one great heaven-and-earth community; it is the full manifestation of the One Church." It also stresses the living tradition: "Tradition is not something old, static, and life-less; it is the life of the Church . . . with the presence of Christ and the Holy Spirit in it." It "is not just a body of knowledge, but a way of life and worship and service."[3]

The reason for considering these older traditions is that evangelicalism in the West has become theologically problematic and may not provide the best resources for articulating an Asian evangelical ecclesiology. The studies of George Marsden[4] and David Bebbington[5] seek to trace the historical roots of evangelicalism in the USA and UK respectively. They succeeded to the extent

---

1. E.g. FABC Papers nos. 19, 69, and others (FABC, "Central Secretariat," accessed 14 February 2018, www.fabc.org/offices/csec/ocsec_fabc_papers.html). This emphasis is also apparent in the number of dissertations on the FABC documents devoted to the issue of dialogue. See James H. Kreoger, ed., *Theology from the Heart of Asia: FABC Doctoral Dissertations*, 2 vols. (Quezon City: Claretian, 2008).

2. For a brief history of Thomas Christianity, see C. P. Mathew and M. M. Thomas, *The Indian Churches of St. Thomas*, rev. ed. (Delhi: ISPCK, 2005). The phrase "Thomas Christianity" is used for churches that trace their roots to the Apostle Thomas, who was believed to be the founder of the church in India.

3. From the website of the Malankara Orthodox Syrian Church, "What Do We Believe?" accessed 15 January 2018, http://mosc.in/the_church/what-do-we-believe.

4. George M. Marsden, *Fundamentalism and American Culture: The Shaping of Twentieth-Century Evangelicalism, 1870–1925* (New York: Oxford University Press, 1980); *Understanding Fundamentalism and Evangelicalism* (Grand Rapids: Eerdmans, 1991).

5. David Bebbington, *Evangelicalism in Modern Britain: A History from the 1730s to the 1980s* (London: Unwin Hyman, 1989).

that they have demarcated a period of history in which movements denominated "evangelical" share certain historical links and family resemblances. But within the last twenty years, evangelicalism has become so theologically fluid and fragmented that it is becoming increasingly difficult to pin down. This problem was highlighted recently by Gerald McDermott, who identifies a deep faultline running through the evangelical world: those who maintain an evangelical orthodoxy in line with faithful Catholic and Orthodox Christianity and those he terms "meliorists," whose theologies show closer affinities with the father of liberal theology, Friedrich Schleiermacher, than with the historic Christian tradition.[6] In this state of affairs, on whose evangelical ecclesiology should the study be based?

Fortunately, in Asia, evangelicalism is less heterogeneous compared with the West. Much of Asian evangelicalism is largely the result of evangelical missions and therefore tends to follow its historical Western counterparts from the days when mainline Protestant denominations were still basically evangelical.[7] But from the late nineteenth and early twentieth centuries, evangelicalism is mostly the product of parachurch organizations and non-denominational mission agencies which share a common evangelical faith. But this common faith is not without its problems as far as ecclesiology is concerned. In the mission field, cooperation often means de-emphasizing denominational distinctiveness and focusing on their common theological heritage – which often means arriving at theological consensus at the lowest common denominator. The already weak ecclesiology of these mission organizations is further exacerbated by exigencies in the mission field. For instance, if a Baptist and a Presbyterian missionary from the same mission organization were to start a church in the Philippines, what would be its polity, leadership structure, and practices relating to the sacraments – and should they even be called sacraments? Thus, "church" is reduced to a gathering of people who confess Jesus as Lord and Savior. Anything deemed controversial is excluded. The result is a theologically hazy notion of the church.

A more broad-based theological definition of "evangelical" would make the discussion of ecclesiology more fruitful. By "theological definition" we are

---

6. Gerald McDermott, "The Emerging Divide in Evangelical Theology," *Journal of the Evangelical Theological Society* 56, no. 2 (2013): 355–377. McDermott calls them "meliorist" because they are constantly thinking of the need to make the faith *better*, more relevant, etc. What distinguishes them from orthodox Christians is their attitude toward Scripture and tradition. For meliorists, the theologian is the final authority, not the consensus of the church.

7. According to Marsden, much of Protestantism in America before the Civil War was evangelical (Marsden, *Understanding Fundamentalism*, 2).

referring to what orthodox Christians from the major traditions – whether Catholic, Protestant, or Orthodox – hold in common regarding the centrality of the gospel of Jesus Christ. The engagements between evangelicals and Catholics (Evangelicals and Catholics Together) and between evangelicals and Orthodox Christians (the Lausanne–Orthodox Initiative) have resulted in greater appreciation that faithful Catholics, Orthodox, and evangelicals have much more in common than do evangelicals and liberals, whether Protestant or Catholic. For example, if one compares the Catholic George Weigel's *Evangelical Catholicism: Deep Reform in the 21st Century Church* (New York: Basic Books, 2013) and the evangelicals Matt Jenson and David Wilhite's *The Church: A Guide for the Perplexed* (London: T&T Clark, 2010), one cannot help noticing that they have more in common theologically with each other than with their liberal counterparts. Evangelicals can heartily assent to Weigel's definition of "Evangelical Catholicism" as "a personal meeting with and knowledge of the Lord Jesus Christ, whom the believer has met in faith and with whom the believer has entered in friendship."[8] Similarly, an evangelical Catholic will have no difficulty when Jenson and Wilhite make the following assertion: "we need to embody the sacred; church that does not embody the sacred is not the church. Sacred embodiment by any other name is sacramentalism."[9] It is from a broad-based understanding of what it means to be evangelical that a more theologically robust evangelical ecclesiology can emerge. In other words, an evangelical ecclesiology must take full cognizance of the doctrine of the church in the larger Christian tradition. To this concern we must now turn.

Essentials of the Church in the Christian Tradition

The doctrine of the church forms part of the third article of the Apostles' Creed: "I believe in the Holy Spirit, the holy catholic church, the communion of saints." In the ancient church, the Creed was taught to baptismal candidates as part of catechetical instruction. In this process, the Creed was "handed over" (*traditio*: "traditioned"), memorized, and recited (*reditio*: "handed back") as the personal confession of faith at baptism.[10] The candidate was asked: "Do you believe in God the Father almighty, maker of heaven and earth?" To which the candidate would answer: "I believe [Latin: *credo*] in God the Father . . . "

---

8. George Weigel, *Evangelical Catholicism: Deep Reform in the 21st Century Church* (New York: Basic Books, 2013), 57.

9. Matt Jenson and David Wilhite, *The Church: A Guide for the Perplexed* (London: T&T Clark, 2010), 39.

10. See *Rite of Christian Initiation of Adults* (Collegeville: Liturgical Press, 1988), §148.

After each confession, the candidate would be immersed.[11] What is of interest is the way the third article is framed in some baptism rituals. The question posed to the candidate was: "Do you believe in the Holy Spirit *in* the Catholic Church . . . ?"[12] There was thus from early times an understanding that the Spirit and the church are so closely linked as to be inseparable.

This intimate connection between the Spirit and the church is more fully developed in Orthodoxy than in Catholicism. The identities of the church and the Holy Spirit are so closely linked that they are mutually conditioning.[13] We cannot properly think of the Spirit apart from his indwelling the church, neither can we think of the church apart from its being indwelled by the Spirit. As the Orthodox theologian John Zizioulas puts it, the church is instituted by Christ and constituted by the Spirit.[14]

The Spirit of Pentecost who comes to indwell the church is the "giving Gift."[15] He is the one Gift of the Father through the Son, and his presence in the church fills the church with diverse spiritual gifts (1 Cor 12; Rom 12). It is from within the ecclesial context that we can develop a better theological basis for the church's mission, including its social engagement. While evangelicals since the Lausanne Convention in 1974 have given serious attention to the church's social responsibility, their functional understanding of the church has meant that social justice and responsibility are related to the church as one of its functions rather than as intrinsic to the church's life and being. Evangelicals would generally agree that social concern is a good in itself and not to be used as a means of evangelism. But on what basis can evangelicals make such a claim? Much of the current understanding of the church's social responsibility is based on such biblical teachings as the *imago Dei*, on divine justice, God's care for the poor, and so on. While these teachings are themselves true, they are predicated on a functional understanding of the church – what the church does rather than what the church is. If the church is a spiritual reality existing

---

11. Triple immersion seemed to be a common practice in the early church, but baptismal rituals differed considerably. See Paul F. Bradshaw, *The Search for the Origins of Christian Worship: Sources and Methods for the Study of Early Liturgy* (New York: Oxford University Press, 2002).

12. J. A. Jungmann, *The Mass of the Roman Rite: Its Origin and Development*, vol. 2, trans. Francis A. Brunner (New York: Benziger, 1955), 265.

13. I have explored this theme in my book *Pentecostal Ecclesiology: An Essay on the Development of Doctrine* (Blandford Forum: Deo Publishing, 2011).

14. John Zizioulas, *Being as Communion: Studies in Personhood and the Church* (Crestwood: St Vladimir Seminary Press, 1995), 140.

15. Tom Smail, *The Giving Gift: The Holy Spirit in Person* (London: Hodder & Stoughton, 1988).

in union with the Trinity through the Spirit, it makes a difference as to how these social responsibilities are to be understood and practiced.

An intrinsic relationship between the Spirit and the church implies that *whatever* the Spirit is doing in the world, he is working *ultimately* to draw people into communion, that is, to Christ and his church, the communion of saints. All the works of the Spirit in the world are a preparation for the gospel (*praeparatio evangelica*). This is strongly emphasized in John Paul II's encyclical *Redemptoris Missio*. The Spirit is at work in the world, even in the religions of the world, but it is not to make the religions or social movements salvific in themselves but to prepare them to receive the knowledge of Christ. This understanding is in keeping with the spirit of evangelicalism.[16]

At the same time we need to resist the temptation of making *praeparatio evangelica* an excuse to use social work as a pretext to preach the gospel or to induce conversion. The gifts of the Spirit, whether they are operative within or outside the ecclesial community, are the sovereign work of the Spirit. We must have confidence in the Spirit to work as he wills rather than using God's gift to serve our own ends. We must trust the sovereign work of the Spirit, that ultimately it is he who will work in his own mysterious ways to draw all people to glorify Christ. From the pneumatological perspective, social justice, caring for the poor, and so on, are intrinsic goods not only because they are commanded by God and bear witness to God's goodness, but also because they are the gifts of the Spirit of the church which the Spirit sovereignly uses to lead to their proper end: the glory of God. The nature of the Spirit is to seek the highest good (*summum bonum*) for all people and all creation, which is to bring them into communion with God. The Spirit will eventually draw the whole created order to its ultimate end: the new heavens and the new earth.

The church indwelled by the Spirit should thus have the stamp of the Spirit's character, which is to draw people into the Trinitarian communion without drawing attention to himself: the Spirit is the person "without a personal face."[17] Similarly, the church which ministers the gifts of the Spirit in the world must do so without drawing attention to itself, without an ulterior motive to convert, but in self-forgetful love for the other.

In summary, if there is to be an Asian ecclesiology that could make its distinctive contribution to the global church, it needs to be based on a consensual evangelical theology drawing from the best in the larger Christian

---

16. See, e.g. Gerald R. McDermott and Harold A. Netland, *A Trinitarian Theology of Religions: An Evangelical Proposal* (New York: Oxford University Press, 2014).

17. Yves Congar, *I Believe in the Holy Spirit*, trans. David Smith (London: Chapman, 1983), III:5.

tradition. Without it, all we could offer would at best be an emaciated and parochial ecclesiology.

With this broader definition in view, we now examine the Asian context which needs to inform an evangelical ecclesiology. Asia is a complex reality, and so we can at most paint it in broad strokes.

The Asian Family and the Evangelical Problematic

An Asian ecclesiology must take full cognizance of the importance of the family. This means understanding not only the church to be the household of faith, but also that the constituents of the church are not just individuals but families. Much of life in Asia, including religion, is family-based. Yet the inherited evangelicalism in Asia is largely derived from the Free Church tradition with its emphasis on individual decision, believer's baptism, and a memorialist view of the "ordinances." While these features of the Christian life have a deeply spiritual dimension (who can deny the spiritual reality of the evangelical experience of being "born again"?), nevertheless, on the whole, the church is seen largely as a collectivity of individuals. In short, the Christian life of the individual may well be spiritual, but the church is understood largely in sociological terms and its *modus operandi* also tends to be governed more by pragmatic than by theological considerations. The result is a dangerous disconnect between individual spirituality and the corporate life shaped largely by social convention and the culture of the times.

When the church is understood sociologically, it is conceived as largely ancillary to the faith of the individual. Church is simply a way of organizing individuals to meet their spiritual needs and harness their collective resources to carry out the central task of evangelism and mission, which may even include a social dimension. By seeing the church in this way, evangelicals feel no qualms about reinventing the church in whatever way most effectively meets their members' needs and common concerns. Thus, if running a separate youth service would keep them in the church, then, by all means, let the youth run their own services; if old forms of worship are no longer attractive, replace them with new forms, which usually means "contemporary" songs accompanied by an electronic keyboard, guitars, and drums. The altar is transformed into a performer's stage.

If Asian evangelicals are to develop an ecclesiology that is resonant with their contexts, they first need to move beyond a sociological understanding of the church to an ontology of the church that takes into consideration the "evangelical" contributions of Catholicism and Orthodoxy. Since the church's essential nature is determined by the personal indwelling of the Spirit, the church is a spiritual reality transcending space and time. This means that the communion of saints also transcends space and time. Saints both in heaven and on earth belong to the one church.[18]

The logic of the communion of saints is the same as the logic of tradition. To recognize the role of tradition is to heed the voices of saints who have gone before us. As Chesterton puts it: "Tradition is democracy extended through time . . . Tradition means giving votes to the most obscure of all classes, our ancestors. It is the democracy of the dead. Tradition refuses to submit to the small and arrogant oligarchy of those who merely happen to be walking about."[19] What Chesterton calls "democracy," when applied to the church, is what the church catholic calls the *sensus fidelium* (the sense of the faithful). It is historical pride, or, more likely for evangelicals, a lack of historical consciousness, that has led them to canonize one particular period of history or movement (usually the sixteenth-century Reformation) instead of listening to the voices of the faithful saints and martyrs throughout church history.

The church, indwelled by the Spirit who is the firstfruits of the new creation, the Gift of the "last days" (Joel 2), is also an eschatological community. Our present communion is at best partial. In the Eucharist we have a foretaste of the eschatological marriage supper. In fact, the whole liturgical celebration culminating in the Eucharist is eschatologically oriented.[20] The Spirit acts as the invisible "glue" binding the church together as the communion of saints through space and time. It is the *person* of the Spirit in the church that makes the church a communion of persons. Thus, Spirit, church, and communion form an unbreakable chain in the third article of the Creed.

The Spirit's presence makes the church an ontological reality and communion is its defining attribute. The answer to the first question of the Westminster Shorter Catechism ("What is man's chief end?") is "Man's chief end is to glorify God and enjoy him forever." If humanity's chief end is to glorify God and enjoy him forever, then we cannot think of the church apart from its ultimate end, namely, the worship of God and face-to-face communion with him. These are eternal acts which define the very essence of the church. All other works of the church insofar as they are not related to eternity must find their point of reference in these eternal acts of worship and

---

18. For a more detailed discussion of these points, see Simon Chan, *Liturgical Theology* (Downers Grove: InterVarsity Press, 2006), 21–40.

19. G. K. Chesterton, *Orthodoxy* (Garden City: Image Books, 1959), 47–48.

20. Geoffrey Wainwright, *Eucharist and Eschatology* (New York: Oxford University Press, 1981); Joseph Ratzinger, *The Spirit of the Liturgy* (San Francisco: Ignatius, 2000), esp. 35–50.

communion. Thus, while evangelicals have rightly emphasized the importance of mission, the proclamation of the evangel, even mission is not the most defining characteristic of the church because mission will end one day when the gospel of the kingdom has been preached to the ends of the earth. Mission is a penultimate but not an ultimate goal of the church.

Worship and communion are not two separate acts but are closely integrated in the liturgy. In the liturgy of Word and sacrament, the church proclaims the redemption story and enters into communion with God in the Eucharist. In the communion of the body and blood of Christ, the church is being transformed into the body of Christ by the Spirit to glorify the Father. The liturgy is explicitly Trinitarian and draws the church on earth into communion with the church in heaven. It is in the liturgy that the church truly has a foretaste of catholicity in time and through time. Evangelicals must learn to cultivate an appreciation of the spirit of the liturgy even if they don't observe the letter of the liturgy.

The church as an ontological reality entails a certain way of looking at church practices. Take, for instance, church order. Church order is not just a practical arrangement based solely on best management practice. Jenson and Wilhite have argued that whether we call the leader of the church bishop, elder, or pastor, church order has an undergirding theology. There has to be a leader and people to make the church, with the leader acting *in persona Christi* (as representative of Christ) in relation to the congregation as members of Christ's body.[21] The problem with evangelicals is that without an *explicit* theology of church order, they end up with *ad hoc* arrangements usually borrowed from the world of business. The pastor functions as either a CEO or a mere employee. If the leader is acting *in persona Christi*, certain roles become definitive of his calling. As the head of the liturgical assembly, his work is proclaiming revelation while the assembly responds to the revelation proclaimed. Since worship is what defines the church as church, the pastor, by virtue of his office, is the worship leader, not so much the one who directs the "praise and worship" or plays the music as the head of the liturgical assembly.[22] He is the minister of Word and sacrament which are the two main constitutive elements of the liturgy. As shepherd of the flock, his main duty is pastoral care. Traditionally, this is expressed in such practices as spiritual direction, the cure of souls, and teaching prayer. In the Asian church, church leadership is more personal-

---

21. Jenson and Wilhite, *Church*, 33.
22. Zack Hick, *The Worship Pastor: A Call to Ministry for Worship Leaders and Teams* (Grand Rapids: Zondervan, 2016).

relational and the pastor often takes on the role of father of the household of faith.[23]

What makes the church the church are the objective "marks of the church," namely, the Word faithfully proclaimed and the sacraments rightly administered. Faithful proclamation of the Word and right administration of the sacraments are predicated on church orders. Thus, in some ordination services, ministers are specifically ordained to be ministers of Word and sacrament. These are the objective core practices from which other ecclesial practices are derived, such as spiritual nurture, prayer, and pastoral care leading to purity of life or subjective holiness. Western evangelicals tend to operate with a docetic ecclesiology, where the essence of the church is found in its "spiritual" activities, while the visible aspects like church orders and leadership are not considered part of the "real" church.[24]

Evangelicals also need to take seriously the sacramentality of the "ordinances." Most evangelicals practice believer's baptism which is usually understood as a sign of what has already occurred: death to sin and rebirth to new life. Baptism is also usually understood individualistically. This understanding and practice is quite foreign to Asian sensibilities. Most Asians understand better the "sacramentality" of the rite of baptism than most evangelicals. This is why many Chinese families are quite willing to allow their children to attend church but not be baptized. For them, baptism is no mere ritual; it is the point of no return. It is what makes a person a "real" Christian.

Besides understanding baptism and the Eucharist as sacraments, that is, as outward signs that convey spiritual realities, the Asian evangelical church must seriously rethink the place of infant baptism in shaping church life in line with the Asian emphasis on the family. Infant baptism understands that the church as the household of faith consists not just of individuals, but that whole families are incorporated into the household of faith. If infant baptism is too big a step to take, the practice of child dedication should function as its near equivalent. It needs to be made mandatory, not an option.

In light of the church's objective and visible character, the whole structure, format, and theology (if there is one) of the so-called "contemporary" worship with its thirty to forty minutes of standalone "praise and worship" followed by another thirty to forty minutes of motivational sermon needs to be thoroughly revamped. Its implicit ecclesiology is that the church is there to serve the needs

---

23. See Otto Lui, *Development of Chinese Church Leaders: A Study of Relational Leadership in Contemporary Chinese Churches* (Carlisle: Langham Monographs, 2013).

24. Docetism is an ancient heresy that denies that Christ has a material body since the material world is believed to be sinful.

of individuals; worship too is largely a way of meeting individual needs – which is why worship is modeled after the pop concert. The people on stage function as motivators and performers for the congregation-audience. It also carries an implicit dualism which exalts the "spiritual" and downplays the material. The "real" Christ is encountered subjectively in the "worship experience" whereas the eucharistic bread and wine is only a symbol of Christ's body and blood.

Communion of Saints and Ancestral Veneration

The doctrine of the church as the communion of saints (*sanctorum communio*) may provide Asian evangelical Christians with the needed impetus to rethink their practice of ancestral veneration. By "ancestral veneration" I have in view filial piety accorded to those who are no longer alive on earth. If the church exists in both heaven and earth, if the church triumphant and militant is one church, then the communion of saints must involve saints on earth and in heaven. Our doctrine of the communion of saints requires us to affirm that they are in fact in communion, even if the nature of their communion and practices associated with it may differ in various Christian traditions.[25]

I have chosen ancestral veneration as a test case as this is one of the most intractable problems in many East Asian societies. The main problem for evangelicals is not only their failure to understand the church ontologically, but also their constricted view of the communion of saints. They think of the communion of saints as communion in time rather than in and through time.

If communion of saints exists through time, what implications would this have on evangelical ecclesial practices? First, it would mean that saints in heaven (not dead saints!) are as important as, if not more important than, saints living on earth. They have attained a certain level of perfection that is perhaps not yet available to saints on earth, since they no longer see "through a glass darkly" (1 Cor 13:12). This is why Catholic, Orthodox, and some Anglicans ask for the intercession of the saints in heaven. Most evangelicals, however, will find such a practice quite foreign to their own tradition. Second, by logical extension, we remember and venerate those Christians whom we know (friends, relatives, etc.) who have gone before us. The crucial question is, can we also venerate relatives who died without receiving Jesus as Lord and Savior *as far as we can*

---

25. The issue is not very different from other doctrinal issues where we distinguish between doctrines and theories associated with them, e.g. the doctrine of the atonement (the *fact* that Christ's death saves) and theories of the atonement (*how* his death saves); the doctrine of the sacramentality of created things (the *fact* that the physical conveys the spiritual) and theories about the sacraments (*how* the physical communicates the spiritual).

tell while they were on earth? The italicized phrase envisages one possibility offered by the evangelical theologian Terrance Tiessen, that those who do not know Christ are given the opportunity to encounter Christ at or just before the point of death.[26] If this is the case, we cannot foreclose the possibility of anyone becoming a Christian even if they were not known to be Christian while on earth. This means that the communion of saints could include those with whom we had no communion while they were on earth. Finally, even if the status of our ancestors is uncertain, could we still not give them the honor they deserve *as* our ancestors?

Ancestral Veneration and Ritual Action

The phrase *sanctorum communio* could also be translated "communion of holy things."[27] This suggests an intimate connection between the communion of saints and the sacraments. The church as communion of saints expresses its life concretely in communion in holy things: sacramental rites involving water, eating, and drinking.[28] It is another way of affirming the point made earlier that the church is constituted by the objective practices of Word and sacrament. The two are inseparable. The mistake of most evangelicals is to separate what cannot be separated. When Word is divorced from sacramental ritual, worship becomes largely a cerebral event. Truth is reduced to concepts, whereas the truth of the Word must be embodied in ritual actions (sacrament). For Asian evangelicals, it is ritual actions that need to be given more prominence to correct their current ritual deficit. It will not do for Christians to *say* that they honor their dead; their non-Christian neighbors will not be convinced unless they can demonstrate their filial piety through concrete ritual acts.

In the Word-dominated world of evangelicals, sacred rites tend to be regarded as mere "add-ons" serving as object lessons ("visible words" as Calvin would put it) or for illustrative purposes. But if there is anything to be learned from our postmodern culture, it is that ritual practices are *more* important ways of learning than mere instruction. Pierre Bourdieu has argued that practice is

---

26. Terrance Tiessen, *Who Can Be Saved? Reassessing Salvation in Christ and World Religions* (Downers Grove: InterVarsity Press, 2004), 221–222. There are alternatives to Tiessen's suggestion; see my *Grassroots Asian Theology: Thinking the Faith from the Ground Up* (Downers Grove: InterVarsity Press, 2014), 196–197.

27. Stephen Benko, *The Meaning of* Sanctorum Communio (London: SCM, 1964).

28. In fact, Benko has shown that *sanctorum communio* as communion of saints was a later development (Benko, *Meaning*, 98–108); its early and primary meaning was the communion in the holy things, the equivalent to "baptism for the forgiveness of sins" found in the Eastern creed (64–78).

an irreducible, precognitive form of knowing, not just a consequence of prior thought. It is very much like the way a child learns to speak his mother tongue long before he *thinks* about what he is saying (i.e. learning the grammar of the language).[29] Similarly, Michael Polanyi has shown that we know more than we can tell. A lot more knowledge is implicit in the things we do than in what we are able to express.[30] The simplest objects are often the most difficult to put into words. It's easier to use a pair of scissors than to describe their shape and how they work.[31]

Asians live in a world pervaded by ritual actions, and long before the postmodern philosophers the Chinese *Book of Rites* had already recognized the formative effect of ritual actions:

> The rules of propriety serve as instruments to form men's characters, and they are therefore prepared on a great scale. Being so, the value of them is very high. They remove from a man all perversity, and increase what is beautiful in his nature. They make him correct, when employed in the ordering of himself; they ensure for him free course, when employed towards others. They are to him what their outer coating is to bamboos, and what its heart is to a pine or cypress. These two are the best of all the productions of the (vegetable) world. They endure through all the four seasons, without altering a branch or changing a leaf. The superior man observes these rules of propriety, so that all in a wider circle are harmonious with him, and those in his narrower circle have no dissatisfactions with him. Men acknowledge and are affected by his goodness, and spirits enjoy his virtue.[32]

"The rules of propriety" refers to ritual actions that are observed in varied situations and social relationships. They shape and form us in ways that no amount of verbal exhortations can.

But in the formation of the church, rites and their meaning always go together. Not only is the church constituted by the liturgy of Word and

---

29. Pierre Bourdieu, *The Logic of Practice*, trans. Richard Nice (Stanford: Stanford University Press, 1990), esp. 66–79.

30. Michael Polanyi, *The Tacit Dimension* (London: Routledge & Kegan Paul, 1966).

31. The example comes from C. S. Lewis, *Studies in Words* (Cambridge: Cambridge University Press, 1990), 313.

32. James Legge, trans., *Book of Rites* (Oxford: Oxford University Press, 1885), available online, http://www.sacred-texts.com/cfu/liki/index.htm , VIII.1.1.

sacrament,[33] catechetical instruction which consists in large part in explaining the meaning of the liturgy is integral to preparing converts for initiation into the church. This has been the pattern from early times.[34]

The ritual impoverishment of evangelical ecclesiology is seen most glaringly in evangelical worship. This is no mere coincidence. An ecclesiology that has excised the sacramental component as part of regular worship is a truncated church that can only result in an impoverished worship. If "rules of propriety" can transform a person, then ritual actions that lack propriety can only lead to serious deformity. Much of modern evangelical worship that goes "contemporary" is *ad hoc*, constantly in flux, and modeled after the rock concert. It suffers from the same flattening effects seen in other institutions brought on by globalization.

Conclusion

The way forward to a robust evangelical ecclesiology in Asia is to mine the resources of the Christian tradition. This means essentially retrieving a theologically normative liturgy. The liturgy is where rites and their meanings cohere in the ancient practice of catechesis. Here I must make clear that I am not referring just to a form of worship, but to the essential core of truth that takes a certain shape. There is a "deep structure" in the liturgy that has remained more or less stable throughout much of Christian history.[35] It revolves around the biblical story of creation, redemption, and consummation. In this story the triune God is the main actor. The liturgy enacts and worshippers "indwell" this story which shapes the church's basic identity. In other words, if we are to ask what the church is theologically, the answer is that it is the people of God who worship the Father, Son, and Holy Spirit in the work of creation, redemption, and consummation. As a doctrine, evangelicals would no doubt agree with this definition; what they lack is a liturgy that faithfully enacts, practices, and "ritualizes" it. The Asian evangelical church has more compelling reason to do this than the church in the West because it exists in a world where the

---

33. Word and sacrament should not be misconstrued as corresponding to explanations and actions respectively. In the liturgy of Word and sacrament, meanings and actions interpenetrate.

34. For a concise history of the catechumenate (i.e. the process of initiating and tutoring new Christians), see Michel Dujarier, *A History of the Catechumenate: The First Six Centuries*, trans. Edward J. Haasl (New York: Sadlier, 1979). For the connection between liturgy and catechesis, see Regis Duffy, *The Liturgy in the Catechism* (London: Geoffrey Chapman, 1995).

35. See Robert Taft, *Beyond East and West: Problems in Liturgical Understanding* (Washington, DC: Pastoral Press, 1984).

concatenation of corporate life, family, and the veneration of ancestors finds concrete expressions in a multiplicity of rites.

With regards to ancestral rites, a further qualification is needed. It is not sufficient to look for specific ritual equivalents to specific ritual practices in Asian ancestral veneration, asking, for example, "What is the Christian dynamic equivalent to the use of joss sticks in honoring the dead?" This approach to contextualizing is what Schreiter and Bevans describe as the "translation model."[36] We need to go beyond the "translation model" to what Schreiter calls the "adaptation model" which involves understanding ancestral veneration as part of a worldview or a way of being and relating that worldview to the Christian worldview. We need to understand its underlying ethos in East Asian cultures. The doctrine of the communion of saints provides Christians with a theological basis for ancestral veneration as a way of being saints. In other words, to be saints entails a way of relating to our ancestors whether they are Christians or non-Christians. Such a view of the communion of saints entails a view of the church not merely as a sociological but as an ontological reality.

References

Bebbington, David. *Evangelicalism in Modern Britain: A History from the 1730s to the 1980s*. London: Uniwin Hyman, 1989.

Benko, Stephen. *The Meaning of* Sanctorum Communio. London: SCM, 1964.

Bevans, Stephen B. *Models of Contextual Theology*. Maryknoll: Orbis, 1992.

Bourdieu, Pierre. *The Logic of Practice*. Translated by Richard Nice. Stanford: Stanford University Press, 1990.

Bradshaw, Paul F. *The Search for the Origins of Christian Worship: Sources and Methods for the Study of Early Liturgy*. New York: Oxford University Press, 2002.

Chan, Simon. *Grassroots Asian Theology: Thinking the Faith from the Ground Up*. Downers Grove: InterVarsity Press, 2014.

———. *Liturgical Theology*. Downers Grove: InterVarsity Press, 2006.

———. *Pentecostal Ecclesiology: An Essay on the Development of Doctrine*. Blandford Forum: Deo Publishing, 2011.

Chesterton, G. K. *Orthodoxy*. Garden City: Image Books, 1959.

Congar, Yves. *I Believe in the Holy Spirit*, translated by David Smith. London: Chapman, 1983.

Duffy, Regis. *The Liturgy in the Catechism*. London: Geoffrey Chapman, 1995.

Dujarier, Michel. *A History of the Catechumenate: The First Six Centuries*. Translated by Edward J. Haasl. New York: Sadlier, 1979.

---

36. Robert J. Schreiter, *Constructing Local Theologies* (London: SCM, 1985); Stephen B. Bevans, *Models of Contextual Theology* (Maryknoll: Orbis, 1992).

Federation of Asian Bishops' Conferences. FABC Papers. www.fabc.org/offices/csec/ocsec_fabc_papers.html.

Hick, Zack. *The Worship Pastor: A Call to Ministry for Worship Leaders and Teams*. Grand Rapids: Zondervan, 2016.

Jenson, Matt, and David Wilhite. *The Church: A Guide for the Perplexed*. London: T&T Clark, 2010.

John Paul II. "*Redemptoris Missio*." http://w2.vatican.va/content/john-paul-ii/en/encyclicals/documents/hf_jp-ii_enc_07121990_redemptoris-missio.html.

Jungmann, J. A. *The Mass of Roman Rite: Its Origin and Development*. Vol. 2. Translated by Francis A. Brunner. New York: Benziger, 1955.

Kroeger, James H., ed. *Theology from the Heart of Asia: FABC Doctoral Dissertations*. 2 vols. Quezon City: Claretian Press, 2008.

Legge, James, trans. *Book of Rites*. Oxford: Oxford University Press, 1885. http://www.sacred-texts.com/cfu/liki/index.htm.

Lewis, C. S. *Studies in Words*. Cambridge: Cambridge University Press, 1990.

Lui, Otto. *Development of Chinese Church Leaders: A Study of Relational Leadership in Contemporary Chinese Churches*. Carlisle: Langham Monographs, 2013.

Malankara Orthodox Syrian Church. "What Do We Belive." Accessed 15 January 2018, http://mosc.in/the_church/what-do-we-believe.

Marsden, George M. *Fundamentalism and American Culture: The Shaping of Twentieth-Century Evangelicalism, 1870–1925*. New York: Oxford University Press, 1980.

———. *Understanding Fundamentalism and Evangelicalism*. Grand Rapids: Eerdmans, 1991.

Mathew, C. P., and M. M. Thomas. *The Indian Churches of St. Thomas*. Rev. ed. Delhi: ISPCK, 2005.

McDermott, Gerald R. "The Emerging Divide in Evangelical Theology." *Journal of the Evangelical Theological Society* 56, no. 2 (2013): 355–377.

McDermott, Gerald R., and Harold A. Netland. *A Trinitarian Theology of Religions: An Evangelical Proposal*. New York: Oxford University Press, 2014.

Polanyi, Michael. *The Tacit Dimension*. London: Routledge & Kegan Paul, 1966.

Ratzinger, Joseph. *The Spirit of the Liturgy*. San Francisco: Ignatius, 2000.

Rite of Christian Initiation of Adults. Collegeville: Liturgical Press, 1988.

Schreiter, Robert J. *Constructing Local Theologies*. London: SCM, 1985.

Smail, Tom. *The Giving Gift: The Holy Spirit in Person*. London: Hodder & Stoughton, 1988.

Taft, Robert. *Beyond East and West: Problems in Liturgical Understanding*. Washington, DC: Pastoral Press, 1984.

Tiessen, Terrance. *Who Can Be Saved? Reassessing Salvation in Christ and World Religions*. Downers Grove: InterVarsity Press, 2004.

Wainwright, Geoffrey. *Eucharist and Eschatology*. New York: Oxford University Press, 1981.

Weigel, George. *Evangelical Catholicism: Deep Reform in the 21st Century Church.* New York: Basic Books, 2013.

Zizioulas, John. *Being as Communion: Studies in Personhood and the Church.* Crestwood: St Vladimir Seminary Press, 1995.

8

Eschatology and Hope in Asia

Roland Chia[1]

Trinity Theological College

Introduction

Hope is essential to human life. Some have compared it to oxygen for the lungs: without oxygen, death occurs through suffocation; without hope, humanity plunges into despair and is overwhelmed by purposelessness and meaninglessness. Hope energizes human life and serves as the essential fuel that empowers humankind's intellectual and spiritual endeavors. Hope is no less essential for communities than it is for individuals. Politically, hope may be said to be the source of civic consciousness and behavior because it makes the future of our society, city, or country inviting. Without hope, each person will simply recoil to his or her private life and seal himself or herself off hermetically from society and the common life. On the other side of the spectrum, hopelessness may "motivate" a kind of fanaticism that ruthlessly, if despairingly, tries to remove every obstacle that stands in the way of the future. Only with hope will there be forbearance, on which all good human life depends and on the basis of which civility is possible. Hope teaches patience and creates that temperament which enables us to listen and speak to those with whom we disagree. For in hope we know that in the end everything will work out and that we need not fear taking our time.[2] Hopelessness is a kind of death because it opens the door to fear, and fear weakens and immobilizes.

---

1. Material in this essay previously appeared in sections of Roland Chia, *Hope for the World: The Christian Vision* (Carlisle: Langham Global Library, 2012), and is reprinted here with permission.

2. Glenn Tinder, *The Fabric of Hope* (Atlanta: Scholars Press, 1999), 14.

More than half a century ago, the great philosopher Gabriel Marcel wrote these words regarding the nature of hope: "The truth is . . . there can be no hope except when the temptation to despair exists. Hope is the act by which this temptation is actively and victoriously overcome."[3] These words imply that hope is never abstract but always emerges from a specific historical and cultural context. The context from which I write, Southeast Asia, now contains more than 600 million people with diverse cultures and languages, despite their shared history. Southeast Asia is also made up of numerous nations, some of which, like Thailand, have histories that stretch across more than a thousand years, while others, like Singapore, are only a few decades old. Southeast Asia also represents a diversity of religions, from animism to more philosophically sophisticated religions, including, of course, Christianity. The region also has a rich cultural and intellectual ethos, as traditional cultures and ideas blend and clash with modern Western ones.

In his sobering account of the consequences of modernity, Anthony Giddens argues that modernity brings to the collective psyche a disconcerting sense of ambivalence and anxiety because it introduces such radical discontinuities and fragmentations to society. The sheer pace of change it brings about and the scope of these changes, as different areas of the globe are drawn together in a complex network of connections that brings with it the clashing waves of social and cultural transformation across the globe, are unprecedented in human history. Vast institutional changes result as older institutions are transformed into something different, and new social orders, such as the nation state, emerge.[4] Paradoxically, the clashing of civilizational and cultural waves in the tempestuous sea of modernity brings about a new kind of integration, one that has political, economic, and cultural dimensions, and therefore also implications.

Thus, in the modern situation, where "countless bits of the world conflict with other bits," to use the graphic language of Patricia Crone,[5] a new integration is fostered, not by traditional values and outlook, but by the new "isms" – rationalism, pluralism, secularism, individualism, and relativism. It is an integration based on the present and not on the past, for it is the tendency of the modern mindset to be preoccupied with the immediacy of the present, thus only worsening its own rootlessness and instability. "Being fragmented,

---

3. Gabriel Marcel, "Sketch of a Phenomenology and a Metaphysic of Hope," in *Homo Viator: Introduction to a Metaphysics of Hope*, trans. Emma Graufurd (London: Gollancz, 1951), 36.

4. Anthony Giddens, *The Consequences of Modernity* (Cambridge: Polity, 1990), 6.

5. Patricia Crone, *Pre-Industrial Societies: Anatomy of the Pre-Modern World* (Oxford: Blackwell, 1989), 196.

the industrial world is unstable. More precisely, it is kept fragmented because it wishes to be unstable, the expansion of cognitive, technological and economic boundaries being its aim . . . Far from being anchored in a tradition, the modern individual is likely to drift: he has to decide for himself where he is going."[6]

This dilemma, which characterizes Western societies so well, is not alien to societies in Southeast Asia caught in the nexus of the old and the new, and any survey of hope in Asia must give due recognition to it. The sea change brought about by modernity, the new challenges that present themselves in the changing geopolitical situation, and long-standing issues and problems that flood the collective psyche of those in the region give shape to new fears, as well as new hopes.

Terrorism and peace

On 11 September 2001 (9/11), when the United States of America was struck by the worst act of terrorism in its history, the world entered a new phase, characterized by President Bush as a "war against terror." To be sure, terror is not new, and its seeds can be traced to the origin myths of most cultures and religions. Indeed, history is full of tyrants and conquerors and the terror they wielded. But when the passenger planes flew into the twin towers in New York and the Pentagon in Washington DC, killing thousands of innocent people, not only were the images of that act of terror permanently embedded in our minds; they, as most commentators and political leaders agree, changed our world forever.

With terrorism, we are confronted with a new kind of enemy, the kind that cannot be seen. On 12 October 2002, two exclusive Bali nightspots frequented by Australian and European clients were bombed by members of the region-wide clandestine radical Islamist group called Jemaah Islamiyah (JI), killing 202 people, mostly Australian. This attack, which proved to be the most devastating in the world since 9/11, came only ten months after a previous JI plot to blow up Western targets in Singapore in December 2001 was foiled. Terror has become our narrative in Asia.

Since these two seminal events, attention has been increasingly focused on Southeast Asia as the "second front" in the war against terrorism. This is especially because of the region's large Muslim population and the many thousands of islands in the Indonesian and Philippine archipelagos that could

---

6. Crone, *Pre-Industrial Societies*, 196–197.

provide hiding places for Al-Qaeda operatives fleeing from Afghanistan. Furthermore, it is known that Osama bin Laden made efforts to spread the influence of Al-Qaeda in the region by developing networks in Southeast Asia for over a decade. With the world's largest Muslim population, Southeast Asia could provide Al-Qaeda with an endless supply of jihadists that would help it to achieve its revolutionary objective of a pan-Islamic community.[7] In the Philippines, Al-Qaeda has provided ideological indoctrination, training, and funding for radical separatist rebel groups like the Moro Islamic Liberation Front (MILF) and the Abu Sayaf Group, although MILF distanced itself from the latter after 9/11. Al-Qaeda has also penetrated JI, which is a regional organization with extensive networks extending from southern Thailand to Australia, and that has infiltrated groups like Jemaah Salafiyah (southern Thailand) and Kumpulan Militan Malaysia.[8]

The member countries of the Association of South-East Asian Nations (ASEAN) recognize that it is in their own interests to fight Al-Qaeda and its associate organizations, and have developed a unified strategy to do so. That strategy has at least five levels: the national level, the subregional level, the regional (ASEAN) level, the ASEAN Regional Forum (ARF) level, and the international level. In Indonesia, for example, the government issued two presidential decrees after the Bali bombing to facilitate investigations and detention, thereby strengthening its legal and administrative infrastructures for dealing with terrorism. At a regional level, Singapore and Malaysia have good intelligence cooperation with each other against the terrorist threat, and both countries are working closely with Indonesia and the Philippines, and with friendly powers like the USA and Australia.[9] The most important vehicle for combating terrorism is the ASEAN Ministerial Meeting on Transnational Crime (AMMTC), which is headed by the ministers of Home Affairs and which forms the core of the ASEAN counter-terrorism cooperation. At international levels, ASEAN has been working with the Financial Action Task Force (FATF) or the Asia-Pacific Group (APG) to deal with the complex issue of terrorist financing.

---

7. Andrew Tan, "The Indigenous Roots of Conflict in Southeast Asia: The Case of Mindanao," in *After Bali: The Threat of Terrorism in Southeast Asia*, eds. Kumar Ramakrishna and See Seng Tan (Singapore: Institute of Defence and Strategic Studies, 2003), 97.

8. Rohan Gunaratna, "Understanding Al Qaeda and Its Network in Southeast Asia," in *After Bali: The Threat of Terrorism in Southeast Asia*, eds. Kumar Ramakrishna and See Seng Tan (Singapore: Institute of Defence and Strategic Studies, 2003), 125.

9. Daljit Singh, "ASEAN Counter-Terror Strategies and Cooperation: How Effective?," in *After Bali: The Threat of Terrorism in Southeast Asia*, eds. Kumar Ramakrishna and See Seng Tan (Singapore: Institute of Defence and Strategic Studies, 2003), 211.

Regardless of the effectiveness or otherwise of these strategies to counter terrorism, what has become clear in the events of 9/11, and in many subsequent events, is that everyone is threatened and that no one is safe anymore. With these attacks, the political has become personal and the personal, political: religion itself, as one theologian exclaims, is no longer just a "private matter." As theologian Jürgen Moltmann wrote in the aftermath of 9/11, "There is no personal life any longer without danger. Personal life has no meaning without political engagement in the necessary resistance against public terror and death, as well as the no-less-necessary work of justice world-wide."[10] The phrase "apocalypse now" has been used to describe human-made catastrophes like the nuclear catastrophe and the ecological catastrophe. With this new form of violence, an apocalyptic terrorism has emerged. The modern–antimodern apocalypses, however, have nothing to do with the biblical apocalyptic tradition, because the former have to do with the hopeless self-annihilation of humans and the annihilation of living space on earth, while the latter is full of hope. To quote Moltmann again: "the biblical visions keep hope alive in God's faithfulness to the creation in the terrors of the end-time: 'The one who endures to the end will be saved' (Mt 10:22). 'When these things begin to take place, stand up and raise your heads, because your redemption is drawing near' (Lk 21:28). Prophetic hope is hope in action. Apocalyptic hope is hope in danger, a hope that is capable of suffering, a patient, enduring, and resistant hope."[11]

Social Challenges

It is probably true to say that few other regions in the world have such extremes of wealth and poverty as Asia in general, and Southeast Asia in particular. Countries in the region with large agricultural sectors are generally poor, and those that opted for insular state-run development after the Pacific War are doubly poor, having severed themselves from the emerging global economy.[12] When the region's economies are measured in terms of the Gross National Product, the range is from Laos, with US$17 billion, to Indonesia, at US$1 trillion. But when population is brought into the equation, the range greatly increases. For instance, Singapore, with a population of 4 million, has a larger economy than that of Malaysia, which has seven times the number of

---

10. Jürgen Moltmann, "Hope in a Time of Arrogance and Terror," in *Strike Terror No More: Theology, Ethics and the New War*, ed. Jon L. Berquist (St Louis: Chalice, 2002), 185.

11. Moltmann, "Hope," 184.

12. Ronald Hill, *Southeast Asia: People, Land and Economy* (Sydney: Allen & Unwin, 2002), 138.

people. Similarly, while Indonesia's population is more than forty times that of Singapore, its economy is only three times as large. Instead of bringing benefits to the developing nations, globalization has exacerbated the inequalities and accentuated the extremes of wealth and poverty between and within nations. To be sure, globalization has brought instant prosperity to a few, but it has also marginalized and excluded many. In his paper "Asian Societies in the Age of Globalisation" Professor Randolph David from the Philippines points out that globalization has "brought tremendous dislocation in the lives of the poor and of indigenous communities. It has made the sufferings and misfortunes of its victims appear as if they were part of the natural order of things."[13]

Sociologists have in recent years been describing the emergence of a new middle class, a new bourgeoisie, in Asia. The West has welcomed this phenomenon because it constitutes new markets for Western products, from processed foods to computer software to educational services. These people are conceived as the new tourists who will bring foreign exchange in difficult times, the new economic dynamizers of the twenty-first century who can revitalize the ailing world economy. Appropriately described as the "new rich," these private entrepreneurs have created an enormous impact, particularly in countries like China and Vietnam, where economic power has long been embodied in the bureaucratic hierarchies of the state apparatus. However, they have an ambivalent relationship with the state. As Richard Robison and David Goodman put it, "The new rich do not constitute a monolithic and homogeneous category, and cannot automatically be assumed to have a vested interest in subordinating the state to society and making accountable its officials. They are both new allies and new enemies for old power centres."[14]

Be that as it may, the fact remains that the majority of the people in Asia are poor, and most Asian countries belong to the so-called developing countries. The message presented in the 1980 gathering of the Christian Conference in Asia (CCA), that "Asia is affected in a particularly acute fashion by the vast problem of poverty, one which afflicts indeed a large proportion of humanity throughout the entire world,"[15] still holds true. In his 1968 study on the problem

---

13. Randolph David, "Asian Societies in the Age of Globalisation," in *Faith and Life in Contemporary Asian Realities*, eds. Feliciano V. Carino and Marina True (Hong Kong: Christian Conference of Asia, 2000), 23.

14. Richard Robison and David S. G. Goodman, "The New Rich in Asia: Economic Development, Social Status and Political Consciousness," in *The New Rich in Asia: Mobile Phones, McDonald's and Middle-Class Revolution*, eds. Richard Robison and David S. G. Goodman (London: Routledge, 1996), 7.

15. "Message to the Asian Communities: Final Statement of the Kandy Conference," *Dialogue* 7 (Sept–Dec 1980): 119.

of poverty in Asia entitled *Asian Drama: An Inquiry into the Poverty of the Nations*,[16] Gunnar Myrdall argues persuasively that despite the varieties of cultures and background, poverty and inequality are the general phenomena in Asia. Not every program that aims to bring nations to affluence has succeeded in eradicating poverty. The long era of colonialism during which the peoples of Asia were placed under Western imperialism, and which, according to one analyst, caused the breakdown of the confidence and creativity of the Asian people, is often cited as one of the major causes of poverty. But, as A. A. Yewangoe has rightly argued:

> This is not to say, however, that the era of colonialism was the only producer of all these troubles, or that once this era passed, the people enjoyed an era of affluence, released from poverty. As has been pointed out before, the control of the economic life of the people is still in the hands of the few, the authorities and/or owners of huge capital. They then form a small elite among impoverished masses, enjoying life and ignoring justice, often in collaboration with the new form of Western and Japanese colonialism, through the power of capital.[17]

Religious and Secular Hope

Any attempt to understand hope in Asia must give cognizance to the role of religions because, despite the growing influence of secularism, the people in Asia continue to be profoundly religious. My purpose here is to sketch, in the broadest strokes, the way in which great religions like Buddhism and Hinduism offer their adherents hope in the face of suffering and uncertainty. The fact that these religions have a long and profound influence on Asian cultures cannot be emphasized enough. In many ways they serve as powerful, if subtle, forces that have shaped and will continue to shape the Asian worldview. As Roman Catholic theologian Hans Küng has rightly argued, religion cannot be seen as a purely theoretical affair. It is "a lived life, inscribed in the hearts of men

---

16. Gunnar Myrdall, *Asian Drama: An Inquiry into the Poverty of Nations*, 3 vols. (London: Allen Lane, 1968).
17. A. A. Yewangoe, *Theologia Crucis in Asia* (Amsterdam: Rodopi, 1987), 11.

and women, and hence for all religious persons something that is supremely contemporary, pulsing through every fibre of their everyday existence."[18]

Most religions, including Christianity, develop their idea of hope in the light of their conception of human suffering and evil. This strategy is especially prominent in Buddhism, particularly with reference to its key concepts, *dukkha* (suffering) and *nirvana* (extinction). In the Pali *Dhammacakkappavattana Sutta*, one of the holy books recognized by Buddhists as scripture, the Buddha states: "Birth is *dukkha*, decay is *dukkha*, disease is *dukkha*, death is *dukkha*, to be united with the unpleasant is *dukkha*, to be separated from the pleasant is *dukkha*, not to get what one desires is *dukkha*. In brief the five aggregates [*khandha*; Sanskrit: *skandha*] of attachment are *dukkha*."[19] Although there has been some debate regarding the meaning of *dukkha*, many scholars maintain that "suffering" is an appropriate translation. However, it is important to have a clear grasp of what constitutes suffering in the Buddhist view. According to Buddhism, anything impermanent and liable to become otherwise is *dukkha*. Thus even happiness is *dukkha*, because happiness is liable to change.[20]

According to the *Dhammacakkappavattana Sutta*, the origin of suffering is craving (*trsnā*): "It is craving which produces rebirth, accompanied by passionate clinging, welcoming this and that (life). It is craving for sensual pleasures, craving for existence, craving for non-existence."[21] Notice that it is not just craving for sensory pleasures that produces suffering, but also craving for continued existence (eternal life), and even for nonexistence. This concept therefore refers to a deep-rooted form of grasping that is the intrinsic trait of the unenlightened person from the time of his or her birth. Craving leads to attachment, which is grouped into four types by the Buddhist tradition: attachment to (1) the objects of sense-desire, (2) views, (3) precepts and vows, and (4) the doctrine of the self. Notice also that it is not the *object* of the craving but the craving and attachment themselves that are the determinative factors. Because suffering has to do with the state of mind, it cannot be eliminated by physical disciplines like extreme asceticism, but only by the transformation of the mind. And this is achieved only by meditation.

---

18. Hans Küng, "Toward Dialogue," in *Christianity and World Religions: Paths of Dialogue with Islam, Hinduism, and Buddhism*, eds. Hans Küng, Josef Van Ess, Heinrich von Stietencron, and Heinz Bechert (London: SCM, 1993), xvii.

19. Translated by Narada Maha Thera (1980), *The Buddha and His Teachings* (Singapore: Stamford Press charitable reprint [n.d.]).

20. Paul Williams and Anthony Tribe, *Buddhist Thought* (London: Routledge, 2000), 42.

21. Williams and Tribe, *Buddhist Thought*, 44.

If suffering is the result of craving, it follows that if all craving can be eradicated or put to an end, suffering will also cease. In the Buddhist tradition, the state of total release from suffering is called *nirvana*, which literally means "extinguishing," as in "extinguishing a flame." Briefly stated, *nirvana* is the result of the permanent cessation of all suffering, which is brought about by the cessation of craving. *Nirvana* is therefore an occurrence or an event as a result of which all the forces that lead to suffering are extinguished. Some critics wrongly interpret Buddhism as nihilistic because they think that *nirvana* refers to the annihilation of the self. Achieving *nirvana* does not cause an individual to cease to exist; rather it brings that person into the state of absolute peace and entirely cuts him or her off from the world. A famous passage from the *Dhammacakkappavattana Sutta* describes this state thus:

> There is in monks a domain where there is no earth, no water, no fire, no wind, no sphere of infinite space, no sphere of nothingness, no sphere of infinite consciousness, no sphere of neither awareness nor nonawareness; there is not this world, there is not another world, there is no sun or moon. I do not call this coming or going, nor standing or lying, nor being reborn; it is without support, without occurrence, without object. Just this is the end of suffering.[22]

Williams points out that a distinction must be made between "nirvana with remainder" and "nirvana without remainder."[23] According to him the *nirvana* that the Buddha attains in this life through the eradication of greed and delusion is referred to by the tradition as "nirvana with remainder." When an enlightened person like the Buddha dies, there will be no rebirth. That is to say, the psychophysical elements that make up this individual will cease and will not be replaced by further psychophysical elements. This is called "nirvana without remainder."

Like Buddhism, Hinduism also offers hope for adherents in the form of liberation from the cycle of birth, death, and rebirth. It teaches that enlightened souls travel along the "paths of the gods," eventually reaching their destination in the world of Brahman. Those who have achieved this, according to the tradition, have been liberated from the cycle of rebirth and have attained oneness with God. Those who have lived morally mixed lives, however, travel the "road of the fathers" after death, and undergo a complicated process of

---

22. R. Gethin, *Foundations of Buddhism* (Oxford: Oxford University Press, 1998), 76–77.
23. Williams and Tribe, *Buddhist Thought*, 48–49.

reincarnation into various forms of life in the world, including vegetation.²⁴ The kind of birth that awaits a person depends on the good works or "karmic residue" that this person has performed or possesses. Good conduct would mean that he or she will attain a "good womb" (e.g. that of a Brahmin, Kzatriya, or Vaisya). But bad conduct would result in the attainment of a bad womb (e.g. that of a dog or a pig). For the entirely lawless, the tradition points to a third possible post-mortem eventuality: they are reborn as tiny creatures with no chance whatsoever of breaking the cycle.

Hinduism presents two different basic human attitudes in the struggle for salvation, which are often described as the way of the monkey and the way of the cat. The baby monkey, according to the tradition, is active from the start, clinging on to its mother and finding security in her. The cat, by contrast, is passive, always depending on its mother for protection from danger. Human beings are accordingly divided into two categories: some try to reach salvation by their own efforts, while others simply cry out for deliverance. The way of the monkey comprises asceticism, the way of action, while the way of the cat points to the way of the love of God.²⁵

It is important to note that the notion of *karma-samsara* is very pervasive in Indian religions like Hinduism (*samsara* = "change") and that such a notion militates against the idea of human free will. Although Hinduism presents the idea of God's supervising the operation of karma, it has very little scope for the concept of God's providential guidance of history toward an ultimate goal. Although, according to the "monkey" and "cat" schools, divine grace could be stimulated by human devotion, there is no conception of divine providence as set forth in the Judeo-Christian tradition. As Brian Hebblethwaite explains, "without denying the reality of God, Hinduism has tended to regard the consequences of human action as falling under the impersonal automatic operation of the law of *karma*."²⁶

Any discussion of hope in Asia must give due attention to the influence of communism, especially in China. To be sure, communism in China is an intricate blend of Marxist socialism and Chinese religious and philosophical culture, resulting in a distorted version of the secularized eschatology proposed by Marx. The main tenets of the communist ideology can be gleaned from

---

24. Julius Lipner, *Hinduism: Their Religious Beliefs and Practices* (London: Routledge, 1994), 230.

25. Heinrich von Stietencron, "Hindu Perspectives," in *Christianity and World Religions: Paths to Dialogue with Islam, Hinduism, and Buddhism*, eds. Hans Küng, Josef van Ess, Heinrich von Stietencron, and Heinz Bechert, trans. Peter Heinegg (London: SCM, 1993), 217–218.

26. Brian Hebblethwaite, *Evil, Suffering and Religion* (London: SPCK, 2000), 58.

the writings of Mao Zedong that were canonized during the rectification campaigns of 1942-44 as the orthodox ideology of the Chinese Communist Party. The canonical status of Mao's writings is clearly evident in the imperative issued by Lin Bao and others before the Cultural Revolution of 1964-65: "study Chairman Mao's writings, follow his teachings, act according to his instructions."[27] Thus although *Maoism* does not appear in Chinese, Western scholars use it to refer to the thought (*sixiang*) of Mao.

Mao Zedong joins Karl Marx and Ludwig Feuerbach in rejecting religion. The Chinese communist view of religion betrays the influences of these two philosophers: "Religion is a social ideology, 'the fantastic reflection in men's minds of those external forces which control their daily life' . . . the fantastic interpretations by religion of natural phenomena, social phenomena, and especially of oppression and class exploitation, play the role of paralyzing the minds of working people, and disintegrating their combat will."[28]

Yet Mao puts so much faith in the masses to bring about a utopia that he in effect divinizes the latter. Thus, in "The Chinese Revolution and the Chinese Communist Party," Mao could declare: "Our Chinese people possess great intrinsic energy. The more profound the oppression, the greater the resistance; that which has accumulated for a long time will surely burst forth quickly. The great union of the Chinese people must be achieved. Gentlemen! We must exert ourselves – we must all advance with the utmost strength. Our golden age, our age of brilliance and splendour lies ahead!"[29]

This is also clearly seen in Mao's idiosyncratic reinterpretation of a classical Chinese fable (*Lie Zi*) during the Seventh National Congress to the Chinese Communist Party in June of 1945 to portray utopia: "We must persevere and work unceasingly, and we, too, will touch God's heart." The traditional interpretation of this fable, which champions hard work and perseverance, is thus blended with Mao's mythology that speaks of God. But the next sentence quickly clarifies what "God" means: "Our God [*Shangdi*] is none other than the masses of the Chinese people."[30]

---

27. Cited in Maurice Meisner, *Marxism, Maoism and Utopianism: Eight Essays* (Madison: University of Wisconsin Press, 1982), 165.

28. Donald MacInnis, *Religious Policy and Practice in Communist China: A Documentary History* (New York: Macmillan, 1972), 60.

29. Mao Zedong, "The Chinese Revolution and the Chinese Communist Party" (December 1939), in *Selected Works of Mao Tse-tung*, vol. 2 (Peking: Foreign Language Press, 1975), 306-307.

30. Mao Zedong, "The Foolish Old Man Who Removed Mountains" (June 1945), in *Selected Works of Mao Tse-tung*, vol. 3 (Peking: Foreign Language Press, 1975), 322.

Mao maintains that the realization of the utopian vision of a Chinese socialist society and universal communist state depends on hard work and perseverance and not on the working out of historical forces. *Datong* (Great Harmony), according to Mao, is achieved by creating a new humanity, uniting the hearts of both the little people (*xiaoren*) and the superior people (*junzi*) in thought and in morality. Is Maoism, with its emphasis on the new humanity (the New China), a substitute religion, an antireligion or a form of atheism? Paul Rule is probably right when he states:

> Perhaps Maoism is a substitute-religion, deliberately usurping the traditional religious ground. The attempt to apply an ultimate criterion, that of transcendence, has revealed an aspect of transcendence but one that is ambivalent and inconclusive. The New China is certainly overtly anti-religious in its policy toward traditional Chinese and foreign religions . . . paradoxically, this very inability to tolerate rivals may be evidence of Maoism's ambitions to be the one, true faith of China. It leaves no room for rivals precisely because of its ambitions to occupy fully all spheres of human activity including that we call religion. If it is not a religion, it looks remarkably like one.[31]

The Fabric of Hope

Hope is by no means the exclusive preserve of religious people or the Christian community, but a universal phenomenon. As a reaction to the challenges and difficulties of life, hope exists at a pre-reflective level of human awareness and activity. Hope, as some theologians have rightly pointed out, belongs to the very essence of the human condition, and is the presupposition and motivation of everything we do. As an "outlook and attitude that influences and shapes and colours all human experiences and activities,"[32] hope is thus essential for human flourishing. In order to attain a proper understanding of hope, a distinction must be made between hope and optimism. Optimism is the naïve and blind acquiescence to the principle of human progress that ignores the ambiguities of our world and the ubiquity of pain, suffering, and evil. Optimism refuses to acknowledge the vulnerability of the human enterprise,

---

31. Paul Rule, "Is Maoism Open to the Transcendent?" in *The New China: A Catholic Response*, ed. Michael Chu (New York: Paulist, 1977), 40.

32. Dermot A. Lane, *Keeping Hope Alive: Stirrings in Christian Theology* (Dublin: Gill & Macmillan, 1996), 59.

preferring to embrace a triumphalism that has lost touch with reality. Hope, in contrast, confronts the world as it is: it embraces a stark realism, struggles with the ambiguity of life, and "responds to it by taking up a particular posture of imagining new possibilities and other alternatives, inspired by the pulses of human experience."[33]

Since the Enlightenment, the confusion of optimism with hope has resulted in the latter being defined in terms of progress, the upward movement of human civilization to its imminent state of perfection. This modern idea of hope is doubtless shaped by the exponential advances in science and technology witnessed from the last decades of the eighteenth century.[34] Philosophically, this idea of progress is given substance by German idealism, which provided its metaphysical and even theological basis. This is seen especially in the philosophy of Hegel, which postulates the development of human civilization as the unfolding of the divine spirit immanent in the human spirit. And, through the theories propounded by Lamarck and Darwin in the nineteenth century about the evolutionary nature of life, the philosophical concept of progress in idealism finds scientific endorsement. To think that these developments have little to do with Asia is to underestimate the influence of ideas and to fail to see that even though modernization and Westernization may be distinguished, they are not always easy to disentangle.

Hope in progress, however, is short-lived, for its decline in the twentieth century is as rapid as its rise in the nineteenth. Even at the end of the nineteenth century, the voices of doubt can be heard in some quarters. But it is in the first decades of the following century that the triumphalistic creed of progress begins to collapse and is replaced by pessimism and anxiety. To be sure, some like Frederic Harrison could continue to be upbeat about the twentieth century. "We are on the threshold of a great time," he could write, "even if our time itself is not great . . . It is the age of great expectation and unwearied striving after better things."[35] But such optimism is not shared by the majority who witness the creed of progress being contradicted again and again by atrocities and tragedies that scar the history of the new century. Tinder, with his usual eloquence and perceptiveness, describes the disappointments that dashed the hope defined by the secular myth of progress: "When the twentieth century began, we were unprepared for the misfortunes and crimes of our age, and

---

33. Lane, *Keeping Hope Alive*, 60.
34. Emil Brunner, *Eternal Hope* (London: Lutterworth, 1954), 19.
35. Quoted in Richard Bauckham and Trevor Hart, *Hope against Hope: Christian Eschatology at the Turn of the Millennium* (Grand Rapids: Eerdmans, 1999), 5.

our disillusionment was more profound than it might otherwise have been. The hope we inherited was laid waste by trench warfare, by totalitarianism in major civilised nations, and by death camps."[36]

Christian hope is defined in terms of transcendence in the sense that true hope presses beyond what we can rationally comprehend and control. The Christian faith maintains that transcendence cannot be attained through the exertion of human powers. For transcendence to be known, as Glenn Tinder has so eloquently argued, transcendence must act. "Transcendence must disclose itself, and call forth the openness in which its disclosures can be freely accepted."[37] Without revelation, our attempts to grasp at transcendence are at best the confession of our ignorance. But the transcendent God has revealed himself in Jesus Christ, and by this revelation, he has shown himself to be profoundly and deeply personal. The hope of the Christian is not in an abstract idea like "the idea of the Good" or the "unmoved Mover." Concepts like "the Absolute" or "being-in-itself" found in different strands of philosophy (Eastern as well as Western) are far removed from the personal God of the Bible. In his revelation, God has presented himself as a conversation partner and invites those whom he has created in his image into a relationship of covenantal love and trust. For Christians, then, God is not just the *object* of hope but its *basis*: we not only hope *for* God but *in* God.

Christian hope is profoundly different from the unbridled optimism of secular "hope" also because it is cruciform: it is founded upon and shaped by the preaching and praxis of Jesus Christ concerning the reign of God. Christian hope does not ignore the reality of pain and suffering, but confronts them in the light of the death and resurrection of Jesus Christ. It is through the paschal mystery of the death and resurrection of Christ that Christian hope understands pain, suffering, and death. As Dermot Lane explains, "Christian hope resides in the crucified Christ, acknowledging that this historical reality includes both darkness and light, tragedy and transformation, sadness and joy, death and resurrection."[38] Furthermore, Christian hope embraces not only the future but also the present, not only otherworldly realities but this-worldly ones as well. In this way, Christian eschatology is profoundly related to the doctrine of creation: if God truly is the creator of this universe, if this cosmos is really God's sanctuary, then eschatology must include the cultivation of creation and humanity in this life as well as their transformation in eternity.

---

36. Tinder, *Fabric of Hope*, 15.
37. Tinder, 31.
38. Lane, *Keeping Hope Alive*, 69.

The Ground of Hope

It should be clear that Christian hope is profoundly different from – even antithetical to – secular expressions of progress and optimism. Christian hope is not founded upon self-confidence or confidence in the human race. Rather Christian hope is established in God, who, through his Word, has promised the renewal and perfection of humankind and the creation. The profound and inextricable relationship between hope and faith is thus paramount. Because it is so rooted in God, Christian hope must always possess that quality of transcendence. As an expression of faith, which is interpreted here as trust, Christian hope transcends our present circumstances and experience and is anchored in the promises of God in Christ. As such, we should be wary of those philosophies and sciences that claim to explain everything, or that seek to unify life and render everything clear and certain. Such claims signal the loss of transcendence, without which hope in the theological sense cannot be understood.

As we noted above, God is never just the *object* of hope but is also the *basis* of hope. It is therefore not enough to claim that God or transcendence is the *ground* of Christian hope. Theologies that speak abstractly of God as the "Absolute" or as "Being-in-itself," or as the "Ground of Being" are often in danger of distorting the concept of God altogether. It is not sufficient to focus merely on the ultimate, indefeasible nature of transcendence; one must also be concerned with its deeply and fully personal character. And this can be known only through God's self-disclosure in Jesus Christ, his incarnate Word. In Jesus Christ, we come to know that God is with us and for us. In the incarnate Word is revealed the essence of God as Trinity – as the communion of Father, Son, and Holy Spirit – and hence also humanity's communal destiny. Christian hope is not just in God, but in God's final reordering of the whole of creation, redeeming it from the perversions of sin, and transforming it into perfection. Human relationships will be ordered under the standard of love. As Glenn Tinder has put it, "The end of the ages must bring a community as deep and immutable as God himself in the perfect life and vitality of the Holy Trinity."[39]

In this way, Christian hope distinguishes itself from philosophical and religious teleologies: it is not established on the basis of a general metaphysics or understanding of history, but on the revelation of God's will for the world in Jesus Christ. For Christians, Christ is the axis of history; that is, in Christ, history has its origins as well as its climax. In Christ are to be found the answers

---

39. Tinder, *Fabric of Hope*, 43.

to the questions human beings have been asking; in him is the fulfillment of their efforts to reach transcendence through their intellect and imagination. As Brunner puts it, "Through this unity of faith and hope the revelation of the inscrutable will of God in Jesus Christ becomes the answer to man's deeply felt question as to the meaning of his existence; an answer which he himself is not capable of providing."[40] Furthermore, because fallen human beings are not so clear-sighted that they are able always to ask the right questions, God's revelation in Christ not only provides answers but also directs the questions. And, insofar as human beings are unable to anticipate the answers, the revelation of God is bound to be surprising and unforeseen. Illustrative of this is the fact that for the Christian faith, the salvation of humankind is bound up with the death of a Jew on the cross, a death that took place on the remote outskirts of Greco-Roman Jerusalem some two thousand years ago.

The Sermon on the Mount, which is a word of hope, shows that Christian hope is not just about a future reality but is one mysteriously hidden in the present.[41] This is because the Sermon's central figure, Christ, has already come into the world and has inaugurated the divine kingdom; and insofar as we are united with him we are capable of fellowship with God. The hope of salvation, of eternal life, is therefore not merely a future utopia, a vision of an ideal that does not exist. Rather eternal life is *real* life, which exists even in the here and now for those who are in communion with Jesus Christ. This is expressed by Paul, who confidently proclaims that the salvation of believers is not just a future reality but one already appropriated by believers in the here and now: "For in this hope we were saved" (Rom 8:24). Paul uses the aorist to bring out the nature of Christian hope,[42] to emphasize the confidence in the purpose and power of God, and to show that the future salvation that Christians hope for is in some sense already a present reality. To be sure, true hope is indefeasible because it is anchored in eternity. And temporal events are significant, not in themselves, but only in relation to eternity. Yet that for which we hope lies not merely in the future, but is already present now, albeit not in full measure. Because the eternal Word of God has become flesh, eternity has penetrated human history, and the kingdom of God has been inaugurated.

---

40. Brunner, *Eternal Hope*, 28.

41. Joseph Ratzinger, *To Look on Christ: Exercises in Faith, Hope and Love* (Slough: St Paul, 1978), 61.

42. James D. G. Dunn, *Romans 1–8*, Word Biblical Commentary (Waco: Word, 1988), 475.

Hope and Discipleship

Finally we turn to the subject of discipleship, and ask how Christian hope should influence the way we live in the world. This question may be put differently: How does our hope in the God who will bring all things to perfection influence our view of the world in which we live and our role in it? Does the vision of the transformed reality lead us somehow to place too little value in this world? I have been discussing the need for transcendence, and the consequences the loss of transcendence has on our perception of the world. We saw that the erosion of belief in transcendence has resulted in the growing concern with this world for its own sake, and that this is seen in every aspect of human culture – science, economics, politics. Does the converse produce the opposite result? Does other-worldliness lead to this-worldly indifference? Some may argue that Paul seems to lean in this direction when he insists that for believers it is preferable to be away from the body and at home with the Lord (2 Cor 5:6, 8). Christians, of course, place more importance on this world than do Hindus, whose concept of *maya* leads them to the conclusion that this-worldly reality is an illusion. Still, the belief that the future holds something better and something "other" than the here and now has led some Christians to view this world as less important. A hymn by James Montgomery in the early nineteenth century hints at this perspective:

> Here in the body pent,
> Absent from Him I roam,
> Yet nightly pitch my moving tent
> A day's march nearer home.
>
> My Father's house on high,
> Home of my soul, how near
> At times, to faith's foreseeing eye
> Thy golden gates appear!
>
> Ah, then my spirit faints
> To reach the land I love,
> The bright inheritance of saints,
> Jerusalem above![43]

True hope, however, does not urge us to take flight of the present for the future, but enables us to face the present with all its suffering, pain, and disappointment with profound realism. True hope enables us to live in the

---

43. James Montgomery, "Forever with the Lord," 1835.

present and never allows us to leave the present for the future. Although Christian hope comprises a vision of the future, the *eschaton*, it nurtures a unique spirituality that strives in humility to be adequate to the circumstances God has placed us in. This means that true hope can never inspire an escapist outlook. When threatened by pain, sorrow, and suffering, he who truly hopes does not immediately try to project himself into the future by imagining some utopia. Rather, he will with resolve face the vicissitudes of life by simply continuing to live his life before God. Cardinal John Henry Newman has expressed this with great poignancy and eloquence in his hymn "Lead, Kindly Light, amid Circling Gloom." Though "the night is dark and I am far from home," yet he pleads that God would "keep Thou my feet; I do not ask to see the distant scene, – one step enough for me."[44]

In Asia, the idea of world denial and separation embodied in either Buddhist or Hindu mysticism is common, especially in countries like Thailand and India where the ubiquity of monumental monasteries and of holy men serves as its constant reminders. Christian hope, however, betokens a very different form of spirituality. Originating as it does from the ancient Hebrews, Christian hope, profoundly rooted in history, believes that God is the sovereign creator of space and time. The same observation may be made when Christian hope and the vision of the Greeks are compared. The Greeks see the world as mere reflections of some eternal order. Jews and Christians see the heavens as the "new heavens and new earth," a new creation in which the evils of this present age, the "night" and the "sea," are eradicated. As Tinder puts it, "such images, drawn from Jewish apocalypse and from the New Testament, suggest how radically different an ontology compared with that of the Greeks, Christian hope rests on."[45] Because it is so rooted in history, Christian hope envisages the story of humankind, not just our personal stories, as part of God's story, a story fashioned by the sovereign and merciful God.

This brings us to the relationship between Christian hope and the cross. Through the cross we come to understand that the worst events can be meaningful and that disappointments and tribulations are part of the course of life in the fallen world. But the cross also enables us to see that every disappointment and suffering we now face can be integrated into the story God fashions, which will ultimately serve our welfare. The dialectic of the cross means that hope is both prepared for disappointments here and is

---

44. Quoted in Ian Ker, *John Henry Newman: A Biography* (Oxford: Oxford University Press, 1988), 79–80.

45. Tinder, *Fabric of Hope*, 56.

sure of eternity in the age to come. The cross and the resurrection of Christ reveal the dialectical nature of hope itself. Hope is dialectical simply because the present conditions are antithetical to those for which we hope. We hope for righteousness in the midst of moral degradation, for justice in the midst of injustice and oppression, and for life in the midst of death. "In the dialectic of destiny, we confront our folly, sinfulness, weakness, and mortality, and in doing this we also confront, through grace, the wisdom, and righteousness, and power, and everlastingness of God."[46]

As a life of hope, the Christian life is therefore lived expectantly. Jesus stresses this when he exhorts his disciples to "keep watch, because you do not know the day or the hour" (Matt 25:13). This emphasis should not be read as an injunction for the disciples to withdraw from the world in order to prepare themselves "spiritually" for his return. Neither does it encourage a fascination for the signs of the end and a misplaced preoccupation with speculating about the date of the *parousia*. Rather Jesus's teaching is purposed to point out that the preparations the disciples must make are essentially of a this-worldly nature, for the presence of the new creation is already hidden in the form of the old. And it can be recognized "not in mystical fervour or some purifying detachment from the world, but precisely in radical involvement in the world through purifying it through initiatives for divine justice, peace and the life to which these lead."[47] The church, to be sure, is not of this world; yet it is called to be in the world and to value the world in the light of its future. This calling is not an optional extra, but is that of every follower of Jesus Christ.

References

Bauckham, Richard, and Trevor Hart. *Hope Against Hope: Christian Eschatology at the Turn of the Millennium*. Grand Rapids: Eerdmans, 1999.
Brunner, Emil. *Eternal Hope*. London: Lutterworth, 1954.
Crone, Patricia. *Pre-Industrial Societies: Anatomy of the Pre-Modern World*. Oxford: Blackwell, 1989.
David, Randolph. "Asian Societies in the Age of Globalisation." In *Faith and Life in Contemporary Asian Realities*, edited by Feliciano V. Carino and Marina True, 21–42. Hong Kong: Christian Conference of Asia, 2000.
Dunn, James D. G. *Romans 1–8*. Word Biblical Commentary. Waco: Word, 1988.
Gethin, R. *The Foundations of Buddhism*. Oxford: Oxford University Press, 1998.
Giddens, Anthony. *The Consequences of Modernity*. Cambridge: Polity, 1990.

---

46. Tinder, 63.
47. Bauckham and Hart, *Hope against Hope*, 207.

Gunaratna, Rohan. "Understanding Al Qaeda and Its Network in Southeast Asia." In *After Bali: The Threat of Terrorism in Southeast Asia*, edited by Kumar Ramakrishna and See Seng Tan, 117–132. Singapore: Institute of Defence and Strategic Studies, 2003.

Hebblethwaite, Brian. *Evil, Suffering and Religion*. London: SPCK, 2000.

Hill, Ronald. *Southeast Asia: People, Land and Economy*. Sydney: Allen & Unwin, 2002.

Ker, Ian. *John Henry Newman: A Biography*. Oxford: Oxford University Press, 1988.

Küng, Hans. "Toward Dialogue." In *Christianity and World Religions: Paths of Dialogue with Islam, Hinduism, and Buddhism*, edited by Hans Küng, Josef Van Ess, Heinrich von Stietencron, and Heinz Bechert, xiv–xx. London: SCM, 1993.

Lane, Dermot A. *Keeping Hope Alive: Stirrings in Christian Theology*. Dublin: Gill & Macmillan, 1996.

Lipner, Julius. *Hindus: Their Religious Beliefs and Practices*. London: Routledge, 1994.

MacInnis, Donald. *Religious Policy and Practice in Communist China: A Documentary History*. New York: Macmillan, 1972.

Maha Thera, Narada, trans. *The Buddha and His Teachings*. Singapore: Stamford Press charitable reprint [n. d.].

Mao Zedong. "The Chinese Revolution and the Chinese Communist Party." December 1939. In *Selected Works of Mao Tse-tung*, Vol. 2. Peking: Foreign Language Press, 1975.

———. "The Foolish Old Man Who Removed Mountains." June 1945. In *Selected Works of Mao Tse-tung*, Vol. 3. Peking: Foreign Language Press, 1975.

Marcel, Gabriel. "Sketch of a Phenomenology and a Metaphysic of Hope." In *Homo Viator: Introduction to a Metaphysics of Hope*. Translated by Emma Graufurd. London: Gollancz, 1951.

Meisner, Maurice. *Marxism, Maoism and Utopianism: Eight Essays*. Madison: University of Wisconsin Press, 1982.

"Message to the Asian Communities: Final Statement of the Kandy Conference." *Dialogue* 7 (Sept–Dec 1980): 119.

Moltmann, Jürgen. "Hope in a Time of Arrogance and Terror." In *Strike Terror No More: Theology, Ethics and the New War*, edited by Jon L. Berquist, 177–186. St Louis: Chalice, 2002.

Myrdall, Gunnar. *Asian Drama: An Inquiry into the Poverty of Nations*. 3 vols. London: Allen Lane, 1968.

Ramakrishna, Kumar, and See Seng Tan, eds. *After Bali: The Threat of Terrorism in Southeast Asia*. Singapore: Institute of Defence and Strategic Studies, 2003.

Ratzinger, Joseph. *To Look on Christ: Exercises in Faith, Hope and Love*. Slough: St Paul, 1978.

Robison, Richard, and David S. G. Goodman. "The New Rich in Asia: Economic Development, Social Status and Political Consciousness." In *The New Rich in Asia: Mobile Phones, McDonald's and Middle-Class Revolution*, edited by Richard Robison and David S. G. Goodman, 1–18. London: Routledge, 1996.

Rule, Paul. "Is Maoism Open to the Transcendent?" In *The New China: A Catholic Response*, edited by Michael Chu, 25–43. New York: Paulist, 1977.

Singh, Daljit. "ASEAN Counter-Terror Strategies and Cooperation: How Effective?" In *After Bali: The Threat of Terrorism in Southeast Asia*, edited by Kumar Ramakrishna and See Seng Tan, 201–220. Singapore: Institute of Defence and Strategic Studies, 2003.

Tan, Andrew. "The Indigenous Roots of Conflict in Southeast Asia: The Case of Mindanao." In *After Bali: The Threat of Terrorism in Southeast Asia*, edited by Kumar Ramakrishna and See Seng Tan, 97–116. Singapore: Institute of Defence and Strategic Studies, 2003.

Tinder, Glenn. *The Fabric of Hope*. Atlanta: Scholars Press, 1999.

von Stietencron, Heinrich. "Hindu Perspectives." In *Christianity and World Religions: Paths to Dialogue with Islam, Hinduism, and Buddhism*, edited by Hans Küng, Josef van Ess, Heinrich von Stietencron, and Heinz Bechert, 137–288. Translated by Peter Heinegg. London: SCM, 1993.

Williams, Paul, and Anthony Tribe. *Buddhist Thought*. London: Routledge, 2000.

Yewangoe, A. A. *Theologia Crucis in Asia*. Amsterdam: Rodopi, 1987.

Part II

Contemporary Concerns

9

A Theology of Suffering and Mission for the Asian Church

Kar Yong Lim
Seminari Theoloji Malaysia

Introduction

According to the 2018 World Watch List published by Open Doors, trends suggest that Christians in Asia and the Middle East are the most vulnerable in terms of suffering.[1] Now in its twenty-sixth year, this annual ranking tracks fifty countries where it is most dangerous to be Christian. Out of the fifty countries ranked, twenty-two are in Asia while twelve are in the Middle East, and a large number of these countries are Muslim-majority with Christianity as a minority. The report highlights that suffering in Asia has risen to unprecedented levels, with Bangladesh, Laos, Bhutan, and Sri Lanka joining the list for the first time in 2017 and Nepal in 2018. The magnitude of persecution is clearly illustrated by the sobering statistic that 215 million Christians experienced high levels of persecution in the fifty countries listed. This means that 1 in 12 Christians live in places where Christianity is either illegal, forbidden, or persecuted. The 2018 Watch List also reports that 3,066 Christians were killed, 1,253 were abducted, and 1,020 were raped or sexually harassed; and 793 churches were attacked during the reporting period. In addition, there is also increasing persecution of women and those who are marginalized and living in poverty.

---

1. See "World Watch List," Open Doors, accessed 25 November 2018, https://www.opendoorsusa.org/christian-persecution/world-watch-list/.

Reasons for the Rise of Suffering and Persecution in Asia

One of the primary reasons for the rise in suffering of Christians in Asia is the spread of radical Islam and Islamic resurgence in recent decades. This radical Islamic movement often embraces a clear anti-Western political agenda and attempts to bring the nations under Muslim domination and *sharia* law. The movement, which often results in Islamic militancy and persecution of Christians, is rapidly expanding in many parts of Asia, notably in Pakistan, Bangladesh, Indonesia, and Malaysia. However, this movement is not limited to Muslim-majority nations but also includes locations where Muslims are a minority, such as southern Thailand, and Mindanao and Palawan in the Philippines. On 27 May 2001, Martin and Gracia Burnham, missionaries with the New Tribes Mission (now known as Ethnos360) serving in the Philippines, were taken captive by a Muslim terrorist group known as Abu Sayyaf near Palawan Island. While Gracia survived the year-long captivity, her husband sadly perished. In her autobiography, Gracia shared their story and admitted that as missionaries, they had been warned of the possibility of suffering and martyrdom, but the reality of it did not strike her until she was held captive in the jungles of the Philippines.[2] The grassroots revival of Islam in Central Asia also leads to religious persecution, as seen in countries like Uzbekistan, Tajikistan, and Kazakhstan. In these countries, persecution has spread due to both Islamic extremism and efforts by the government to restrict the growth of and conversion to Christianity. Islamic groups such as Al-Qaeda, Boko Haram, Jemaah Islamiyah, Islamic State of Iraq and the Levant (commonly known as ISIS or IS), and the Taliban are some of the active radical Islamic movements seen in our world today.

The rise of ethnic and religious nationalism is a second reason for the suffering of Christians who are in a minority in Asia. In countries like India, the rise of Hinduism and Indian nationalism has led to increasing levels of persecution toward the Christian minority. This has spilled over into neighboring Hindu-majority Nepal, where in 2017 the government criminalized conversion to Christianity, putting tremendous pressure on the Christian minority. In Myanmar and Sri Lanka, the rise of Buddhist nationalism is also evident. In China, new religious regulations, the "Regulations for Religious Affairs," were passed in 2018.[3] This new legislation has severe implications

---

2. Gracia Burnham, *In the Presence of My Enemies* (Wheaton: Tyndale House, 2003).

3. See "Regulation for Religious Affairs," State Council of the People's Republic of China, accessed 1 December 2018, http://www.gov.cn/zhengce/content/2017-09/07/content_5223282.htm?from=timeline.

for Christianity as churches must now obtain government approval and registration for any religious activities. Underlying this new legislation is the ideology that religions are not compatible with communist ideals and threaten the country's government. Since the new regulations came into force, the Chinese government has implemented a crackdown on unofficial and underground churches in the country. It has been reported that a number of large unofficial churches throughout the country have been shut down.[4]

Intertwined with religious persecution are the issues of gender, caste, and poverty. Christian women from marginalized groups are often the most vulnerable in suffering for the sake of Christ. In Pakistan, the case of Asia Bibi, which gained international attention, is an example of women suffering in an Islamic context.[5] A convert to Christianity, she worked as a farm laborer, but was arrested in 2009 for insulting Islam when, being deemed unclean, she offered water to a Muslim co-worker. She received the death penalty in 2010 for blasphemy. After winning an appeal before the highest court in the land she was finally freed, but only after nine years of imprisonment, including an extended period of time in solitary confinement. Yet it remains unlikely that her suffering will soon come to an end. She will most likely have to start life afresh outside of her home country together with her family, possibly adopting a new identity. In addition, officials known to have supported her acquittal are also at risk.[6]

The rise in suffering in Asia is unprecedented and is a cause for profound concern. In light of this, there is urgent need for a robust understanding of suffering for the sake of the gospel that is biblically rooted and contextually relevant. This essay hopes to offer some reflections on this issue. First, I will offer a brief survey and evaluation on the theme of suffering and mission based on some recent works on mission theology from missiologists and biblical

---

4. See "China Bans One of Beijing's Biggest Underground Protestant Churches," *South China Morning Post*, 10 September 2018, accessed 1 December 2018, https://www.scmp.com/news/china/politics/article/2163489/china-bans-one-beijings-largest-underground-protestant-churches; Mimi Lau, "Members of Unofficial Chinese Church Vow to Defy Crackdown and Keep Meeting," *South China Morning Post*, 11 December 2018, accessed 12 December 2018, https://www.scmp.com/news/china/politics/article/2177520/underground-chinese-church-members-vow-defy-crackdown-and-keep.

5. See Memphis Barker, "Asia Bibi: Pakistan Court Overturns Blasphemy Death Sentence," *The Guardian* online, 31 October 2018, accessed 1 December 2018, https://www.theguardian.com/world/2018/oct/31/asia-bibi-verdict-pakistan-court-overturns-blasphemy-death-sentence.

6. See Harriet Sherwood, "Quashing of Asia Bibi's Blasphemy Charge Will Not End Her Suffering," *The Guardian* online, 31 October 2018, accessed 1 December 2018, https://www.theguardian.com/world/2018/oct/31/quashing-of-asia-bibis-blasphemy-charge-will-not-end-her-suffering.

scholars. Following this, I will turn my attention to focus on the apostle Paul and his thoughts on suffering. Through Paul's life, I aim to propose a biblical and theological framework for understanding suffering and mission. Finally, I will offer some reflections on the relationship of suffering and mission, and its implications for Christian witness in the contemporary world, using Malaysia, a Muslim-majority nation, as a case study.

Is There a Place for Suffering in the Theology of Mission?

Although suffering for the sake of the gospel is a prominent theme in the New Testament, and particularly in Paul's epistles, this theme has received too little attention from scholars of missions and the New Testament. Otherwise comprehensive and commendable works on the theology of mission give only passing attention to the theology of suffering.[7] Similarly, while New Testament scholars have noted the importance of suffering for Paul's self-understanding, this theme is often underdeveloped in comparison to its prominence in Paul's thought and practice.[8] While there are, of course, exceptions to this rule,[9] it unfortunately remains the case that suffering as a part of Paul's ministry often receives less attention than his purported methods for missionary "success."[10] These emphases have a tendency to pay attention to models that generate growth and success in mission or church planting rather than persecution and suffering.

Thankfully, there are signs of change on the horizon. Timothy Tennent suggests that the changing context of missions in the era of global Christianity

---

7. George W. Peters, *A Biblical Theology of Missions* (Chicago: Moody, 1972); David J. Bosch, *Transforming Mission: Paradigm Shifts in Theology of Mission* (Maryknoll: Orbis Books, 1991); Roger Hedlund, *The Mission of the Church in the World: A Biblical Theology* (Grand Rapids: Baker, 1991); Christopher J. H. Wright, *The Mission of God: Unlocking the Bible's Grand Narrative* (Downers Grove: InterVarsity Press, 2006); and *The Mission of God's People: A Biblical Theology of the Church's Mission* (Grand Rapids: Zondervan, 2010).

8. Thus, in an almost 2,000-page study of early Christian mission, the chapter on "Mission and Persecution" comprises only about six pages in length in Eckhard J. Schnabel, *Early Christian Mission*, vol. 2 (Downers Grove: InterVarsity Press, 2004), 1533–1538. A similar absence is notable in Andreas J. Köstenberger and Peter T. O'Brien, *Salvation to the Ends of the Earth: A Biblical Theology of Mission* (Downers Grove: InterVarsity Press, 2001).

9. See, for example, Scott Hafemann, "'Because of Weakness' (Galatians 4:13): The Role of Suffering in the Mission of Paul," in *The Gospel to the Nations: Perspectives on Paul's Mission*, eds. Peter Bolt and Mark Thompson (Downers Grove: InterVarsity Press, 2000), 131–146.

10. For example, see J. Herbert Kane, *Christian Missions in Biblical Perspective* (Grand Rapids: Baker, 1976), who devotes a chapter on "Missions in the Ministry of Paul" (72–93) under the section "The Biblical Basis of Missions" where Pauline mission is methodically reduced to Paul's missionary strategy and factors in his success.

points us in a different direction.[11] Tennent laments that, tragically, most mission training and textbooks written by Western authors have not included persecution or suffering as a theme for serious reflection, and even if this theme is included, it has not been understood within a larger biblical and theological framework.[12] In light of these realities, Tennent offers a theological framework that places suffering and persecution within the larger context of the mission of God. His exposition on suffering and mission is timely and welcome. Another recent addition to mission textbooks is the work by Scott Sunquist, *Understanding Christian Mission*, focusing on Christian mission and its historical, biblical, and theological foundations. Sunquist's central thesis is that mission is from the heart of God and this is carried out in suffering in this world for the redemption of the nations for God's eternal glory.[13] While Sunquist's aim is to see mission history and contemporary issues in mission from the perspective of suffering and glory, how this is reflected in the discussion on contemporary issues in mission could have been further developed.

Yet there is still room for a biblical and theological framework to be further explored and developed for various parts of the Majority World, especially Asia, by taking into account the challenges and uniqueness of mission in these contexts. Moreover, while there is general agreement about the significant role suffering played in Paul's mission, and acknowledgment of the dominance of the theme of suffering in both his epistles and the Lukan record in Acts, there remains a lack of any specific serious study on the place of suffering in Paul's missionary calling. The relationship between suffering and mission remains a neglected theme that needs to be further explored. What is urgently needed is a development of a biblical and theological framework on suffering and mission rooted in Asian soil. Admittedly, this is not an easy task as Asia is not only a large continent but diverse as well.

Paul's Perspective on Suffering

Throughout the pages of the New Testament, we read accounts of suffering and persecution as a result of Christian witness. Jesus warns us about the

---

11. Timothy C. Tennent, *Invitation to World Missions: A Trinitarian Missiology for the Twenty-First Century* (Grand Rapids: Kregel, 2010).

12. Tennent, *Invitation to World Missions*, 462.

13. Scott W. Sunquist, *Understanding Christian Mission: Participation in Suffering and Glory* (Grand Rapids: Baker, 2013).

cost of following him.[14] The experience of the early Christians testifies to the reality of suffering in Acts.[15] In his epistles, Paul provides detailed description of his apostolic suffering: prolonged imprisonments, near-death experiences, numerous beatings, trying tribulations, extreme dangers in his travels, physical pains and depravations, as well as daily anxiety for the churches he established.[16] The most detailed descriptions of them are found in 2 Corinthians. I have argued elsewhere that Paul develops the theme of suffering at critical points in his argument in 2 Corinthians. The theme of suffering introduced in the epistolary thanksgiving section of 2 Corinthians 1:3–11 is subsequently expanded in 2:14–16; 4:7–12; 6:1–11; 11:23 – 12:10 and finally recapitulated in 13:4. Therefore, Paul's apostolic suffering is the unifying theme that unites the entire argument of this letter.[17] A number of questions could be raised in light of Paul's sufferings: How did Paul understand the nature of his own suffering? What role did Paul's understanding of his suffering play in his mission to the Gentiles? What kind of mission theology can be constructed for the effectiveness of Christian witness in the contexts of opposition and persecution in Asia?

First of all, Paul's understanding of his suffering is not to be divorced from his apostolic mission. Whenever Paul mentioned his suffering, particularly in 2 Corinthians, it was directly related to his apostolic mission. His suffering was a direct result of the proclamation of the gospel of the crucified Messiah (2 Cor 2:14–15; 4:10) in which the power of God was revealed (2 Cor 4:7; 12:9–10; 13:4).[18] For Paul, the proclamation of the gospel was not done out of convenience nor in a context of comfort. His missionary activities were often met with fierce opposition and persecution, yet none of these ever diminished his zeal for the gospel or stifled his evangelistic efforts. As such, Paul viewed his suffering as necessary and integral to his Gentile mission, rather than as impediments to the progress of the gospel (2 Cor 6:3). Likewise, as heralds of

---

14. For example, see Matt 10:16–42; 25:31–46; Mark 13:5–23; Luke 8:13–15; 9:23; 14:25–35; 18:8; 21:10–19; John 15:18–21.

15. For example, see Acts 4:1–22; 5:12–41; 6:7–15; 7:54–8:4; 12:1–18; 13:49–14:7; 16:16–34; 17:1–15; 19:23–32; 21:27–36.

16. See 1 Cor 4:9–13; 2 Cor 1:3–11; 2:14–17; 4:7–12; 6:4–10; 11:23b–33; 12:10; Phil 3:10; Col 1:24. See also Rom 12:14–21; 1 Cor 4:9–13; Phil 1:12–14; 3:7–11; 1 Thess 1:6; 2 Tim 2:3–13; 3:10–12.

17. For further discussion, see Kar Yong Lim, *"The Sufferings of Christ Are Abundant in Us": A Narrative Dynamics Investigation of Paul's Sufferings in 2 Corinthians*, Library of New Testament Studies 399 (London: T&T Clark, 2009).

18. See also Acts 14:19–20; 16:16–24; 18:12–17; 19:23–41; 21:27–36; 23:12–15; 27:13–44; 28:16–31.

the gospel today, we must be prepared for the event that we are called to suffer in our Christian witness.

Second, Paul claimed that his suffering had positive missiological benefits for the Corinthians. Paul clearly states that it was through his suffering that the Corinthians received comfort and salvation (2 Cor 1:6) and even life (2 Cor 2:15–16; 4:10–12; and 13:4. Cf. Col 1:24). There is no ambiguity in Paul's language when he states that the Corinthians were the direct beneficiaries of his sufferings. The fact that "death is at work in [Paul], but life is at work in you" (2 Cor 4:12) is testimony to the reality that his sufferings resulted in the awakening of life in those who believed in the gospel, and in giving birth to a Christ-believing community in Corinth. Suffering could possibly be the instrument through which God makes his glory known.

Third, Paul's understanding of his suffering was also inspired by the Hebrew Scriptures. Paul's references to Scripture demonstrate that he lived in the world of the Scriptures, allowing them to shape his understanding of his suffering and mission to the Gentiles. This can be seen in Paul's citation of Isaiah 49:8 in 2 Corinthians 6:2. Isaiah 49 has been widely understood as the second Servant Song in which the Servant of the Lord is the instrument appointed by Yahweh to be a light to the Gentiles and to bring his salvation to the ends of the earth (Isa 49:6). Paul viewed his apostolic mission in the same light, as bringing the Gentiles back to God in a way analogous to the tradition of the Servant of the Lord and in fulfillment of God's promises.[19] In other words, the mission of Paul was an extension of the mission of Jesus (John 14:12). In this way, we are reminded that we are instruments God uses to advance his kingdom. As Jesus suffered, we should not expect to be spared similar treatment.

Next, Paul also identified his suffering as the sufferings of Christ. It is interesting to note that when Paul mentions his sufferings in 2 Corinthians, he explicitly makes reference to the sufferings of Christ as well. In 2 Corinthians 1:5 Paul declares, "the sufferings of Christ are abundant for us" (NRSV).[20] Further on, in 2 Corinthians 4:10–11 Paul states that he always carries in his body the "death of Jesus" so that the life of Jesus might be manifested in his body. In 2 Corinthians 13:4 Paul again identifies his weakness with that of Christ's being "crucified in weakness." Thus, it is not surprising that Paul was able to declare: "for Christ's sake, I delight in weaknesses, in insults, in hardships, in persecutions, in difficulties. For when I am weak, then I am

---

19. For further discussion, see Lim, *Sufferings of Christ*, 123–157.
20. For further discussion, see Lim, 43–57. See also Wright, *Mission of God's People*, 239–241, for a discussion on the relation between mission and the suffering God.

strong" (2 Cor 12:10). Paul wanted the Corinthians to understand that the nature of his apostleship and his ministerial lifestyle was transformed by his understanding of the cross of Christ. If the Corinthians could not understand and appreciate his cruciform life and ministry as demonstrated by weakness and suffering grounded in the cross and gospel of Christ see 2 Cor 11:23 – 12:10), how would they understand the weakness and suffering of Christ and apply it to their own lives as well? After all, to follow Jesus is to take up one's cross and bear that cross in the path of Christian discipleship. There is no other option.

Furthermore, Paul's suffering clearly demonstrated his deep love not only for the Gentiles but also for his own people, the unbelieving Jews. While Paul might be better known as the Apostle to the Gentiles, this does not mean that he ceased to be a Jew and that he completely ignored the spiritual needs of the Jews. This is demonstrated through Paul's willingness to subject himself to the "forty lashes minus one" a total of five times (2 Cor 11:24), a punishment that was meted out by synagogue authorities upon the Jews for various offenses. This strongly suggests that Paul never abandoned his own people, but continued his evangelistic activities within the Jewish synagogues. Paul's action clearly demonstrates his deep love and concern for the Jews to the extent of being willing to suffer for their sake (see Rom 9:1–4). This could only be the response of one who had been gripped by the love and grace of the Lord, and it was that gratitude and debt to Christ's love that propelled him to love others so deeply (see 2 Cor 5:14–15).

This is the same debt for all of us who call ourselves Christians, people bearing the name of the one who calls us to be his ambassadors and spokespersons (2 Cor 5:18–20): that we should love others deeply to the extent that we are willing to suffer for the sake of the gospel so that those who have yet to hear the good news might come to experience the redemption that Christ offers.

Finally, it was through Paul's very weakness in suffering that the power of God was manifested in his life. In bringing the gospel to the Corinthians, Paul did not subject himself to the prevailing social values and conventions of his days. Paul declared that he did not proclaim the gospel with eloquence or superior wisdom, but in weakness, fear, and trembling (1 Cor 2:1–5). The only message Paul proclaimed was "Jesus Christ and him crucified" (1 Cor 2:2), and Paul's ministerial style clearly reflected the humility of Christ (see 2 Cor 13:4). In the eyes of a society that placed a high value on physical appearance, his physical wounds and scars resulting from years of suffering (see Gal 6:17) were not marks of honor but of dishonor and weakness. Therefore, it is not surprising that all these factors worked against Paul when the nature of his apostleship was called into question, and that they subsequently became a crucial point of contention between him and the opponents within the Corinthian church. Paul charged these super-apostles with preaching "a[nother] Jesus . . . a different spirit . . . a different gospel" (2 Cor 11:4). At the root of this charge is that Paul saw a massive incongruence between the true gospel and the lifestyle of these super-apostles. The message of Christ's cruciform life simply did not square with their preoccupation with rhetorical eloquence, which sought to impress the audience rather than to transform lives to be Christlike.

Based on the above observations, we can draw a key insight into Paul's mindset with regard to suffering: far from viewing himself as a cracked and useless vessel, Paul saw his sufferings and weaknesses as the very vehicle that God used "to show that this all-surpassing power is from God and not from us" (2 Cor 4:7). Paradoxically, it was through his suffering that Paul was able to identify with the sufferings of Christ, and experience the power of God working through his weakness and the power of the Holy Spirit in the proclamation of the gospel.

If taken seriously, Paul's life continues to tell a story of endurance and patience in ministry, love and devotion to the churches, faithfulness and obedience to the gospel message, sacrifice and service for his Lord, sincerity and integrity before God, and, above all, a rejection of triumphalism and its accompanying pride and self-focus. Moreover, Paul's perspective on suffering is modeled directly on that of Jesus (see Phil 2:1–11). For Paul, suffering is an ongoing reflection of and participation in the sufferings of Christ (2 Cor 1:5; Col 1:24). As such, Paul's cruciform life challenges us to a re-examination of our understanding of the relationship between suffering and the proclamation of the gospel. Like Paul and Jesus, we must view suffering as one of the ways in which we embody and bear witness to the gospel of Christ in the world.

Contemporary Reflections

Paul's understanding of his suffering as necessary and integral to his proclamation of the gospel may be difficult for some to accept, and may even sound irrelevant in the contemporary world. In the proceeding section, I offer some reflections on suffering and mission from the perspective of a Christian minority living in the multireligious, multiethnic, and multicultural context of Malaysia, where Islam is not only the dominant religion but also the official religion enshrined in the Federal Constitution. While the Constitution provides for freedom of religion, the propagation of religious faith other than Islam is prohibited.[21] The uniqueness of Malaysian society is that religious belief, identity, and ethnic boundaries are intricately interconnected. The Malays, who are the dominant racial group, are Muslims, and defined as Muslims in the Constitution.[22] In general, those of Chinese origin are Buddhists or practice Chinese-related religious faiths, and those of Indian origin are Hindus. Since Islam is the official religion of the nation, its influence has been keenly felt, with the rapid implementation of Islamic programs since the early 1980s. Islamic values and practices have also been introduced into the administration of the country. Subsequently, educational programs, financial institutions, and legal frameworks based on Islamic principles have been progressively introduced. Increasing symbolic and external signs of Islamic resurgence and Islamization are also seen in the building of mosques, observance of public holidays based on the Islamic calendar, Islamic architecture of both public and private buildings, and the dress codes of many adherents of Islam.[23] In September 2001, Prime Minister Dr Mahathir Mohamad declared that Malaysia was an Islamic state.[24]

In this context, how can a re-examination of a missiological understanding of suffering be applied in Malaysia where strong Islamic resurgence and rapid Islamization are presently being experienced? How can the church be an effective and credible witness in an Islamic context?

In the wake of the strong Islamic resurgence in Malaysia, Christian mission and witness has become increasingly difficult. Religious conversion from Islam to Christianity has become both a very sensitive and an emotional issue that leads to persecution and suffering. The experiences of Jamaluddin Othman, Hilmy Nor, and Pua Boon Seng are somber reminders of the reality of suffering and persecution following religious conversion from Islam. Jamaluddin

---

21. For further discussion, see Lee Min Choon, *Freedom of Religion in Malaysia* (Petaling Jaya: Kairos, 1999); and Abdullah Saeed and Hassan Saeed, *Freedom of Religion, Apostasy and Islam* (Aldershot: Ashgate, 2004), especially chs. 9–12 on their case study of religious freedom and Islam in Malaysia.

22. Article 160(2) of the Federal Constitution of Malaysia defines a Malay as a "person who *professes the religion of Islam*, habitually speaks the Malay language, [and] conforms to Malay custom" (emphasis mine).

23. For further discussion, see Sadayandy Batumalai, *Islamic Resurgence and Islamization in Malaysia: A Malaysian Christian Response* (Ipoh: St John's Church, 1996); Hussin Mutalib, *Islam in Malaysia: From Revivalism to Islamic State* (Singapore: Singapore University Press, 1993); Chandra Muzaffar, *Islamic Resurgence in Malaysia* (Petaling Jaya: Penerbit Fajar Bakti, 1987); and Albert Sundararaj Walters, *We Believe in One God? Reflections on the Trinity in the Malaysian Context* (Dehli: ISPCK, 2002), 11–86, especially his analysis on Islamic resurgence, Islamization, and Christian–Muslim relations (60–86).

24. Mahathir Mohamad's political agenda in making Malaysia an Islamic country is well documented. See his *Islam and the Muslim Ummah: Selected Speeches of Dr. Mahathir Mohamad, Prime Minister of Malaysia*, updated ed. (Petaling Jaya: Pelanduk Publications, 2001).

Othman and Hilmy Nor are Malay Muslims who converted to the Christian faith, while Pua Boon Seng is a Christian of Chinese origin. They were detained in 1987 as part of the *Operasi Lalang*, a codename for the police operation in which more than one hundred people were arrested for professing and practicing their religious faith, which was viewed as an act that threatened the national security of Malaysia.[25] Lina Joy, another Malay Muslim convert to Christianity, also faced persecution, harassment, and tremendous difficulty in her application to strike out the word "Islam" from her national identity card. Her case attracted international attention.[26]

More recently, Pastor Raymond Koh, a Christian activist, was abducted in broad daylight on 13 February 2017 in what appeared to be a well-planned and professionally executed operation.[27] Pastor Koh was involved in an earlier controversy in 2011 when, after being accused of proselytizing Muslims by the Selangor State Islamic Religious Department, a box containing two bullets accompanied by a note threatening his life was sent to his house. The case was subsequently dropped because of lack of evidence.[28] At the time of writing, Koh remains missing and there are no further leads on his case. A number of vigils and prayer meetings have been organized for Koh, and churches have also extended help to stand in solidarity with Koh's family.

There are other incidents that demonstrate challenges in the practice of one's faith. We have witnessed controversies surrounding the use of the word "Allah" in the Malay-language translation of the Bible that resulted in the warrantless raid of the office of the Bible Society of Malaysia by the Selangor Islamic Religious Department on 2 January 2014, resulting in the confiscation

---

25. For further information, see the case of Minister of Home Affairs, Malaysia and Another v. Jamaluddin bin Othman [1989] 1*MLJ* 418. See also the testimonies of Hilmy Nor, *Circumcised Heart* (Petaling Jaya: Kairos: 1999); and Pua Boon Sing, *Fragments from Kamunting: 325 Days in Police Custody for the Christian Faith* (Serdang: Good News Enterprise, 1990) recounting their experiences in solitary confinement during their police detention. Lee, *Freedom of Religion in Malaysia*, 85–88, provides helpful commentary on these cases.

26. See Jalil Hamid and Syed Asman, "Malaysia's Lina Joy Loses Islam Conversion Case," Reuters, 30 May 2007, accessed 15 March 2018, https://www.reuters.com/article/us-malaysia-religion-ruling/malaysias-lina-joy-loses-islam-conversion-case-idUSSP20856820070530; and Jane Perlez, "Once Muslim, Now Christian and Caught in the Courts," New York Times online, 24 August 2006, accessed 15 March 2018, http://www.nytimes.com/2006/08/24/world/asia/24malaysia.html.

27. Footage of the abduction of Pastor Raymond Koh can be viewed at, "CCTV Footage Captures Pastor Raymond Koh's Abduction," *The Star Online*, YouTube, 4 March 2017, accessed 15 March 2018, https://www.youtube.com/watch?time_continue=7&v=Y-jcxSZGS-8.

28. See "An Agonising Wait for Hubby's Return," *Daily Express*, 2 April 2017, accessed 15 March 2018, http://www.dailyexpress.com.my/news.cfm?NewsID=116851.

of more than three hundred copies of the Bible in the Malay language.[29] On 11 May 2008, customs officers at Kuala Lumpur airport seized some teaching materials containing the word "Allah" in a Christian context from Jill Ireland, a Christian native from the tribe of Melanau. After a seven-year legal battle, these materials were finally returned to her upon court order.[30]

These incidents are not simply isolated events but clearly highlight that, without a doubt, the Christian church in Malaysia faces an increasingly challenging task of being a faithful witness as a religious minority within a dominant Islamic context.[31] We are reminded that the proclamation of the gospel of Christ, the crucified and risen Savior, has never been an easy task in a world steeped in religious pluralism, and particularly so in an Islamic majority context. As in Paul's day in Corinth, the gospel of Jesus Christ remains a stumbling block and a scandal (1 Cor 1:23–24) today. The Acts of the Apostles contains numerous stories that serve to remind us that suffering and dying for the gospel was not only the price paid by the apostles and the early Christ-followers, but was also the instrument used by God for the expansion of the gospel. Focusing on the triumphalist aspects of the gospel and idealizing the values of power, eloquence, and appearance are naturally more attractive and easily accommodated. As Christ-followers, we would rather remain in our comfort zones than experience unnecessary hardship and inconvenience, and would rather be recipients of God's abundant blessings than be the Master's suffering ambassadors for the sake of the gospel. Our worship sometimes reflects our preference for a Jesus Christ superstar – the hero and miracle-worker – than for the Jesus Christ who died on the cross and now summons us to take up our cross and follow him daily.

If suffering is necessary and integral to Christian witness, churches, and especially ministers of the gospel, need to evaluate whether their lives

---

29. See "Jias Raids Bible Society of Malaysia," *The Star* online, 2 January 2014, accessed 15 March 2018, https://www.thestar.com.my/news/nation/2014/01/02/jais-raid-bible-society/. The word "Allah" has been used in the vernacular Bible translation in the Malay language for more than four hundred years, since the earliest translation of the Gospel of Matthew was completed in 1612. It is only in recent decades, following the Islamic resurgence, that this matter has been fueled into a controversial issue.

30. See "Jill Ireland Back in Court as Malaysia Considers Christians' Right to Call God 'Allah,'" World Watch Monitor, 27 October 2017, accessed 15 March 2018, https://www.worldwatchmonitor.org/2017/10/jill-ireland-back-court-malaysia-considers-christians-right-call-god-allah/.

31. For a discussion on the challenges and restrictions confronting the church in Malaysia, see Walters, *We Believe in One God?*, 74–80 and 234–284; Göran Wiking, *Breaking the Pot: Contextual Responses to Survival Issues in Malaysian Churches*, SMS 96 (Lund: Swedish Institute of Missionary Research, 2004); and Kairos Research Centre, *Doing the Right Thing: A Practical Guide on Legal Matters for Churches in Malaysia* (Petaling Jaya: Kairos, 2004).

and ministries conform to the prevailing social conventions and cultural expectations or reflect a faithful and living exegesis of the gospel of Jesus Christ. They are called to live the cruciform life by embracing the cross of Christ. They are to demonstrate that the power of the gospel is at work in their lives so that a clear cruciform pattern results. Any preaching of the cross that focuses on the resurrection while denying the suffering of Christ is to be rejected. Thus, any elimination from Christian witness of suffering grounded in the gospel of Jesus Christ may well be the "other gospel" that Paul speaks against (2 Cor 11:4). The Christian church in Malaysia is reminded that without the cross, there is no Christian gospel, no church of Christ. Without suffering, there is no Pauline mission, no Christian proclamation. For this very reason, it is all the more urgent that we hear Paul's radical call to the embodiment of the gospel of Jesus Christ.

A prominent missiologist once made the following comment on the *Operasi Lalang* in Malaysia: "Christian leaders in Malaysia have come to erroneous conclusions about ministry among Malay Muslims there. Their position is based on their awareness that in the past some have been imprisoned or expelled for evangelism. It is commonly concluded that because of persecution, not biblical injunction, it is not God's will to attempt evangelism among the Malays."[32] In this respect, Tennent's call for greater awareness of and emphasis on suffering in mission is spot on as we move toward post-Christendom and an increasingly post-Christian context where "we need to better prepare students to understand the dynamics of persecution and to develop a theological understanding of persecution as a normative part of the church's life and witness."[33]

Christian witness today is in a very different position than it was a century ago. The majority of Christians today live in countries marked by religious pluralism and political subjugation. This changing face of mission demands that we read the Bible from the grassroots perspective of a religious minority experiencing social injustice and political powerlessness rather than from an elite position of prestige and power.[34] Any credible Christian witness today cannot ignore religious persecution and suffering. Therefore, Tennent is right

---

32. Greg Livingstone, *Planting Churches in Muslim Cities: A Team Approach* (Grand Rapids: Baker, 1993), 78.

33. Tennent, *Invitation to World Missions*, 96.

34. For example, Simon Chan, *Grassroots Asian Theology: Thinking the Faith from the Ground Up* (Downers Grove: InterVarsity Press, 2014); and Sebastian C. H. Kim, ed., *Christian Theology in Asia* (Cambridge: Cambridge University Press, 2008) are excellent examples of constructing theology from the ground up within the Asian context.

to suggest that we may have finally come full circle to a situation that is closer to the vibrancy and holistic perspective of the first-century Christians where the advancement of the gospel is always accompanied by suffering.[35] In this respect, I wonder whether any of us would be interested in responding to the following recruitment advertisement that caught my attention many years ago:

> Wanted: Missionaries . . . Bitter cold, scorching heat, long hours. Sickness almost certain. Possible imprisonment. Safe return not guaranteed. Honor and recognition from peers doubtful. Eternal rewards. Interested parties apply.[36]

Conclusion

In this essay, I have suggested that the relationship of suffering and mission remains an area that is largely unexplored, based on a survey of significant works on mission theology from the disciplines of missiology and biblical studies. Therefore, I proposed that we should seriously consider Paul's understanding of his suffering in his Gentile mission, from which we can draw relevant insights and a robust understanding and theological framework for suffering within the context of Christian mission. For the decades ahead, we will certainly witness increasing difficulty for credible Christian witness in the Majority World, where heightened opposition, especially from Islamic and Hindu groups, is to be expected. Therefore, we cannot ignore suffering or fail to incorporate it in our theological framework for what it means to be faithful Christ-followers in Asia.

The Christian church needs to be reminded that while suffering for the gospel may be an abstract idea for those who live in relatively peaceful and secure environments, it is a daily reality for Christ-followers in many parts of the world, and especially in Asia. We need a fresh reading of Paul's perspective on suffering and an urgent rediscovery of the missiological significance of suffering. Paul's message of suffering, grounded in the gospel of Jesus Christ, serves as a timely reminder to all of us who are commissioned to proclaim the saving drama of God in Jesus Christ. May we have the courage and boldness to remain faithful to the gospel of Christ and, through our lives, spread the aroma of Christ that comes from knowing him (2 Cor 2:14–16).

---

35. Tennent, *Invitation to World Missions*, 406.

36. A recruitment advertisement for missionaries that appeared in *International Journal of Frontier Mission* 11 (1994): 58.

References

Allen, Roland. *Missionary Methods: St Paul's or Ours?* Grand Rapids: Eerdmans, 1962.
"An Agonising Wait for Hubby's Return." *Daily Express*, 2 April 2017. Accessed 15 March 2018, http://www.dailyexpress.com.my/news.cfm?NewsID=116851.
Asia Mission Conference. *The Mission of God in the Context of the Suffering and Struggling Peoples of Asia*. Osaka: CCA, 1988.
Barker, Memphis. "Asia Bibi: Pakistan Court Overturns Blasphemy Death Sentence." *The Guardian* online, 31 October 2018. Accessed 1 December 2018, https://www.theguardian.com/world/2018/oct/31/asia-bibi-verdict-pakistan-court-overturns-blasphemy-death-sentence.
Basri, Ghazali. *Christian Mission and Islamic Da'wah in Malaysia*. 2nd ed. Kuala Lumpur: Nurin Enterprise, 1992.
Batumalai, Sadayandy. *Islamic Resugence and Islamization in Malaysia: A Malaysian Christian Response*. Ipoh: St John's Church, 1996.
Bolt, Peter, and Mark Thompson, eds. *The Gospel to the Nations: Perspectives on Paul's Mission*. Downers Grove: InterVarsity Press, 2000.
Bosch, David J. *Transforming Mission: Paradigm Shifts in Theology of Mission*. Maryknoll: Orbis Books, 1991.
Burnham, Gracia. *In the Presence of My Enemies*. Wheaton: Tyndale House, 2003.
"CCTV Footage Captures Paster Raymond Koh's Abduction." *The Star Online*, YouTube, 4 March 2017. Accessed 15 March 2018, https://www.youtube.com/watch?time_continue=7&v=Y-jcxSZGS-8.
Chan, Simon. *Grassroots Asian Theology: Thinking the Faith from the Ground Up*. Downers Grove: InterVarsity Press, 2014.
"China Bans One of Bejing's Biggest Underground Protestant Churches." *South China Morning Post*, 10 September 2018. Accessed 1 December 2018, https://www.scmp.com/news/china/politics/article/2163489/china-bans-one-beijings-largest-underground-protestant-churches.
Colaco, J. M. *Jesus Christ in Asian Suffering and Hope*. Madras: CLS, 1977.
Gilliland, Dean S. *Pauline Theology and Mission Practice*. Grand Rapids: Baker, 1983.
Hafemann, Scott. "'Because of Weakness' (Galatians 4:13): The Role of Suffering in the Mission of Paul." In *The Gospel to the Nations: Perspectives on Paul's Mission*, edited by Peter Bolt and Mark Thompson, 131–146. Downers Grove: InterVarstiy Press, 2001.
Hamid, Jalil, and Syed Asman. "Malaysia's Lina Joy Loses Islam Conversion Case." Reuters, 30 May 2007. Accessed 15 March 2018, https://www.reuters.com/article/us-malaysia-religion-ruling/malaysias-lina-joy-loses-islam-conversion-case-idUSSP20856820070530.
Hedlund, Roger. *The Mission of the Church in the World: A Biblical Theology*. Grand Rapids: Baker, 1991.

"Jias Raids Bible Society of Malaysia." *The Star* online, 2 January 2014. Accessed 15 March 2018, https://www.thestar.com.my/news/nation/2014/01/02/jais-raid-bible-society/.

"Jill Ireland Back in Court as Malaysia Considers Christians' Right to Call God 'Allah.'" World Watch Monitor, 27 October 2017. Accessed 15 March 2018, https://www.worldwatchmonitor.org/2017/10/jill-ireland-back-court-malaysia-considers-christians-right-call-god-allah/.

Kairos Research Centre. *Doing the Right Thing: A Practical Guide on Legal Matters for Churches in Malaysia*. Petaling Jaya: Kairos, 2004.

Kane, J. Herbert. *Christian Missions in Biblical Perspective*. Grand Rapids: Baker, 1976.

Kim, Sebastian C. H., ed. *Christian Theology in Asia*. Cambridge: Cambridge University Press, 2008.

Kirk, J. Andrew. *What Is Mission? Theological Explorations*. Minneapolis: Augsburg, 2000.

Köstenberger, Andreas J., and Peter T. O'Brien. *Salvation to the Ends of the Earth: A Biblical Theology of Mission*. Downers Grove: InterVarsity Press, 2001.

LaHaye, Tim, and Jerry Jenkins. *Left Behind: A Novel of the Earth's Last Days*. Carol Stream: Tyndale, 1995.

Larkin, William J. Jr., and Joel F. Williams, eds. *Mission in the New Testament: An Evangelical Approach*. Maryknoll: Orbis, 1999.

Lau, Mimi. "Members of Unofficial Chinese Church Vow to Defy Crackdown and Keep Meeting." *South China Morning Post*, 11 December 2018. Accessed 12 December 2018, https://www.scmp.com/news/china/politics/article/2177520/underground-chinese-church-members-vow-defy-crackdown-and-keep.

Lee, Min Choon. *Freedom of Religion in Malaysia*. Petaling Jaya: Kairos, 1999.

Lee, Young Kee. "God's Mission in Suffering and Martyrdom." PhD diss., Fuller Theological Seminary, Pasadena, 1999.

———. "A Missiological Perspective on Suffering." In *Footprints of God: A Narrative Theology of Mission*, edited by Charles Van Engen, Nancy Thomas, and Robert Gallagher, 92–102. Monrovia: MARC, 1999.

Lim, Kar Yong. *"The Sufferings of Christ Are Abundant in Us": A Narrative Dynamics Investigation of Paul's Sufferings in 2 Corinthians*. Library of New Testament Studies 399. London: T&T Clark, 2009.

Livingstone, Greg. *Planting Churches in Muslim Cities: A Team Approach*. Grand Rapids: Baker, 1993.

Mohamad, Mahathir. *Islam and the Muslim Ummah: Selected Speeches of Dr. Mahathir Mohamad, Prime Minister of Malaysia*, updated ed. Petaling Jaya: Pelanduk Publications, 2001.

Mutalib, Hussin. *Islam in Malaysia: From Revivalism to Islamic State*. Singapore: Singapore University Press, 1993.

Muzaffar, Chandra. *Islamic Resurgence in Malaysia*. Petaling Jaya: Penerbit Fajar Bakti, 1987.

Nor, Hilmy. *Circumcised Heart*. Petaling Jaya: Kairos, 1999.

Perlez, Jane. "Once Muslim, Now Christian and Caught in the Courts." *New York Times* online, 24 August 2006. Accessed 15 March 2018, http://www.nytimes.com/2006/08/24/world/asia/24malaysia.html.

Peters, George W. *A Biblical Theology of Missions*. Chicago: Moody, 1972.

Priest, Robert J., and Robert DeGeorge. "Doctoral Dissertations on Mission: Ten-Year Update, 2002–2011." *International Bulletin of Missionary Research* 37 (2013):195–202.

Pua, Boon Sing. *Fragments from Kamunting: 325 Days in Police Custody for the Christian Faith*. Serdang: Good News Enterprise, 1990.

Ro, Bong Ring, ed. *Christian Sufferings in Asia*. Taichung: ATA, 1989.

Saeed, Abdullah, and Hassan Saeed. *Freedom of Religion, Apostasy and Islam*. Aldershot: Ashgate, 2004.

Schnabel, Eckhard J. *Early Christian Mission*. Vol. 2. Downers Grove: InterVarsity Press, 2004.

Schreiner, Thomas R. *Paul, Apostle of God's Glory in Christ: A Pauline Theology*. Downers Grove: InterVarsity Press, 2001.

Senior, Donald, and Carroll Stuhlmueller. *The Biblical Foundations for Mission*. London: SCM, 1983.

Sherwood, Harriet. "Quashing of Asia Bibi's Blasphemy Charge Will Not End Her Suffering." *The Guardian* online, 31 October 2018. Accessed 1 December 2018, https://www.theguardian.com/world/2018/oct/31/quashing-of-asia-bibis-blasphemy-charge-will-not-end-her-suffering.

Skreslet, Stanley H. "Doctoral Dissertations on Mission: Ten-Year Update, 1992–2001." *International Bulletin of Missionary Research* 27 (2003): 98–133.

Sunquist, Scott W. *Understanding Christian Mission: Participation in Suffering and Glory*. Grand Rapids: Baker, 2013.

Tennent, Timothy C. *Invitation to World Mission: A Trinitarian Missiology for the Twenty-First Century*. Grand Rapids: Kregel, 2010.

Thomas, T. K., ed. *Testimony amid Asian Suffering*. Singapore: Christian Conference of Asia, 1977.

Tieszen, Charles L. *Re-examining Religious Persecution: Constructing a Theological Framework for Understanding Persecution*. Kempton Park, SA: AcadSA, 2008.

Van Engen, Charles, Nancy Thomas, and Robert Gallagher, eds. *Footprints of God: A Narrative Theology of Mission*. Monrovia: MARC, 1999.

Von Zychlin, Christa, ed. *Suffering: Eyes to See and Ears to Hear: A Theological Consultation from the Mekong*. Hong Kong: Lutheran Theological Seminary, 2015.

Walters, Albert Sundararaj. *We Believe in One God? Reflections on the Trinity in the Malaysian Context*. Delhi: ISPCK, 2002.

Wiking, Göran. *Breaking the Pot: Contextual Responses to Survival Issues in Malaysian Churches*. SMS 96. Lund: Swedish Institute of Missionary Research, 2004.

"World Watch List." Open Doors. Accessed 25 November 2018, https://www.opendoorsusa.org/christian-persecution/world-watch-list/.

Wright, Christopher J. H. *The Mission of God: Unlocking the Bible's Grand Narrative*. Downers Grove: InterVarsity Press, 2006.

———. *The Mission of God's People: A Biblical Theology of the Church's Mission*. Grand Rapids: Zondervan, 2010.

Yewangoe, A. A. *Theologia Crucis in Asia: Asian Christian Views on Suffering in the Face of Overwhelming Poverty and Multifaceted Religiosity in Asia*. Amsterdam: Rodopi, 1987.

10

Cultural Identity and Theology in Asia

Lalsangkima Pachuau
Asbury Theological Seminary

While there are several pockets in Asia where communities are dominantly Christian, Asia as a whole is the only continent in the world where Christianity is a minority religion. Asia's greatest distinction among the world's continents is the religiosity of the people and their strong cultural traditions. Most Asians are deeply rooted in each of their own cultural traditions and religions. Unsurprisingly, the majority of today's living religions including Christianity are Asian-born. While other living religions of Asia remain firmly Asian, Christianity seems to have lost its grip on its birth culture of Asia. Many Asians view Christianity as foreign to their cultures and traditions, as illustrated by Indian historian K. M. Panikkar. In his 1953 book, Panikkar declared, "in spite of the immense and sustained effort made by the churches . . . of the European countries and America, the attempt to conquer Asia for Christ has definitely failed."[1] He blamed the foreignness of Christian teachings and its imperialistic attitude to Asians as the main factors. Developments between the early 1950s when the book was written and today have cast serious doubts on Panikkar's statement. Yet Christianity's stance in relation to the firmly held traditions of Asia is as critical a question as it was decades ago. In this essay, we will explore Christianity's relation to Asian cultures and consider what it is called to be theologically.

---

1. K. M. Panikkar, *Asia and Western Dominance: A Survey of the Vasco Da Gama Epoch of Asian History, 1498–1945* (London: George Allen & Unwin, 1953), 454.

Asian Religiosity, Cultural Traditions, and Christian Faith

If we are to identify some important distinctive features of Asia, the religiosity of the people and the grip of cultural traditions on their lives would be one of the top distinctions. Europeans were quick to learn of the firm hold Asian cultural and religious traditions had on the Asian people when they first came into contact with them. Pioneer Jesuit (Society of Jesus) missionaries such as Francis Xavier in Japan, Matteo Ricci in China, Alexandre de Rhodes in Vietnam, and Roberto de Nobili in India clearly made changes in their missionary approaches when they realized the sturdiness of the cultural traditions of the Asians they encountered. They all came to adapt Christianity to the local traditions, and some accommodated aspects of the traditions within the Christian understanding and teaching. Though there were differences in emphases among them, the Jesuits came to be known for their adaptation and accommodation of cultural practices within Christianity especially after the papal visitor Alexandro Valignano. The Jesuit missionaries who embraced accommodation of certain Asian religious and cultural practices were soon opposed by other Christian missionaries and church leaders. What came to be called the "rites controversy," which lasted more than a century, exemplified this conflict.[2] The controversy also contributed to the suppression of the Society of Jesus in 1773 until the restoration in 1814.

The British later became the most successful colonizers of Asian countries among the Europeans. Arguably, one reason for their success in the early years was their consciousness of the religions and cultures of the people. For instance, the British East India Company did not permit Christian missionaries to work in its colonies for fear of disturbing the cultural and religious sentiments of the people. That policy impacted the subsequent history quite significantly. Had it not been for that policy, William Carey and his friends would not have had to establish their center in the Danish colony of Serampore in Bengal. They could have worked in the city of Calcutta. Had it not been for that policy through which Adoniram Judson and his company were driven out of Calcutta, they may not have gone to Burma to establish a long-lasting missionary work there. This, however, is not to say that Western colonialists were respectful of the cultural traditions of Asia. In fact, quite the opposite. The policy was a strategy of the company to colonize the people effectively only to achieve its

---

2. On the advocation of accommodation by Matteo Ricci and Roberto de Nobili in their own words, see Klaus Koschorke, Frieder Ludwig, and Mariano Delgado, eds., *A History of Christianity in Asia, Africa, Latin America, 1450–1990: A Documentary Sourcebook* (Grand Rapids: Eerdmans, 2007), 33–38.

vested interests. Western political and cultural systems entered Asia through imperialism and clashed with the cultures and religions of Asians; and the fault lines they created between Western and Asian cultures impacted Asian Christian identity enormously.

A common tale among early generations of Asian Christian converts is of a struggle to reconcile their newfound faith with their cultural traditions. Depending on how they relate Christian faith to their cultures, Christians come to reconcile their faith with their social and cultural lives differently. Such a reconciliation always involves a degree of change to and continuity of their indigenous cultures. In some cases, thoughtful converts soon realize the importance of the culture they felt they were abandoning and return. Some never accept that they have abandoned their culture, yet the new faith does change their culture. Many pass through different stages to come to their reconciling point. Others who may have thought that they had abandoned their cultures were, in actuality, operating thoroughly within their cultures without realizing it. The stories of two individuals who experienced radical conversion to Christianity illustrate the differences and similarities of converts' journeys. These are the stories of Yisu Das Tiwari (1920–1987) of India and John Sung (1901–1944) of China. The stories of each of these men are especially illustrative when we contrast them with the story of another of their fellow countrymen.

Prompted by the reading of the book *Christ in the Silence*, Yisu Das felt the need to pray in Christ's name. As a Hindu Brahmin, he first resisted the idea but eventually prayed, saying, "O Lord, if you are a living Lord, save me from my sins. Save me from myself." Then, "[a]t once there is a gracious Personality by my side on whom I may repose my feverish head, one who is closer than the closest friend,"[3] he declared. Despite the fact that Yisu Das was banished from his home after his baptism, he continued associating with Hindus and later recalled his thought. "When I decided to be baptized, I did not think that I was 'leaving' Hindu society. I thought I was adding something new; something glorious to my Hindu heritage . . . Soon, I discovered this was not possible . . . [M]y own family shut the door, literally, on my face. I was driven out."[4] While he struggled with integration into Christian community, his faith in Jesus Christ never wavered. "I became a Christian because of my faith in the person of Christ. Him I regarded as my Saviour. He had the devotion of my heart and the obedience of my will."[5] Asked before his death, sixty-

---

3. Ravi Tiwari, *Yisu Das: Witness of a Convert*, (Delhi: ISPCK, 2000), 4.

4. Tiwari, *Yisu Das*, 5–6.

5. Quoted in Ravi Tiwari, *Reflections and Studies in Religion* (Delhi: ISPCK, 2008), 178.

four years after his conversion and baptism, if he would "still take the same course," Yisu Das replied, "Christ is my 'ishta,' he has never left me, I will never leave him, but I would have not joined the Christian community; I would have lived with my people and my community and been a witness to them."[6] Yisu Das understood the hardness of such a witness among caste Hindus in general, and Brahmins in particular. As illustrated by the life story of another Indian convert, a lowly outcaste by the name of Ditt, whose refusal to leave his community after conversion led to the mass conversion of his Chuhra people,[7] such a witness to one's own people was relatively easier in low caste or outcaste communities. Today, almost three-quarters of Indian Christians are of outcaste or non-caste origins. The sacrifices of persons like Ditt are often overlooked in the story.

John Sung, from Fujian province in China, was, in the words of John T. Seamands, "one of the most colorful and effective evangelists of the Christian Church in China" in the twentieth century.[8] Somewhat close to a child prodigy, John Sung topped his high school class, then went to the United States of America for college at the age of nineteen.[9] Recognizing his academic excellence, the faculty of Ohio Wesleyan University permitted him to complete his college degree in three years instead of the normal four. In another three years, he also completed his PhD in Chemistry at Ohio State University. Rather than practicing or teaching science, he went to study theology at Union Theological Seminary, New York, where he experienced a major faith crisis and a nervous breakdown. He had experienced a profound conversion as a child during the Hinghwa Revival, and in New York, he experienced a sort of second rebirth leading him to some strange expressions of his faith. His outspoken and judgmental way of expressing his faith, his strange behavior of singing, weeping, and preaching, and the "other bizarre things" he did led the leadership at Union to admit him to a mental hospital, where he was kept more than six months.[10] Once discharged from the hospital at the intervention of the Chinese Consulate, Sung headed back to China and began his evangelistic ministry. Remarkably, he tossed his academic diplomas in the sea before reaching China.

---

6. "An Interview," in Tiwari, *Yisu Das*, 24.

7. On the story of Ditt and the Chuhra mass movement, see J. Waskom Pickett, *Christian Mass Movements in India* (Lucknow: Lucknow Publishing, 1933), 22–23, 42–45; John C. B. Webster, *The Dalit Christians: A History*, rev. and enlarged ed. (Delhi: ISPCK, 2009), 56–63.

8. John T. Seamands, *Pioneers of the Younger Churches* (Nashville: Abingdon, 1967), 83.

9. For a detailed study of John Sung, see Lim Ka-Tong, *The Life and Ministry of John Sung* (Singapore: Genesis Books, 2012). The brief account provided here is drawn from the pages of this book.

10. Ka-Tong, *Life and Ministry*, 66–67.

A fiery preacher at home comfortable in the Chinese folk culture and convinced of modernism's threat to Christianity in China, Sung appealed most to the popular Christians and lay people. Before dying at the young age of forty-three, he ministered publicly for twelve years, during which time he touched many lives. At the heart of his message was a call to radical discipleship and vital spirituality. He was shunned many times by pastors and church leaders for his blazing message and confrontational style of engagement. Sung's style represented an indigenous evangelism of grassroots-level Chinese Christianity. It took him a few years to relearn Chinese culture after he came back to China. He described the change between his times in America and China as his transition from being "modernized" to "indigenized." Often despised as a "country bumpkin," he wore simple indigenous clothes and communicated his message clearly in indigenous terms.[11] Sung has been criticized for his "other-worldly" message which was not necessarily foreign to the Chinese popular culture. His message reached and touched millions of Chinese people in both China and the surrounding nations. As Lim Ka-Tong has persuasively argued, Sung's message was contextual while not compromising to the demands of the modernizing impulse. "Contextualization in the Chinese soil cannot be done purely at the level of elite culture. Contextualization happens when a vibrant faith that requires nothing less than radical discipleship touches the mind as well as the heart [of the people]. John Sung portrayed this in his short life and ministry,"[12] Lim concluded.

If one compares John Sung's way of indigenizing Christianity with that of another famous Christian thinker and leader in China, Bishop K. H. Ting, one sees a very different approach to indigenization. Bishop Ting's commitment to serve the Chinese church is undoubted. While he was serving in Geneva with the World Students' Christian Federation, China became communist. The new China expelled missionaries and persecuted Christians. Against the tide and the advice of his colleagues and friends, Ting returned to China to serve the church and the nation. Quite opposite to Sung's ministry approach, Ting ministered through political authority and power to make Christianity Chinese. He devoted his life to drawing together Christianity and Chinese identity through the communist government. By his retirement in 1996, to quote his biographer Philip Wickeri, "Ting [had] become the most significant voice in China for the interests of the church, making use of his important

---

11. Ka-Tong, 113.
12. Ka-Tong, 278–279.

government position and personal prestige to enhance religious freedom and give attention to reforming church structures."[13]

Progressive liberals typically take a critical stance against oppressive state powers for the sake of Christ's liberation of the people in other parts of the world. Characteristically, liberalism generally embraces liberation theology. But in China, by siding with the state's authority, liberal theologians opposed Western Christianity to claim its indigeneity, and, consequently, worked against the liberation of the people from oppression. This phenomenon not only complicates how the Three-Self Church partners with other churches outside China, it also defies its theological liberalism.

Major Asian Cultural and Religious Traditions

Most living religions of today originated in Asia. At the risk of oversimplifying the very complex religious systems of Asia, I will make some regional simplification just for the purposes of the present discussion. By dividing the entire continent of Asia into East, West, and South, we may broadly differentiate the origins of the religions into these regions. West Asia (called the "Middle East" by people in America and Europe) has what some have broadly categorized as the "Abrahamic religions" of Judaism, Christianity, and Islam. Of course, Christianity has become a small minority religion in the land of its origin. In South Asia originated what we may broadly call the *Dharmic* religions of Hinduism, Buddhism, Jainism, and other amalgamated ones. East Asia has the harmonizing religious philosophies of Confucianism, Daoism, and the spiritually embedded Shintoism and Shamanism. Akin to Shamanism are a variety of primal and indigenous religions which spread throughout Asia and beyond. Because our purpose is to relate Christianity with the religious and cultural traditions of Asia, I will limit the scope to the religions of South and East Asia.

In each of these religious groups, there are important commonalities and significant differences. In some cases, such as Hinduism and Buddhism, the neighboring religion within the category may provide an opposing alternative religious teaching while sharing strong common presuppositions and worldviews. In other cases, the provided ways are just very similar, such as the *Tao* (or *Dao*) of Taoism and *Dharma* of Hinduism and Buddhism. Here we will briefly highlight broad viewpoints of major religious systems of South

---

13. Philip L. Wickeri, *Reconstructing Christianity in China: K. H. Ting and the Chinese Church* (Maryknoll: Orbis Books, 2007), 3.

and East Asia to provide comparative traditions for Christianity. We should highlight one common viewpoint which has influenced our approach here, namely the relationship between religion and culture. Unlike contemporary Christianity, which commonly differentiates culture from religion, these Asian religions largely treat culture and faith as a unity. Therefore, any attempt to deal with cultures and cultural traditions cannot avoid dealing with the religions.

With no common doctrine or exclusive authoritative scripture, Hinduism is a difficult religion to define. An amalgam of a variety of traditions accumulated over centuries, it is often difficult to determine what Hinduism includes and excludes. While the diverse beliefs and practices may not identify a Hindu, as K. M. Sen has rightly noted, Hinduism does have certain common "religious assumptions," as it is governed by certain "modes of conduct" and "behaviour."[14] Hindus are thus defined more by the structure of their faith and conduct than by the content of their beliefs.

Deeply embedded in the belief that they are in a cycle of birth and death (*samsara*), Hindus live their lives governed by *karma* (cause and effect between actions in the present life and status in the next life) and driven by *dharma* (living according to one's identity). At the heart of the social structure is *dharma*, the natural and universal order of being which one ought to follow. There are two sets of social obligations which govern a Hindu's life. One is caste (or *varna*) obligation, and the other is how one ought to live at different stages of life (*asrama*). This is essentially how Hinduism is practiced and is often called *varnasramadharma* (the *dharma* of *varna* and *asrama*). In practice, *dharma* is often translated as "duty" (what one ought to do in being one) and is closely associated with the *karmic* law of cause and effect in the cycle of death and rebirth. Living as one ought to live (faithful to one's *dharma*) leads one to a better or higher life (higher caste) in the next birth. Consequently, to disobey one's *dharma* is believed to result in rebirth in a lower caste or as an animal. Functionally, Hinduism is a religious or social system that classifies every person into hierarchically defined caste and generational identities. The system somewhat harmonizes society by finding a place for each and insisting on enforcing that order.

Much of the Hindu worldview and structural elements are shared by Buddhism, Jainism, and Sikhism. While Sikhism differs in its monotheistic faith, Buddhism goes the opposite way in a nontheistic direction. In the history of Hindu philosophy, Buddhism and Jainism are listed among the heterodox philosophies. Sharing many of its structural beliefs with Hinduism, Buddhist

---

14. K. M. Sen, *Hinduism* (London: Penguin, 1961), 15.

teaching is built on the importance of suffering and desire in the cycle of death and rebirth (*samsara*). Liberation from endless suffering can be obtained by following the eightfold path, a combination of moral living, meditation, and wisdom. If the way of doing what is right leads to better lives in the next birth, meditation toward achieving enlightenment is the way of liberation. The three major schools of Buddhism – *Theravada* (mostly in South-Southeast Asia: Sri Lanka, and Myanmar to Cambodia), *Mahayana* (China, Japan, Korea), and *Vajrayana* (Tibet and Mongolia)[15] – differ in many respects, yet their core teaching is the same. If the Hindu *dharma* has to do with the social structure of caste and generational hierarchies, the Buddha-*dharma* opposes such hierarchy by teaching the universal "truth" of existential suffering and how to overcome it through the prescribed eightfold path. Be it the well-developed Mahayana *Bodhisattva* (helper in the spiritual path) or the Engaged Buddhism of the Dalai Lama, the basic eightfold path remains. So focused on human effort to overcome the conditioned existence, Buddhism does not really bother much about God. If not atheistic, it is largely nontheistic as some Buddhists claim. The social structure of Buddhism rests on mutual supports among the monastic (the Sangha), political leadership, and the society. Even though the Buddha strongly opposed the caste hierarchy of Hinduism, Buddhism does construct a new spiritual hierarchy between lay people and the monastics.[16]

The two Chinese religious philosophies, Taoism (or Daoism) and Confucianism, are most often discussed as a pair. The entry on "Daoism" in the online *Encyclopedia Britannica* begins with a comparison with Confucianism: "In the broadest sense, a Daoist attitude toward life can be seen in the accepting and yielding, the joyful and carefree sides of the Chinese character, an attitude that offsets and complements the moral and duty-conscious, austere and purposeful character ascribed to Confucianism."[17] Even as they provide very different – in some respects opposing – solutions, the two philosophical religions seek to answer the same riddle of human life, namely how human beings can be their best, especially in relation to other people and creatures. At the heart of the quest is communal harmony in the interests of the society. Scholars have differentiated the Taoist philosophy (Tao Chia) of the classic text

---

15. On the three schools, see Terry Muck, "Buddhism: History, Belief, Practices," in *Handbook of Religion: A Christian Engagement with Traditions, Teachings, and Practices*, ed. Terry C. Muck, Harold A. Netland, and Gerald R. McDermott (Grand Rapids: Baker Academic, 2014), 84.

16. Muck, "Buddhism," 85.

17. Anna K. Seidel, Michel Strickmann, and Roger T. Ames, "Daoism: Chinese Philosophy and Religion," *Encyclopaedia Britannica*, accessed 5 March 2018, https://www.britannica.com/topic/Daoism.

Tao Te Ching by the sage Lao Tzu, from the Taoist religion (Tao Chiao), which seeks immortality.[18] While Taoism as a religion has declined considerably, especially after communism, its influence remains strong. In fact, its popularity has risen in recent years through martial arts (*kung-fu*), "self-exercise and therapy" (*Ch'i-kung*).[19] The Tao which Taoists believe underlies the universe is an impersonal energy or spiritual principle. Through the Tao, harmony is sought with the environment and the world by aligning one's true essence with the nature of the universe. Taoism is mystical and unorganized as a religion.

Confucianism, on the other hand, is highly organized and seeks harmony through well-defined relationships. In very simple terms, Confucianism holds that by empathy and understanding others, people gain a sense of righteousness and produce a harmonious society. One expert defines Confucianism as a "faith in the creative transformation of our human condition as a communal act and as a dialogical response to Heaven. This involves the integration of four dimensions of humanity: self, community, nature, and Heaven."[20] The "five relationships"[21] of Confucianism as taught by an early teacher, Mencius, show a hierarchical structure of duty and relationships for the division of labor. Four of the five relationships, namely father–son, ruler–minister, husband–wife, and old–young, show relationship obligations between superior and subordinate. Only the fifth, which is friend–friend, shows equal relationship. Filial piety, related to the first relationship, is considered "the first step to moral excellence," and a core value in Confucianism.[22] Mutuality is sought even in the hierarchically ordered relationships.

All these religious and cultural traditions of East and South Asia exemplify the diverse and rich traditions of Asia. They also show how different they are from the Abrahamic monotheistic faith originating from Western Asia in general and Christianity in particular. Religious scholars have characterized these two groups of religions variously as "mystic religions" (South and East Asian religions) and "prophetic religions" (Abrahamic faith). For theological purposes, Asian theologian M. M. Thomas categorized the two groups as "Unitive" religions and "Messianic" religions. He explained as follows: "The broad division is between the Judaeo-Christian-Islamic traditions which take

---

18. Liu Xiaogan, "Taoism," in *Our Religions*, ed. Arvind Sharma (New York: HarperCollins, 1993), 234–235.

19. Xiaogan, "Taoism," 237.

20. Tu Wei-ming, "Confucianism," in *Our Religions*, ed. Arvind Sharma (New York: HarperCollins, 1993), 142.

21. Wei-ming, "Confucianism," 186–193.

22. Wei-ming, 186.

history as the fundamental sphere of the self-revelation and saving action of God, and the other religious traditions of African, Indian and Chinese origins which see salvation in the enduring vision of an undifferentiated spiritual unity or harmony of nature, man, spirits, and gods."[23] As described above, Asian religions prioritize unity and seek the harmony of human beings and creation. Christianity, on the other hand, believes in the supreme and gracious God whose will it seeks to follow and on whose covenant it depends. Perhaps the most contrasting aspect of Christian faith in comparison with other Asian religions is its insistence on being saved by God by being converted to him. Christians believe that human beings cannot do anything to accomplish their salvation, that God has acted graciously through his Son Jesus Christ, and that they can live as his people with the help of God's Spirit. Conceptually, the conversion of human beings as a result of God's work of salvation is a very foreign concept for most Asian religions. Yet this is at the heart of the Christian faith with which we seek to relate the cultural traditions of Asia.

Contextual Theologies and Indigenous Practices of Faith

In their differing stances and experiences, Asian Christians commonly recognize the significance of their culture in relation to their faith. While there have been some serious efforts to indigenize theology in religio-cultural contexts, there has also been natural indigenization, in which Christians do not even recognize what they are doing. In contexts where Christians have become the majority or significant minority of the population, such natural indigenization seems to have occurred intuitively. In areas where Christians are a small minority, concerted efforts are often needed to indigenize the faith. In her study on the work of the University Bible Fellowship (UBF) in the USA, South Korea's largest nondenominational mission organization, Rebecca Kim identified some distinct characteristics of the UBF, such as a strong hierarchy and a commitment to disciplined and active work, which she said reflected the influence of Confucianism.[24] Until they are exposed to a different cultural context, Korean Christians may not recognize the deep influence Confucianism has on their Christianity. I have also reflected on the Christianity of my own community, the Mizo Christian community, and found that a great deal of our

---

23. M. M. Thomas, *Man and the Universe of Faiths* (Madras: CLS, 1975), 33–34.
24. Rebecca Y. Kim, *The Spirit Moves West: Korean Missionaries in America* (Oxford: Oxford University Press, 2015), 45.

traditional worldviews have flowed into our Christian thoughts and impacted the underlying theology of the people.[25]

Following efforts to indigenize Christianity, indigenous theologies have also been in the making in several regions where Christians are in the minority, such as India and Japan. We may mention some early attempts by Indian Christians to indigenize Christian faith,[26] among which are the works of Brahmabandhab Padhyaya, Sandhu Sundar Singh, and A. J. Appasamy. Upadhyaya interpreted Christ as *Chit* and the Trinity as *Saccitananda* using the Hindu Vedantic expression of the Supreme Being.[27] Sadhu Sundar Singh advocated reception of Christ's water of life in an Indian cup, a symbol of his desire to make Christianity Indian. A. J. Appasamy attempted to interpret Christianity in terms of the Hindu religious way of devotion called *Bhakti marga*. The struggles to birth new indigenous theologies were difficult. A critical observation of Japanese Christian students by a German scholar in the mid-1930s is revealing:

> The [Japanese] students certainly study our European books with dedication, and thanks to their intelligence, they understand them; but they fail to draw any consequences from them for their own Japanese identity. . . . They live on two stories, as it were: a lower, fundamental one, in which they feel and think in the Japanese manner, and an upper one, in which they line up with European knowledge from Plato to Heidegger, and the European teacher wonders: Where is the staircase, to take them from one to the other?[28]

Even if there were no obvious staircases, early Japanese scholars did find narrow passageways to connect the two stories in some ways. Among several examples are Danjo Ebina (1866–1937) and Kanzo Uchimura. Ebina employed *Fushi Ushin*, one of the five basic moral precepts of Confucianism, using the father–son relationship as a way of expressing relation with God.[29]

---

25. See Lalsangkima Pachuau, "Mizo '*Sakhua*' in Transition," *Missiology: An International Review* 34, no. 1 (January 2006): 41–57.

26. See M. M. Thomas, *The Acknowledged Christ of the Indian Renaissance* (London: SCM, 1969); Robin Boyd, *An Introduction to Indian Christian Theology*, rev. ed. (Madras: CLS, 1975).

27. On Upadhyaya's work, see Timothy Tennent, *Building Christianity on Indian Foundations: The Legacy of Brahmabāndhav Upādhyāy* (Delhi: ISPCK, 2000).

28. These are the words of Karl Löwith who taught for five years in Japan from 1936, quoted with translation by Yasuo Furuya, "Introduction," in *A History of Japanese Theology*, ed. Yasuo Furuya (Grand Rapids: Eerdmans, 1997), 4–5.

29. Yasuo Furuya, ed., *A History of Japanese Theology* (Grand Rapids: Eerdmans, 1997), 14.

Kanzo Uchimura connected Christian ethics with Confucian morality and founded the "Non-church" movement to suit the Japanese worldview.[30] On the Catholic side, we see similar development after Vatican II in the 1960s. The Catholics' preferred term is "inculturation," which was employed in both liturgical renewal and theology by Indian scholars like D. S. Amalorpavadass.[31] Indigenization progressed in postcolonial Asia when Christianity came to be challenged by various social and national revolutions. Out of that development came a new chapter under the rubric of "contextualization."

It was the Asian leaders of the newly reenergized Theological Education Fund (TEF) who conceptualized and propounded the new concept called contextualization in the early 1970s. The name itself was ridiculed at first by some,[32] and the idea did not easily gain acceptance in some quarters as some versions seemed too radical. But today, the concept is widely accepted. Taiwanese theologian Shoki Coe, then the director of the TEF, initiated and championed the concept by introducing it as a decadal theme of the TEF in 1972. He said the intention was "to convey all that is implied in the familiar term *indigenization*, yet seek to press beyond for a more dynamic concept which is open to change and which is also future-oriented."[33] Indigenization, he said, is a "missiological necessity" and should not be abandoned. Yet indigenization "tends to be used in the sense of responding to the Gospel in terms of traditional culture. Therefore, it is in danger of being past-oriented."[34] With "the new phenomenon of radical change" the context had changed and a new concept was needed. "The new context is not that of static culture, but the search for the new, which at the same time has involved culture itself,"[35] for which the concept of contextualization was introduced.

Today, contextualization has been used in more than one way. Some use it exclusively in connection with cross-cultural communication of the gospel, close to the meaning of indigenization. Others connect it mostly to theology in reference to a broad variety of contextual theologies, among which are some

---

30. Furuya, *History*, 18–19.

31. See D. S. Amalorpavadass, *Gospel and Culture: Evangelization and Inculturation* (Bangalore: National Biblical Catechetical and Liturgical Centre, 1985).

32. For instance, the English missionary-historian Stephen Neill once called contextualization one of "the worst ecumenical barbarisms by which the English language has of late been debased." Stephen Neill, *Salvation Tomorrow: The Originality of Jesus Christ and the World's Religions* (Nashville: Abingdon, 1976), 109n5.

33. Shoki Coe, "In Search of Renewal in Theological Education," *Theological Education* 9, no. 4 (Summer 1973): 241.

34. Coe, "In Search of Renewal," 240.

35. Coe, 240.

who limit it to liberation theologies. Broadly speaking, contextualization of the gospel is about reading the Bible and the gospel in a context and constructing contextual theology which takes into serious consideration the social and cultural contexts.

Recognizing that numerous contextual theologies have already been developed in Asia, we reiterate the question of how best to relate the gospel to religious and cultural traditions. In some ways, the question has been newly asked in evangelical communities during the past few decades as evangelical scholars have come to accept contextualization as a theological challenge.[36] Progressive ecumenist theologians have produced numerous works on Asian theology, and Asia may have one of the richest bodies of theological works in the non-Western world. From the Christ-centered syncretistic theology of M. M. Thomas of India to the culturally insightful and symbolically rich theology of Kosuke Koyama of Japan[37] and the fiercely anti-Western "transpositional" theology of C. S. Song of Taiwan,[38] progressive theologians have developed Asian theology in conversation with Asian social and political movements. In the large three-volume *Asian Christian Theologies*, the development of these theologies to the early twenty-first century has been profiled and documented quite thoroughly.[39] The target contexts of the progressives have largely been sociopolitical impact and religious plurality, and, correspondingly, they have produced enormous works on liberation and interreligious theologies. Creative theologies for the liberation of the poor and marginalized have been constructed under such rubrics as *minjung, dalit*, tribal, indigenous, as well as various feminist theologies. While the intents are for the people, this body of work has largely been secluded from the spiritual and ecclesial disposition of the laity and popular Christianity.[40] In recent years, we have seen more collaboration with Pentecostal and evangelical Christians.

---

36. One of the earliest and most comprehensive efforts from an evangelical perspective in conversation with progressive liberal thinkers of Asia is Hwa Yung's *Mangoes or Bananas? The Quest for an Authentic Asian Christian Theology* (Oxford: Regnum, 1997).

37. See, for instance, Kosuke Koyama, *Water Buffalo Theology*, rev. ed. (Maryknoll: Orbis Books, 1999).

38. See Choan-Seng Song, *The Compassionate God* (Maryknoll: Orbis Books, 1982).

39. John C. England et al., eds., *Asian Christian Theologies*, 3 vols. (Maryknoll: Orbis Books, 2002–2004).

40. For an attempt to construct an Asian grassroots theology, see Simon Chan, *Grassroots Asian Theology: Thinking the Faith from the Ground Up* (Downers Grove: InterVarsity Press, 2014).

An Evangelical Theology of Culture for Asia

Insisting on the primacy of the Scriptures over human experience or systems, evangelical Christians used to have a tendency to withdraw from cultural studies. William Dyrness has vividly captured evangelicals' reputation on the issue: "Throughout their history evangelicals have displayed ambivalence toward their cultural context. The world was something to be won over in the name of Christ, or to be avoided as a source of temptation, but it could also represent a resource to be exploited in pursuit of their evangelical calling."[41] Through the influence of missionary Bible translators and anthropological missiologists, evangelical Christian scholars and institutions have become open to interacting with social and cultural traditions. The Lausanne Movement has also highlighted the importance of the relationship between the gospel and culture since the late 1970s. The Lausanne Committee organized a consultation on Gospel and Culture in January 1978 and produced a rich document called the Willowbank Report.[42] Later that year, *Evangelical Missions Quarterly* dedicated an entire volume to "contextualization."[43] These two marked a major turning point in evangelical theology and set a new agenda. The approach to contextualization in these writings emphasizes culture's importance for the communication of the gospel and is less concerned with social change, reflecting the common usage of the concept among evangelicals especially in the West. Some Asian evangelicals, together with their compatriots in other non-Western nations, started important initiatives in the Lausanne Movement and beyond by embracing social and cultural factors in interpreting the gospel.[44]

During the past few decades, we have seen scores of discussions on contextualization and contextual theologies in evangelical and adjoining circles. One of the best acknowledged and most helpful studies is *Models of Contextual Theology* by Stephen Bevans. Bevans locates various models according to their proximity either to "faith experience" as recorded in Scripture and preserved in Christian traditions or to "experience of the present . . . context" of culture

---

41. William A. Dyrness, "Evangelical Theology and Culture," in *The Cambridge Companion to Evangelical Theology*, ed. Timothy Larsen and Daniel J. Treier (Cambridge: Cambridge University Press, 2007), 145.

42. See John Stott and Robert T. Coote, eds., *Down to Earth: Studies in Christianity and Culture* (London: Hodder & Stoughton, 1981).

43. *Evangelical Missions Quarterly* 54, no. 1 (Jan–Mar 1978). The issue is available online at MissioNexus, accessed 16 March 2018, https://missionexus.org/category/emq/emq-volumes/volume-14-issue-1/.

44. See Vinay Samuel and Chris Sugden, eds., *Sharing Jesus in the Two Thirds World: Evangelical Christologues from the Contexts of Poverty* (Bangalore: Partnership in Mission-Asia, 1983).

and social lives.[45] The closer a model hews to the present cultural context, the further it is from Scripture and tradition.[46] As a way of locating different plausible theological stances, this is a very helpful work. Yet, as Bevans himself insists, none of the models needs to be exclusive. While most open-minded evangelicals may identify themselves under the Synthetic or Translation models, they do relate to aspects of other models such as Anthropological and Praxis. For our purposes, what is important is how we understand human culture and society from a scriptural and theological viewpoint, and how we view God's call on them. In what follows, I will make a theological case for what I call a transformational theology of culture.

Bevans's work is particularly helpful in laying out the different ways by which Scripture and Christian traditions have been related to human cultures and social lives in recent years. It is an empirical observation regarding how various scholars have related Scripture and accompanying church tradition to existential culture and social lives. It does not pretend to be a theology of culture, and does not deal with the theological call to human culture and society.

Yet what *do* Scripture and Christian tradition say that God wants human culture and society to be? In responding to this question, we operate on the assumption that culture is intrinsically related to human beings. Societies and cultures are extensions of human living. Asian theologian Carver Yu made a good theological observation on culture: "humanity does not live *in* culture, but its very being is actualized and concretized as culture. Insofar as humanity is a gift from God, culture is also a gift from God."[47] The fall of humanity into sin is the fall of culture too. "In the face of the reality of sin," Yu further observes, "all cultures, including those deeply touched by the Christian gospel and even those which claim to be Christian cultures, are mixtures of what is reminiscent of God's promise, God's preserving grace and human distortion."[48] Consequently, what God does salvifically for human beings is what he does for human culture and society. What he calls humanity to be is also what he expects culture to be. God's work of redemption aims at restoring human beings, including their structure of existence, to his image.

---

45. Stephen B. Bevans, *Models of Contextual Theology*, rev. and expanded ed. (Maryknoll: Orbis Books, 2002), 5.

46. Bevans, *Models of Contextual Theology*, 32. The models are Anthropological, Transcendental, Praxis, Synthetic, Translation, and Countercultural.

47. Carver T. Yu, "Culture from an Evangelical Perspective," in *Christianity and Cultures: Shaping Christian Thinking in Context*, eds. David Emmanuel Singh and Bernard C. Farr (Oxford: Regnum, 2008), 7.

48. Yu, "Culture from an Evangelical Perspective," 9–10.

I contend that God's call to be born anew, that is, to be converted to him, and his offer of salvation in Christ are directed not only to human beings as individuals, but to entire human communities and their structures of existence, that is, their social and cultural traditions. Here an old theological adage may be restated for our purposes: God acts in his Son in the power of the Holy Spirit to redeem and reconcile the world to himself, and he calls the entirety of humanity to turn back to him and to live in covenantal relationship with him. By his redemptive and reconciling work in Christ, God is calling the entirety of humanity, together with their structures of existence (society) and ways of living (culture), back to his image. Through his gracious act of redemption in Jesus Christ, God has made it clear that he wants to bring human beings to be united to him, to transform them into his likeness, and to enable them to witness to him and his glory. In Jesus Christ, God not only acted to save the world, but also modeled the way of saving the world in his self-emptying incarnation. God's offer of covenantal relationship and his call for humankind to live with, in, and for him is also his call to the culture and society of every human group. God's call to humanity is to turn to him and be transformed into his likeness. That is what God calls culture to be.

As mentioned before, much of the non-Abrahamic Asian traditional religions we have discussed seek harmony among human beings and harmony with surroundings. The communal and generational harmony sought in Hinduism produces a social and generational hierarchy. Confucian harmony is built on familial and social hierarchy. Alignment with *dharma* in Hinduism or *Tao* in Taoism are the ways to communal and environmental harmony. The Confucians pragmatically seek such through the relational integration of the self, community, nature, and heaven, while the Buddhists strive for true liberation by following the path of morality, meditation, and wisdom.

Christianity, on the other hand, believes that God the Creator has intervened in human history in the person of Jesus Christ to save and transform the world to his likeness. None of the religious goals we listed above contradict Christian faith as such. They do not completely oppose God's gracious act of salvation in Jesus Christ, though they do not have it and do not teach it. Many of the cultural practices related to these religious teachings are admirable and good, and they could be excellent ways to express God's image. Yet they are not borne by faith in God, nor do they respond to God's loving act of redemption.

Toward a Transformational Theology of Culture

Our assertion here is for the conversion of human cultures to God. Conversion, broadly speaking, is about change in one's orientation and direction. Biblically, it is a turn or return and re-orientation of life to God (*subh* [return] in Old Testament Hebrew and *metanoia* [repentance] in New Testament Greek).[49] Practically, it also involves both rejection of and continuity with one's life before and after. In her study of New Testament teaching on conversion, Beverly Gaventa categorizes conversion into three types, each of which is found in the New Testament. She calls them "Alternation," which shows a limited form of change; "Pendulum-like Conversion," showing radical change which results in rejection of past affiliations; and "Transformation," where there is a radical change which does not reject the past but reinterprets it.[50] If the conversion of the Ethiopian eunuch as described in Acts 8 is an example of the "Alternation" type, Luke's descriptions of Paul's experience in Acts 9 is a "Pendulum-like conversion." Yet Paul's own descriptions, which we find in bits and pieces in his letters, show the "Transformation" type.[51] The stories we have narrated earlier relate closest to Transformation, which also is the most comprehensive way to describe conversion theologically. The God Paul served before his conversion was the same God to whom he dedicated his entire life after his conversion. His view of God changed radically when he realized that the God he feared had graciously reached out and redeemed him in the person and work of Jesus of Nazareth whom he had been scorning.

The kenotic incarnation as God's way of reaching the world is itself a theological model. The historic Christian faith as articulated by the Chalcedonian Creed of AD 451 pronounced this powerfully when it declared Jesus Christ to be "fully God and fully human." This is perhaps one of the hardest faith statements of Christianity. The incarnated Jesus was not half God and half human, nor was he fully God deceptively appearing in human form. He was both fully God and fully human. The depth by which he identified himself with human beings is the depth by which we are called to identify with the cultures we serve. Never giving up his divinity, he became one of us, fully taking our being into himself. He is, therefore, both a stranger and a native.

---

49. The prophets in the Old Testament persistently called the people of Israel to "return" to their covenantal relationship with God, and Jesus's call to "repent and believe the good news" of the kingdom (Mark 1:15) can be understood similarly.

50. Beverly R. Gaventa, *From Darkness to Light: Aspects of Conversion in the New Testament* (Philadelphia: Fortress, 1986), 8–14.

51. Gaventa, *From Darkness to Light*, 148–149.

As Andrew Walls has persuasively shown, he came to us as a "pilgrim" or stranger as well as an "indigenous" or full-blooded native.[52] The model Christ left us is clear. Our call is both to identify with the cultures of the people and to transform them toward Christlikeness in the power of the Holy Spirit. Carver Yu captures this tension well: "Evangelical theology, by virtue of the fact that it is a theology of the good news, has the task of affirming the world as God would affirm it, as it is. We thus have the task of identifying God's preserving and redeeming grace at work in culture . . . However, in the face of the reality of sin, affirmation is not enough." He proposes a critical affirmation: "To take culture seriously, one cannot avoid the critique of culture."[53]

What can we propose as a way of reaching our people embedded in cultures which are fed by non-Christian religious traditions? In what way can we identify with, and be transformative of, the cultures of Asians which are deeply entrenched in the religious traditions of Hinduism, Buddhism, Taoism, Confucianism, Shintoism, Islam, and others? I conclude with thoughts on what Asian Christians should hold firm in ministering to the religious and cultural traditions of their neighbors. I do this under three categories: cooperation, encounter, and communication.

To Cooperate

The gospel and culture discussions have taught us that the gospel is as much a culture as it is divine. Culture as a meaning-making entity is required if the gospel is to be gospel for any human being. Until it is meaningful to the whole person, the gospel is not fully realized. It is meaningful only in the cultural framework some call "worldview." There is thus only one true and real incarnation, and that is the incarnation of Jesus Christ (John 1:14). Our "ministry of incarnation," then, is an extension of this theological truth, and more a symbol than a reality. There is one fundamental communication of the gospel of God, and that is the communication in Jesus Christ in the power of the Holy Spirit. From this one vertical communication, every other communication of the gospel is pursued horizontally.

The "fully human" dimension of the gospel calls for a full cooperation with cultures by full identification. In other words, every culture provides a

---

52. Andrew Walls, *The Missionary Movement in Christian History* (Maryknoll: Orbis Books, 1996), 7–9.

53. Carver T. Yu, "The Bible and Culture in the Shaping of Asian Theology," in *Christianity and Cultures: Shaping Christian Thinking in Context*, eds. David Emmanuel Singh and Bernard C. Farr (Oxford: Regnum, 2008), 60.

ground where the gospel can be rooted, and cultures are redeemable for God's work and glory. The religious traditions we have described are very different in orientation from Christian faith. But the values and morality they carry can be transformed for the service of Christian faith. In his letter to the Colossians, Paul insists that God was pleased to reconcile all things to himself by making peace through the blood of Jesus in his cross (Col 1:20). Christ is all and in all (Col 3:11).

To Encounter

In their attempt to relate to Asian religious traditions and cultures, progressive liberal theologians in Asia have tended to accept much of Asian traditions and cultures while harshly criticizing Western theologies. Swayed by the emerging spirit of relativism under the rubric of pluralism, a number of theologians have made the case for uncritical acceptance of Asian religious and cultural traditions. The desire to embrace what is indigenous can easily lead one to take the side of the native for the sake of being native. This may be one reason why some theologians embraced communism in China in the name of the Three-Self Patriotic Movement. Hitler's Nazism was also embraced by many Christians, including well-known theological thinkers.

The gospel criticizes all cultures as much as it accepts them as ground in which to root itself. It accepts, condemns, transforms, and uses cultures all at the same time. While we should admit that we can easily misuse the authority of the gospel for our own vested interests, we should also allow the gospel to confront the cultures and traditions of the people to whom we minister. The gospel becomes gospel by converting every thought to Christ and transforming every life to Christlikeness (2 Cor 10:5).

To Communicate

Missionary religions are burdened by the call to communicate their message to others. A religion is missionary when its teachings are addressed to all.[54] The good news that God has acted favorably in his Son for the salvation of the world is a message for all humankind. Those who have heard it are charged to pass that good news on to others (Mark 16:15). The joy of the good news itself compels recipients to pass on the gospel (Rom 10:12–15). Yet in

---

54. See my argument for this point in Lalsangkima Pachuau, "Vulnerability and Empowerment in Crossing Frontiers: A Christian Theology of Mission," *Asbury Journal* 68, no. 2 (2013): 78–94. This article is freely available online.

communicating that good news, Christians have often made it sound like bad news. More than ever, we desperately need communication that is fair and just. Modes of communication that deride or dominate others are not acceptable. Unfortunately, the domineering manner by which Christians often "evangelized" in the past were not evangelical by nature. As a result, the word "evangelical" came to assume negative connotations. What is needed, then, is a gospel-transformed manner of communicating the gospel of transformation. We are called to communicate the gospel justly, fairly, and faithfully, and to bear joyful witness to the transformative power of the good news.

Conclusion

In this chapter, I have argued that new Christians come to reconcile their newfound faith with their cultures one way or another. The process involves change and continuity. In fact, that is what Christians are called to do: to identify with their cultures and to transform them toward Christlikeness. Even in the midst of this transformation, our religious and cultural traditions will continue to characterize the nature and identity of the community. Yet no culture is accepted as it is; every culture – and every life, for that matter – needs conversion to God, transformation toward God-likeness. Thus, even as distinctive cultural traits must persist, Christians must also consciously redirect personal and communal ways of life toward God by centering their lives on the triune God.

References

Amalorpavadass, D. S. *Gospel and Culture: Evangelization and Inculturation.* Bangalore: National Biblical Catechetical and Liturgical Centre, 1985.
Bevans, Stephen B. *Models of Contextual Theology.* Revised and expanded ed. Maryknoll: Orbis Books, 2002.
Boyd, Robin. *An Introduction to Indian Christian Theology.* Rev. ed. Madras: Christian Literature Society, 1975.
Chan, Simon. *Grassroots Asian Theology: Thinking the Faith from the Ground Up.* Downers Grove: InterVarsity Press, 2014.
Coe, Shoki. "In Search of Renewal in Theological Education." *Theological Education* 9, no. 4 (Summer 1973): 233–243.
Dyrness, William A. "Evangelical Theology and Culture." In *The Cambridge Companion to Evangelical Theology*, edited by Timothy Larsen and Daniel J. Treier, 145–159. Cambridge: Cambridge University Press, 2007.

England, John C., Jose Kuttianimattathil, John M. Prior, Lily A. Qunitos, David Suh Kwand-Sun, and Janice Wickeri, eds. *Asian Christian Theologies*. 3 volumes. Maryknoll: Orbis Books, 2002–2004.

Furuya, Yasuo, ed. *A History of Japanese Theology*. Grand Rapids: Eerdmans, 1997.

———. "Introduction." In *A History of Japanese Theology*, edited by Yasuo Furuya, 4–5. Grand Rapids: Eerdmans, 1997.

Gaventa, Beverly R. *From Darkness to Light: Aspects of Conversion in the New Testament*. Philadelphia: Fortress, 1986.

Hwa Yung. *Mangoes or Bananas? The Quest for an Authentic Asian Christian Theology*. Oxford: Regnum, 1997.

Kim, Rebecca Y. *The Spirit Moves West: Korean Missionaries in America*. Oxford: Oxford University Press, 2015.

Koschorke, Klaus, Frieder Ludwig, and Mariano Delgado, eds. *A History of Christianity in Asia, Africa, Latin America, 1450–1990: A Documentary Sourcebook*. Grand Rapids: Eerdmans, 2007.

Koyama, Kosuke. *Water Buffalo Theology*. Rev. ed. Maryknoll: Orbis Books, 1999.

Larsen, Timothy, and Daniel J. Treier, eds. *The Cambridge Companion to Evangelical Theology*. Cambridge: Cambridge University Press, 2007.

Lim, Ka-Tong. *The Life and Ministry of John Sung*. Singapore: Genesis Books, 2012.

Muck, Terry C. "Budhism: History, Belief, Practices." In *Handbook of Religion: A Christian Engagement with Traditions, Teachings, and Practices*, edited by Terry C. Muck, Harold A. Netland, and Gerald R. McDermott, 81–86. Grand Rapids: Baker Academic, 2014.

Muck, Terry C., Harold A. Netland, and Gerald R. McDermott, eds. *Handbook of Religion: A Christian Engagement with Traditions, Teachings, and Practices*. Grand Rapids: Baker Academic, 2014.

Neill, Stephen. *Salvation Tomorrow: The Originality of Jesus Christ and the World's Religions*. Nashville: Abingdon, 1976.

Pachuau, Lalsangkima. "Mizo 'Sakhua' in Transition." *Missiology: An International Review* 34, no. 1 (January 2006): 41–57.

———. "Vulnerability and Empowerment in Crossing Frontiers: A Christian Theology of Mission." *Asbury Journal* 68, no. 2 (2013): 78–94.

Pannikar, K. M. *Asia and Western Dominance: A Survey of the Vasco Da Gama Epoch of Asian History, 1498–1945*. London: George Allen & Unwin, 1953.

Pickett, J. Waskom. *Christian Mass Movements in India*. Lucknow: Lucknow Publishing, 1933.

Samuel, Vinay, and Chris Sugden, eds. *Sharing Jesus in the Two Thirds World: Evangelical Christologies from the Contexts of Poverty, Powerlessness and Religious Pluralism*. Bangalore: Partnership in Mission-Asia, 1983.

Seamands, John T. *Pioneers of the Younger Churches*. Nashville: Abingdon, 1967.

Seidel, Anna K., Michel Strickmann, and Roger T. Ames. "Daoism: Chinese Philosophy and Religion." *Encyclopaedia Britannica* online. Accessed 5 March 2018. https://www.britannica.com/topic/Daoism.

Sen, K. M. *Hinduism*. London: Penguin, 1961.

Sharma, Arvind, ed. *Our Religions*. New York: HarperCollins, 1993.

Singh, David Emmanuel, and Bernard C. Farr, eds. *Christianity and Cultures: Shaping Christian Thinking in Context*. Oxford: Regnum, 2008.

Song, Choan-Seng. *The Compassionate God*. Maryknoll: Orbis Books, 1982.

Stott, John, and Robert T. Coote, eds. *Down to Earth: Studies in Christianity and Culture*. London: Hodder & Stoughton, 1981.

Tennent, Timothy. *Building Christianity on Indian Foundations: The Legacy of Brahmabāndhav Upādhyāy*. Delhi: ISPCK, 2000.

Thomas, M. M. *The Acknowledged Christ of the Indian Renaissance*. London: SCM, 1969.

———. *Man and the Universe of Faiths*. Madras: CLS, 1975.

Tiwari, Ravi. *Reflections and Studies in Religion*. Delhi: ISPCK, 2008.

———. *Yisu Das: Witness of a Convert*. Delhi: ISPCK, 2000.

Walls, Andrew. *The Missionary Movement in Christian History*. Maryknoll: Orbis Books, 1996.

Webster, John C. B. *The Dalit Christians: A History*. Rev. and enlarged ed. Delhi: ISPCK, 2009.

Wei-ming, Tu. "Confucianism." In *Our Religions*, edited by Arvind Sharma, 139–228. New York: HarperCollins, 1993.

Wickeri, Philip L. *Reconstructing Christianity in China: K. H. Ting and the Chinese Church*. Maryknoll: Orbis Books, 2007.

Xiaogan, Liu. "Taoism." In *Our Religions*, edited by Arvind Sharma, 229–289. New York: HaperCollins, 1993.

Yu, Carver T. "The Bible and Culture in the Shaping of Asian Theology." In *Christianity and Cultures: Shaping Christian Thinking in Context*, edited by David Emmanuel Singh, and Bernard C. Farr, 51–62. Oxford: Regnum, 2008.

———. "Culture from an Evangelical Perspective." In *Christianity and Cultures: Shaping Christian Thinking in Context*, edited by David Emmanuel Singh, and Bernard C. Farr, 7–16. Oxford: Regnum, 2008.

11

Jesus and Other Faiths

Ivan Satyavrata

Assembly of God Church of Kolkata

Introduction

Covering one-third of the world's land mass and housing almost two-thirds of the world's population, there is perhaps no region of the world as difficult to describe comprehensively as Asia. The cradle of human civilization with a five-thousand-year history, Asia is a rich mosaic of traditions, cultures, and civilizations. Asia is home to all the living religions of the world, including Judaism, Islam, Christianity, Hinduism, Buddhism, Jainism, Sikhism, Confucianism, Taoism, Shintoism, and Zoroastrianism. The religions of Asia have molded the lives and cultures of Asian people for several millennia and continue to give meaning and direction to their lives even today.

Although Asia was the original cradle of the Christian movement, and despite Christianity's being rooted in Asia long before it gained ground in the West, Christianity accounts for less than 10 percent of Asia's teeming millions. Amidst strongly entrenched ancient religious traditions like Hinduism, Buddhism, Confucianism, and Taoism, the church is identified as a foreign presence and viewed with suspicion as a left-over vestige from the colonial era in many parts of Asia. Furthermore, globalization has brought about a mingling of peoples and cultures without parallel in the history of civilization, giving rise to the twin phenomena of multiculturalism and religious plurality.[1] This has intensified the experience of cultural and religious plurality, especially in the urban societies of Asia. A key factor in Christianity's relatively weak

---

1. Harold Netland, *Encountering Religious Pluralism* (Downers Grove: InterVarsity Press, 2001), 9–15.

impact in Asia is its failure to engage the developed cultures and religions of Asia with adequate depth.

Christian Faith and Religions in Conflict

Religious plurality has been an integral part of life within the human community since time immemorial, and while the church has had to address this fact since its inception, the issue today is fraught with critical existential and sociopolitical consequences. In the post-9/11 world, perhaps the most frightening realization that emerged when the shockwaves had subsided was that religion as a major factor in global conflict was here to stay. The upsurge of fundamentalism in all religions became a matter of great concern since fundamentalist ideology in any religion appeared to generate hatred, suspicion, and fear in its followers toward other religions. Many began to observe a close connection between religious fundamentalism and terrorist violence within all of the world's major traditions, including Christianity, Islam, Hinduism, Judaism, Buddhism, and Sikhism.[2]

For instance, in a *New York Times* article soon after 9/11, Thomas Friedman, author of the best-selling *The Lexus and the Olive Tree*, described the real threat as not terrorism per se but "religious totalitarianism" – "a view of the world that my faith must reign supreme and can be affirmed and held passionately only if all others are negated." Friedman places all faiths that come out of the biblical tradition – Judaism, Christianity, and Islam – within this category, and candidly lays the blame for 9/11 squarely at the feet of such faiths because of their tendency to believe that they have access to privileged truth. Friedman himself sees the only hope for future global peace and social harmony in a view that he strongly advocates: the ideology of "pluralism" that embraces religious diversity and allows equal recognition of alternative faith communities without claiming exclusive truth. Quoting Rabbi David Hartman in support of his view, Friedman asks: "Can Islam, Christianity and Judaism know that God speaks Arabic on Fridays, Hebrew on Saturdays and Latin on Sundays, and that he welcomes different human beings approaching him through their own history, out of their language and cultural heritage? Is single-minded fanaticism a necessity for passion and religious survival, or can we have a multilingual view of God – a notion that God is not exhausted by just one religious path?"[3]

---

2. Mark Juergensmeyer, *Terror in the Mind of God*, 3rd ed. (Berkeley: University of California Press, 2003).

3. Thomas L. Friedman, "The Real War," *New York Times*, 27 November 2001, https://www.nytimes.com/2001/11/27/opinion/foreign-affairs-the-real-war.html .

This is a classic pluralist strategy of stereotyping religions that lay claim to absolute truth as "single-minded fanaticism" and trivializing the differences between religions as essentially linguistic, reflecting historically and culturally conditioned responses to ultimate reality. Asian voices such as Peter Phan also call for abandonment of historic Christianity's claims of Christ's decisiveness in light of "the heightened consciousness, ever more widespread since modernity, of the necessarily relational and historically embedded character of all exclusive and absolute claims, including religious ones, a feature that seems to render such exclusive and absolute claims problematic if not impossible."[4]

Most Asian religions have, for the most part, been tolerant of their neighbors of other faiths down through the centuries. However, revival and global expansion of world religions like Islam, Hinduism, Buddhism, and Christianity have contributed to rising communal tensions and religious conflict in recent years.[5] Religious groups in Asia often affirm their identity in violent conflict with one another. Christian missionary activity is often seen as stoking communal passion and as a potential source of religious conflict. In such an environment, nurturing a culture of tolerance seems to take the highest priority and the ideology of pluralism seems hard to resist.

Committed Christians thus find themselves on the defensive, having to give fresh thought to some difficult questions, some of which strike at the jugular of the Christian faith: In the midst of a society that is increasingly multireligious and culturally diverse, what should the Christian posture be toward the diverse faiths of our neighbors? When we confess Jesus as the universal Lord and Savior, are we also saying that Christianity has a monopoly on truth and goodness – that there is no truth or goodness whatsoever in any other religion? What is distinctive about the Christian message in a world of many faiths? Is Christ's decisiveness essential to the Christian faith? If so, how should we affirm it, and are we really compelled to share it with neighbors of other faiths? If every religion claims to be the only true one and sees its mission as converting those of other faiths, will it not intensify religious bigotry, fanaticism, and communal strife?

Our stewardship of the gospel demands that we think about and respond clearly to some of these burning questions which strike at the very heart of

---

4. Peter C. Phan, "Cultural Diversity and Religious Pluralism: The Church's Mission In Asia," *East Asian Pastoral Review* 43, no. 2 (2006), accessed 7 February 2018, http://www.eapi.org.ph/resources/eapr/east-asian-pastoral-review-2006/volume-43-2006-number-2/cultural-diversity-and-religious-pluralism-the-churchs-mission-in-asia.

5. Jehu J. Hanciles, "Migration and Mission: Some Implications for the Twenty-First Century Church," *International Bulletin of Missionary Research* 27, no. 4 (2003): 146.

the Christian faith. While it is not possible to address all of these questions in a single chapter of this nature, this essay attempts to suggest a framework that could enable Christians to continue to witness faithfully to Christ while conveying genuine respect and sensitivity to neighbors of other faiths within our multireligious Asian context. But first we need to consider the serious challenge posed by the growing popularity of the phenomenon called religious pluralism.

The Challenge of Religious Pluralism

While plurality of religions and cultures has always been an integral aspect of human society, the twin forces of modernization and globalization have helped give rise to a phenomenon that is distinctively modern, in terms of both the cultural diversity experienced by societies today and the contemporary response to this reality within the global cultural environment. While "plurality" refers simply to the fact of cultural and religious diversity, "pluralism" more properly describes an egalitarian perspective that maintains a rough parity among religions concerning religious truth. It holds that no one religion can claim to be somehow normative and superior to others: all religions are culturally conditioned human responses to the one divine reality with complex histories, and salvation (or enlightenment or liberation) should be acknowledged as present and effective in its own way in each religion. Pluralism manifests itself in a wide range of expressions, from a rather crude, undeveloped intuition that God will accept sincere and good people of any or no faith, to sophisticated philosophical models, such as those of John Hick and Raimundo Panikkar.[6]

A complex set of historical and sociological factors has led to the growing attraction pluralism holds for people in our world today. For much of the history of the world, most people lived in isolation from the ethnic and cultural "other." The advent of globalization, however, has resulted in the unprecedented proximity of people of different religions and cultures. The cultural "other" has thus become less alien and unfamiliar, resulting in increased acceptance of difference. An important byproduct of this intermingling of cultures is the "idealization" of ethnic and religious diversity and skepticism toward claims of absolute truth in religion.

The modern encounter between cultures can be an exotic and exhilarating experience but it is also fraught with tension and potential for violence.

---

6. John Hick, *God Has Many Names* (Philadelphia: Westminster, 1980); Raimundo Panikkar, *The Trinity and the Religious Experience of Man* (New York: Orbis Books, 1973).

Religion, which is at the heart of most cultures, has emerged as one of the most powerful sources of social conflict in recent times, and the rise of religious fundamentalism has added to the attraction of pluralism. In this context, pluralism appears to offer an adequate ideological basis for communal peace and social harmony. As a result, pluralism has gained widespread credibility and popularity in recent decades. It forms an unofficial orthodoxy in much of academia today, is widespread in popular contemporary culture, and is firmly entrenched within the entertainment and media elite.

A matter of serious concern, however, is the growing acceptance of pluralism among professing Christians, given the fact that it raises crucial questions concerning the nature and purpose of Christian mission and the Christian faith itself.[7] The Christian gospel maintains that all humans are sinners in need of redemption, and that God desires the salvation of peoples of every race, culture, and religion. It also asserts that God's salvation comes to us through a particular person, Jesus Christ, the decisive self-disclosure of God, who took upon himself the sins of the world, and that by faith in him human beings can be restored to right relationship with God. Pluralism rejects this understanding of the gospel as intellectually untenable and morally repugnant. The assumption is that sincere and morally respectable people simply cannot be mistaken about basic religious beliefs, especially when such beliefs and practices seem to have beneficial effects. This perspective understandably has some emotional appeal, but clearly undermines the grounds and motivation for Christian mission.

Pluralism Unmasked

Yet the pluralist position is hard to defend biblically, and has little or no support in church tradition. It strikes at the nerve center of Christian faith at four crucial points.

First, pluralism challenges the historic Christian claim to have privileged access to divine revelation in the unique authority accorded to the Christian Scriptures. Pluralists assert that an irenic approach to other religions requires that the holy scriptures of people of other faiths be accepted as possessing

---

7. A classic illustration is the watershed multi-author work John Hick and Paul F. Knitter, eds., *The Myth of Christian Uniqueness: Towards a Pluralistic Theology of Religions* (New York: Orbis, 1987). One of the earliest cases in the modern period was argued by Alan Race in *Christians and Religious Pluralism* (New York: Orbis Books, 1982), reiterated more recently in his *Making Sense of Religious Pluralism: Shaping Theology of Religions for Our Times* (London: SPCK, 2013).

the same authority as the Bible since they also contain divine revelation. For instance, the influential Indian pluralist theologian S. J. Samartha maintained that Christians in a multireligious world cannot ignore other scriptures that provide spiritual support and guidance to millions of people today. While the Bible remains normative for Christians, its authority cannot be extended to people of other faiths who have their own scriptures: "In a multi-religious society the criteria derived on the basis of one particular scripture of one particular community of faith cannot be used to pass negative judgments on other scriptures regarded as equally authoritative by communities of faith living side by side with Christians."[8]

Second, pluralism lays the axe to the central constitutive claim of the Christian faith: that Jesus of Nazareth was not simply one of many, or even the greatest of all human religious figures, but was the decisive self-disclosure of the eternal God himself. Pluralists regard this as an arrogant claim, an impossible obstacle in the movement toward interreligious harmony so essential to world peace. Samartha thus quite explicitly rejects the full deity of Jesus: "The 'co-equal divinity' of Jesus, that is, the claim that Jesus of Nazareth *is* God, is not taught in the New Testament . . . The closer people came to affirm the full deity of Jesus the further they moved away from the historical Jesus."[9] Like that of many other pluralists, Samartha's quest for a revised Christology is radically reductionist in its approach to the New Testament account of Christ, and effectively empties Jesus of any claims to uniqueness or decisiveness. For him, Jesus of Nazareth is little more than a Teacher-Prophet. While Christians may hold that Jesus is unique and normative *for them*, they cannot claim that Jesus is unique or normative in a universal sense. Jesus may be the savior for Christians, but he is not the only Savior for all peoples.

A third serious problem with pluralism is its view of different religions as representing many different paths leading to the same ultimate goal. The different religious traditions thus merely describe different contexts within which men and women experience essentially the same salvation or liberation. Do the different religions all make essentially the same claims and teach basically the same truth? Even a cursory survey of the world's living religions reveals that they have marked differences in their essential affirmations. Thus, a major problem with which pluralists must contend is *the problem of conflicting*

---

8. S. J. Samartha, *The Search for New Hermeneutics in Asian Christian Theology* (Madras: CLS, 1987), 49.

9. S. J. Samartha, *One Christ – Many Religions: Toward a Revised Christology* (New York: Orbis Books, 1991), 141.

truth claims. This is easily illustrated by even a cursory comparison of three cardinal beliefs in three of the world's major religions.

What is God (the religious ultimate) like? For Islam, Allah is the one eternal creator God, and any attempt to blur the distinction between the Creator and creation is regarded as idolatry. There is no one concept of the religious ultimate common to all Buddhists. In Theravada Buddhism, *nirvana* is the ultimate reality – the condition of complete cessation of attachment; in Mahayana Buddhism, *Dharmakaya*, the all-inclusive essential nature of the Buddha's essence, is the ultimate; and in Zen Buddhism, the ultimate reality is *sunyata* or emptiness. In Hinduism, the highest philosophical conception of ultimate reality is monistic: the absolute, impersonal Being is *nirguna* (without qualities) Brahman of *advaita* (non-dualistic) Vedanta. Popular Hinduism, on the other hand, is polytheistic with a pantheon consisting of a mind-boggling 330 million male and female deities. There are also monotheistic sects within Hinduism as well as atheistic Hindus who are pure materialists.

What is the nature of the human predicament? For Islam, the ultimate sin is *shirk*, associating anything created with Allah, and idolatry is unambiguously condemned. Sin is more a weakness, a defect, or imperfection, than a radical corruption of the nature and will. While there are some minor differences, Hinduism and Buddhism both share the belief that humankind is trapped within *samsara*, a cycle of rebirth and transmigration based on *karma*. The root problem of human existence is thus not moral sin, but innate, primordial ignorance regarding the true nature of reality.

What is the nature of salvation or liberation? According to Islam, a glorious future salvation awaits the faithful: on the Day of Judgment those whom Allah declares worthy will be admitted to the tangible, sensual delights of Paradise. In Hinduism salvation is *moksha*: total liberation from the chains of *karma* and the cycle of rebirth. This may be attained in one of three ways: the way of selfless or disinterested action (*karma marga*); the way of mystical knowledge (*jnana marga*); or the way of devotion to a personal deity (*bhakti marga*). All Buddhists view salvation as release from *samsara* through *nirvana*, the complete elimination of desire and the conditions producing rebirth. But while some regard this as strictly resulting from one's own efforts, others regard self-effort as futile and maintain that only faith in the mercy and merit of another can bring enlightenment.

Is the ultimate reality personal or impersonal? Is there one God, many deities, or no higher being of any kind? Is the human predicament the result of moral sin or cosmic illusion? Is salvation essentially a release from the cycle of rebirths, or the promise of a blissful, sensual paradise awarded to the faithful? There is incredible diversity of beliefs in the various religions, and many essential affirmations are in fact mutually incompatible. Pluralists are forced to resort to a reductionist reinterpretation of religious beliefs and practices in ways often unacceptable to orthodox adherents of religions. The pluralist argument that, despite their divergent beliefs, all religions are more or less equally true is thus clearly untenable. The facts simply do not fit: they have to be "chipped" to fit the theory.

The theological criteria employed in pluralist constructions thus tend to be arbitrary, and the construct fails to stand up to empirical scrutiny. Finally, and perhaps most importantly, the pluralist vision rests on a premise that is seriously flawed logically. The pluralist thesis relies on the assumption that there is no privileged religious tradition, and that if the various religions of the world surrender their "divisive," tradition-specific distinctives in favor of pluralist approaches, religious harmony will automatically follow. Thus, a critical question with which pluralists must contend is this: *Is there such a thing as a non-tradition-specific approach?*

Samartha's approach here is again illustrative of most pluralists, who insist that all language about God is culture-conditioned. For Samartha, God is essentially a "Mystery" to which there may be different human responses. These responses vary according to the cultural setting, giving rise to different religious traditions. From the point of view of mystical experience, language is a limitation, and all our language of God is symbolic. God, *Brahman*, Trinity, *Sat-cit-ananda*, and so on, are all culture-conditioned descriptions of the ultimate "Mystery" that lies at the heart of the meaning of the universe. Hence, one human response to this "Mystery" cannot claim to be truer than another. But here is the problem: Samartha's view of God is clearly not Christian; rather, it is clearly derived from the Hindu *advaitic* tradition in which the ultimate reality of *Brahman* is an impersonal, ineffable mystery. On the other hand, his view of God is inconsistent with his distinctly Christian view of mission as "God's continuing activity through the Spirit to mend the brokenness of creation, to overcome the fragmentation of humanity, and to heal the rift between humanity, nature and God."[10]

So Samartha's view of ultimate reality is from *advaitic* Hinduism, while his view of mission is Christian. The crux of the matter here is simple: What criteria does he employ in such eclectic judgments? More specifically, how does Samartha know all that he asserts about the nature of the "Mystery"? His definition of "Mystery" is intended to be all-inclusive, but in effect it excludes

---

10. Samartha, *One Christ*, 149.

all forms of orthodox religious belief, Christian or otherwise, which may claim that "Mystery" has revealed itself. On what basis does he reject all contrary claims as false? He can do so only on the basis of the tradition-specific starting point of *advaitic* Hinduism, influenced by liberal Christian theology.

This is typical of the pluralist strategy and is the point at which the pluralist project fails miserably: the flawed assumption that it is possible to have a "helicopter" vantage point above all of the religions from which transcendent, theologically neutral criteria for evaluating religious truth claims can be formulated. The fact is that there is no such privileged high ground in any theological evaluation of religious truth claims. Like all other religious truth claims, pluralist truth claims are also inevitably tradition-specific. This, then, is the most serious weakness of the pluralist position: the huge logical inconsistency inherent in its attempt to deny the right of other worldviews to make any privileged claims, even as pluralism itself employs tradition-specific criteria in evaluating religious beliefs.[11]

The privileged high ground which pluralism claims thus simply does not exist, and since pluralist claims are also inevitably tradition-specific, nothing called pluralism really exists. The pluralist solution must thus be viewed in all honesty for what it really is: not just a new interpretation of any of the world religions, but a distinctive way of viewing reality. When unmasked, it turns out to be an alternative, syncretistic religious ideology which makes exclusive truth claims about the nature of reality just like any other religious belief system.

An Alternative Proposal

The social context of cultural and religious plurality thus presents the church in Asia with what is undoubtedly its greatest test: How should it responsibly steward the faith legacy entrusted to it and witness to the universality of Christ's lordship within the Asian context of cultural diversity and religious plurality? The challenge facing Christian witness in Asia, then, is to hold together an uncompromising allegiance to the truth of the gospel with an unyielding commitment to foster genuine harmony amid people of other faiths.

Christian responses to issues that arise in interreligious engagement generally tend to be positioned between two poles. At one extreme is the relativistic pole we have just considered – religious pluralism, which regards all religions as more or less true, and leading to the same reality. Pluralism

---

11. See Gavin D'Costa's incisive critique in *The Meeting of Religions and the Trinity* (Edinburgh: T&T Clark, 2000), 19–47.

celebrates cultural, moral, or religious differences in their own right, and the only absolute is the conviction that there are no absolutes. Tradition-specific approaches – such as any claims of Christ's finality or decisiveness – must be abandoned in the interests of religious and social harmony.

The reaction to the pluralist position from the opposite "restrictivist" pole asserts that only one single revelation or one single religion is true – Christianity – and that all other revelations or religions are false. Salvation is related exclusively to one particular tradition, restricted to one particular community, with the rest of humankind either left out of account or explicitly excluded from the sphere of salvation. Out of their concern to preserve the decisiveness of Christ, restrictivists tend to dismiss outright the existence and empirical data of other religions without proper trial. Inaccurate and unfair *a priori* judgments are made on the data of other faiths. They tend to have little or no concern to make fair judgments or offer logical explanations for "truths" in other religions and cultures which find correspondence with and attestation in the authoritative revelation we have in Christ.[12]

Is there a way to relate Christian faith and experience to other religions that takes both the "fact" of Christ and the "fact" of religions seriously? Can we propose a theological framework that affirms effectively the decisiveness of Christ while ascribing value to the genuine aspirations within the religious traditions and experience of people of other faiths?

The "Fulfillment" Approach in the Indian Context

Based originally on Jesus's attitude to Judaism in Matthew 5:17 – "Do not think that I have come to abolish the Law or the Prophets; I have not come to abolish them but to fulfil them" – the belief that Christ "fulfils" other religions can be traced almost continuously throughout the history of the church. Although the theme in its original New Testament context applied primarily to the fulfillment of Jewish messianic expectations in the incarnation of Christ,[13] resources for a secondary application to other non-Christian cultures may be found in certain New Testament evangelistic texts: the concept of *Logos* in the prologue of John's

---

12. J. Andrew Kirk, *Loosing the Chains: Religion as Opium and Liberation* (London: Hodder & Stoughton, 1992), 180–186; Dewi Arwel Hughes, *Has God Many Names?* (Leicester: Apollos, 1996), 228–229.

13. Richard N. Longenecker, *The Christology of Early Jewish Christianity* (Grand Rapids: Baker, 1970), 65–66, 79–81.

Gospel,[14] the addresses of Paul to Gentile audiences in Acts 14 and 17,[15] and Paul's creation theology in Romans 1-2.[16] The early fathers' approach to non-Christian philosophy and religion was also based on a "fulfillment" reading of the New Testament.[17]

Followers of Christ in India have struggled for centuries to find a way to resolve the tension between attraction to Christ and love for their ancestral tradition. Beginning in the mid-nineteenth century, we observe a consistent response emerging from within the experience of Indian converts to Christian faith who viewed their faith in Christ as fulfilling the highest aspirations of their pre-Christian religious experience. Various forms of the basic fulfillment approach thus emerge frequently within the Indian tradition, with little or no evidence of mutual influence between these different views. The only common factor appears to have been their experience of Christ as mediated through the Christian Scriptures. The early Christian attitude to the Jewish scriptures seemed to have shaped their own approach to their pre-Christian religion and culture. We cite a few examples by way of illustration before looking at one representative convert's journey a little more closely.

Keshab Chandra Sen was the first to speak of Christ as "fulfilling" other religions, of his coming to India as an "Asiatic in race" and "Hindu in faith." Despite his deep attraction to Christ, he remained within the Hindu fold all of his life.[18] Following Sen's line, *Manilal Parekh* maintained that the teaching of the nineteenth-century Gujarati reformer Swami Narayana convinced him "that God incarnates himself for the redemption of mankind," leading him first to faith in Christ and then eventually to Christian baptism.[19]

Nehemiah Goreh consciously resisted Western influence upon his traditional culture and lifestyle, and despite the influence of rationalism and Western orthodoxy on his thought, affirmed the presence of divine light within the Hindu tradition. The absolute decisiveness of Christ was clearly the starting point of his approach, and his fulfillment view was a tentative attempt to build

---

14. Leon Morris, *The Gospel According to John* (Grand Rapids: Eerdmans, 1995), 102–108.

15. F. F. Bruce, *The Acts of the Apostles* (Grand Rapids: Eerdmans, 1990), 379–380, 354–356, 381–385.

16. James D. G. Dunn, *Romans 1-8*, Word Biblical Commentary 38A (Dallas: Word, 1988), 57–58, 71, 105.

17. Chrys Saldanha, *Divine Pedagogy: A Patristic View of Non-Christian Religions* (Rome: LAS, 1984), 158–186; Paul Hacker, *Theological Foundations of Evangelization* (St Augustin: Steyler, 1980), 35–50.

18. D. C. Scott, *Keshub Chunder Sen* (Madras: CLS, 1979), 215–216.

19. Robin Boyd, *Manilal C. Parekh, 1885-1967; Dhanjibhai Fakirbhai, 1895-1967* (Madras: CLS, 1974), 25, 37.

a bridge from the light of God in general revelation within Hinduism to an acceptance of the full revelation of God in Christ.[20]

Bramabandhab Upadhyay's lifelong quest for a Hindu-Catholic theology and personal identity made him a patriotic nationalist all his life. The Vedanta, in his expression of the *Logos* fulfillment model, represented the highest point which unaided reason has been able to attain in the Indian context, providing the foundation for a natural theology, and finding fulfillment in the supernatural revelation in Christ.[21]

Krishna Mohan Banerjea refutes the charge that Christianity is a foreign religion and that Hindu converts to Christianity have betrayed their ancestral Hindu faith and tradition. He discerns the presence of a "divine pedagogy" in the Vedic teaching on sacrifice, and especially in the self-sacrificing *Prajapati* as a prefigurement of Christ. He uses the idea of an original universal primeval revelation to assert the universal scope of the divine covenant and to include Vedic religion within the sweep of a cosmic salvation-history scheme. His theory affirms, moreover, the decisive fulfillment of the Vedic concept of *Prajapati* in the historic figure of Christ.[22]

Sadhu Sundar Singh's fulfillment approach has its basic impulse in the *bhakti* mystical quest for a personal experience of communion with God. God reveals his pure and self-giving love especially in the incarnation and redemption accomplished by Christ. Humanity's need for communion with God is fulfilled through a mystical encounter with the living Christ, by means of which they experience a transformation of heart and discover true peace and happiness. The universality of God's concern for humanity's salvation and the particularity of the means he employs in Christ are thus held together in a form of the *Logos* fulfillment view. In his interpretation of *Logos* fulfillment, not only are *bhakti* aspirations fulfilled in Christ, but some aspects of Christian faith also find their fulfillment in the sadhu ideal.[23]

---

20. Robin Boyd, *An Introduction to Indian Christian Theology* (Delhi: ISPCK, 1991), 55–57.

21. Julius J. Lipner, *Brahmabandhab Upadhyay: The Life and Thought of a Revolutionary* (New Delhi: Oxford University Press, 1999), 178–183.

22. K. P. Aleaz, *From Exclusivism to Inclusivism: The Theological Writings of Krishna Mohun Banerjea (1813–1885)* (Delhi: ISPCK, 1998), 594–612.

23. Perumalla Surya Prakash, *The Preaching of Sadhu Sundar Singh* (Bangalore: Wordmakers, 1991), 46–51.

A Bhakti Christian Response: Narayan Vaman Tilak (1862–1919)[24]

The *bhakti* school in Hinduism has held great attraction for Indian Christians because of its conception of God as a loving, personal being distinct from his creation who bestows grace upon his creatures and can be worshiped with feelings of deep love and personal devotion.[25] A significant number of Hindu converts from the *bhakti* tradition seem to have viewed the *bhakti* framework as providing the most appropriate preparation for and expression of the Christian faith in the Indian context. Several of the proponents of this school were poet-mystics, and the best known of these Christian *bhakti* poets was Narayan Vaman Tilak.

Narayan Vaman Tilak, a Chitpavan Brahmin convert and renowned Maharashtrian poet, was a saint and activist. Although we do not find structured theological statements on any aspect of his thought, his poetry and hymns express original theological insights of considerable value in the quest for a deeper understanding of the Christian–Hindu religious encounter.[26] Tilak's patriotism was the starting point for an ardent quest for the ideal religion that would provide a suitable spiritual foundation for a great and prosperous India. At the end of his search and his study of the New Testament, he found himself irresistibly attracted to Christ, and became convinced that Christ was the Guru for whom India and the world were looking.[27]

Tilak was passionately devoted to Christ and deeply committed to his Hindu spiritual heritage, and his intense love for both remained with him all his life. He did his best to dispel the misconception that becoming a Christian involved renouncing one's traditional cultural heritage and separating oneself from the Hindu community.[28] According to Winslow, Tilak was convinced that "if Christ could be presented to India in His naked beauty, free from the disguises of Western organisation, Western doctrines and Western forms of

---

24. Two early definitive biographies of Tilak are by J. C. Winslow, *Narayan Vaman Tilak: The Christian Poet of Maharashtra* (Calcutta: Association Press, 1930), henceforth cited as *Tilak*; and by his wife, Lakshmibai Tilak, *I Follow After*, trans. E. Josephine Inkster (Madras: Oxford University Press, 1950). For other helpful introductions, see Plamthodathil S. Jacob, *The Experiential Response of N. V. Tilak* (Madras: CLS, 1979), henceforth cited as *Response*; and H. L. Richard, *Christ-Bhakti: Narayan Vaman Tilak and Christian Work among Hindus* (Delhi: ISPCK, 1991), henceforth cited as *Christ-Bhakti*.

25. See A. J. Appasamy, *Christianity as Bhakti Marga* (Madras: CLS, 1930); S. Neill, *Bhakti: Hindu and Christian* (Madras: CLS, 1974).

26. Richard, *Christ-Bhakti*, 81; Jacob, *Response*, x.

27. Jacob, *Response*, 108.

28. Hans Staffner, *Jesus Christ and the Hindu Community* (Anand: Gujarat Sahitya Prakash, 1988), 65.

worship, India would acknowledge Him as the supreme Guru, and lay her richest homage at His feet."[29]

In the early years following his conversion, Tilak's attitude toward Hinduism was essentially confrontational, and his criticism of certain aspects of Hinduism often expressed itself in anti-Hindu rhetoric. His overall approach was, nevertheless, sensitive: "There is truth in Hinduism and we must not accuse and hurt Hindus, but find common points and then present the gospel . . . Always study their side. Do not say all is false, idol worship is sin, there is no life in it, and so on . . . Look for similarities to build a bridge."[30]

Some seven or eight years after his conversion, Tilak underwent a spiritual crisis which radically deepened his personal experience of communion with Christ. Richard observes that the spiritual and emotional resources of *bhakti*, which lay suppressed in the depths of his being, were now released in a deeply Indian lyrical and musical expression of devotion to Christ.[31] This phase in Tilak's experience led him to break out of traditional Christian worship styles into more contextually relevant approaches, and to reinterpret his Hindu devotional heritage in the light of his experience of Christ.[32]

Tilak's earlier critical attitude thus gave way to a more positive approach to Hinduism in later years, when he became convinced that the knowledge of God imparted to India through the *bhakti* poet-saints had prepared India for the gospel of Christ. He thus recommended the study of older Hindu literature and devotional poetry, believing that the devotional writings of Namdev, Tukaram, Jnanesvara, and other saints of Maharashtra could serve as preparation for the reception of the Christian gospel. He thus cautioned Christian missionaries against imposing a foreign version of the Christian faith in India, and advised them to show respect and reverence for the ancient religious traditions and sages of India.[33]

The significance of this attitude is clarified when he says, "We esteem all the world's saints as prophets of God, and the sayings of the Hindu saints form our first old testament."[34] For Tilak, the Hindu scriptures thus seem to have functioned as a kind of Old Testament, preparing Hindus to receive the truth of the gospel message.[35] Tilak illustrates this from his own experience

---

29. Winslow, *Narayan Vaman Tilak*, 118.
30. *Dyanodaya* 57, no. 25 (23 June 1898), quoted in Richard, *Christ-Bhakti*, 65–66.
31. Richard, *Christ-Bhakti*, 77.
32. Richard, 78–80.
33. Winslow, *Narayan Vaman Tilak*, 60.
34. Quoted in Jacob, *Response*, 45.
35. Richard, *Christ-Bhakti*, 85; cf. Staffner, *Jesus Christ*, 67.

with his famous claim, "I have come to the feet of Christ over the bridge of Tukaram," indicating that his study of Tukaram had prepared him to receive the message of Christ.[36]

In further elaborating this understanding of the relationship between Christian and *bhakti* Hindu experience based on his own spiritual pilgrimage, Tilak explains how the teaching of *bhakti* saints like Tukaram and Jnanesvara positively influenced his movement toward Christ: "The traditional way of union with the Supreme through *bhakti*, which Hindu mystics have conceived and Hindu devotees experienced, may be summed up in the four words, *samipata* (nearness), *salokata* (Association), *Sarupata* (likeness), and *sayujyta* ('yokedness' or union); this has helped me to enter into the meaning of that series of Christ's sayings – 'Come after Me,' 'Take My yoke upon you,' 'Become like unto Me,' 'Abide in Me.'"[37]

Tilak's positive attitude to the Hindu tradition is, however, balanced by a clear conviction regarding the decisiveness of God's revelation in Christ. He affirms that in contrast to Tukaram and other *bhakti* saints, Jesus alone spoke with a clear voice about God and is the only Savior: "Nothing but the religion of Jesus . . . can enable our beloved India to understand what God's idea of sin is, nor reclaim the sinner, nor regenerate, nor make him perfect as his Father in heaven is perfect."[38]

He was, however, convinced that Hindus must be invited to accept Christ not as the destroyer of their spiritual heritage, but as its fulfillment: "Christ came not to destroy, but to fulfil and his learned disciples have ever interpreted the literature of the world in a discerning and constructive way. Our task is not to condemn indiscriminately, but rather to appreciate the best that there is in persons, to hold up to them their own acknowledged best, and then to try lovingly to make that best of theirs still better."[39]

Tilak's thought is couched in poetic language and embedded in lyrical verse, making a conceptual analysis of his ideas somewhat difficult. His attempt led him to make a decisive break with the established church toward the closing years of his life, following which he launched an indigenous Christian movement called *Devacha darbar*.[40] This step was the climax of a

---

36. Reported by Winslow, *Narayan Vaman Tilak*, 59.

37. Quoted in Winslow, *Narayan Vaman Tilak*, 56–57.

38. *Dyanodaya* 59, no. 23 (7 June 1900) and 76, no. 21 (24 May 1917); quoted in Richard, *Christ-Bhakti*, 86.

39. *Dyanodaya* 71, no. 37 (12 September 1912); quoted in Richard, *Christ-Bhakti*, 12.

40. He described this as "a brotherhood of the baptized and unbaptized disciples of Christ" (Winslow, *Narayan Vaman Tilak*, 100).

lifelong struggle to free the person and message of Christ from its Western image, and his deep identification with the Indian culture and tradition.[41] The main strength of Tilak's fresh and creative approach was not its theological sophistication but its contextual authenticity, emerging from his attempt to assert the continuity of his Christian experience with his pre-Christian religious and cultural heritage. The value of his contribution must be measured largely in terms of his effective application of the fulfillment approach in practical interreligious engagement.

The fulfillment approach thus emerged among converts in pre-independence India as a response to the need to contextualize the gospel in the Indian context, and to assert the relevance of Christ against the charge of cultural "foreignness" and irrelevance of Christian faith. This impulse then led them to explore and winnow the Hindu tradition for resources which would enable them to affirm meaningfully the relevance of Christ within the Hindu context. Their research uncovered various aspects of the Hindu tradition and experience which they then began to regard as "pedagogy" to Christ. The implications of this will be explored further in the following evaluation.

Where Christ Meets Other Faiths: A Brief Assessment[42]

Christ's Decisiveness and Universality

The fulfillment view is grounded in the decisive moment for Christian faith: the incarnation event. The central constitutive claim of the Christian faith – that in the person and event of Jesus Christ God has spoken and acted decisively for the benefit of the whole world – is normative and decisive in shaping the logic and presuppositions of Christian theological discourse. The inevitable starting point in any attempt to come to grips with the message of Jesus must always be Jesus himself: What did Jesus say? What did Jesus claim to do? Who did Jesus claim to be? The New Testament portrait of Jesus is of a man without any equal (John 1:1–14). His birth is miraculous (Luke 1:30–38). He makes claims to deity (John 5:17–18; 10:30–33): authority to forgive sins (Mark 2:5–7), to give life to the dead (John 5:21–29), and to judge the world (John 5:22, 27). He predicts his own death and resurrection, and then fulfils the prediction (Mark 10:32–34; cf. 16:1–6). Those who recorded the details of Jesus's life were convinced that

---

41. Richard points out that Tilak himself was "living proof of at least partial validity in the fulfilment school" (Richard, *Christ-Bhakti*, 18–19, 89–90).

42. For a more detailed description and assessment of the "fulfillment approach" in the Indian context, see Ivan Satyavrata, *God Has Not Left Himself without Witness* (Oxford: Regnum, 2011); *To Fulfil, Not to Destroy: Christ as the Fulfilment of Hindu Religious Experience in Indian Christian Theology* (Oxford: Regnum, 2018).

he was God in the flesh, and that in his life, death, and resurrection God has provided salvation for all people (John 14:6–10; Acts 4:12).[43]

In the fulfillment approach, God's self-disclosure in Christ is definitive as the normative criterion of truth and the starting block of a universal quest for truth wherever it may be found. Based on the truth as revealed in the Christ event, the genuine work of the Spirit can be discerned and affirmed as various religious experiences are judged on the basis of their orientation toward Christ. The decisiveness of the Christ event and the universality of the *Logos*-Christ in creation are thus held closely together in the fulfillment view. The Christ event discloses God's universal concern to redeem all humanity and restore the world back to himself, and Christ is thus presented as the fulfillment of the religious aspirations of people of all faiths and cultures. This provides the theological basis for the Spirit's work in actively drawing people to God and to Christ, enabling the church to pursue its evangelistic mandate.

Revelation in Other Religions

Fulfillment approaches neither absolutize nor demonize religions. The degree of value ascribed to non-Christian religions varies, but they are viewed objectively as containing some elements of the true knowledge of God, and subjectively, reflecting legitimate expressions of the need for self-transcendence. These religions, however, express human anticipations of something fuller: the fullness offered only in Christ.

Paul's address to the Greeks at Athens in Acts 17:22–31 offers a classic illustration of this. Paul avoids any direct reference to the Old Testament, but makes use of several concepts of distinctly pagan origin. The first is the inscription on the altar to the "unknown god," probably one of several such altars at Athens integral to the religious consciousness of the Athenians. It served as a point of contact – a text Paul used to launch his speech. Although the ignorance rather than the worship is underlined, Paul clearly intended to convey that he was now making known to them this "unknown god" whom they worshiped in ignorance. Paul's speech also employs two consecutive quotations from Greek poets to illustrate his argument: "in him we live and move and have our being" – a reference traced back to the sixth-century BC poet Epimenides, the Cretan; and "we are his offspring" – a citation from a

---

43. If for whatever reason we doubt the reliability of the New Testament and are not convinced by its witness to Jesus's life and ministry, we should simply walk away from Christ and the Christian faith. What we have no right to do is select facts arbitrarily from the New Testament record and fashion a Jesus of our own making who can be accommodated within our prefabricated presuppositions.

third-century BC poet, Aratus of Cilicia (Acts 17:28). A further reference to pagan sources is the allusion to Stoic philosophy in the expression "they (men) should seek God, in the hope that they might feel after him and find him" (Acts 17:27, RSV).

Paul is here interacting with the specific traditions of Athenian religion. The inculturation impulse is evident in his selection and employment of specific non-Christian notions familiar to his Gentile audience. In their original context, none of these pagan concepts used by Paul expressed pure, "Christian" knowledge of God. But the fact that each of them contained an element of truth is recognized by him, and utilized to relate the Christian gospel to such knowledge of God as they possessed. These fragments of truth are, however, identified on the basis of christological criteria, loosened from their original context and reoriented in the communication of the Christian message.[44]

But not only do the aspirations of other religions find fulfillment in Christ; conversely, Christocentric criteria are applied in identifying elements of truth, goodness, and beauty in cultures of people of other faiths. This is an essential dimension of the ongoing Christian contextualization project, entailing criticism, purification, and growth of the existing tradition and practice of the church. In the course of this ongoing process, elements of truth in other cultures may thus enrich and complement aspects of Christian truth and bring them to their full expression. The end result of such a Christ-centered process of inculturation is that rather than destroying what is of value in culture and religion, Christ becomes the restorer of all that is true and good in the traditional cultural heritage.

The Scope of Salvation

Although there are distinctive views of salvation held by different religions, there are strands in some faiths which reflect aspirations which overlap with the Christian understanding and may serve as helpful points of contact in communicating the good news. The Spirit's activity in pointing to Christ may be discerned in the spiritual hunger evidenced among people of other faiths but interpreted in relation to the New Testament account of Christ and the Spirit. A clear instance is the Roman centurion Cornelius's journey to faith in Christ, in which the fuller revelation in Christ was accorded to him as a natural outcome of his devotion to God based on his pre-Christian spiritual aspirations (Acts 10:1–7, 24–48). Although pre-Christian mediations of the Spirit may sometimes be real, they are essentially provisional and preparatory in nature.

---

44. For further reflection, see Satyavrata, *God Has Not Left Himself*, 204–205.

The Christ event manifests God's universal redemptive concern and at the same time represents the prophetic focus and medium of God's redemptive action. But Christ is viewed as the Savior not just of Christians, but potentially of people of any and all faiths who put their trust in him. The Spirit draws people of all faiths toward a relationship of loving communion with Christ and the Father. Faith in Christ is thus viewed not as a tribal religion but as a cosmic faith with a universal orientation, open to all who will accept Christ's lordship, and in which christologically attested truths, values, and aspirations of all religions can be incorporated.

How can salvation in Christ be applied to those who have never heard of Christ? Indian fulfillment thinkers generally concur that those invincibly ignorant – those individuals who could not have understood the Christian message, even through reasonable diligence – will not automatically be excluded from the grace of God. They leave room for the possibility that they could be judged on the basis of their response to the light they possess apart from explicit knowledge of and faith in Christ.

Intolerance and Communal Harmony

The commitment of fulfillment theology to the decisiveness of Christ has sometimes exposed it to the charge of imperialism and intolerance.[45] There is, however, no *a priori* reason why the claim of Christianity (or of any other faith or ideology) to have access to universal truth should be regarded as imperialistic or intolerant, unless it asserts this claim coercively, denying the same privilege to others. The fulfillment position attempts to offer a theological interpretation of the phenomenon of religion on the basis of a Christian interpretive framework. All the major religions are, likewise, universalistic in vision, but not for that reason regarded as intolerant or imperialistic.

There is nothing in the fulfillment claim to Christ's decisiveness that is in itself intolerant of or detrimental to communal harmony. Although the fulfillment view has its original impetus in God's initiative to re-establish his kingdom rule over humankind, God's rule need not be interpreted in terms of a coercive elimination of human freedom or of religio-political conquest. The Trinity discloses the rule of God as a rule of love, which seeks communion without repressing freedom.[46] The goal of Christian mission thus need never be the "destruction" of Hinduism or of any other faith or worldview. Other

---

45. Race, *Christians and Religious Pluralism*, 68.

46. Jürgen Moltmann, *The Trinity and the Kingdom of God*, trans. Margaret Kohl (London: SCM, 1981), 174–176.

religions have a right to exist and to express themselves in a universe where God concedes to every human being the right to choose to obey him or to reject him, and permits even Satan himself the freedom to work against his purposes.

The fulfillment approach proceeds unapologetically from an *a priori* commitment to christological criteria when engaging in dialogue with neighbors of other faiths. In working toward global peace and a just, egalitarian, and socially inclusive world order, Christians must dialogue with other faiths in defining a universally acceptable "global" ethic, but Christian commitment to this "global" ethic will be necessarily nuanced, based on its convergence with christological criteria.

Christian Mission in a Pluralistic Society

The church's evangelistic mandate requires it to announce the arrival of the kingdom decisively in Christ. As followers of Jesus Christ, what we have to share is not essentially a set of timeless truths or a sophisticated ethical system, but a story – his-story, the story of Jesus! We did not invent or create this story; it has been entrusted to us as a stewardship, and we have no right to either change it or to keep it to ourselves (1 John 1:1–2; Acts 4:19–20). But being followers of Jesus is no reason to have feelings of religious superiority or cultural arrogance. We must be willing to exercise tolerance as we allow others the same freedom to practice their faith as we desire for ourselves. Furthermore, Christ-followers must be committed to discern and willing to celebrate any rays of truth, goodness, or beauty that we observe in the devotion, cultures, or lifestyles of people of other faiths.

Called to be the "salt of the earth" and "light of the world," the church is duty-bound to cooperate with people of all faiths in working for peace, justice, and equality, to advance the kingdom purpose of God for a better world: a world free of poverty, injustice, and strife. But our stewardship of the gospel requires that we remain faithful to our mission of sharing the story of the saving love of God in Christ – a story that has transformed millions of lives and revolutionized societies down through the centuries.

Conclusion

Cultural diversity and religious pluralism, from both without and within the church, are increasingly the hallmarks of contemporary society, and present both formidable challenges and enormous opportunities for the church's mission in Asia. The rise of religious pluralism as an ideology does represent an ominous threat to the church's mission and could even put the future survival of the church in Asia in peril. On the other hand, with close to two-thirds of the global population within its borders and home to some of the earliest and most resilient Christian communities, Asia represents the world's greatest evangelistic opportunity in this millennium.

As the center of Christianity has shifted away from its traditional Western base to multiple new centers across the world, there is a growing realization that Christianity in the third millennium might be the most culturally diverse in history.[47] The emergence of such multiple centers must compel us to think in new ways about the shape of Christian mission in the twenty-first century. More than ever before, Christianity will need to be understood as a multicultural and global movement that has found new life in the lived realities of the Majority World. The diverse cultures and religions of Asia make it an exciting living laboratory to explore new avenues of doing mission, as followers of Christ discover fresh ways to connect the gospel with the lived experience of Asians. Let us continue to share the story of Jesus with our neighbors of other faiths with conviction and courage, but also sensitivity and humility. This story must not just be told in words but attested by living evidence of its transforming power in the lives of those who claim to be Christ-followers in Asia today.

References

Aleaz, K. P. *From Exclusivism to Inclusivism: The Theological Writings of Krishna Mohun Banerjea (1813–1885)*. Delhi: ISPCK, 1998.
Appasamy, A. J. *Christianity as Bhakti Marga*. Madras: CLS, 1930.
Boyd, Robin. *An Introduction to Indian Christian Theology*. Delhi: ISPCK, 1991.
———. *Manilal C. Parekh, 1885–1967; Dhanjibhai Fakirbhai, 1895–1967*. Madras: CLS, 1974.
Bruce, F. F. *The Acts of the Apostles*. Grand Rapids: Eerdmans, 1990.
D'Costa, Gavin. *The Meeting of Religions and the Trinity*. Edinburgh: T&T Clark, 2000.
Dunn, James D. G. *Romans 1–8*. Word Biblical Commentary 38A. Dallas: Word, 1988.
Friedman, Thomas L. "The Real War." *New York Times*, 27 November 2001. https://www.nytimes.com/2001/11/27/opinion/foreign-affairs-the-real-war.html.
Hacker, Paul. *Theological Foundations of Evangelization*. St Augustin: Steyler, 1980.
Hanciles, Jehu J. "Migration and Mission: Some Implications for the Twenty-First Century Church." *International Bulletin of Missionary Research* 27, no. 4 (2003): 146–153.
Hick, John. *God Has Many Names*. Philadelphia: Westminster, 1980.

---

47. Philip Jenkins, *The Next Christendom: The Coming of Global Christianity* (New York: Oxford University Press, 2002).

Hick, John, and Paul F. Knitter, eds. *The Myth of Christian Uniqueness: Towards a Pluralistic Theology of Religions*. New York: Orbis Books, 1987.

Hughes, Dewi Arwel. *Has God Many Names?* Leicester: Apollos, 1996.

Jacob, Plamthodathil S. *The Experiential Response of N. V. Tilak*. Madras: CLS, 1979.

Jenkins, P. *The Next Christendom: The Coming of Global Christianity*. New York: Oxford University Press, 2002.

Juergensmeyer, Mark. *Terror in the Mind of God*. 3rd ed. Berkeley: University of California Press, 2003.

Kirk, J. Andrew. *Loosing the Chains: Religion as Opium and Liberation*. London: Hodder & Stoughton, 1992.

Lipner, Julius J. *Brahmabandhab Upadhyay: The Life and Thought of a Revolutionary*. New Delhi: Oxford University Press, 1999.

Longenecker, Richard. N. *The Christology of Early Jewish Christianity*. Grand Rapids: Baker, 1970.

Moltmann, Jürgen. *The Trinity and the Kingdom of God*. Translated by Margaret Kohl. London: SCM, 1981.

Morris, Leon. *The Gospel According to John*. Grand Rapids: Eerdmans, 1995.

Neill, S. *Bhakti: Hindu and Christian*. Madras: CLS, 1974.

Netland, Harold. *Encountering Religious Pluralism*. Downers Grove: InterVarsity Press, 2001.

Pannikar, Raimundo. *The Trinity and the Religious Experience of Man*. New York: Orbis Books, 1973.

Phan, Peter C. "Cultural Diversity and Religious Pluralism: The Church's Mission in Asia." *East Asian Pastoral Review* 43, no. 2 (2006). Accessed 7 February 2018, http://www.eapi.org.ph/resources/eapr/east-asian-pastoral-review-2006/volume-43-2006-number-2/cultural-diversity-and-religious-pluralism-the-churchs-mission-in-asia.

Race, Alan. *Christians and Religious Pluralism*. New York: Orbis Books, 1982.

———. *Making Sense of Religious Pluralism: Shaping Theology of Religions for Our Times*. London: SPCK, 2013.

Richard, H. L. *Christ-Bhakti: Narayan Vaman Tilak and Christian Work among Hindus*. Delhi: ISPCK, 1991.

Saldanha, Chris. *Divine Pedagogy: A Patristic View of Non-Christian Religions*. Rome: LAS, 1984.

Samartha, S. J. *One Christ – Many Religions: Toward a Revised Christology*. New York: Orbis Books, 1991.

———. *The Search for New Hermeneutics in Asian Christian Theology*. Madras: CLS, 1987.

Satyavrata, Ivan. *God Has Not Left Himself without Witness*. Oxford: Regnum, 2011.

———. *To Fulfil, Not to Destroy: Christ as the Fulfilment of Hindu Religious Experience in Indian Christian Theology*. Oxford: Regnum, 2018.

Scott, D. C. *Keshub Chunder Sen*. Madras: CLS, 1979.

Staffner, Hans. *Jesus Christ and the Hindu Community*. Anand: Gujarat Sahitya Prakash, 1988.
Surya Prakash, Perumalla. *The Preaching of Sadhu Sundar Singh*. Bangalore: Wordmakers, 1991.
Tilak, L. *I Follow After*. Translated by E. Josephine Inkster. Madras: Oxford University Press, 1950.
Winslow, J. C. *Narayan Vaman Tilak: The Christian Poet of Maharashtra*. Calcutta: Association Press, 1930.

12

God's *Basileia* in Asia's *Res Publica*
Situating the Sacred in Asia's Public Sphere

Aldrin M. Peñamora

Philippine Council of Evangelical Churches

Introduction

Christianity occupies an ambivalent and amorphous place in Asia's public sphere. As Felix Wilfred observes, Christianity suffers isolation from public life, and has "little influence on the political life of the Asian countries, and on their economic policies."[1] Part of the reason for this has to do with views fracturing God's heavenly realm from the earthly, the spiritual from the political, the sacred from the secular, the private from the public, the present from the future. This essay addresses such fractures. As Timoteo D. Gener writes, "Theology ought not to remain exclusively in the church."[2]

This essay proceeds thus: first, it gives an overview of the Asian public situation, underscoring the need to perceive Jesus in light of that situation; second, it discusses the importance of religion in the public sphere; third, a social–spatial understanding of God's kingdom is presented, exemplified

---

1. Felix Wilfred, *Asian Public Theology: Critical Concerns in Challenging Times* (Delhi: ISPCK, 2010), "Introduction," Kindle.

2. Timoteo D. Gener, "With/Beyond Tracy: Re-Visioning Public Theology," *Evangelical Review of Theology* 33, no. 2 (April 2009): 121.

by Jesus's performative action of proclaiming it in the Markan episode of temple cleansing (Mark 11:15–17); and finally, it sketches modes of Christian engagement in Asia's public spaces.

Asia's Anguish

In a recasting of a Chinese folktale about Lady Meng, whose tears brought down a portion of the Great Wall and uncovered the bones of her husband interred under it, Taiwanese theologian C. S. Song powerfully paints a picture of the oppressions and struggles that Asians continually confront, of which the Wall is a formidable symbol. As Song writes, "there have grown around this monument of cruelty stories and legends depicting the endless tragedies that invaded the lives of common people, humiliating them, uprooting them, and destroying them. Reflected in these stories of the people . . . is not only the remote past, but the immediate present and perhaps the distant future. Projected in them is the universal struggle of people to be human, free, and authentic."[3]

Hence, a number of theologies have emerged in Asia grappling with Asia's oppressions. Among these are Korea's *minjung* (people) theology, India's *dalit* theology, and the Philippines' *theology of struggle*, with each movement emphasizing the distinct historical, social, political, and cultural locations of its origin.[4] Two emphases are clear in these reflections: first, they consistently seek to give voice to the marginalized members of Asian society: Dalits, *minjung*, women, tribal peoples, and similarly situated people groups. Second, these approaches reflect a significant shift in the method of doing theology, one influenced by the hermeneutic of liberation.[5] As Aloysius Pieris avers, theological attempts that do not take seriously the coalescence of faith and poverty in Asia have proven to be misdirected.[6]

---

3. C. S. Song, *The Tears of Lady Meng: A Parable of People's Political Theology* (New York: Orbis Books, 1982), 25.

4. The *minjung* in Korea are the poor, not only in terms of finances but also in power and social status. Similarly, the Dalits of India are society's outcasts, whose status is so low that they are not even included in India's traditional division of four castes. See Yeow Choo Lak, ed., *Doing Theology with God's Purpose in Asia*, ATESEA Occasional Papers no. 10 (Singapore: ATESEA, 1990), 21–23, 104–110. See also Manohar Chandra Prasad, "Dalit Theology: Methodological Issues in a Contextual Theology of Liberation," *Asia Journal of Theology* 23, no. 1 (April 2009): 166–175; Jin-kwan Kwon, "Minjung (the Multitude), Historical Symbol of Jesus Christ," *Asia Journal of Theology* 24, no. 1 (April 2010): 153–171.

5. R. S. Sugirtharajah, ed., *Frontiers in Asian Christian Theology: Emerging Trends* (New York: Orbis Books, 1994), 2.

6. Aloysius Pieris, *An Asian Theology of Liberation* (London: T&T Clark, 1988), 69.

These emphases grew out of Asian experiences, and while crucial differences necessarily exist in these experiences, there are also commonalities that connect diverse Asian realities. According to William Dyrness, these are the following: first, most Asian nations harbor a disproportionate population living in poverty; second, many Asian countries have unequal and debilitating relations with developed and richer Western nations; third, Asian nations were once the home of sophisticated civilizations; and fourth, the peoples of Asia have a deeply religious outlook on life.[7]

The Federation of Asian Bishops' Conference (FABC) made similar observations. The bishops pointed out that Asia's economic system is largely under the control of foreign investors in collaboration with the local elites, whose interests are protected by the political system. Deprivation and the poverty of the masses are therefore the natural outcomes of such exploitative alliances. In terms of the political aspect, the FABC observed that Asia's traditions were being eroded by atheistic communism, colonialism, feudalism, and classical Western capitalism. And in regard to the religious dimension, they perceived that fundamentalism and religious hegemony were serious challenges.[8] Indeed, religion has often been a factor in military conflicts in Asia.

To these Asian realities must be added the culture of violence that, as James Haire observes, manifests itself in various forms. Economic violence, for instance, has led to a widening of the gap between the rich and the poor, and structural violence based on patriarchy has often led to forced labor migration, gender discrimination, and marginalization of people groups due to caste, race, ethnicity, and class.[9] Violence against nature and the environment is also a common reality in Asia. Regrettably, such forms of violence sometimes occur with religious legitimation. Amid these urgent concerns, Christians in Asia need, like Lady Meng, to shed tears for the multitudes suffering under oppressive rule, and to point to Jesus, recalling that he has an Asian face.

---

7. William Dyrness, *Learning about Theology from the Third World* (Grand Rapids: Zondervan, 1990), 15–16.

8. A. Alangaram, *Christ of the Asian Peoples: Towards a Asian Contextual Christology: Based on the Documents of the Federation of Asian Bishops' Conference*, rev. ed. (Bangalore: Asian Trading, 2001), 14–19. See also A. A. Yewangoe, *Theologia Crucis in Asia: Asia Christian Views on Suffering in the Face of Overwhelming Poverty and Multifaceted Religiosity in Asia* (Amsterdam: Rodopi, 1987), 9–12.

9. James Haire, "Public Theology – A Latin Captivity of the Church: Violence and Public Theology in the Asia-Pacific Context," *International Journal of Public Theology* 1, no. 3 (2007): 457.

The Asian Visage of Jesus

Recalling the Asian face of Jesus requires re-conceptualizing many of our inherited portrayals of Christ. This need not require vitiating entirely Western conceptions of God. Indeed, Asian Christians must learn from, appreciate, and respond to fellow Christians around the world regarding who God is. As Hwa Yung rightly notes, mutual interdependence – between the East and the West – must undergird this task in order for the church to "come to a greater and more wholesome perception of the wonder and majesty of God."[10] Moreover, as the FABC pointed out, the process of contextualization does not mean closing the doors to the outside world, for analogous social transformations through the Word that are occurring around the globe must be allowed to influence and shape local theological and ethical convictions.[11] Rather, we must be open to rediscovering who Jesus is and what following Jesus means for Asian Christians, in light of their embeddedness in the particularities of their locations.

Such a task is essential, for conceptions about Jesus are never neutral, but always culturally and historically conditioned. As Song notes, such neutral and ahistorical conceptions of Christian doctrine have the effect of leaving it "homeless."[12] A similar point can be seen in the heart-rending question that Elie Wiesel recalls being uttered by a bystander upon seeing a little boy

---

10. Hwa Yung, *Mangoes or Bananas?: The Quest for an Authentic Christian Theology* (Oxford: Regnum, 1997), 239–240. Yung's position is based on his view that the approach of the East is relational while that of the West is rational. Melba Maggay also sees some differences on the cognitive level between Asians and Westerners. She remarks that the former think synthetically or try to harmonize contradictions and seeming opposites, while Westerners demonstrate the mental habit of logical negation or either–or thinking (*Filipino Religious Consciousness: Some Implications to Missions* [Quezon City: Institute for Studies in Asian Church and Culture, 1999], 29–42). But see Kosuke Koyama, "The Asian Approach to Christ," *Missiology* 12, no. 4 (October 1984): 435–447. Koyama contends that "there is no fundamental difference – philosophically, metaphysically, psychologically, spiritually, culturally or religiously – between what we call East and West," (Koyama, "Asian Approach," 436). The differences that we perceive, says Koyama, are actually the distinct responses of the people to the disturbances to their culture, which were caused by the presence of God, who puts into question the spiritual (*mythos*) and the intellectual (*logos*) life of the people.

11. Alangaram, *Christ of the Asian*, 93. Michelle Tooley writes from a similar perspective and remarks: "By hearing the story of Guatemalan women, women in the United States can draw hope from their story and recognize and confront the violence and injustice in our society." Michelle Tooley, *Voices of the Voiceless: Women, Justice and Human Rights in Guatemala* (Scottdale: Herald, 1997), 19.

12. C. S. Song, *Tell Us Our Names: Story Theology from an Asian Perspective* (New York: Orbis Books, 1984), 11. Song was pointing to the theological task or to theology in general, which I applied to the conception of Jesus.

(*pipel*) dangling slowly to his death on the gallows: "Where is God?"[13] At that *particular* time and situation, the nameless person grappled not with the mere concept of God, but with finding the concrete reality of his presence.

Asian Christians are similarly situated in recognizing the visage of their crucified and risen Lord in disheartening circumstances. The question of Jesus's presence is, simultaneously, for the suffering people of Asia, a question that deals with his absence, for he has often been portrayed as being present *powerfully* only among society's elite, and present in *weakness* among the outcasts. Such was the portrait of the Christ that came primarily through the West, reflected in colonial politics, wherein the church allied itself with the country's rulers. As a result, the Christ-image became captive to the powerful and was viewed as white, patriarchal, elitist, and Western-oriented.[14] The playwright Kim Chi Ha depicted the Western captivity of Christ in his stirring play *The Gold-Crowned Jesus*, in which the statue of Jesus cries out for liberation from a stone image with a golden crown. He cries out that only the downtrodden, represented by a leper, can liberate him so he can wear again his crown of thorns.[15] Such is a depiction of what it means to be in solidarity with society's oppressed, of the suffering that may be involved, of the tears, and at times blood, that will need to be shed in resisting and transforming oppressive situations and powers. Dietrich Bonhoeffer knew this well, famously arguing that "only a suffering God can help."[16]

Religion and the Public Space

Recognizing Jesus's face in Asia's public space, which is characterized by the suffering and cries of its people, means entering that space. This entails reconstruing the very notion of *res publica* (or "public sphere") from which religion has often been driven out. In modern times, the notion of a *res publica* is often associated only with the notion of "state," particularly exemplified in republican government. However, it has historically referred to a broad range

---

13. Elie Wiesel, *Night*, trans. Marion Wiesel (New York: Hill & Wang, 2006), 64–65.
14. See Sugirtharajah, *Frontiers in Asian Theology*, chs. 1, 2, and 4.
15. Kim Chi Ha, *The Gold-Crowned Jesus and Other Writings* (New York: Orbis Books, 1978), 85, cited in Kuribayashi Teruo, "Recovering Jesus for Outcasts in Japan," in Sugirtharajah, *Frontiers in Asian Theology*, 18–19. See also C. S. Song, "Oh, Jesus, Here with Us!," *Ecumenical Review* 35, no. 1 (1983): 59–74.
16. Dietrich Bonhoeffer, *Letters and Papers from Prison*, ed. Eberhard Bethge (New York: Collier, 1972), 361.

of things and denoted those matters that are everyone's business.[17] Moreover, as Cicero remarked incisively, where there is no justice, there can be no *res publica*:

> So who would call that a republic, i.e., the property of the public, when everyone was oppressed by the cruelty of a single man, and there was not one bond of justice nor any of that social agreement and partnership which constitute a community? . . . Therefore, whenever there is a tyrant, one cannot say, . . . that there is a defective republic; logic now forces us to conclude that there is no republic at all.[18]

The participation of the people in activities, deliberations, and decision making concerning matters of public significance is thus a key feature of the Roman notion of public sphere. In more recent times, the role of religion in this public sphere has become the source of significant disagreement. Some have called for the banishment of religion entirely, such as Richard Rorty, who considers religion to be a "conversation stopper" for public discourse.[19] Others have suggested that it will be a source of "open-ended conflict and possible anarchy."[20] Jürgen Habermas's influential work has been accused of minimizing the "relevance of religion for the emergence of a public sphere in politics,"[21] though he explicitly rejected the secularist conception of religion as an essentially private matter that has no place in the public conversation. Habermas ultimately offers a commendable mediating view that acknowledges the validity of religion in public conversations while also affirming the importance of finding "secular translations" for religious discourse in the public political domain. Discerning the place of religion in the public sphere, especially in Asia, where Christianity is generally a minority faith, is of course an ongoing project. Nevertheless, recognizing its legitimate place in the *res publica* is a necessary first step.

---

17. Peter Keegan, *Graffiti in Antiquity* (New York: Routledge, 2014), 173; Luiz Carlos Bresser-Pereira, "Citizenship and *Res Publica*: The Emergence of Republican Rights," *Citizenship Studies* 6, no. 2 (2002): 152–153; Cicero, *The Republic and the Laws*, trans. Niall Rudd (Oxford: Oxford University Press, 1998), 1.39.

18. Cicero, *Republic* 3.43. See Robert T. Radford, *Cicero: A Study in the Origins of Republican Philosophy* (Amsterdam: Rodopy, 2002), 28–29.

19. Richard Rorty, *Philosophy and Social Hope* (London: Penguin, 1999), 170–171.

20. Richard John Neuhaus, *The Naked Public Square: Religion and Democracy in America*, 2nd ed. (Grand Rapids: Eerdmans, 1986), 21.

21. David Zaret, "Religion, Science, and Printing in the Public Spheres in Seventeenth-Century England," in *Habermas and the Public Sphere*, ed. Craig Calhoun (Cambridge: MIT Press, 1992), 212–213; Craig Calhoun, "Introduction," *Habermas and the Public Sphere*, ed. Craig Calhoun (Cambridge: MIT Press, 1992), 35–36.

Basileia "in" *Res Publica*

This situatedness of the Christian faith in the public space requires attending to a further question: How does that public space stand in relation to the "sacred space" where God dwells and reigns – God's *basileia*, or kingdom? So far we have noted that what designates a space as "public" are the activities and the discourses (usually among competing voices) regarding affairs or properties of public character – those things that are "everyone's business."

How should we understand the kingdom of God? The biblical concept, *basileia tou theou*, is often understood in terms of God's "kingly rule or reign" in a spiritual or abstract sense, an interpretation largely drawing from Gustaf Dalman. Dalman's reading, Sverre Aalen remarks, has to do with showing how the Hebrew *malkuth* or the Aramaic *malkutha* in the Jewish texts, when referring to God's kingdom, always meant God's kingly rule or kingship and never territorial rule.[22] This understanding has become firmly established in biblical scholarship as represented in influential works on the Synoptics.[23] In the process, the spatially oriented, this-worldly understanding of "kingdom" has been relegated to a secondary meaning in New Testament lexicons.[24]

According to Aalen, who was one of the first to argue against this consensus, "kingdom" in the Old Testament indeed often refers to "reign," expressed through Jewish parallelisms showing the correspondence between *malkuth* and *melech* (king) (e.g. Isa 24:23; Zech 4:7; 14:16, 17).[25] However, when it comes to the New Testament, he notes an absence of expressions connecting God's kingdom with the abstract notion of "reign" or "kingship."[26] Rejecting also the "de-territorialization of Jesus and the kingdom,"[27] Hans Kvalbein perceptively saw a "non-reign/kingship" description from Dalman himself when he said

---

22. Sverre Aalen, "'Reign' and 'House' in the Kingdom of God in the Gospels," *New Testament Studies* 8, no. 3 (A52 1962): 215–216.

23. Hans Kvalbein, "The Kingdom of God in the Ethics of Jesus," *Communio Viatorum* 40, no. 3 (1998): 204. See George Eldon Ladd, *A Theology of the New Testament*, rev. ed. (Grand Rapids: Eerdmans, 1993); Joachim Jeremias, *New Testament Theology* (London: SCM, 1971). Jeremias writes, "The central theme of the public proclamation of Jesus was the kingly reign of God" (Jeremia, *New Testament*, 4).

24. Kvalbein, "Kingdom of God," 204; Karen J. Wenell, "Kingdom, Not Kingly Rule: Assessing the Kingdom of God as Sacred Space," *Biblical Interpretation* 25, no. 2 (2017): 209. Kvalbein observes that the entry in J. P. Louw and E. A. Nida's *Greek–English Lexicon of the New Testament Based on Semantic Domains* warns without any explanation against using the spatial "kingdom" over "rule" as the proper interpretation of the term.

25. Aalen, "'Reign' and 'House' in the Kingdom of God," 216–217.

26. Aalen, 219.

27. Nicholas R. Brown, *For the Nation: Jesus, the Restoration of Israel and Articulating a Christian Ethic of Territorial Governance* (Eugene: Pickwick, 2016), 8.

that in the New Testament God's kingdom is more aligned with the rabbinic phrase *olam habbah*, or "the coming world," which, when translated properly, should have yielded "kingdom" and not God's "reign."[28] While acknowledging "reign" as a proper rendition in many instances (e.g. Luke 1:33; Rev 17:12, 14–18), J. C. O'Neill draws attention to the necessary link (which Dalman denied) between reign and realm. "The right to reign," he says, "is the right to reign over a designated realm."[29]

Situating the kingdom of God in spatial terms, however, does not simply mean identifying it with a specific geographical location. It is helpful at this point to link it with notions of place and sacred space. According to David Harvey, from a socio-spatial perspective, "places are constructed and experienced as material ecological artefacts and intricate networks of social relations. They are an intense focus of discursive activity, filled with symbolic and representational meanings, and they are a distinctive product of institutionalized social and political economic power."[30] As social constructions, places are filled with decodable signs or interpretable meanings. While on the one hand space points to distance, boundaries, and extensions, on the other hand, places are also storied. According to Walter Brueggemann, they are imbued with historical meanings, providing people across generations with identity, continuity, defined vocation, and envisioned destiny.[31] In the Old Testament, Scripture often portrays places becoming sacred upon being marked by God's epiphanic presence, thus becoming places of divine self-disclosure (e.g. Bethel in Gen 28:10–22; Mt Horeb in Exod 3:1–5).[32]

Seth D. Kunin notes that sacred space in the Old Testament is tied up not only with God's unique presence, but also with God's glory. The ark, tabernacle, and temple are sacred because they are the places where God's glory is specially present and revealed.[33] Sacred space is also connected intrinsically to God's people. Indeed, the connection between sacred place and people is such that

---

28. Kvalbein, "Kingdom of God," 206–208.

29. J. C. O'Neill, "The Kingdom of God," *Novum Testamentum* 35, no. 2 (1993): 131. See Wenell, "Kingdom, Not Kingly Rule," 210.

30. David Harvey, *Justice, Nature and the Geography of Difference* (Cambridge: Blackwell, 1996), 316.

31. Walter Brueggemann, *The Land* (Philadelphia: Fortress, 1982), 4–5.

32. John Inge, "Toward a Theology of Place," *Modern Believing* 40, no. 1 (Jan 1999): 46–47. See Gerald S. Sloyan, "The Bible on Sacred Space," *Liturgy* 3, no. 4 (1983): 23–35.

33. Seth D. Kunin, "Sacred Place," in *Themes and Issues in Judaism*, ed. Seth Kunin (London: Cassell, 2000), 35. See also Karen J. Wenell, "Jesus and the Holy Land," in *Handbook for the Study of the Historical Jesus*, 4 vols., eds. Tom Holmén and Stanley E. Porter (Leiden: Brill, 2011), 2773–2799.

the sanctity of a place depends on the actions of the people – that is, whether or not they faithfully maintain the grounds that honor their status as storied and sacred.[34]

It is in this ethical sense that the notion of people is a vital component of God's kingdom, because God's kingdom is ultimately performative.[35] Kingdom is thus a linkage of "God-people-land," as Karen J. Wenell aptly puts it, where people, because of their relationship with God as Father,[36] demonstrate the values and ways of the kingdom. As a sacred place, the Jerusalem temple was supposed to function as a manifestation of God's rulership on earth, and thus occupied a preeminent role in Jewish life. Sadly, as in Jesus's time, its form and function failed to match.

The Cleansing of the Temple: Reclaiming God's Space

The Gospel of Mark's telling of the temple "cleansing episode" in 11:15–17 (cf. Matt 21:12–13; Luke 19:45–46; John 2:13–17) portrays Jesus reclaiming the sacred function of Israel's most prized sacred space. While the dominant groups dictated how the temple should be understood in terms of thought and practice, its public character left its meaning open to shifts, reinterpretations, and revisions.[37] In this light, by unmasking the temple's oppressive character in its current form, Jesus was proclaiming and reclaiming God's "space" in that contested space.

As the site of the climax of Jesus's conflict with the Jewish religious leaders (e.g. Mark 3:22–29; 7:1–23), the temple's political and theological significance stands out. Politically, it symbolizes the immense religious and political power of the authorities; theologically, it represents the very place of God's dwelling. From the viewpoint of the religious leaders, the enforcers of God's will, Jesus's conflict with the temple's status quo was a conflict with God himself.[38] Central therefore to the conflict is the issue of *authority*, best summarized by the double

---

34. Susan J. White, "Can We Talk about a Theology of Sacred Space?," in *Searching for Sacred Space: Essays on Architecture and Liturgical Design in the Episcopal Church*, ed. John Ander Runkle (New York: Church, 2002), 33–34.

35. Glen H. Stassen and David P. Gushee, *Kingdom Ethics: Following Jesus in Contemporary Context* (Downers Grove: InterVarsity Press, 2003), 21. See G. R. Beasley-Murray, *Jesus and the Kingdom of God* (Grand Rapids: Eerdmans, 1986), 184–185.

36. Wenell, "Kingdom, Not Kingly Rule," 213–214.

37. Karen J. Wenell, "Contested Temple Space and Visionary Kingdom Space in Mark 11–12," *Biblical Interpretation* 15, no. 3 (2007): 329.

38. Ira Brent Diggers, "The Politics of Divine Presence: Temple as Locus of Conflict in the Gospel of Mark," *Biblical Interpretation* 15, no. 3 (2007): 238, 241.

question the religious leaders posed to Jesus: "By what authority are you doing these things? . . . And who gave you authority to do this?" (Mark 11:28). "These things," of course, points to Jesus's earlier action at the temple that similarly questioned the legitimacy of the temple activities and the religious leaders behind them.[39]

The actions mentioned above refer to Jesus's "driving out" the buyers and sellers in the temple courts, "overturning" the tables of money changers and sellers of doves, and not allowing the carrying of merchandise through the temple courts (Mark 11:15–16). In doing these things, Jesus was disrupting activities directly connected with temple worship. Scholars are divided as to the meaning of the action: Was it a ritual cleansing, a prophetic action, a judgment of destruction, a portent of God's coming, or something else?[40]

Without belaboring the point, it is essential to note that Jesus's action was not directed at the temple per se – for he continued going to and teaching in the temple courts after this event (Mark 11:27; 12:35) – but at the religious authorities who sanctioned practices that subverted the temple's very purpose. That Jesus's denunciation referred to the religious authorities is clarified by the fig-tree narrative (Mark 11:12–14, 20–21).[41] It is also important to interpret Jesus's action in relation to his overarching message about God's kingdom (Mark 1:15). His action was a protest, in line with prophetic denunciations, highlighting the dissonance between the oppressive temple practices and his teaching about God's kingdom.[42] In short, it was an action that proclaimed the presentness, the inbreaking, of God's kingdom through his coming.

In this way, Jesus's action at the temple, which Mark presents as leading to his death, serves to highlight his kingdom-centered counter-perception of the temple in contrast to the economic-centered perspective of the religious

---

39. Timothy C. Gray, *The Temple in the Gospel of Mark: A Study in Its Narrative Role* (Tübingen: Mohr Siebeck, 2008), 55–56.

40. A good discussion on the different views is provided in Alexander J. M. Wedderburn, "Jesus' Action in the Temple: A Key or a Puzzle?," *Zeitschrift für die neutestamentliche Wissenschaft und die Kunde der älteren Kirche* 97, no. 1 (2006): 1–6. E. P. Sanders's view also gained attention, rejecting the notion of "cleansing." See his *Jesus and Judaism* (Philadelphia: Fortress, 1985). Craig Evans engaged with key points Sanders raised and found them uncompelling. Craig Evans, "Jesus' Action in the Temple: Cleansing or Portent of Destruction?," *Catholic Biblical Quarterly* 51, no. 2 (Apr. 1989): 237–270.

41. Clinton Wahlen, "The Temple in Mark and Contested Authority," *Biblical Interpretation* 15, no. 3 (2007): 259–263.

42. Wenell, "Contested Temple Space," 335; Francis D. Alvarez, "The Temple Controversy in Mark," *Landas* 28, no. 1 (2014): 125–127. That Jesus's acts were a prophetic announcement of judgment carried out from his self-understanding as a prophet was the position taken by N. T. Wright in *Jesus and the Victory of God* (Minneapolis: Fortress, 1996), 413–427.

leaders. In contrast to the oppressive present, Jesus's kingdom sayings offer a glimpse of an "imagined place," presenting visions for the alternative outworking of structured places and just practices. In short, the cleansing is a pointed criticism of present unjust conditions.[43] Through prophetic, symbolic action, Jesus fervently expressed, like the Old Testament prophets before him, God's displeasure with (1) Gentile exclusion; (2) unjust economic practices; and (3) religious authoritarianism.

Situating the Sacred in Asia's Public Spaces

Thus, in the temple-cleansing incident, Jesus demonstrates in a concrete way the inbreaking of God's kingdom. The kingdom, as we have contended, has at least a partial spatial dimension, pointing to God's kingship in time and space. But while it includes space, in its proleptic character, it cannot be confined to it. As Kunin observes, the dynamic character of God's presence or *Shekinah* allows for sacred places to be mobile and multiple. The tabernacle exemplifies the former. The latter can be seen during the exile when, after the destruction of the Jerusalem temple, sacred space "became primarily dynamic, following the community rather than being a specific place or places."[44] In the same way, the geographical dimension of God's kingdom cannot be delineated, for it is like a seed that is growing (Mark 4:26–34), but it is linked to those who enter it, who understand its character, and who aspire to live and abide by it. The kingdom, then, is *spatially located*, *mobile*, and *performative* in character.[45] And if it is among us, Emily Askew reflects, "then we should continue to train our eyes to see its marks."[46] In the following we seek to see its marks through Jesus's actions, which carry important implications for the public spaces of Asia.

First and foremost, it is notable that Jesus rejected *exclusion*. As a whole, the Markan Gospel underlines Jesus's concern for and mission of opening God's kingdom to the Gentiles, despite the disciples' failure to understand this throughout Jesus's life and ministry.[47] The temple arrangement, with an

---

43. Halvor Moxnes, *Putting Jesus in His Place: A Radical Vision of Household and Kingdom* (Louisville: Westminster, 2003), 109–110.

44. Kunin, "Sacred Place," 37, 40.

45. Wenell, "Kingdom, Not Kingly Rule," 227–229. See Stassen and Gushee, *Kingdom Ethics*, 21–42.

46. Emily Askew, "Critical Spatiality: Mhay's Room and the Kingdom of God," *Lexington Theological Quarterly* 45, no. 34 (Winter 2013): 70.

47. Kelly R. Iverson, *Gentiles in the Gospel of Mark: "Even the Dogs under the Table Eat the Children's Crumbs"* (London: T&T Clark, 2007), 186.

outer court called the "Court of the Gentiles," reflected YHWH's concern to draw the nations to himself. It was a place where foreigners were allowed so that they could participate in the temple prayer and worship activities.[48] Yet the proliferation of commercial activities in the area prevented this. That Jesus described his action using Isaiah 56:7 is insightful, for while that passage points to a future anticipation of the radical inclusiveness of the Gentiles on God's holy mountain, Jesus used it as a litmus test for the present.[49]

In Asia, some of the people groups suffering wide-ranging exclusion or discrimination include the *Dalits* (broken people) of India, the *Minjung* (oppressed masses) of Korea, the *Lumads* (indigenous people groups in Mindanao) of the Philippines, and the *Rohingyas* (Muslims) of Myanmar. Each of these groups experiences a denial of their rights to participate in the social, economic, and political institutions because of race, ethnicity, religion, or social position.[50] Just as the commercialism in the Court of the Gentiles resulted in elimination of Gentile identity in the temple, so in Asia the nonrecognition or derogation of identity is a key feature of exclusionary practices. The Rohingyas exemplify this, having been considered Bengali aliens and subjected to ethnic cleansing. As Azeem Ibrahim points out, the alienation of the Rohingyas was spun early in Myanmar's history by military, fundamentalist Buddhists and ethnic extremists, and has now become ingrained in the minds of the people.[51] In 2014, Myanmar's government did not include them in the census, thereby denying them recognition as a people and making way for the subsequent elimination of a non-people. India's Dalits are similarly considered non-people, and are "discriminated against, denied access to land, forced to work in degrading conditions, and routinely abused . . . legislations and constitutional protections serve only to mask the social realities of discrimination and violence faced by those *living below* the 'pollution line.'"[52] Sadly, Keith Hebden observes, Christians also participate in the exclusion of others such as the Dalits, so that

---

48. Wahlen, "Temple in Mark," 267.

49. Driggers, "Politics of Divine Presence," 240; Holly J. Carey, "Teachings and Tirades: Jesus' Temple Act and His Teachings in Mark 11:15–19," *Stone-Campbell Journal* 10, no. 1 (2007): 103.

50. Chittaranjan Senapati, *Exclusion and Poverty in India and Central Asia: A Diversity and Development Perspective* ([India]: Partridge, 2016), ch. 2.3, Kindle ed.

51. Azeem Ibrahim, *The Rohingyas: Inside Myanmar's Hidden Genocide* (London: Hurst & Co., 2016), 3–4.

52. Human Rights Watch Report, *Broken People: Caste Violence Against India's "Untouchables"* (New York: Human Rights Watch Report, 1999), 1–2; quoted in Peniel Rajkumar, *Dalit Theology and Dalit Liberation: Problems, Paradigms and Possibilities* (Farnham: Ashgate, 2010), 5.

they find themselves not only "'outside the temple' but also often 'outside the Church.'"[53]

In such exclusionary situations, an important way the church in Asia can emulate Jesus's actions in the temple is through fighting for the inclusion of the oppressed in the public sphere, forging a "culture of empowerment,"[54] and demanding a recognition of their identity in accordance with their status as *imago Dei*. Where the public discourse will not allow for such radical claims to be made, overturning the tables may entail creating or participating in what Nancy Fraser calls *subaltern counterpublics*, or alternative public spaces, where the oppressed can utter and find their own voice, as well as hear those of others.[55] This means intentionally seeking the oppressed and going to the margins, just as the Markan Jesus visited Gentile territory to bring them God's compassion, healing, and kingdom (e.g. Mark 5:1–20; 7:24 – 8:9; 8:22 – 9:29).[56] Indeed, through *being with* and understanding those who have fallen through society's cracks – or have been thrust into them, as it were – Christians in Asia can genuinely advocate for the legitimate concerns *for*, *and*, and *with* the excluded ones, thus situating kingdom values or the sacred in the public square.

Second, aside from rejecting exclusion, Jesus denounced *unjust economic practices*. In the temple incident, Jesus rejected the commercialism being carried out in the outer Court of the Gentiles, especially as it had already crept into the inner areas of the temple (Mark 11:16).[57] Such commercialism was initiated by Herod and sanctified by the religious authorities, for the Second Temple was, in actuality, the third rendition, grandiosely rebuilt by Herod from Zerubbabel's modest reconstruction. It was a monumental undertaking, both externally with respect to the building and internally with respect to the materialization of cultic temple practices. As Bertz remarks based on the writings of Josephus, "Herod had succeeded in Hellenizing and romanizing it at its very center. . . . The new Temple had acquired new functions: It was

---

53. Keith Hebden, *Dalit Theology and Christian Anarchism* (Farnham: Ashgate, 2011), 145.

54. C. S. Song, *Jesus and the Reign of God* (Minneapolis: Fortress, 1993), 114–150.

55. Nancy Fraser, "Rethinking the Public Sphere: A Contribution to the Critique of Actually Existing Democracy," *Social Text* 25/26 (1990): 66–67. This approach of seeking justice through counterpublics for marginalized Asian-Americans is advocated by K. Christine Pae and James W. McCarty III in their insightful essay, "The Hybridized Public Sphere: Asian American Christian Ethics, Social Justice, and Public Discourse," *Journal of the Society of Christian Ethics* 32, no. 1 (2012): 93–114.

56. See Iverson, *Gentiles in Mark*, 182–186.

57. P. M. Casey, "Culture and Historicity: The Cleansing of the Temple," *Catholic Biblical Quarterly* 59, no. 2 (1997): 310.

now Herod's Temple, a divine manifestation of Herodian legitimacy."[58] More of a commercial institution than a house of worship, the temple had become a source of wealth, including for the high priests, who were able to legally obtain tithes even from the very poor.[59] In short, it had become, Jesus says, citing Jeremiah 7:11 a "den of robbers." Jesus thus rejected the Herodian temple for its worship of Mammon instead of God.

Poverty is prevalent in most postcolonial Asian nations. Felix Wilfred is therefore right to assert that "there is no Asian public theology without addressing the economy."[60] Indeed, while some countries, like Japan, Singapore, Hong Kong, and South Korea, are home to robust economies, most Asian nations are immersed in dire poverty due in large part to the effects of colonization, the economic and political domination (and unjust management) of the elite, and exploitation of multinational corporations. Hence the issue of poverty is intrinsically intertwined with the struggle for economic justice.[61] In the public spaces of Asia, an essential element of the struggle is what Walter Wink calls "unmasking the Domination System,"[62] a process illustrated by Jesus's prophetic deprivation of the temple's excessive and unjust commercialism. Unmasking requires the rejection of a posture of silence common in Asian cultures and Christian traditions. This "scandal of silence" too often has the effect of perpetuating and legitimizing unjust conditions.[63] Conversely, the aim of unmasking is the cultivation of a "culture of conscience,"[64] so as to make visible or unveil the outworking of oppressive forces in society for the explicit purpose of social transformation.[65] It is therefore a vital task of the churches in

---

58. Hans Dieter Betz, "Jesus and the Purity of the Temple (Mark 11:15–18): A Comparative Religion Approach," *Journal of Biblical Literature* 116, no. 3 (1997): 464–465.

59. Casey, "Culture and Historicity," 314, 315.

60. Wilfred, *Asian Public Theology*, ch. 8, Kindle. It has been observed that the main focus, therefore, of most Asian theologies has been development and particularly "liberation." Catalino G. Arevalo, "Some Pre-Notes to Doing Theology on Man, Society and History in the Asian Context," *Landas* 25, nos. 1/2 (2011): 39.

61. See Roland Chia, *Hope for the World: The Christian Vision* (Carlisle: Langham Global Library, 2012), 5–7.

62. Walter Wink, *Engaging the Powers: Discernment and Resistance in a World of Domination* (Minneapolis: Fortress, 1992), 87–108.

63. Tooley, *Voices of the Voiceless*, 182. According to Virginia Fabella, many Filipino women suffer gender oppression because they see Jesus primarily as a victim who was silent in his sufferings. Virginia Fabella and Sun Ai Lee Park, eds., *We Dare to Dream: Doing Theology as Asian Women* (Kowloon: Asian Women's Resource Centre for Culture and Theology, 1989), 10.

64. Song, *Reign of God*, 104.

65. Timothy Rutzou, "Strange Bedfellows? Ontology, Normativity, Critical Realism, and Queer Theory," in *Critical Realism, History, and Philosophy in the Social Sciences*, eds. Timothy Rutzou and George Steinmetz (Bingley: Emerald, 2018), 136.

Asia. As Michael Walzer remarks, the biblical prophets invented the practice of social criticism, that is, of unmasking hypocritical norms, behavior, and institutions.[66] Prophetic unmasking of the causes of economic oppression is thus invaluable and can be an initial step toward responsible actions based on a more realistic sense of society's economic contradictions.

Third, and finally, Jesus's prophetic action was a denunciation of *religious authoritarianism*. As the temple incident shows, not only were the religious authorities intolerant of Gentiles; they were also deeply intolerant of Jewish religious dissenters, prompting them to plan to kill Jesus, "for they feared him, because the whole crowd was amazed at his teaching" (Mark 11:18). Violence in the name of religion is a reality in many Asian nations, particularly in relation to "majority–minority" politics that play an important role in shaping the nation and ideas of the common good and citizenship.[67] Often, the secular nature of a government is compromised to serve the interests of the dominant religion, as in the case of the Rohingya in Myanmar. In the Philippines, decades of conflict has taken place between the government, representing the nation's Christian majority, and the *Moros* (Muslims), who have been repeatedly oppressed. India has seen communal violence break out, as illustrated by the deadly Gujarat riots. Pakistan's blasphemy laws, which are often wielded arbitrarily to punish members of the Christian minority, likewise illustrate the volatile majority-minority relations in the country.

Following Jesus in the religiously charged public spaces of Asia requires the rejection of authoritarian tendencies characteristic of the religious leaders who ultimately plotted to kill him. Indeed, whereas the authorities shunned Jesus, seeing in him a religious "other" who could only threaten their well-being, Jesus sought out social and religious "others," and even had meals with them. Jesus valued their identity as human persons and pointed to the possibility of a shared life across traditional boundaries. In engaging the public sphere of Asia, Christians should therefore seek "greater human solidarity, not just toleration or the protection of individuals in their solitude."[68] Interreligious dialogue has been one approach to fostering solidarity, with some measure of success in countries like Indonesia and the Philippines. Nevertheless, as Paul Hedges observes, while dialogue may not always provide the common ground

---

66. Michael Walzer, *Interpretation and Social Criticism* (Cambridge: Harvard University Press, 1987), 87.

67. Rowena Robinson, "The Politics of Religion and Faith in South Asia," *Society and Culture in South Asia* 3, no. 2 (2017): vii.

68. David Hollenbach, *The Common Good and Christian Ethics* (Cambridge: Cambridge University Press, 2002), 136.

for deliberative rational discourse, it can still promote understanding among different groups and lead to greater empathy for others, important goods in the cultivation of a healthy public sphere.[69]

Conclusion

Cognizant of the multiple oppressive forces that continue to plague many nations in Asia, as a Filipino Christian I have attempted in this essay to answer the question, "What does it mean to be a citizen of God's kingdom in Asia?" To be sure, the full unfolding of God's kingdom lies in the future; nevertheless, as argued in this essay, its present manifestation is not merely spiritual, but has spatial, this-worldly implications. In particular, the kingdom must be characterized by certain values and performative actions, such as those displayed by Jesus in the Markan account of the temple-cleansing incident. In Jesus's defense of the rights of the Gentiles in the sacred public space of the Jerusalem temple, we see that for him, God is not only Lord of our private places, but he is also Lord over all that is public, and, indeed, over all creation. Perceiving the kingdom in this way should prompt us to engage in Asia's public spaces, and in particular to pursue the inclusion and dignity of the oppressed and marginalized, for whom the kingdom's advent is good news with public implications.

References

Aalen, Sverre. "'Reign' and 'House' in the Kingdom of God in the Gospels." *New Testament Studies* 8, no. 3 (1962): 215–240.
Alangaram, A. *Christ of the Asian Peoples: Towards an Asian Contextual Christology: Based on the Documents of the Federation of Asian Bishops' Conference*. Rev. ed. Bangalore: Asian Trading, 2001.
Alvarez, Francis D. "The Temple Controversy in Mark." *Landas* 28, no. 1 (2014): 115–152.
Arevalo, Catalino G. "Some Pre-Notes to Doing Theology on Man, Society and History in the Asian Context." *Landas* 25, nos. 1/2 (2011): 37–55.
Askew, Emily. "Critical Spatiality: Mhay's Room and the Kingdom of God." *Lexington Theological Quarterly* 45, no. 34 (2013): 69–78.
Beasley-Murray, G. R. *Jesus and the Kingdom of God*. Grand Rapids: Eerdmans, 1986.

---

69. Paul Hedges, "Can Interreligious Dialogue Provide a New Space for Deliberative Democracy in the Public Sphere? Philosophical Perspectives from the Examples of the UK and Singapore," *Interreligious Studies and Intercultural Theology* 2, no. 1 (2018): 20.

Betz, Hans Dieter. "Jesus and the Purity of the Temple (Mark 11:15–18): A Comparative Religion Approach." *Journal of Biblical Literature* 116, no. 3 (1997): 455–472.

Bonhoeffer, Dietrich. *Letters and Papers from Prison*. Edited by Eberhard Bethge. New York: Collier, 1972.

Bresser-Pereira, Luiz Carlos. "Citizenship and *Res Publica*: The Emergence of Republican Rights." *Citizenship Studies* 6, no. 2 (2002): 145–164.

Brown, Nicholas R. *For the Nation: Jesus, the Restoration of Israel and Articulating a Christian Ethic of Territorial Governance*. Eugene: Pickwick, 2016.

Brueggemann, Walter. *The Land*. Philadelphia: Fortress, 1982.

Calhoun, Craig, ed. *Habermas and the Public Sphere*. Cambridge: MIT Press, 1992.

Carey, Holly J. "Teachings and Tirades: Jesus' Temple Act and His Teachings in Mark 11:15–19." *Stone-Campbell Journal* 10, no. 1 (2007): 93–105.

Casey, P. M. "Culture and Historicity: The Cleansing of the Temple." *Catholic Biblical Quarterly* 59, no. 2 (1997): 306–332.

Chandra Prasad, Manohar. "Dalit Theology: Methodological Issues in a Contextual Theology of Liberation." *Asia Journal of Theology* 23, no. 1 (April 2009): 166–175.

Chia, Roland. *Hope for the World: The Christian Vision*. Carlisle: Langham Global Library, 2012.

Cicero. *The Republic and the Laws*. Translated by Niall Rudd. Oxford: Oxford University Press, 1998.

Diggers, Ira Brent. "The Politics of Divine Presence: Temple as Locus of Conflict in the Gospel of Mark." *Biblical Interpretation* 15, no. 3 (2007): 227–247.

Dyrness, William. *Learning about Theology from the Third World*. Grand Rapids: Zondervan, 1990.

Evans, Craig. "Jesus' Action in the Temple: Cleansing or Portent of Destruction?" *Catholic Biblical Quarterly* 51, no. 2 (1989): 237–270.

Fabella, Virginia, and Sun Ai Lee Park, eds. *We Dare to Dream: Doing Theology as Asian Women*. Kowloon: Asian Women's Resource Centre for Culture and Theology, 1989.

Fraser, Nancy. "Rethinking the Public Sphere: A Contribution to the Critique of Actually Existing Democracy." *Social Text* 25/26 (1990): 56–80.

Gener, Timoteo D. "With/Beyond Tracy: Re-Visioning Public Theology." *Evangelical Review of Theology* 33, no. 2 (April 2009): 118–138.

Gray, Timothy C. *The Temple in the Gospel of Mark: A Study in Its Narrative Role*. Tübingen: Mohr Siebeck, 2008.

Haire, James. "Public Theology – A Latin Captivity of the Church: Violence and Public Theology in the Asia-Pacific Context." *International Journal of Public Theology* 1, no. 3 (2007): 455–470.

Harvey, David. *Justice, Nature and the Geography of Difference*. Cambridge: Blackwell, 1996.

Hebden, Keith. *Dalit Theology and Christian Anarchism*. Farnham: Ashgate, 2011.

Hedges, Paul. "Can Interreligious Dialogue Provide a New Space for Deliberative Democracy in the Public Sphere? Philosophical Perspectives from the Examples of the UK and Singapore." *Interreligious Studies and Intercultural Theology* 2, no. 1 (2018): 5–26.

Hollenbach, David. *The Common Good and Christian Ethics*. Cambridge: Cambridge University Press, 2002.

Human Rights Watch Report. *Broken People: Caste Violence against India's "Untouchables."* New York: Human Rights Watch Report, 1999.

Hwa Yung. *Mangoes or Bananas?: The Quest for an Authentic Christian Theology*. Oxford: Regnum, 1997.

Ibrahim, Azeem. *The Rohingyas: Inside Myanmar's Hidden Genocide*. London: Hurst & Co., 2016.

Inge, John. "Toward a Theology of Place." *Modern Believing* 40, no. 1 (1999): 42–50.

Iverson, Kelly R. *Gentiles in the Gospel of Mark: "Even the Dogs under the Table Eat the Children's Crumbs"*. London: T&T Clark, 2007.

Jeremias, Joachim. *New Testament Theology*. London: SCM, 1971.

Keegan, Peter. *Graffiti in Antiquity*. New York: Routledge, 2014.

Kim, Chi Ha. *The Gold-Crowned Jesus and Other Writings*. New York: Orbis Books, 1978.

Koyama, Kosuke. "The Asian Approach to Christ." *Missiology* 12, no. 4 (1984): 435–447.

Kunin, Seth D. "Sacred Place." In *Themes and Issues in Judaism*, edited by Seth D. Kunin, 22–55. London: Casell, 2000.

———, ed. *Themes and Issues in Judaism*. London: Cassell, 2000.

Kvalbein, Hans. "The Kingdom of God in the Ethics of Jesus." *Communio Viatorum* 40, no. 3 (1998): 197–227.

Kwon, Jin-kwan. "Minjung (the Multitude), Historical Symbol of Jesus Christ." *Asia Journal of Theology* 24, no. 1 (April 2010): 153–171.

Ladd, George Eldon. *A Theology of the New Testament*. Rev. ed. Grand Rapids: Eerdmans, 1993.

Lak, Yeow Choo, ed. *Doing Theology with God's Purpose in Asia*. ATESEA Occasional Papers no. 10. Singapore: ATESEA, 1990.

Maggay, Melba. *Filipino Religious Consciousness: Some Implications to Missions*. Quezon City: Institiute for Studies in Asian Church and Culture, 1999.

Moxnes, Halvor. *Putting Jesus in His Place: A Radical Vision of Household and Kingdom*. Louisville: Westminster, 2003.

Neuhaus, Richard John. *The Naked Public Square: Religion and Democracy in America*. 2nd ed. Grand Rapids: Eerdmans, 1986.

O'Neill, J. C. "The Kingdom of God." *Novum Testamentum* 35, no. 2 (1993): 130–141.

Pae, K. Christine, and James W. McCarty, III. "The Hybridized Public Sphere: Asian American Christian Ethics, Social Justice and Public Discourse." *Journal of the Society of Christian Ethics* 32, no. 1 (2012): 93–114.

Pieris, Aloysius. *An Asian Theology of Liberation*. London: T&T Clark, 1988.

Radford, Robert T. *Cicero: A Study in the Origins of Republican Philosophy*. Amsterdam: Rodopy, 2002.

Rajkumar, Peniel. *Dalit Theology and Dalit Liberation: Problems, Paradigms and Possibilities*. Farnham: Ashgate, 2010.

Robinson, Rowena. "The Politics of Religion and Faith in South Asia." *Society and Culture in South Asia* 3, no. 2 (2017): vii–xx.

Rorty, Richard. *Philosophy and Social Hope*. London: Penguin, 1999.

Rutzou, Timothy. "Strange Bedfellows? Ontology, Normativity, Critical Realism, and Queer Theory." In *Critical Realism, History, and Philosophy in the Social Sciences*, edited by Timothy Rutzou and George Steinmetz, 119–158. Bingley: Emerald, 2018.

Sanders, E. P. *Jesus and Judaism*. Philadelphia: Fortress, 1985.

Senapati, Chittaranjan. *Exclusion and Poverty in India and Central Asia: A Diversity and Development Perspective*. [India]: Partridge, 2016.

Sloyan, Gerald S. "The Bible on Sacred Space." *Liturgy* 3, no. 4 (1983): 20–27.

Song, C. S. *Jesus and the Reign of God*. Minneapolis: Fortress, 1993.

———. "Oh, Jesus, Here with Us!" *Ecumenical Review* 35, no. 1 (1983): 59–74.

———. *The Tears of Lady Meng: A Parable of People's Political Theology*. New York: Orbis Books, 1982.

———. *Tell Us Our Names: Story Theology from an Asian Perspective*. New York: Orbis Books, 1984.

Stassen, Glen H., and David P. Gushee. *Kingdom Ethics: Following Jesus in Contemporary Context*. Downers Grove: InterVarsity Press, 2003.

Sugirtharajah, R. S., ed. *Frontiers in Asian Christian Theology: Emerging Trends*. New York: Orbis Books, 1994.

Tooley, Michelle. *Voices of the Voiceless: Women, Justice and Human Rights in Guatemala*. Scottdale: Herald, 1997.

Wahlen, Clinton. "The Temple in Mark and Contested Authority." *Biblical Interpretation* 15, no. 3 (2007): 248–267.

Walzer, Michael. *Interpretation and Social Criticism*. Cambridge: Harvard University Press, 1987.

Wedderburn, Alexander J. M. "Jesus' Action in the Temple: A Key or a Puzzle?" *Zeitschrift für die neutestamentliche Wissenschaft und die Kunde der älteren Kirche* 97, no. 1 (2006): 1–22.

Wenell, Karen J. "Contested Temple Space and Visionary Kingdom Space in Mark 11–12." *Biblical Interpretation* 15, no. 3 (2007): 323–337.

———. "Jesus and the Holy Land." In *Handbook for the Study of the Historical Jesus*, edited by Tom Holmén and Stanley E. Porter, 2773–2799. 4 Vols. Leiden: Brill, 2011.

———. "Kingdom, Not Kingly Rule: Assessing the Kingdom of God as Sacred Space." *Biblical Interpretation* 25, no. 2 (2017): 206–233.

White, Susan J. "Can We Talk about a Theology of Sacred Space?" In *Searching for Sacred Space: Essays on Architecture and Liturgical Design in the Episcopal Church*, edited by John Ander Runkle, 19–36. New York: Church, 2002.

Wiesel, Eli. *Night*. Translated by Marion Wiesel. New York: Hill & Wang, 2006.

Wilfred, Felix. *Asian Public Theology: Critical Concerns in Challenging Times*. Delhi: ISPCK, 2010. Kindle edition.

Wink, Walter. *Engaging the Powers: Discernment and Resistance in a World of Domination*. Minneapolis: Fortress, 1992.

Wright, N. T. *Jesus and the Victory of God*. Minneapolis: Fortress, 1996.

Yewangoe, A. A. *Theologia Crucis in Asia: Asian Christian Views on Suffering in the Face of Overwhelming Poverty and Multifaceted Religiosity in Asia*. Amsterdam: Rodopi, 1987.

Zaret, David. "Religion, Science, and Printing in the Public Spheres in Seventeenth-Century England." In *Habermas and the Public Sphere*, edited by Craig Calhoun, 212–235. Cambridge: MIT Press, 1992.

13

Finding Home for the Unhomed
Helping Diaspora Communities Discover Identity and Belonging

Juliet Lee Uytanlet
Biblical Seminary of the Philippines

Discovering Diaspora and Diaspora Missiology

The movement of people from one place to another, whether near or far, can be traced back to the beginning of human life on earth. The biblical account describes how, after Adam and Eve fell short of God's glory with their deliberate disobedience, they had to move out of the beautiful garden of Eden and move into a new, unfamiliar place where thorns and thistles grew (Gen 3:23). Other biblical stories also present the movement of people across geographical and cultural boundaries, such as Abraham's sojourning to Canaan, Joseph's being sold as a slave to Egypt, the Israelites leaving Egypt for Canaan, and the exile of the Jews to Babylon. Humans have always been moving from one place to another in search of sustenance, shelter, and security. As intelligent beings, humans do not simply seek sustenance to stay alive, but long for both physical well-being and a meaningful understanding of their identity and belonging.

There are several terms used to refer to the movement of people. "Migration" is a general term that describes humans moving from one place to another. Migration can either be internal, movement within one's country, or external, going abroad. It can be voluntary, such as those seeking better employment opportunities abroad, or involuntary, such as refugees, asylum seekers, and internally displaced people (IDP) who are forced out of their homes for various reasons. It can also be temporary or permanent. International students go abroad temporarily for studies and tourists for pleasure and cultural experiences. Migrant workers or overseas workers work abroad temporarily or on a contractual basis. "Immigration" is the act of entering and settling in a country that is not your country of birth or origin. Immigration usually connotes the idea of permanent settlement. "Emigration" is the act of leaving one's country of birth to enter another country. An emigrant is one who has left his or her country to enter another country as a migrant or immigrant.[1]

"Diaspora" is a phenomenon that includes both migration and immigration. The word "diaspora" comes from the Greek *speiro* and *dia*, meaning "to scatter abroad." The Greeks used this word to refer to migration and colonization. Lawrence J. Ma notes that "Historically, the word connotes the loss of homeland, uprootedness, expulsion, oppression, moral degradation, a collective memory of the homeland and a strong desire to return to it one day."[2]

The word "diaspora" was used mainly with regard to religious groups until the 1950s. It did not gain popularity until the mid-1980s, when it was used to refer to a population living outside their original territory. Today, diaspora loosely means ethnic communities divided by state boundaries or transnational communities.[3] According to Robin Cohen, there are five main types of diaspora: victims (refugees and internally displaced people), laborers (migrant workers), traders (transnational businessmen and women), imperial settlers (colonizers), and deterritorialized people (those culturally hybridized due to colonization).[4] It is possible for an ethnic group to have more than one type of diaspora.

Lawrence J. C. Ma highlights the need to reconceptualize diaspora in the twenty-first century. He proposes that diaspora must be understood as "a process, a group of people, a geographic area and a spatial network."[5] Diaspora is first of all a process: migrants have to go through a series of events, situations, and experiences. They have to go through relocation and, sometimes even re-migration as they adapt, adopt, innovate, and negotiate for survival and prosperity. Such is the case of the Chinese diaspora in Southeast

---

1. Rayna Bailey, *Immigration and Migration* (New York: Infobase Publishing, 2008), 306–307.

2. Lawrence J. C. Ma, "Space, Place, and Transnationalism in the Chinese Diaspora," in *The Chinese Diaspora: Space, Place, Mobility, and Identity*, eds. Lawrence J. C. Ma and Carolyn Cartier (Lanham: Rowman & Littlefield, 2003), 7.

3. Stephanie Dufoix, *Diasporas* (Berkley: University of California Press, 2008), 17–19, 23, 30.

4. Robin Cohen, *Global Diasporas: An Introduction* (London: Routledge, 2008), 18.

5. Ma, "Space, Place, and Transnationalism," 2.

Asia who re-migrated to the United States, Canada, European countries, and Australia during the 1960s onward. The desire for re-migration, in this case, was primarily due to discrimination, hostility, and violence against them.[6]

Second, diaspora is about groups of people or ethnic groups from the same homeland moving to different parts of the world.[7] Hutchinson and Smith define ethnicity as a "named human population with myths of common ancestry, shared historical memories, one or more elements of common culture, a link with a homeland and a sense of solidarity among at least some of its members."[8] The strength or weakness of each characteristic defined by Hutchinson and Smith varies for each ethnic group, generation, and individual. First-generation immigrants generally have a strong sense of homeland. The second-generation ethnic group may still hold on to the many traditions and customs passed on to them by their parents. They can often speak their mother tongue fluently. However, the third, fourth, and fifth generations may not necessarily be fluent in their ethnic language or culture. The longer the ethnic group lives in and adapts to the host country, the more likely that they will either lose their ethnic culture or mix their culture with that of the host country. Unless there is a constant streaming of new immigrants of the same ethnicity or other intentional actions undertaken to promote and preserve their ethnic culture and language, it is difficult for future generations to preserve their ethnic language and culture.

Third, diaspora has to do with a geographical area and spatial network. Space is more than just a "container" for people to live in; it is a place for identification and belonging. Space is affected by complex factors – economic, political, ecological, social, and cultural dimensions – that intersect and constantly challenge the space and the people within it. Diaspora is thus not just about space or geographical location, but also the relationships and connections emerging in that complex multilayered space.[9]

Thus, we can define diaspora as a process of migration or re-migration by a community of people who share common cultural linkages in one location fostering connections and relationships. What, then, is diaspora missiology? Missiology is a multidisciplinary study of mission that incorporates theology, history, and social sciences, so diaspora missiology is "a missiological

---

6. Ma, 7–8.

7. Ma, 7.

8. John Hutchinson and Anthony D. Smith, eds., *Ethnicity* (Oxford: Oxford University Press, 1996), 7.

9. Ma, "Space, Place, and Transnationalism," 7–12.

framework for understanding and participating in God's redemptive mission among people living outside their place of origin."[10]

The importance of the relationship between diaspora and missions has been recognized by evangelical Christians around the world:

> The Third Lausanne Congress on World Evangelization (Cape Town 2010) recognized the importance of diaspora missions and missiology. Consequently, many denominations and mission organizations are adjusting their structures, re-calibrating their strategies, and realigning their resources (personnel and funds) for effective delivery to help fulfill the Great Commission. Several seminaries such as Ambrose University (Calgary, Canada), Alliance Graduate School (Manila, Philippines), and Ukraine Evangelical Theological Seminary (Kiev, Ukraine), are now offering courses in Diaspora Missiology. More doctoral students are writing their dissertations on diaspora or migration related issues. Diaspora study is no longer restricted to the domains of history, economics, law, political, and social sciences. Today, it is exciting to see the fast emergence of diaspora missiology. Clearly, the Lausanne Movement has catalyzed the academy, the local church, and the marketplace.[11]

Individuals like Sadiri Joy Tira and Sam George have been catalysts for this movement, zealously mobilizing churches and Christians around the world to participate in the work of diaspora missions. Tira is a Filipino Canadian while George is an Indian American. Both attest to the importance of diaspora missions as they themselves are living and ministering in diaspora communities. Tira puts it this way:

> Today, people from the 10/40 Window are scattered all over the globe. The Chinese and the South Asian diasporas are two of the largest in the world. Who would have predicted the recent political explosions in North Africa, driving Egyptians, Tunisians, Syrians, Libyans, and Iraqis into exile? The refugee situations of recent months are staggering – not to mention the millions of Jewish people, Africans, Armenians, and Palestinians who have

---

10. The Lausanne Movement, "The Seoul Declaration on Diaspora Missiology," 14 November 2009, https://www.lausanne.org/content/statement/the-seoul-declaration-on-diaspora-missiology.

11. The Lausanne Movement, "Diasporas," https://www.lausanne.org/networks/issues/diasporas.

been scattered for centuries. All these people are from the 10/40 Window, the area on the map that was known in early Protestant missions as the "region beyond."[12]

With globalization and urbanization, the nations and ethnicities are coming to our cities. They live among us. We need not travel far to do cross-cultural missions because the Lord has brought them right across our streets. The challenge is whether we are taking this opportunity to minister to the strangers among us. Do we see them as souls who need to hear the good news of our Lord Jesus Christ? Do we love our "new" neighbor who may be seeking to form new identities and belonging?

We need to be reminded that God has the nations in mind and in his heart when we talk about mission or doing missions. He called Abraham out of Ur so that through him the nations would be blessed. As his witness to the nations he used the nation Israel, set apart to worship the only one true God. He sent his prophets to prophesy to both Israel and the nations. When we say that God loved "the world" (John 3:16) this includes all nations; when Jesus issues the Great Commission, it is a call to reach all ethnic groups (Matt 28:19–20). We follow the example of Paul, who conscientiously preached to both Jews and Gentiles and diligently traveled all over the Roman world. With diaspora missions, we need to realize the great opportunities we have to witness to the nations who could be our neighbors.

The Diaspora Community: Finding Identity and Belonging

According to the United Nations in 2017, India has the largest diaspora of international migrants in the world, with 16.6 million living outside their country. The other nations with large diaspora populations are Mexico (13 million), the Russian Federation (10.6 million), and China (10 million).[13] However, this data on China excludes Taiwan, Hong Kong, and Macao. Furthermore, Chinese immigrants have a multi-century history of being

---

12. Sadiri Joy Tira, "Every Person (From Everywhere)," in *Regions Beyond and Regions Around: Diaspora Missions and the Christian and Missionary Alliance in Canada*, ed. Sadiri Joy Tira (Calgary: Jaffray Centre for Global Initiatives, 2018), 3.

13. "By definition, an international migrant is a person who is living in a country other than his or her country of birth." United Nations, Department of Economic and Social Affairs, Population Division (2017), *International Migration Report 2017 (Highlights)* (New York: United Nations, 2017), http://www.un.org/en/development/desa/population/migration/publications/migrationreport/docs/MigrationReport2017_Highlights.pdf, 3, 12–13. Others estimate the Indian diaspora as 20 to 25 million. Sam George, *Understanding the Coconut Generation: Ministry to the Americanized Asian Indians* (Niles: Mall Publishing, 2006), 14.

scattered throughout different parts of the world, commonly referred to as the Overseas Chinese or *huaqiao* 華僑.[14] Among the billions of people in this world, the Chinese people are the most scattered today.[15] They can be found in 130 countries outside of China.[16] As Allen Yeh puts it, the Chinese diaspora "has often gone unnoticed" when in fact they are "the largest diaspora in the history of the world."[17] "[T]he Overseas Community Affairs Council estimates in 2015 that there are 43 million ethnic Chinese living beyond China, Taiwan, Hong Kong, and Macao. The Chinese people is then the largest group dispersed in the world, having the largest world population of 1.39 billion in China in 2015."[18]

Ma classifies Chinese international migration into two broad periods: the pre-1960s and the post-1960s. The pre-1960s goes as far back as the nineteenth century when migrants were mostly from Fujian and Guangdong and serving as laborers, traders, and farmers. The post-1960s migrants are the Chinese diaspora of Southeast Asia and from different parts of China. They are generally educated and well-off, very different from the images of migrants in the pre-1960s. Their reasons for migration are political instability, economic development, changing immigration policies in Western countries, and modern globalization. Nonetheless, the Chinese in diaspora have often experienced unwelcoming situations in the past and even in the present, despite the fact that they carry images of billionaires and rich transnationals rather than coolies and merchants.[19]

---

14. Ma, "Space, Place, and Transnationalism," 2. The *huaqiao* or Overseas Chinese is the immigrant who arrives from China. Back in the colonial period, these migrants considered their host country a temporary home, a transient place. While they wanted to return back to their homeland, unforeseen circumstances led them to settle and flourish in their host countries for generations. Juliet Lee Uytanlet, *The Hybrid Tsinoys: Challenges of Hybridity and Homogeneity as Socio-Cultural Constructs among the Chinese in the Philippines* (Eugene: Pickwick, 2016), 75.

15. Chinese people or *huaren* 華人 refers to Chinese in diaspora. This classification includes immigrants and their descendants. See Uytanlet, *Hybrid Tsinoys*, 73.

16. Peter S. Li and Eva Xiaoling Li, "Chinese Overseas Population," in *Routledge Handbook of Chinese Diaspora*, ed. Tan Chee Beng (London: Routledge, 2013), 20–21.

17. Allen Yeh, "The Chinese Diaspora," in *Global Diasporas and Mission*, eds. Chandler H. Im and Amos Yong (Oxford: Regnum, 2014), 89.

18. Juliet Lee Uytanlet, "Transit, Transient, Transition: How the Lexington Chinese Christian Church Became an Instrument of Conversion," in *Reaching New Territory: Theological Reflections*, eds. Samson Uytanlet, Thomas R. V. Forster, and Susan Tan (Valenzuela City: Biblical Seminary of the Philippines, 2017), 21–39.

19. "Coolie" means cheap labor. The Coolie Trade was instrumental in the late nineteenth century in the dispersion of cheap Chinese laborers to different parts of the world. Uytanlet, *Hybrid Tsinoys*, 44–45, 223, 225–229.

Bhabha's Unhomed Theory

As a member of the Chinese diaspora community, I wish to highlight how this group can be a case study in how the church can see diasporic communities as special places for the reception and transmission of the gospel. First, however, we need to understand how two theoreticians – Homi Bhabha and Meredith McGuire – help us understand the nature of identity formation in diasporic communities.

Bhabha's discussion of the unhomed provides an important framework in understanding diaspora people. For Bhabha, the unhomed are not those without homes, but those who are not at home. I picture someone at a party who feels out of place and not welcomed. In the Filipino lingo, we sometimes shorten the term as "o-p" and say "*na-o-o-p ako*" (I feel o-p, or out of place).

As a Chinese Filipino born and raised in the Philippines, I have experienced discrimination and prejudice that has led to feelings of being unhomely. Before I got my Philippine citizenship, I questioned my identity, especially my citizenship. To which country do I belong? The Philippines is where I identify, but I am classified as a Chinese citizen. Yet I do not have a Chinese passport but a Taiwanese passport. However, I still need to get a Taiwan visa to enter Taiwan or other countries. I find myself identifying with Bhabha, who grew up in Bombay as a member of a small minority group, and now lives and works in the West. Reflecting the feelings of countless diaspora community members, he wonders "what it would be like to live without the unresolved tensions between cultures and countries that have become the narrative of my life, and the defining characteristic of my work."[20]

Bhabha describes the experience of the unhomed as a feeling of displacement and even "terror" upon recognizing that one is not at home, nor even where one "should" be. He creatively describes this phenomenon not just with sociological analysis, but by referring to characters in literature who find themselves trapped in homes not of their own choosing.[21]

Bhabha's discussion of liminality (in-betweenness), ambivalence, and displacement describes familiar situations and realities for diasporic people. In the case of the Chinese in the Philippines, I can personally bear witness to the struggle with identity and belonging, constantly negotiating between two identities and two cultures. This process can also lead to a sense of displacement.

---

20. Homi Bhabha, *The Location of Culture* (Oxford: Routledge, 2004), x.
21. Bhabha, *Location of Culture*, 13–15.

In my fieldwork conducted in 2012, I classified Chinese Filipinos into six groups:

1. Old Immigrants: those who entered the Philippines from 1898 to 1975.
2. New Immigrants: those who entered the Philippines from 1976 onwards.
3. *Tsinoys*: a colloquial term meaning children or descendants of Old and New Immigrants who were born and grew up in the Philippines.
4. Chinese Citizens and Overseas Chinese Filipino Workers: the minority among the minority who experience marginalization and unhomeliness.
5. Chinese Spouses in interethnic marriages.
6. Chinese Mestizos/as: children of mixed parentage of a Chinese and a Filipino.

Based on the data gathered in the field, all of these groups have experienced various degrees of unhomeliness:

> The OIs [Old Immigrants] and NIs [New Immigrants] are unhomed with their sojourning nature. The Tsinoys are unhomed with their dual identities as both Chinese and Filipino. The Chinese citizen Tsinoys have "imaginary" citizenship as they truly have no permanent country to call their own. Their unhomely situations are likely to remind them of their difference from the dominant Filipinos but also push them to seek a place of belonging. Hence, this unhomely nature also makes them desire citizenship and identify with Filipinos as one people in one nation. The Chinese and Filipino spouses in inter-ethnic marriages are unhomed as they were ushered either into a dominant Chinese or Filipino community and culture. The Chinese Mestizos have these unhomely feelings when neither the Chinese or Filipino community accepts them because of physical appearance or language fluency. The Overseas Chinese Filipino Workers all the more feel unhomed in other countries as they adjust to new environments and try to identify themselves in terms of ethnicity and nationality.[22]

---

22. Uytanlet, *Hybrid Tsinoys*, 164.

While every diasporic community has its own story, the categories of experience here are likely similar to those of other diasporic communities around the globe. Diasporic people's ambiguous identities can expand their opportunities for identity formation, and their dual identities can give them a unique ability to negotiate two or more cultures. Yet this uncertainty can also create barriers with other communities, creating feelings of unhomeliness when they are victims of prejudice, distrust, and misunderstanding. This unhomeliness leads to the desire to find belonging and acceptance.

McGuire and Finding Belonging

While Bhabha's theory helps us understand one aspect of diasporic experience – finding oneself displaced and not "at home" – diasporic communities also find themselves in a constant process of forming a new identity. To understand this process, we turn to Meredith McGuire, whose work examines the formation of identity and belonging from sociological and religious perspectives. McGuire's theory starts with the process whereby individuals form personal meaning – that is, is an interpretation of the situations or events of their lives.[23]

The individual's meaning, for the most part, is influenced by family, friends, institutions, and the larger society. Therefore, in the context of a family, children first discover their belonging to understand their identity. The social group, whether the family or community, provides the framework by which a child relates his or her practices, beliefs, and meanings to being "one of them." The individual formulates a meaning system to know the operative values and norms of the social group or larger society. The individual can choose to accept, reject, or modify the meanings received. It is when the individual agrees and identifies with the group's meaning system that he or she finds belongingness.[24]

To return to the case study of the Chinese diaspora in the Philippines, Chinese Filipinos were given labels and names throughout their history, and they also gave themselves labels and names to construct their identity and belongingness.

> The Spaniards called them *Sangleys* then *Chinos*. The Americans called them Chinamen and Coolies. They were also classified as Non-Christian Tribe and Aliens. The Filipinos called them *Tsino, Kabise, Tsekwa, Intsik, Beho, Barok, Bulol, Butsekik, Singkit*

---

23. Meredith B. McGuire, *Religion: The Social Context*, 5th ed. (Long Grove: Waveland, 2008), 26.

24. McGuire, *Religion*, 25–32, 37, 52–57.

or *Singkot*, *Tsinito* or *Tsinita*, Chinky-eyed, Chinks, Tsinoy, or Chinoy . . . In academics, proper reference to the Chinese in the Philippines has evolved as well from mere "Chinese" to "Philippine Chinese" to "Filipino-Chinese" to "ethnic Chinese" to "Chinese-Filipino" to "Chinese Filipino," dropping the hyphen. The Chinese Filipinos referred to themselves in Minnanhua as *lanlâng*, *Tiong kok lâng*, *Banlam lâng*, *Hua-din*, *Hua-è*, Chinese, Tsinoy, or Chinoy. There were those who called other Chinese or even themselves *hoan-á*.[25]

The construction of identity and finding of belonging are important for diasporic people who are in a process of transition. Transition unavoidably causes unhomeliness and even a crisis of meaning through a meaning-threatening experience.[26] According to McGuire, meaning-threatening experiences include the "death of a loved one, painful illness, or serious economic misfortune." Other circumstances can be "oppression by an enemy, famine, earthquake, or economic depression," or even ongoing conditions such as long-term injustice and inequality.[27] All these events can bring about unhomeliness and even meaninglessness for members of diasporic communities.

McGuire notes that for those who believe in a loving God, it may be especially difficult to reconcile disastrous events and their faith. In response, theodicies offer "religious explanations that provide meaning for meaning-threatening experiences."[28] Thus, when crisis threatens the order in the meaning systems of individuals or social groups, theodicies help provide answers to these crises and affirm that there is a larger meaning system of order in this world. The individual or group may not be fully satisfied with the explanations, but the assurance that order exists behind the chaos may suffice. In cases where individuals experience total disorder and no theodicies can offer sufficient

---

25. Uytanlet, *Hybrid Tsinoys*, 73. The meaning of the Minnanhua or Amoy names and labels given by the Chinese Filipinos to themselves is as follows: *lanlâng* [our people], *Tiong kok lâng* [Chinese], *Banlam lâng* [Banlam Region people or from Southern Min], *Hua-din* [Chinese people], *Hua-è* [Chinese descent], Chinese, Tsinoy [Chinese and Filipino], Chinoy, and *hoan-á* [barbarians].

26. "Transitions may be geographical (country to country, rural to city), relational (marriage, separation, leaving home), chronological (adolescence to adulthood, becoming parents, children leaving home), cultural (different job or educational context), etc." Irene Alexander, "God in the Transitions," in *God at the Borders: Globalization, Migration and Diaspora*, eds. Charles R. Ringma, Karen Hollenbeck-Wuest, amd Athena Gorospe (Mandaluyong City: OMF Literature, 2015), 160.

27. McGuire, *Religion*, 32–33.

28. McGuire, 33.

meaning, a state of anomie (a crisis in moral order) can emerge, sometimes leading to suicide as the ultimate struggle against disorder.[29]

Diasporic people are discovering and constructing their identities in relation to space and the complex relationships with people, networks, and environments. Crisis further displaces the already unhomely position of diasporic people. In light of these conditions, what can Christianity offer as a theology for unhomed diasporic people? Can the church embrace and accept these strangers and help them find meaning and belonging in Christ?

Finding Home for the Unhomed

The church ought to be the best people to understand the unhomed people in diaspora. Second Corinthians 4:16 – 5:1 reminds us that Christians are also unhomed in this world because our true and eternal home is with God in heaven. In this world we shall have tribulations, crises that will threaten our faith, but we have hope in God through his Word, his Spirit, and the church. Paul uses a list of opposites in this passage to show contrast and to bring out the beauty of having our hope and faith in Christ Jesus:

> Therefore we do not lose heart. Though *outwardly* we are wasting away, yet *inwardly* we are being renewed day by day. For our *light and momentary troubles* are achieving for us an *eternal glory* that far *outweighs* them all. So we fix our eyes not on what is *seen*, but on what is *unseen*, since what is seen is *temporary*, but what is unseen is *eternal*. For we know that if the *earthly tent* we live in is destroyed, we have a building from God, an *eternal house in heaven*, not built by human hands [emphasis added].

Paul reminds his readers that even as their physical bodies are growing older, withering, and dying, this should be an occasion for their faith to grow deeper. Trials and tribulations are difficult crises, but they must view them as "light" and "temporal" in light of what is unseen and eternal. While we may be without homes for now (living in tents), we can count on God's promise of an eternal home in heaven, one built by God himself. Thus, Christianity can offer a theology of the unhomed in view of our ultimate identity and belonging in Christ. Moreover, the church can open its doors to receive the unhomely because we understand that we ourselves are unhomed in this world, and we can offer them hope and meaning in Christ.

---

29. McGuire, 34–35. See also Emile Durkheim, *Suicide: A Study in Sociology*, trans. John A. Spaulding, and George Simpson (New York: Free Press, 1951), 241–276.

Helping Diaspora Communities Find Their Ultimate Identity in Christ

Moreover, Jesus himself is unhomed. He was unhomed when he was on earth, among a people who did not receive him or acknowledge his divine identity. The King of kings and Lord of lords was born in a humble manger and not long afterward became a refugee to Egypt, fleeing from those who wanted to kill him. When Jesus started his ministry, he was unhomed and rejected in his hometown. He constantly faced opposition and rejection from the very people he created and sought to save. Finally, the Jewish religious leaders plotted to kill him. They falsely accused him and successfully had him crucified. Christ's embrace of an unhomely life and death assures us that he understands the unhomed, for he himself was one, in the worst possible way. Further, his resurrection gives us hope that he is victorious and can provide a new identity and new eternal home for all who receive him.

Christianity provides one enduring identity in which individuals in diaspora can find hope, solace, assurance, and home. The Christian identity rests solely in Christ alone. For Christians, being "in Christ" supplies an ultimate identity, one that offers a meaningful, abundant life (John 10:10; 17:3). This identity also unites us into one body as God's children. There is neither Jew nor Gentile, slave nor free, male nor female, for we are all one in Christ (Gal 3:26–29). In Christ, we are followers of Jesus (Eph 5:1–2), forgiven and reconciled because of his death and resurrection (Rom 5:9–11). Along with believers from every tongue and tribe, we are moved to repentance because of God's kindness (Rom 2:4), and believe that Christ alone is the propitiation for our sins (Rom 3:25–26). We are loved, saved, and blessed (1 John 4:10–12) in order to be sent out as witnesses to this good news (Matt 28:19–20).

Helping Diaspora Communities Find Their Eternal Belonging in Christ

Christianity provides eternal belonging with God as our Father in heaven and Christ Jesus as our Lord (2 Cor 4:18; 5:1). Christianity enables believers to wait on the Lord and trust in his goodness and faithfulness despite the fact that life on earth is not a bed of roses (John 16:33; 14:27). It provides the rationale for enduring and persevering in their faith in God (Jas 1:2–8). It helps put into right perspective the chaos that threatens the meaning system and assures believers that the God of order still reigns (1 Pet 1:3–9). Christianity offers diasporic people an eternal home where their pilgrimage ends, "the city with foundations, whose architect and builder is God" (Heb 11:10).

References

Alexander, Irene. "God in the Transitions." In *God at the Borders: Globalization, Migration and Diaspora*, edited by Charles R. Ringma, Karen Hollenbeck-Wuest, and Athena Gorospe, 160–167. Mandaluyong City: OMF Literature, 2015.

Bailey, Rayna. *Immigration and Migration*. New York: Infobase Publishing, 2008.

Bhabha, Homi. *The Location of Culture*. Oxford: Routledge, 2004.

Cohen, Robin. *Global Diasporas: An Introduction*. London: Routledge, 2008.

Dufoix, Stephanie. *Diasporas*. Berkley: University of California Press, 2008.

Durkheim, Emile. *Suicide: A Study in Sociology*. Translated by John A. Spaulding and George Simpson. New York: Free Press, 1951.

George, Sam. *Understanding the Coconut Generation: Ministry to the Americanized Asian Indians*. Niles: Mall Publishing, 2006.

Hutchinson, John, and Anthony D. Smith, eds. *Ethnicity*. Oxford: Oxford University Press, 1996.

The Lausanne Movement. "Diasporas." https://www.lausanne.org/networks/issues/diasporas.

———. "The Seoul Declaration on Diaspora Missiology." 14 November 2009. https://www.lausanne.org/content/statement/the-seoul-declaration-on-diaspora-missiology.

Li, Peter S., and Eva Xiaoling Li. "Chinese Overseas Population." In *Routledge Handbook of Chinese Diaspora*, edited by Tan Chee Beng, 15–28. London: Routledge, 2013.

Ma, Lawrence J. C. "Space, Place, and Transnationalism in the Chinese Diaspora." In *The Chinese Diaspora: Space, Place, Mobility, and Identity*, edited by Lawrence J. C. Ma and Carolyn Cartier. Lanham: Rowman & Littlefield, 2003.

McGuire, Meredith B. *Religion: The Social Context*. 5th ed. Long Grove: Waveland, 2008.

Tira, Sadiri Joy. "Every Person (From Everywhere)." In *Regions Beyond and Regions Around: Diaspora Missions and the Christian and Missionary Alliance in Canada*, edited by Sadiri Joy Tira, 2–4. Calgary: Jaffray Centre for Global Initiatives, 2018.

United Nations Department of Economic and Social Affairs, Population Division (2017). *International Migration Report 2017: Highlights*. New York: United Nations, 2017. http://www.un.org/en/development/desa/population/migration/publications/migrationreport/docs/MigrationReport2017_Highlights.pdf.

Uytanlet, Juliet Lee. *The Hybrid Tsinoys: Challenges of Hybridity and Homogeneity as Socio-Cultural Constructs among the Chinese in the Philippines*. Eugene: Pickwick, 2016.

———. "Transit, Transient, Transition: How the Lexington Chinese Christian Church Became an Instrument of Conversion." In *Reaching New Territory: Theological Reflections*, edited by Samson Uytanlet, Thomas R. V. Forster, and Susan Tan, 21–39. Valenzuela City: Biblical Seminary of the Philippines, 2017.

Yeh, Allen. "The Chinese Diaspora." In *Global Diasporas and Mission*, edited by Chandler H. Im and Amos Yong, 89–98. Oxford: Regnum, 2014.

14

Hans Frei's Typology of Theology for Religious Encounters in Asian Contexts

Kang-San Tan[1]

BMS World Mission

The aim of this chapter is to propose a heuristic field map to assist mission practitioners as they seek to enter into an authentic and Christian encounter with non-Christian religious worldviews in Asian contexts. Using Hans Frei's typology of theological methods, I hope to encourage an approach that promotes a range of context-specific responses that are deemed tenable for a religious encounter. Current polarizations between pluralist and particularist categories are reflected, on the one hand, in relativistic attitudes toward religions and, on the other, in rejectionist responses to all religions. Unless we develop a more adequate "way of seeing," both parties will find it difficult to move beyond a culture of distrust, closed categories, and misdirected conclusions.

An appropriate theological framework and understanding of non-Christian religions is important not merely for theological clarity but also for the authentic witness of the church in the midst of many faiths. Although Christians are aware of multireligious existence, deeper dialogue and discussions between adherents of disparate faiths have tended to be limited to a one-directional approach of evangelism or pronouncements about other beliefs rather than genuine and deep encounters of faith. In a pluralist world, there is a need for

---

1. Portions of this chapter originally appeared in K.-S. Tan, "The Christian Challenge of Religious Encounter," *Connections Journal* 5, no. 2–3 (April 2006): 54–58.

a more adequate Christian typology or framework for engaging meaningfully and deeply with people from different faiths.

Although the Asian church is not unfamiliar with religious plurality, the modern phenomenon of religious pluralism transcends any earlier Christian sense in at least three distinct ways.[2] First, the old conceptions of faiths as existing as isolated blocks within historical geographical boundaries have been shattered. Second, the wealth of religious studies and knowledge makes any ignorance about the beliefs of non-Christian religions inexcusable. Gavin D'Costa highlighted that while religious pluralism existed in the past, "since the dawn of Christianity,"[3] our modern context presents a different circumstance because "Christians have both intellectual and experiential access to the religions of the world."[4] Third, Hinduism and Buddhism have now joined Christianity and Islam in "becoming almost as energetic in their missionary endeavours."[5] Today, when Christianity seeks to engage seriously with people from different faiths, it demands a different approach, one in which theological reflections must account for the new awareness, doctrines, and perspectives of other faiths.

All theologies are developed out of personal context, and no type of theology can be developed in a purely academic and objective sense. I am writing from an evangelical Christian perspective, holding to the finality of Jesus for salvation. I grew up in a loving Buddhist home in Malaysia, which is a Muslim-majority country. For over twenty-six years I have mostly worked as a missiologist and mission trainer in Southeast Asia.

In Search of a New Typology for Theology of Religions

Traditionally, categories of a theology toward other religions are grouped in the threefold typology of pluralism, inclusivism, and exclusivism.[6] Among others, there are three main criticisms against the threefold typology.[7] First, the history of world religions, and the unique contexts of interreligious relations, are far

---

2. Alan Race, *Christians and Religious Pluralism: Patterns in the Christian Theology of Religions* (Maryknoll: Orbis Books, 1983), 1–2.

3. Gavin D'Costa, *Theology and Religious Pluralism: The Challenge of Other Religions* (Oxford: Blackwell, 1986), 1.

4. D'Costa, *Theology and Religious Pluralism*, 2.

5. D'Costa, 2.

6. The terms "pluralism," "inclusivism," and "exclusivism" as a typology for theology of religion were popularized over thirty-five years ago by Alan Race, *Christians and Religious Pluralism*.

7. Race, *Christians and Religious Pluralism*, 150.

too complex to be neatly categorized into three typologies. Second, due to the complexity of religions and diversity of contexts, the options for Christian responses are far more diverse than could be simply limited to three options or theological paradigms. Third, the focus of the typology has been mostly on doctrinal comparison between religious systems rather than on people and relationships between faith practitioners. In particular, the typology does not allow a sufficient role for the process of encounter between people from different religions.[8] Fourth, evangelicals have also criticized the typology for its association of exclusivism with a pejorative force, implying arrogance toward non-Christian religions, for its sharp distinctions between each position, and for its failure to take into account the complexities and differences between religions. For example, many evangelicals will be exclusivist in their position on the finality of Jesus for salvation, but will be open to incorporating the insights from other religions for life and faith. Nevertheless, from the perspective of people from different faiths, the charges of arrogance and insensitivity leveled at evangelicals are often not unfounded.

Veli-Matti Kärkkäinen acknowledges the challenge of classifying theologians within one typology or another. "I am increasingly unhappy with this taxonomy as it tends to obscure subtle, but significant differences."[9] Harold Netland illustrates the difficulty in trying to classify scholars as diverse as Max Warren (1904–1977), Stephen Neill (1900–1984), Kenneth Cragg (1913–2012), and Lesslie Newbigin (1909–1998) all in the exclusivist camp. Each of these writers combined a clear commitment to Christian orthodoxy with a sensitivity to the work of the Holy Spirit in non-Christian religion, treating different religions with sympathy rather than intolerance. Kenneth Cragg, for example, demonstrated a deep appreciation for the value of the Qur'an as a source for Christian reflection.[10]

Fifth, citing forms of universalism commonly held by Karl Barth (exclusivist), Karl Rahner (inclusivist), and John Hick (pluralist), Gavin D'Costa asserts that "the threefold typology fails to deliver on the question of the salvation of the unbeliever in a precise enough sense," whereby "all hold

---

8. Race, 150.

9. Veli-Matti Kärkkäinen, *An Introduction to the Theology of Religions: Biblical, Historical, and Contemporary Perspectives* (Downers Grove: InterVarsity Press, 2003), 171.

10. Harold Netland, *Encountering Religious Pluralism: The Challenge to Christian Faith and Mission* (Downers Grove: InterVarsity Press, 2001), 47–54.

virtually similar views about the outcome of the salvation of the world, but in the threefold typology, they are categorized in very different ways."[11]

Sixth, some scholars, especially those in the school of comparative religions, criticize the typology as too focused on the question of salvation rather than actual engagement between religions.[12] Seventh, in a devastating critique, D'Costa argued that all three positions are exclusive, "operating with a particular notion of truth."[13] For example, John Hick and Paul Knitter are indebted to "agnostic liberalism, thus imposing upon all religions an exclusive hurdle which they must conform to if they are to grow out of their parochial adolescence."[14]

Hans Frei's Five Types of Theology

If the threefold typology is inadequate, then perhaps a different way of describing the relationship between Christianity and other faiths is still possible. In this section, I will use Hans Frei's model of Five Types of Theology to help us develop a more critical appreciation for the variety of approaches toward non-Christian religions.[15] Frei was frustrated with how different categories of theologies were lumped together without accounting for the nuances and differences in their respective theological approaches.

Similarly, the impasse among evangelical approaches to other religions may be due to our inability to account for the different nuances between pluralism and exclusivism.

So, instead of engagement, evangelicals find it easier to retreat to forms of rejectionism or isolationism. Because we continue to adopt traditional categories in thinking about non-Christian religions, evangelicals find it difficult to move outside of our theological boxes. In an age of increased religious tensions, we are faced with the danger of erecting more fences than bridges for interreligious encounters. Instead of labeling various approaches

---

11. Gacin D'Costa, *Christianity and World Religions: Disputed Questions in the Theology of Religions* (Chichester: Wiley-Blackwell, 2010), 34.

12. D'Costa, *Christianity and World Religions*, 37–39.

13. D'Costa, 35.

14. D'Costa, 35.

15. I am indebted to David Ford, *Theology: A Very Short Introduction* (Oxford: Oxford University Press, 1999) for introducing Hans Frei's types of theology.

as liberal, evangelical, catholic, or confessional, it may be helpful to evaluate our approaches to people of other faiths through Hans Frei's typology.[16]

Two Extreme Types: From Outsider to Insider Orientation

Frei's basic idea is that there are two extreme and opposite ways in which Christianity relates to modernity, and there are three mediating points in between these polarities.

In Type 1, Christian theology develops from some modern philosophy, worldview, or agenda such as Enlightenment thinking, materialism, atheism, ecology, poverty, or justice. Proponents are confident in the rightness of their position according to evidence derived from science, genetics, psychology, or some other particular discipline. In the theology of religions, we may find an analogue to the Type 1 approach whenever pluralistic approaches rely on concepts of tolerance, or the supposition that all religions are vaguely Christian at their core. Proponents of this approach run the risk of developing a perspective that is lacking in biblical or Christian foundations. People in this category then judge all perspectives according to how they fit into their point of reference. Sometimes, they will pick and choose those acceptable elements in Christian theologies as long as they support their agenda or perspective!

The other extreme pole is Type 5, which is an attempt to repeat a classic theology (Calvinistic, Lutheran, Barthian, Wesleyan) or denominational theological position (Catholic, Reformed, Pentecostal, Baptist), and to see all realities in those terms. The Bible becomes the only reference for encountering people of other faiths, ignoring any nuances in the real beliefs of other cultures. From such a vantage point, proponents of this view will reject any new attempts at formulating theological engagement with non-Christian religions. For example, non-Western theologies or contextual theologies are rigorously evaluated based on "foundational" truths of Western theological interpretations and categories. Some conservative evangelicals operate along this line of thinking in its extreme forms. Therefore, we judge Islam, Buddhism, and Hinduism through Western theological categories. We compare the best of Christianity with the worst of other religions. The result is that irrelevant and deep-seated belief systems are seldom addressed. Nominalism, legalism,

---

16. In using Frei's typology, I am not relying on Hans Frei's theological presuppositions; rather, I am using his theological categories as a heuristic tool for finding new ways of seeing and engaging with people of other faiths.

fundamentalism, and parochialism thrive within communities that operate under this Type 5 approach.

At the local church level, one could argue that Type 5 theology is the dominant approach among Christians in Asia. Christians in Muslim-majority nations such as Indonesia, Malaysia, and Brunei typically adopt Western views of Islam as primarily an evil religion to be replaced by Christianity. Newly founded churches in Thailand, Myanmar, Vietnam, Cambodia, and Laos generally reject local cultures, festivals, and rituals as primarily religious. Therefore, new converts from Buddhism are encouraged not to participate in many social and cultural activities. Such isolationist behaviors reinforce Buddhist views that Christianity is a Western religion.

Three Mediating Types of Theology

In between these two types of theology are approaches which seek to engage with non-Christian cultures or religions. These three types of theology are at the heart of those who seek some form of engagement. The Type 2 approach engages with Christian theology through interaction with social sciences, management theories, psychology, or non-Christian religious studies, and applies these to Christianity in order to discern the relevance of the gospel for today. Sometimes embracing extreme forms of this approach, mission practitioners may allow specific agendas or pet projects such as dialogue, holistic mission, justice, modernity, management, strategies-in-mission, and spirituality to be the sole integrative framework for engaging with people of other faiths. In this case, neither the Christian gospel nor the real beliefs of non-Christian faiths play any primary function in the development of approaches or strategies for mission.

For Type 2 approaches, both Christianity and non-Christian religions are appendices or illustrations of social scientific realities. On the one hand, when we listen to some pluralists committed to a politically correct framework of tolerance or New Age writings, one gets the sense that there is no serious religious encounter taking place. On the other hand, evangelicals can be susceptible to similar reductionism when mission is defined narrowly in terms of evangelism and conversion, or driven by ideologies such as completing the Great Commission, speeding Jesus's second coming. In most cases, a critical evaluation of these mission programs and projects will reveal that limited interest or investments are placed in the study of non-Christian religions, or in the interaction between the history and culture of the people groups.

Type 3 is in the middle because it refuses to allow any single agenda or framework to dominate, embracing multiple perspectives and engaging with the social, cultural, and religious worlds of people. It recognizes that there is no such thing as a purely religious encounter. Real engagement with Islam must include an understanding of its distinctive sects, political structures, historical meanings, economic realities, and the future envisaged by adherents of these concrete communities. On this view, the best way forward in encountering people of other faiths is not coming with a set of presuppositions, doctrines, or projects, but setting up dialogues between Christians and people of other faiths. The key idea is correlation: "the aim is to correlate issues raised by the Christian faith and practice with other approaches to those issues."[17] Are there correlations between Buddhists' vision for *nirvana* and enlightenment with the Christian's vision of salvation? We cannot arrive at simplistic conclusions without the needed engagements in speaking with Buddhists and the study of the religiously shaped meanings of these terms. In poverty-alleviation projects among Hindus, we need to take into account predominant Hindu worldviews on *karma* and the social structures of classes currently operating in Hindu society.

Thus, other faiths are not merely points for polemics; they help us to see if there are aspects of these religious beliefs that can contribute to building appropriate models for such relief projects. In seeking correlation, we need not buy wholesale into another religious belief system. Rather, we can recognize the intricate balance between religion and culture and seek to authenticate the gospel in diverse social contexts. Based on intimate knowledge and careful study of the real beliefs of other faiths, evangelicals are then in a reliable position to make judgments, to come up with truth validations, and to allow the Christian gospel to interact with any contradictory truths.

Frei highlights Paul Tillich (1886–1965) as the best-known exponent of a theology of correlation. Tillich used "religious symbols to meet the fundamental questions raised about the meaning of life and history."[18] The symbol of the kingdom of God correlates with the meaning of history, and the symbol of "Jesus as the Christ." Inclusivists such as Gavin D'Costa and Marcus Borg may be generally comfortable with this position, but so would others, such as theologian Terrance Tiessen, missiologist Lesslie Newbigin, Islamicist Kenneth Cragg and anthropologist Charles Kraft. They are examples of theologians who fit into Type 3. People who describe themselves as radical

---

17. Ford, *Theology*, 24.
18. Ford, 25.

or open evangelicals, or those experimenting with forms of new communities within insiders movements will most likely be launching from this Type 3 base of mission theology. The key liberating fact is that these folk are no longer operating on one metanarrative, but have a capacity to engage with people at their contextual realities, believing that God is far bigger than their Christianity.

Type 4 tries to avoid the middle path of correlation by giving priority to the Christian narrative and position. It is "faith seeking understanding" based on a prior commitment to Scripture and the gospel. Such a faith commitment does not exclude the need for dialogue. Instead, it seeks to find new ways of being believers in the midst of non-Christian cultures while maintaining roots and identities within the historic Christian community. Mainstream evangelicalism will be most comfortable with this position, and scholars such as Timothy Tennent and Gerald McDermott typify this approach.

Most evangelicals move between the Type 5 and Type 4 continuum, with pragmatists and dogmatists more likely to fall into Type 5. Missiologists and practitioners who place a priority on cultural understanding and the study of other religions tend to operate in Type 4, and the innovative radicals and scholars of religions tend toward Type 3. Of course, every theologian or missionary cannot be typecast into one category, nor are we suggesting that once one adopts a position on one issue, one is unable to move between types of approaches. The value of Frei's model is in helping us reflect on the way we think about issues surrounding interreligious encounter. At the least, it should help us to be self-critical about our presuppositions when we disagree with people on this complex subject.

Some Implications for Religious Encounters in Southeast Asia

In this section, using Frei's Types of Theology, we seek to illustrate how evangelicals may explore fresh ways of thinking about engaging people of other faiths. Christian encounters need to move beyond the superficial level of Christian behaviors and religious identification. The first level of engagement is in a person-to-person exchange of views. Over time and depending on context, these religious conversations may move into discovery of deeply held beliefs, rituals, and religious symbols. Ultimately, genuine religious encounter aims at worldview transformation.[19] Where possible, we will discuss some practical

---

19. For further discussion, see my essay "Elements of a Biblical and Genuine Missionary Encounter with Diaspora Chinese Buddhists in Southeast Asia," in *Sharing Jesus in the Buddhist World*, eds. David Lim and Steve Spaulding (Pasadena: William Carey Library, 2003), 19–30.

outworking in interfaith relations arising from this need for the Christian gospel to engage with other-faith worldviews. Non-Western contributions to the debate about religious encounter are not normally focused on doctrinal study or philosophical approaches. Rather, such reflections are best focused on the daily interactions between firm believers who seek to engage with their neighbors on every aspect of life. However, it will be a mistake to think that there is no theoretical framework for such folk-level engagements. The remaining discussion is an attempt to bring together both theories of religious encounter with the kind of religious conversation which is happening daily between people of different faiths.

The Move from Dialogue-as-Witness to Dialogue-Is-Witness

Dialogue-as-witness refers to methods of approaching people of other faiths that are primarily dialogical rather than monological, rooted in the belief that the non-Christian is a partner in religious encounter. On this view, all religions, including Christianity, are simultaneously expressions of a genuine search for God as well as a form of rebellion against God. Therefore, simplistic acceptance or total rejection of mutual learning is irresponsible and untenable in today's globalized context. In contrast, dialogical approaches allow for input, responses, and agenda-setting from non-Christian partners.

However, dialogue is still a problem for many missionaries who may be trapped in neo-colonialist and triumphalist approaches. Even though old positions of power no longer exist, neo-colonialism still has an impact, methodologically and substantively contributing to a mentality of power and control. New strategies for mission and evangelism are still perpetuated and manufactured in the West without being driven by genuine agendas from national partners. Networks and new alliances are still a means for the richer partners to recruit poorer national churches to adopt foreign programs and ideas. Often, the last group to enter our minds or to give any input would be those non-believers whom we are trying to reach! Should not the Muslims, Buddhists, and Hindus be the first "contributors" to our methods and thinking about evangelistic strategies and approaches?

In contrast to the dialogue-as-witness approach, dialogue-is-witness is a resulting testimony arising from religious encounters where non-Christian beliefs and views intersect and are eventually transformed by the Christian gospel. Initially, such dialogue is an expression of Christian testimony that cares deeply for the historical and religious belief systems of non-Christians. In this sense of "dialogue is witness," we are no longer trapped in discussions about whether the method should be monological or dialogical, or the state of the unevangelized. Our concern is primarily to live authentically as Christians in the midst of the non-Christian world.

This approach denies that there is one method, whether dialogical or not; rather, it asserts that humility and willingness to acknowledge God in the act of witness is a testimony of faith and trust in God. Proponents of this approach are not relativist, but we are open evangelicals: open for God's Spirit to work through worshippers of all religious backgrounds, releasing us to be true witnesses for the gospel.

In some sense, behind every model for mission lie theological presuppositions about non-Christian religions. Giving thought to the interplay between dialogue-as-witness and dialogue-is-witness is the result of our willingness to acknowledge the complexities of engaging with social, religious, and cultural dimensions of Christian work among non-Christians. We cannot settle these controversial issues at the level of methods for evangelism, historical labels, or predetermined outcomes. Depending on the nature of the relationship, the purpose of religious engagement, or the issues at stake, Christians could move between a continuum of correlation, faith seeking understanding, and resolute commitment to historic Christianity.

Theology of the Kingdom of God and Islam

Muslims, Jews, and Christians share similar roots in monotheism, Judeo-Christian prophetic traditions, and interreligious civilizations. The Kingdom of God, Covenant, the Holy Spirit, and Cross-Textual readings of the Holy Scriptures are promising symbols for breaking the impasse within evangelicalism in exploring religious encounters. In this section, I will discuss how the theology of the kingdom of God may be used as a framework for engaging with people of other faiths. Jesus's message of the kingdom is an invitation to follow God's ways rather than nationalistic aspirations of establishing a political Jewish kingdom. Rather than spiritual promises of heaven, his parables break open the Jewish worldview, confirming that the true people of God are not just the Jews but also Gentiles. Parables act not merely as stories about the kingdom, but also as the very means for inviting Jews as well as Gentiles into the kingdom of God. The miracles of Jesus are another tool for worldview transformation, when these miracles are signs of God's surprising inclusion of the poor and the lepers who exhibited faith in Jesus as the Messiah. In addition to proclaiming Jesus's divinity, these miracles and healings are signs that God is vindicating Jesus's way of life and mission.

Muslims more than other religionists need to encounter true faith and become followers of such a radical kingdom. When they see faith and ethics embodied in life witness that exceeds religious righteousness, like the Jewish audience to whom Jesus told the story of the Good Samaritan (Luke 10), Muslims will discover that Christians are also people of the book. Religious encounter in this way cannot be achieved without long-term friendship, without living in the midst of Muslims and exhibiting that "righteousness" of faith. The kingdom of God must therefore include not just the religious but every aspect of life of the Christian. It will be like a pearl, precious and pursued by the merchant who is willing to surrender everything for the sake of possessing it. Over time, the signs of the kingdom will give a coherent and consistent message, lived out in the humble obedience of a follower of Isa-Al-Masih, and speaking powerfully and relevantly to Muslim mindsets. God's kingdom will necessarily be broader than the local church in its life and expression of worship.

Christians and Muslims can focus together on contextual problems such as Jesus's divinity, the meaning of life, drug addiction, corruption in society, or the Palestinian–Israeli conflict. Correlation requires both Christians and Muslims contribute their respective perspectives and responses to these issues. Evaluation of these issues is necessarily linked with many other social and political factors, including the religious meanings brought by both religions. Dialogue takes place at personal, attitudinal, religious, and societal levels. In the process, there will be both points of correlation as well as points of tension. The goal is not to win a convert or argument, but mutual witness. The truth, veracity, and final vindication of the Christian vision of the kingdom of God is something which belongs to the realm of God's sovereign power, rather than being dependent on human ingenuity. This process of mutual witness is repeated over and over in the daily relationship, and with intentionality, training in apologetics, and listening skills, Christian–Muslim dialogue can enable both parties to grow in their faith and knowledge of God.

Finding Our Way Forward

Rudolph Otto, Emil Brunner, and Wilfred Cantwell Smith have all written on the luminous nature of religious truths which cannot be purely captured in propositional statements. Certain things have been revealed to us in Scripture and can be known, but there are other truths which can only be known progressively; and there are still other truths about God outside our experiences which we can probably discover through non-Christian religions.

Such discoveries are only available when we move out of our comfortable paradigms of Christendom.

In an unpublished lecture given at Trinity Evangelical Divinity School in 1995, Peter Beyerhaus introduced the Tripolar Approach to other religions. According to Beyerhaus, a monopolar perspective says that all religions are human inventions rather than due to the existence of a God. This is the position taken by communists like Karl Marx, and by rationalist thinkers such as Descartes or Kant. Bipolars are people who say that the sources of religions are humans and God. They recognize the role of the transcendent or Supreme Being, such as God in Christianity, or Islam, which caused humans to desire communion with the luminous. Religions are intimately linked due to the dynamic interplay between culture and religions. Finally, Beyerhaus proposed a tripolar view of non-Christian religions which takes into account three sources of all religions: humans and their cultures, God and the supernatural elements in all religions, and the works of the devil in all religions. In a tripolar view of religions, we take seriously the supernatural elements within all religions. There are powerful forces at work, principalities that have brought people into bondage. These demonic forces are at work in both Christendom as well as in non-Christian religions. Therefore, Christian encounter is not merely an exchange of reasoned arguments and theological debates.

Type 5 theology will brand all non-Christian religions as demonic, failing to distinguish religious aspects from cultural, while Type 1, when combined with a monopolar perspective of other religions, will fail to grapple with the reality of demonic influences in religions. Likewise, Type 4 theology, when combined with a bipolar view of religions, will merely engage in religious and philosophical exchanges, and will again dismiss the beliefs in spirits in Asian traditional religions. Daniel Tong, a Singaporean Anglican priest, demonstrated a good example of Type 4 theology by seeking to evaluate Chinese beliefs and cultural practices in light of God's Word.[20] Evangelicals rooted in a Western epistemology seem good at analyzing but not very good at synthesis; good at splitting fine doctrinal hairs, but not very good at allowing new shoots to grow into indigenous Christianity within the parameters of orthodoxy. In his excellent book *Grassroots Asian Theology*, Simon Chan, a Singaporean Pentecostal theologian, rightly identifies "the chief ecclesiological problem in Asia [as] how to be church in the midst of more ancient family-based

---

20. See Daniel Tong's conservative judgment on the value of ancestor veneration in *A Biblical Approach to Chinese Traditions and Beliefs* (Singapore: Genesis Books, 2003), 96–107.

religious communities."[21] Yet while his analysis is correct, Chan's proposal in developing authentic Asian family-based religious communities may benefit from further attention to the intimate link between Asian cultures and religions. Methodologically, Chan considers Scripture, tradition, and grassroots Asian Christians as primary sources for theology (Type 4 and Type 5). Type 3 theologies, in contrast, will regard Asian religious traditions as valuable resources for developing Christian theology. Thus, K. K. Yeo, a Malaysian-Chinese theologian who has taught in North America and China, demonstrates what I consider a Type 3 approach when he uses Confucius and Paul's writings as equally rich theological resources for constructing a Chinese Christian identity. In fact, Yeo argues that such a distinct Chinese-Confucian Christian identity will eventually transform Western Christianity.[22]

Concluding Reflections: Toward a Mutual Transformation of Religious Encounters

Historically, Christian formulations from the early church fathers to the Reformation period have postulated their creeds within Christendom and from a context where the "religious other" lived in distant lands. That context is no longer with us today. In almost every continent, including the post-Christian West, Christians live and work in the midst of other religionists.

First, the changed context of the public square resulting from migration, diaspora communities, and the Internet revolution means that every Christian truth will need to be rearticulated missiologically and in conversation with other religious and secular ideologies. As indicated in this chapter, a rearticulation of Christian truths must include so-called "in-house" matters relating to the nature of the church, doctrines of Christ, and salvation. For example, it is one thing to say within the confines of the church that the Qur'an is inspired by the devil, but quite another to express such views in the marketplace. Complicating matters, in light of the Internet revolution and podcasting, every sermon and church position espoused privately may now be contested publicly.

Second, in many parts of Asia, Christians are minorities who need to find new ways of relating to their neighbors in order to develop indigenous Christianities. It is my contention that Christian theological reflection on God,

---

21. Simon Chan, *Grassroots Asian Theology: Thinking the Faith from the Ground Up* (Downers Grove: InterVarsity Press, 2014), 204.

22. K. K. Yeo, *Musing with Confucius and Paul: Toward a Chinese Christian Theology* (Cambridge: James Clarke, 2008), 253–303.

faith, and mission should include critical correlations (Type 3 theology) to local social and cultural contexts. In a multicultural future, moreover, I contend that no theologian or mission theoretician can develop an adequate and robust theology without also being at home in another religious tradition, or without the disciplined study of another religion. Therefore, expanding dialogue and witness means that cross-cultural workers, due to their multicultural outlook, will become valuable change agents for the Christian church in rethinking Christian positions for the new world order.

Third, we note that expanding dialogue and witness also means that religious encounter is not just about purely religious conversations. Through religious encounter, we must enter into every aspect of life, whether social, political, or religious. The problems of poverty and AIDS, rampant materialism in the Asia-Pacific, rising debt, consumerism, and the proliferation of ecological waste are not merely Christian concerns but issues of common humanity. The promotion of religious-liberty issues for both Muslims in the West and Christian minorities in Muslim-majority countries is an example of new and interrelated issues where members of different faiths can come together and share resources in making this world a better place.

Terry Muck writes: "We do live in a dialogical age. . . . Diverse cultures, religions and worldviews are the stuff of which our countries and neighborhoods are made. We simply cannot change that. The question is whether we let the techniques of dialogue required for living in such a culture drive Christianity or whether Christianity discovers in a dialogical culture forms that can be useful in communicating the gospel, forms that do not violate the basic tenets of faiths."[23]

Reflecting on my own religious background as an Asian Christian, I seek to illustrate the contextual nature of all theologies. If both Western and Asian Christians recognize the intimate links between religions and cultures, then mission workers from the West as well as Asian Christians will be liberated to return to Asian philosophies and Asian traditions as treasure hunters. I contend that the creation of an authentic Asian Christian identity cannot be done without a more positive evaluation of the Asian philosophical and religious traditions of Confucianism, Taoism, and Buddhism. The Western Christian traditions of Christianity, particularly among pietistic and conservative Christian missions, have tended to emphasize the radical discontinuity of the early church father Tertullian, who famously asked, "What has Athens

---

23. Terry Muck, "Evangelicals and Interreligious Dialogue," Journal of the Evangelical Theological Society 36, no. 4 (1993): 522.

to do with Jerusalem?" Other models of continuity, best represented in the early centuries of the church by Justin Martyr and Clement of Alexandria, demonstrate that a more positive evaluation of other religious traditions has been fruitfully employed in our Christian tradition, and may pay dividends again today.

Anselm of Canterbury described theology as "faith seeking understanding" (Type 4). Theology begins with God's revelation and proceeds with our human response of understanding God in faith. In espousing "faith seeking understanding," we are actually proposing a "new way of knowing," whereby traditional evangelical theology is complemented by a quest for new theological understanding of complex realities. Such a theological venture involves two dimensions: an historical investigation into what evangelical theologians of religion have developed, and new reflection on our own religious traditions. This new reflection is grounded in biblical, historical, and systematic theology that informs and instructs a *Christian* identity, particularly in recalling an evangelical heritage.

Yet it is crucial that in such investigation, a commitment to the Christian gospel must be distinguished from a commitment to Western forms of Christianity. When one *uncritically* exports foreign forms of Christianity, then the expansion of Christian mission and new movements to Christ will inevitably rob local communities of their past, whether that is their culture – which is widely recognized as an undesirable result – or their religion – which is generally presumed to be necessary. Yet because of the intimate connection between religion and culture, I believe such *total replacement* approaches will eventually do damage to the integrity and identity of new converts from another faith. Instead, the challenge for Christian theology is to construct self-understandings and identities which are actually capable of transforming non-Christian religions. Such integrative theological analysis will result in some elements of their past faiths being rejected as incompatible with Christian commitment, while other elements of their past faiths will be integrated, albeit with a Christian reinterpretation. Such borrowings are part of the long process of the transmission of faith, which is not to be confused with syncretism, which I see essentially as the mixture of incompatible belief systems into one's faith.

When we move from assured Christian beliefs (Type 5) into mission evaluation of other religions, then "faith seeking understanding" must move from the domain of analysis (Type 4) to synthesis (Type 3). Theologies must move from the domain of academic reflections to new synthesis that is contextual and related to real-life situations.

Contextual theologies need to be developed by followers of Jesus from mixed religious identities. New forms of Christian communities need to grow without Pharisees or elder brothers of supposed prodigals acting as theological watchdogs. Typically, the process of faith integration, from initial self-theologizing through deeper stages of identity formation, will take place over a few generations.

In this chapter I used Hans Frei's Types of Theology to emphasize the need for Christians to be more aware of the range of theological assumptions we adopt unconsciously whenever we approach people from different faiths. I indicated that Type 4, "faith seeking understanding," is a good model for evangelicals in engaging sensitively with different faiths. However, in some specific contexts, Type 3's "correlation" approach may bring added advantages in helping Christians to treat different belief systems on their own terms rather than judging other beliefs *a priori*. It is my prayer that this theological reflection may help open up new vistas for deepening our Christian witness as we seek to honor God and love our neighbors from different faiths.

References

Burnett, David. *The Spirit of Buddhism*. Crowborough: Monarch, 1996.

———. *The Spirit of Hinduism*. Tunbridge Wells: Monarch, 1992.

Chan, Simon. *Grassroots Asian Theology: Thinking the Faith from the Ground Up*. Downers Grove: InterVarsity Press, 2014.

D'Costa, Gavin. *Christianity and World Religions: Disputed Questions in the Theology of Religions*. Chichester: Wiley-Blackwell, 2010.

———. *Theology and Religious Pluralism: The Challenge of Other Religions*. Oxford: Blackwell, 1986.

Dulles, Avery. *Models of Revelation*. Garden City: Doubleday, 1983.

Ford, David. *Theology: A Very Short Introduction*. Oxford: Oxford University Press, 2005.

Frei, Hans, and George Hunsburger. *Types of Christian Theology*. Yale: Yale University Press, 1992.

Glaser, Ida. *The Bible and Other Faiths: Christian Responsibility in a World of Religions*. Leicester: Inter-Varsity Press, 2005.

Heim, S. Mark. *Salvations: Truth and Difference in Religion*. Maryknoll: Orbis Books, 1995.

Kärkkäinen, Veli-Matti, *An Introduction to the Theology of Religions: Biblical, Historical, and Contemporary Perspectives*. Downers Grove: InterVarsity Press, 2003.

Knitter, Paul F. *Theologies of Religions*. Maryknoll: Orbis Books, 2003.

Lim, David, and Steve Spaulding. *Sharing Jesus in the Buddhist World.* Pasadena: William Carey Library, 2003.

———. *Sharing Jesus Holistically with the Buddhist World.* Pasadena: William Carey Library, 2005.

Ma, Wonsuk. "Doing Theology in the Philippines: A Case of Pentecostal Christianity." *Asian Journal of Pentecostal Studies* 8, no. 2 (2005): 215–233.

McDermott, Gerald R. *Can Evangelicals Learn from World Religions?* Downers Grove: InterVarsity Press, 2000.

Moucarry, Chowkat. *Faith to Faith.* Leicester: Inter-Varsity Press, 2001.

Muck, Terry. "Evangelicals and Interreligious Dialogue." *Journal of the Evangelical Theological Society* 36, no. 4 (1993): 517–529.

Neibuhr, Richard. *Christ and Culture.* New York: HarperCollins, 2001.

Netland, Harold. *Encountering Religious Pluralism: The Challenge to Christian Faith and Mission.* Downers Grove: InterVarsity Press, 2001.

Race, Alan. *Christians and Religious Pluralism: Patterns in the Christian Theology of Religions.* Maryknoll: Orbis Books, 1983.

Tan, Kang-San. "Elements of a Biblical and Genuine Missionary Encounter with Diaspora Chinese Buddhists in Southeast Asia." In *Sharing Jesus in the Buddhist World*, edited by David Lim and Steve Spaulding, 19–30. Pasadena: William Carrey Library, 2003.

———. "Kingdom-Oriented Framework for Encountering Buddhist Worldviews." *Connections: The Journal of the WEA Mission Commission* 3, no. 1 (Apr 2006), 43–50.

Tennent, Timothy C. *Christianity at the Religious Roundtable.* Grand Rapids: Baker Academic, 2002.

Tiessen, Terrance L. *Who Can Be Saved? Reassessing Salvation in Christ and the World Religions.* Downers Grove: InterVarsity Press, 2004.

Tong, Daniel. *A Biblical Approach to Chinese Traditions and Beliefs.* Singapore: Genesis Books, 2003.

Yeo, K. K. *Musing with Confucius and Paul: Toward a Chinese Christian Theology.* Cambridge: James Clarke, 2008.

Yong, Amos. *Beyond the Impasse: Toward a Pneumatological Theology of Religions.* Grand Rapids: Baker Academic, 2003.

15

Theology in a Context of Radical Cultural Shift
A Chinese Reflection

Carver T. Yu[1]

China Graduate School of Theology

Theology Contextual and Catholic

Before we plunge into contextual theological reflection, we need to be clear about the task of contextual theology. Why should theology be contextual, and how contextual can it be without undermining the significance of traditional doctrinal formulations of the catholic (universal) church? This question, I believe, is likely to linger in the minds of theological students in Asia. To go about this, let us ask a simple but foundational question: What is theology? In expounding the nature of theology, I have found Karl Barth's articulation most illuminating. Theology, according to Barth, is science. Not "a science," as if it is one science among many, like chemistry, physics, or biology.

What defines science as science is its objectivity in its inquiry. As science, theology has to be objective, and that means it has to be true to the nature of the object it seeks to understand, and that means to follow the object wherever it leads. Edmund Husserl's motto, "to the object itself," has provided a deeper

---

1. Portions of this chapter previously appeared in Carver T. Yu, "Redeemer and Transformer: The Relevance of Christ for China's Cultural Renewal and Liberation," in *Diverse and Creative Voices: Theological Essays from the Majority World*, eds. Dieumeme Noelliste and Sung Wook Chung (Eugene, OR: Pickwick, 2015), 67–83.

understanding of objectivity and therefore of the nature of science. Barth has found such an understanding most relevant to the nature of theology as science.

This means the object theology seeks to understand happens to be the Absolute Subject, who has absolute freedom to choose to be hidden or reveal himself in whatever way he chooses. Theology, then, has to follow the inner logic of the revelation of the sovereign God, who chose to reveal himself by his Word – the Word spoken to us through prophets, and ultimately as the Word incarnate. That means that theology as science has to be guided by God's revelation in the Bible and Jesus Christ.

Now we have to ask further: What sort of science is theology? It is a science of critique. Critique of what? It is a critique of the church's proclamation, examining and testing whether it is faithful to the Word of God revealed in Jesus Christ, the Word incarnate.[2] To be faithful to the Word who became flesh and completely identified himself to a sinful world of perversion, a world rife with oppression and suffering, the proclamation of the church has to follow the incarnate Word where he leads. Theology has the task of ensuring that the gospel proclaimed is the gospel of the Word incarnate. All proclamation of the gospel has to have the Incarnate mode of articulation. That means it has to have the commitment and orientation of identifying with the context where the Word of God is to be preached, being responsive to the life issues in a life situation, not for the expediency of generating quick response and wide acceptance of the gospel, but for real-life transformation, which implies the transformation of the life situation.

The implication is clear. All theological reflections and articulations of the gospel have to be contextual in nature. The burning issues of a context, the sociocultural-spiritual predicaments it faces, and the unique mode of human corruption or aspiration, all affect our proclamation of the gospel. The gospel is certainly the same gospel, but the way it is being proclaimed, the relevant answers coming out of it in response to the life questions being asked, are bound to be context-oriented. Reflecting on the message of the gospel, an Asian theologian cannot avoid having a unique perspective. Certainly, we have to ask: Just how unique can this theological perspective be? The answer is quite simple: it can be unique as much as it is catholic and evangelical at the same time. And that means it has to take the articulation of the gospel in the form of doctrines affirmed by the catholic church as foundational. Contextual theology

---

2. Karl Barth, *Church Dogmatics* I/1, trans. G. W. Bromiley (Edinburgh: T&T Clark, 1973), 4–17.

must be bound by doctrinal theology, which serves as the source from which it draws spiritual and intellectual resources.

The gospel delivered to the Greco-Roman world and articulated by the early church fathers is the same gospel for Asians in their unique contexts. The gospel is whole, impacting all aspects and all dimensions of human life. While human persons in different historical contexts may find themselves in different conditions with different forms of human distortion, which may find different aspects of the gospel more relevant, the gospel is nevertheless an integrated whole. Only the whole gospel can address the human person in a holistic way. However, in different contexts, addressing different human conditions, proclamation of the gospel and theological articulations of it may require emphasis on certain aspects or dimensions of the gospel in order to bring in the full impact of the whole gospel. Putting emphasis on certain aspects does not mean neglecting the other aspects.

Chinese Contextual Issues

Since President Xi became the supreme leader in 2012, to the surprise of many, one of his major projects has been the revival of the Chinese cultural tradition. Prominent propaganda calling for the return to our cultural past can be seen everywhere in China. In response, the church has been making a frantic attempt to "make Christianity more Chinese," seeking a theological construction that is thoroughly Chinese. An indigenous Chinese theology has become an urgent quest for the church in China. This has not come as an accident. To President Xi and many leaders as well as Chinese intellectuals, the erosion of the Chinese cultural tradition has reached an alarming state. As China has become highly modernized and Westernized, the sense of cultural identity crisis, of the discontinuity with its cultural past, has become more and more acute. This problem is in fact nothing new. For more than a century, as China has been forced, like many other Asian countries, to Westernize to the point of rejecting its cultural past, the Chinese have been haunted by this sense of identity crisis. The problem just refuses to go away.

In the middle of the nineteenth century, after humiliating defeats in the Opium Wars (1839–1860), the threat of China being divided among Western powers was real. Whether China as a nation could survive the onslaught of Western imperialism and colonialism was a critical question. As the sense of crisis intensified, a complete cultural overhaul to make China strong again became urgent. China was forced to modernize and Westernize. The Chinese cultural past was severely questioned. As the crisis deepened, questioning of

China's cultural past culminated in an iconoclastic rejection, leading inevitably to a deep sense of identity crisis.

In the course of seeking cultural renewal, there were intensive debates. For many, the Chinese cultural past was a failure and had to be abandoned. For others, the achievement of the Chinese humanistic spirit could not be brushed aside just because of temporary technological setbacks. On the other hand, the Western scientific-mechanistic worldview behind all the technological achievements could in the long run be a real menace not only to China but to humanity as a whole.[3] However, the iconoclastic approach prevailed, and unreserved Westernization was set into motion, leading to the rapid disintegration of Chinese cultural tradition, resulting first in a deep sense of identity crisis and then an axiological crisis – the crisis of values. For many Chinese intellectuals and ordinary people, the old ghost of their cultural past just refused to fade away. It comes back to haunt them continually. What are they to do with the spiritual values and way of life ingrained in their personality for centuries? How can they integrate their historic past with Western elements so as to maintain the historical continuity and thus the integrity of their culture? Perhaps more importantly, how are they to evaluate the Chinese emphasis on "inner life" over against the emphasis on efficiency and functionality in the Western world? Is the life in which efficiency and functionality are the highest values worth living? This is an "axiological crisis," a crisis of values. As the full implications of free market capitalism joining forces with postmodern individualistic liberalism surface, more and more Chinese start to ask: Is not the price of unreservedly adopting Western civilization too high?

An unrestrained form of market capitalism has proven to be devastating in China, as traditional values have been severely undermined, leaving little spiritual strength to offset or minimize the impact. The spiritual and ecological implications can be frightening, not only for China but also for the world. Let me explain briefly, starting from the more obvious to communicate how serious the problem can be. In 2008, Maximilian Auffhammer of UC Berkeley and Richard Carson of UC San Diego projected on the basis of China's economic growth that by 2010, the increase in carbon dioxide emissions in China over

---

3. Liang Su-ming's lectures at Beijing University in 1921, "*Dong Xi Wen Hua Ji Qi Zhe Xue*" ("Eastern and Western Cultures and Their Philosophies"), was prophetic in pointing to the inner problems of Western culture. Liang affirmed unequivocally the value of the Chinese humanistic tradition. In a similar vein, Carsun Chang wrote a book in collaboration with German philosopher Rudolf Eucken defending the Chinese tradition while pointing to the spiritual predicaments in the West (*Das Lebensproblem in China und in Europa* [Leipzig: Quelle, 1922]). Chang's essay in that volume, "The European Cultural Crisis and the Direction of China's New Culture," is highly instructive.

its 2000 level would be 600 million metric tons. This figure dramatically dwarfs the 116-million-metric-ton emission reduction pledged by developed countries (except the USA) in the Kyoto Protocol (2001).[4] Even under rather conservative estimations, by 2030 carbon dioxide emissions in China will exceed the total emissions of all other industrial countries combined. The greenhouse effect by then will be devastating. At the same time, due to improved living standards, the increase in automobiles in China is also a serious concern. In 2001, there were only 16 million cars in China; in 2010, there were 90.86 million; and in 2016 there were already 194 million. Oil reserves will quickly be depleted, but that is a small matter in comparison with the problem of air pollution. If there is no spiritual or moral restraint strong enough to avert such a development, this will be a serious problem not only for China, but for the whole world. But this is merely on the surface; underneath, there is something more serious, and that is the collapse of moral values due to the impact of market capitalism in the context of postmodernity.

Market-driven capitalism is accelerating phenomenally in China as well as in other parts of Asia. Everywhere it goes, in the name of unobstructed freedom to provide maximum choices in the market, any spiritual and moral barrier that stands in the way has to be dismantled. Market capitalism, with functional rationality as its highest value, has had a far-reaching cultural impact in Western society right before our eyes. All values other than functional and marketable values are marginalized. Even the sacred and the sublime are to be commoditized. The moral and spiritual implications are astounding. Very few theologians have come to terms with this problem, and this neglect may prove to be costly.

Cultural Identity Crisis and Theology of Culture

In the face of the cultural identity crisis as well as the axiological crisis, in what way can Christian theology contribute to find a way out? Asian theologians share many common concerns as we share the common experience of witnessing the disintegration of our Asian traditions under the impact of modernization, which is almost synonymous with Westernization. It was in this most agonizing situation that waves of missionary endeavors came into China from 1850 to 1949. Poorly equipped for understanding Chinese tradition and insensitive

---

4. Maximilian Auffhammer and Richard T. Carson, "Forecasting the Path of China's Carbon Dioxide Emissions Using Province-Level Information," *Journal of Environmental Economics and Management* 55, no. 3 (2008): 229–247.

to China's struggle for survival as well as cultural integrity, missionaries proclaimed a gospel infused with a Western mindset and tainted with spiritual and cultural triumphalism, thus causing the gospel to be perceived as part of the cultural invasion from the West. At the same time, with a truncated soteriology, they preached a gospel of pure personal salvation, neglecting the sociocultural dimension of redemption. They were thus totally oblivious to the desperate quest of the Chinese people for sociocultural renewal. Some even saw Chinese culture as both backward and totally depraved. They were not able to feel the pain of identity crisis and the burning desire for cultural renewal.

During this time, the missionaries missed the opportunity to preach a holistic gospel integrating both the personal and the cultural aspects of redemption. As a result, Chinese intellectuals saw the gospel as totally irrelevant to their struggle for national reconstruction and cultural transformation. The lesson for a truncated gospel was costly, and a truncated theology was responsible. They lacked not only a holistic concept of redemption, but also a theology of culture on the basis of a sound theology of creation.

Theology in such contexts has to articulate the relevance of the gospel for affirming cultural tradition while transforming it through the power of Christ. To do so, Asian theology has to first develop a theological framework for affirming and making critical judgments about culture, and then point the way to transformation.

To begin with, we need to develop an evangelical theology of culture. To do so, we have to ask the very basic question: What is culture? Barth has given a most succinct and insightful answer: "Culture means humanity."[5] The human being does not live *in* culture; his or her very being is actualized and concretized *as* culture. Insofar as humanity is a gift from God, culture too is a gift from God. It is given as a mode of our being human. Barth points out that, "seen from the point of creation, the kingdom of nature (*regnum naturae*), culture is the promise originally given to man of what he is to become."[6]

What the human being is to become can only be found in the fulfillment of the image of God, not in abstraction but in the concrete form of life that is both creative and obedient to the Word. "The image is not in the human person; it is the human person."[7] As the image of God, the human being shares the sanctity that belongs to God: a sanctity that even God himself would not violate. We

---

5. See Barth, "Church and Culture," in *Theology and Church: Shorter Writings 1920–1928*, trans. L. P. Smith (London: SCM, 1962), 338.

6. Barth, "Church and Culture," 341.

7. A. J. Heschel, *The Insecurity of Freedom* (New York: Schoken Books, 1972), 152.

can thus even say that the human being shares the kind of absoluteness that belongs to God. In this sense, it is quite understandable that early church fathers like Athanasius and Basil the Great, and subsequently the Eastern Orthodox tradition, put so much emphasis on the idea of the "deification of the human being." Athanasius, referring to the logic of Christ's incarnation, would say, "He was made man that we might be made god." Basil also put it thus: "man is nothing less than a creature that has received the order to become god."[8]

Referring to the biblical tradition, Jewish philosopher Abraham Heschel points out that the Bible, unlike the Egyptian and Babylonian traditions, hardly deals with death as a problem. Its central concern is not how to escape death, but rather how to sanctify life. And the divine image does not enable human beings to attain immortality, but to attain sanctity.[9] If culture is the concrete mode of human existence manifesting the image of God, then ensuring the sanctity of the human person as that which is holy to God is the most fundamental directive for culture as the manifestation of humanity.

A culture, if it is to fulfill its task for the actualization of humanity, has to cultivate a sense of sacredness for all human persons within it. "Love your neighbor as yourself" (Lev 19:18) is an inevitable implication drawn from the fact that behind and above each human person is the Absolute God. At the same time, the human being hears inside him- or herself the call from God, "Be holy because I, the Lord your God, am holy" (Lev 19:2). Culture should also give expression to the sense of the sacred (or holy) intrinsic to human being. Only when a culture cultivates commitment to the unconditional can it be true to its task. A culture that alienates itself from the transcendent grounds itself on itself and ends up absolutizing itself. Self-absolutization is the root of human sinfulness. A society that closes its eyes to the transcendent light starts turning its own darkness into eternal light, justifying all forms of oppression and violence in the name of justice, thus violating the integrity of the image of God.

The reality of sin puts all human endeavors and creativity on the defensive. After the fall, what was originally a promise now hangs over human beings as a judgment. While the freedom of the human being is a real gift from God, his or her will to distort the promise of God is allowed its full effects, though contained within God's providence. And so the distortion of humanity sets in and permeates every aspect of culture. The land still prospers, but prosperity can become destructive. There will be thorns and thistles which will block and

---

8. Georgios I. Mantzaridis, *The Deification of Man* (New York: St Vladimir Press, 1984), 7.
9. Heschel, *Insecurity of Freedom*, 152.

disrupt human beings' attempts to cultivate order and abundance. What should have been positive directives for fulfillment now become guidance toward a blind alley. Culture thus contains the implications of the curse from God as well as the outworking of human beings' own sinful designs. All cultures are to be judged by the Word of God, while at the same time they are to be affirmed by the Word of God as his gift, even in their corrupted forms.

Affirmation and Critique: A Theological Response to the Cultural Identity Crisis

If culture was originally a gift from God, and after the fall it serves the purpose of the preservation of humanity waiting for full redemption by curtailing the power of sin, then there is something we can affirm in culture even after the fall. Contextual theologians need to have an in-depth dialogue with their own cultural tradition to both affirm and critique it. On the one hand, we have to bring out the best from a cultural tradition that manifests God's blessing. On the other hand, we have to point out whatever aspects of that tradition have the potential for the distortion of humanity. Here I venture to show from a dialogue with the Chinese cultural tradition how this may be accomplished. The following brief presentation should only be taken as an illustration designed to point the right direction for further pursuit. As Daoism, Buddhism, and Confucianism have been the three major strands of Chinese culture, we shall examine them briefly to illustrate how affirmation and critique can be exercised.

In both Daoism and Buddhism, the Nothingness of human existence is stressed. In Daoism, *Dao* (a concept overlapping in many ways with the Greek concept of *logos*) is the ultimate reality. Human existence is nothing but a transient manifestation of *Dao*; what appears to be real, with all its shape, form, sound, and motion, lasts merely a fleeting moment before falling back into the formless, shapeless, motionless, undifferentiated *Dao*. All differentiations or individual existence are ultimately nothing but delusions – something very much like a dream. Any attachment to them can only bring about disappointment and pain. Any attempt to ascribe lasting value to anything can only cause disillusion. All claims of truth can only be tentative and relative, fabricated only to sustain a fleeting moment of existence mistaken as really real and everlasting.

Daoism sees cultural fabrications as the cause of inauthentic human existence and therefore the source of human suffering. There is no concept of sin, the concept that human nature has already been distorted or corrupted, before cultural construction. It seeks liberation from the stifling oppressions of cultural constructions as well as from unnatural desires of the human heart, which again come from cultural nurture and orientation. Human culture, which originally aims to cultivate full humanity, becomes oppressive when it imposes on Nature strictures that reflect nothing but human desires and fear, thus rendering Nature unnatural. Human desires and fear, which subvert and work against Nature, are the cause of these strictures.

Even the pursuit of saintliness or the pursuit of wisdom can be obstructive and destructive. They are used as a pretext to boost one's status or fame – in short, one's ego. They may also be desperate responses to the chaotic human condition, but these futile actions can only make things worse. The path to liberation is to return to the simplicity of life, to the natural way, to the approach of "effortlessness" (*Wu-wei*), a state of freedom comparable to what Christians call "beatitude."[10] Again, the key lies in emptying and renouncing the fabricated self. There is a strong sense of judgment on culture. Culture means fabrication, the source of inauthentic human existence. The call to return to Nature is the call to return to *Dao*, which is an undifferentiated whole of reality. All differentiation, all individual existence, is transient and relative, and amounts to Nothing from the perspective of the undifferentiated eternal *Dao*.

Buddhism dwells on the reality of human suffering, the source of which is illusion about the self. Self-attachment is the root of the human predicament and suffering. The self is in reality empty; its "substance" is nothingness. All human inventions and cultural constructions serve to hide this reality from us, and to hold us captive in this castle of illusion. Salvation, therefore, means liberation from this castle of illusion. Self-negation is the key, and the discipline of self-denial is the path to liberation.

As we can see from the narrative above, the core spiritual insights of Daoism and Buddhism can be affirmed. This understanding of the nature of human existence in itself agrees in a profound way with the Christian belief in *creatio ex nihilo*. It points to the fact that if not for God's creative act, the ultimate reality of the world is Nothingness. God called the world out of Nothingness by his Word, his command. Without his Word, the world is Nothing, and we are Nothing. The Nothingness of human existence described by Buddhism and Daoism is indeed true, but this is merely half of the picture. It has left out the creative act of God, the act that confers reality on the world and on the human being. It nevertheless depicts the true condition of human beings as that of sinners who attempt to delude themselves in seeing themselves as

---

10. See Edward Slingerland, *Effortless Action: Wu Wei as Conceptual Metaphor and Spiritual Ideal in Early China* (Oxford: Oxford University Press, 2003), 78–88, 176–182.

the ultimately real, the ground upon which they can ground their existence. This certainly only leads them back to Nothingness, the very ground of their being without God's creative act. Self-attachment is a delusion leading only to endless suffering. In this, the Buddhist and Daoist insight must be affirmed.

And yet there are aspects of Daoism and Buddhism that need to be questioned. Both Daoism and Buddhism uphold a worldview that is utterly impersonal. Daoism can go to the extreme of denying the value of even the most positive human emotion such as love and compassion. Dao has no feeling.[11] Buddhism perceives emotion negatively, seeing it as a form of attachment, the source of suffering.

This does not square with the reality of the human being as a person. Core to our personhood is the capacity to love, and related to that is the capacity to transcend ourselves, to overcome our self-centeredness, and to move beyond ourselves to acknowledge the reality of others and to identify with them. The capacity to transcend is synonymous with freedom. Freedom and the capacity to love, according to Augustine, are the two most precious gifts from God. According to Barth, these reflect God's Being, and are thus fundamental to the human person's being the image of God. God as the Absolute Subject is absolutely free, but God's freedom does not mean the arbitrary exercise of his will; it is freedom bound by covenantal love. His freedom is freedom to love, even to the point of sacrificing himself.[12]

In short, the Christian worldview understands the world as a realm of personal beings. Moreover, the world is full of very real suffering and corruption. However, it is still a world made real by God and sustained by his grace. It is therefore a world full of joy, love, sympathy, and yearning for truth and justice. We cannot let suffering have the last word, allowing it to negate all of these, let alone nullify the reality of what God has created.

Confucianism, on the other hand, has little to say about Nothingness. Rather, it sees the world as concrete and real, manifesting *Dao*, which brings all things to fulfillment. Confucianism puts tremendous emphasis on human participation with heaven and earth to bring fulfillment to all things. The human being does not live in isolation, but in a community of beings who

---

11. "Nature has no emotion, no feeling, all things are straw dogs to it," author's own translation from Lao Zi, *Dao De Jing*.

12. Barth, in *Church Dogmatics*, II/1, §28 (257–321), presents "God as the Being who loves in freedom," bringing freedom and love together in God's being as inseparable and mutually implicated. Love, genuine love, comes out of freedom, and freedom is the capability to transcend oneself, to overcome one's being centered on oneself. When self-transcendence opens oneself to the Other, it becomes the act of love.

should exist and relate to one another in accordance with the mandate of heaven. Participation in the mandate, and participation with one another, is the key. For the Confucian tradition, a fundamental attitude in one's approach to reality and life is *Jing* (reverence, respect). *Jing* is the intuitive confidence in the infinite value of the human being and the cosmos.[13] This attitude opens the human heart to the transcendent dimension, to that which is beyond the human realm. It is a positive directive that points the human person as well as society as a whole to the Lord Creator. Thus, in the Chinese tradition there has been a strong sense of the Mandate of Heaven (*Tien Ming*) that governs all things.

Jing was originally a religious concept, referring to the feeling of *mysterium tremendum* toward that which is the ultimate. This fundamental attitude holds promise for the Chinese people to recognize their dependence on the transcendent. However, in the Confucian tradition, *Tien Ming* is so immanent in the human person that human beings have almost become the *Dao* incarnate, and thus self-affirmation of the human person becomes almost absolute, leaving little space for recognizing the reality of alienation from the transcendent: the reality of sin. *Tien Ming* has even become the human moral order upheld by the Confucian tradition.

The concept of self-denial is rather remote to the Confucian mind.[14] What is necessary is not the restoration of the sense of utter dependence or reconciliation between the human being and heaven, but self-discipline for saving oneself from any inauthenticity. Indeed, the Confucian tradition puts tremendous emphasis on the human being as the locus for the manifestation of *Dao*, which can shine through human existence.

Thus, allowing *Dao* to shine forth is of paramount importance to one's being human. To achieve that one has to go deep into one's being to grasp its heart and nature, in order to focus on it, not allowing oneself to be distracted by desires stirred by sensations. This practice of inwardness is a core spiritual exercise. Such a philosophical anthropology has the potential of echoing the Christian concept of the human person as the image of God. However, the lack of awareness of human depravity and the insistence on self-sufficiency for ultimate fulfillment are mental blocks to be overcome.

On the other hand, Confucius and Mencius placed tremendous emphasis on mutual commitment and mutual enrichment within a community of beings.

---

13. Táng Jūn Yì, *Zhong Guó Wen Hua Zhî Jing Shén Jiá zhí* [The spiritual values of the Chinese culture] (Taiwan: Student Press, 1951), 136.

14. Móu Zōng-sán, *Zhong Guó Zhe Xue Zhī Tè Zhì* [The distinctive character of Chinese philosophy] (Taiwan: Student Press, 2003), 16.

Ren (commitment-communion) is a state of life whereby full humanity is manifested. *Ren*, according to Móu Zōng-sán, one of the most important Chinese philosophers in the modern age, means "life-communion with the aim of enriching one another."[15] It is a life attitude based on a particular perception of reality. To the Confucian, one's being is always being-with others and being-for others. This being-with and being-for is not limited to communion and commitment among human beings, but also includes heaven and earth. The human being, to accomplish full humanity, has to participate with heaven and earth to transform and nourish all things under heaven, thus coming into union with all.[16]

This resonates with the Christian conviction about full humanity. Full humanity is realized in covenantal fulfillment – the fulfillment of the human being as being-with and being-for others, as revealed in Jesus Christ. Here the Chinese tradition can be a challenge to evangelical theology as the latter tends to narrow its soteriological perspective to justification. The theme of alienation and covenantal restoration is particularly relevant here. Salvation through reconciliation, participation, and mystical union can become very powerful. In the face of the Confucian tradition, evangelical theology may need to broaden its soteriological perspective by retrieving theological resources from the early church fathers and the Eastern Orthodox tradition.

Certainly, from the Christian perspective, the Confucian tradition has a serious flaw in its lack of awareness of human depravity. The Confucian tradition always sees the bright side of the human being, even in the face of rampant corruption in society. While corruption in society is acknowledged to be real, it is seen not as stemming from corrupt human nature but as originating in the failure to nurture and direct human nature to fully develop in accordance with its true nature. There is no concept of sin, and therefore no sense of being under its bondage. Liberation therefore comes not from transcendent power, but from self-reflection and self-discipline, the cultivation of an authentic inward self. Proclaiming the gospel to the Confucian tradition means proclaiming the reality of human sinfulness as well as the inability of human beings to save themselves.

---

15. Móu Zōng-sán, *Li Shî Zhé Xué* [Philosophy of history] (Taiwan: Student Press, 1976), 178.

16. "It is only he who is most authentic in his existence that he can cultivate his humanity to the full. Only then can he cultivate others to full humanity. Only then can he cultivate animals and things to their full nature . . . he then can participate with Heaven and Earth to transform and nourish all and come into union with Heaven and Earth." Author's own translation from Confucius, *The Doctrine of the Mean*, ch. 22.

From the discussion above, I hope it is clear that, while making a theological critique of culture to facilitate gospel-shaped cultural transformation is the ultimate goal, we must also recognize and affirm culture as God's gift, a gift full of promise for fulfillment in Christ. If indeed evangelical theology is able to affirm certain aspects of the Chinese cultural tradition, it can give hope to the Chinese people for holding onto their tradition as a gift from God – as a promise waiting for fulfillment in Christ – allowing them to see the possibility of maintaining the historical continuity of their cultural identity.

The Axiological Crisis: A Theological Response to the Sociocultural Impact of Market Capitalism in China

An axiological crisis is deepening in China in the wake of the globalization of market capitalism. If the sociocultural impact of market capitalism proves to be deeply troubling in other parts of the world, it will prove to be much more so in China. Chinese theologians have to take this challenge most seriously.

From 1980 onward, China has taken a new course. Market capitalism was mounted onto an authoritarian sociopolitical system rife with corruption. With the traditional value system torn to pieces, with all forms of spiritual quest suppressed, and with the communist ideology discredited, China was in a spiritual vacuum as it faced the onslaught of market capitalism, which recognizes efficiency and functionality as the measure of all value. When price competition dominates all other concerns, the purpose of economics is narrowly defined as "the science of efficiency," making efficiency the supreme virtue. To facilitate efficiency, moreover, functional rationality becomes the norm of the day.

Economists, however, do not seem to care to ask, "Efficient for what and to whom?" What they do care about is how to stimulate desires to grow consumption so as to sustain continual economic growth. People are thus driven by market dynamics to consume, resulting in a consumer culture. Within such a cultural framework, economics has become a religion. Its article of faith is that people are driven by self-interested economic rationality, and they do things because these actions offer them greater positive benefits than the cost incurred. Market fundamentalists would in principle exclude non-market values, and defend such a position in the name of scientific objectivity and neutrality. But as it turns out, behind such market fundamentalism is a set of unexamined ideological assumptions. In his book *Economics as Religion*, Robert H. Nelson seeks to lay bare the "unexamined ideology" of modern economics, a system of foundational values grounded in particular assumptions.[17]

Surely it is inevitable that one operates with certain basic assumptions. Yet it is one thing to prize efficiency and functional rationality, to regard free markets as indispensable and the most efficient instruments for the operation of an economic system; it is another thing to let them be the measure of all values, to the point of excluding other values in principle. Even George Soros, who defends the free market most vehemently, points out, "Market fundamentalists have transformed an axiomatic value-neutral theory into an ideology, which has influenced political and business behavior in a powerful and dangerous way . . . the idea that some values may not be negotiable is not recognized or, more exactly, such values are excluded from the realm of economics."[18]

The implication is clear, as Rebecca M. Blank states: "Belief in the value of the market leads some to argue for the libertarian position, which is that it is socially acceptable to provide any good for which there is a market . . . pornography is not a valid social concern . . . Similarly, if people wish to engage in prostitution – if some are willing to sell and others to buy – it is no one else's concern."[19]

Under the impact of functional rationality, not only the value of a person is to be assessed entirely in terms of his or her function in the market, but institutions like marriage and family, which are so vital to the integrity of Asian cultures, are doomed to be on the path of disintegration. Economists like Richard Posner blatantly challenge the "sacredness" of marriage and family. Applying his functional rationality, he regards it as rational to treat marriage as a contractual arrangement. From such a perspective, he sees no fundamental difference between prostitution and marriage. The only difference lies in the fact that marriage is a long-term arrangement of mutual service between husband and wife, whereas prostitution is a spot-market transaction.[20] This shows how value can be drained of emotional, moral, and spiritual content, excluding in principle tacit human commitment as relevant to the measure of value.

---

17. Robert H. Nelson, *Economics as Religion: From Samuelson to Chicago and Beyond* (University Park: Pennsylvania State University Press, 2014), xviii–xx.

18. George Soros, *The Crisis of Global Capitalism: Open Society Endangered* (London: Little, Brown & Co., 1998), 43.

19. Rebecca M. Blank, "Viewing the Market Economy through the Lens of Faith," in *Is the Market Moral? A Dialogue on Religion, Economics and Justice*, eds. Rebecca M. Blank and William McGurn (Washington: Brookings Institution Press, 2004), 24.

20. Richard A. Posner, *Sex and Reason* (Cambridge: Harvard University Press, 1998), 131, cited in Nelson, *Economics as Religion*, 180.

For Asian cultures, the institutions of marriage and family have for centuries been guarded as "sacred" for they are regarded as foundational for communal life, and communal life is vital to the integrity of being human. The family is the sacred space where freedom and commitment are woven together in the making of the human person. When marriage is on the path to being reduced to a transactional arrangement, family as the core component of Asian cultures is in severe danger. Community (*Gemeinschaft*) will degenerate into a mode of relation characterized by German sociologist Ferdinand Tönnies as "association" (*Gesellschaft*) of contractual individuals.[21] In a contractual society, the dominant social relation is the exchange of commodities and rational calculation of maximum benefits, and human persons "are essentially separated in spite of the uniting factor . . . here everybody is by himself/herself and isolated, and there exists a condition of tension against all others."[22] There is no mutual familiar relationship among these contractual individuals.[23] Such a shift from community to contractual association is foundation-shaking for Asian cultures, exacerbating their sense of identity crisis.

Contextual theology needs to elaborate the Christian concept of freedom as freedom *for commitment*, for, according to the Christian tradition, freedom is the capability of self-transcendence, the capability to limit and even negate oneself. The content and dynamic of freedom is love. In the incarnation, God has revealed himself to be absolutely free, yet his freedom is bound by his covenantal love to human beings, so much so that he emptied himself to identify with human beings in the very depths of their suffering and desperation. In God, freedom and love go together and are inseparable.

Here, the narrative of the covenantal nature of God's being and action, the gravity of covenantal love as manifested in Jesus Christ, the covenantal nature of the human person as the image of God, and the covenantal nature of the whole creation is highly relevant for upholding the integrity of Asian cultures in general and Chinese culture in particular. For the Christian tradition, unconditional covenantal love is the highest value, the measure of all values. In fact, covenant is the structure of created reality. To use Barth's expression:

---

21. Ferdinand Tönnies, widely regarded as one of the founding fathers of sociology, distinguished between two types of social groups, *Gemeinscchaft* (community) sustained by the bond of mutual commitment, and *Gesellschaft* (association) formed as an instrument for fulfilling individual aims and goals, sustained by functional contractual arrangements. See Ferdinand Tönnies, *Community and Association*, trans. C. P. Loomis (London: Routledge & Kegan Paul, 1974).

22. Tönnies, *Community and Association*, 74.

23. Tönnies, 87.

covenant is the internal basis of creation, and creation is the external basis of covenant.[24]

If it upheld covenantal commitment, "economics" would have an entirely different meaning from its modern understanding. The term "economics" itself is highly suggestive. It is coined by combining two Greek words, *oikos* and *nomia*, with *nomia* referring to "law" or "principle" and *oikos* to "a household." In choosing and combining these two words, "economics" carries the meaning or ideal of serving as the principle or law for regulating the use and sharing of resources within a household. This reflects the Christian ideal of seeing the world as a family under God, in which the right relationship between human beings is a covenantal relationship, a much deeper relationship than a contractual relationship that exists for purely functional purposes. This covenantal perspective is the necessary prerequisite for a Christian understanding of economics. It is only from such a perspective that we can observe how questionable the basic assumptions of our present economic mode truly are. Right here we can show our Chinese friends that the Christian tradition has a great deal of resonance with the Chinese tradition, and that we can join forces to combat the devastating spiritual challenge of market capitalism.

Concluding Remarks

We have walked through a long corridor of theological reflection, from theology as the science of critique to affirming that the proclamation of the church has to be incarnational to be faithful to God's revelation, and thus to affirming that theology has to be contextual. From there we pursued a theological reflection on the Chinese context, highlighting the identity crisis and axiological crisis as major issues Chinese theologians need to address. To resolve the identity crisis of the Chinese culture, theology has to provide a theology of culture that allows us to assess a culture, affirm it while judging it, and facilitate its redemption without disrupting its historical continuity. To deal with the axiological crisis brought about by Westernization, modernization, and globalization, we need to identify the major trends that exacerbate the disintegration of moral and social values so vital to the health of society. Market capitalism in its present form, and the fundamental assumptions behind it, need to be reviewed and challenged. Attempts must be made to redirect it into a covenantal mode.

---

24. Barth, *Church Dogmatics*, III/1, §41 ("Creation and Covenant"), 94–329.

Ultimately, the identity crisis and the axiological crisis are deeply intertwined, for the heart of the matter is the values that a tradition has treasured for centuries. To resolve the axiological crisis today, we cannot deal with the problem purely from the Christian perspective. We have to draw spiritual resources from the Chinese humanistic tradition. If we can affirm certain aspects of the Chinese culture, they certainly can combine forces with the Christian tradition to combat the menace of super-capitalism.

The exercise above is an exploration serving as an illustration of how contextual theology can be done and in what way its contribution is urgent and therefore vital for the well-being of the modern world.

References

Auffhammer, Maximilian, and Richard T. Carson. "Forecasting the Path of China's Carbon Dioxide Emissions Using Province-Level Information." *Journal of Environmental Economics and Management* 55, no. 3 (2008): 229–247.

Barth, Karl. "Church and Culture." In *Theology and Church: Short Writings 1920–1928*, 334–354. Translated by L. P. Smith. London: SCM, 1962.

———. *Church Dogmatics*, I/1, II/1, III/1. Translated by G. W. Bromiley. Edinburgh: T&T Clark, 1973.

Biéler, André. *The Social Humanism of Calvin*. Translated by Paul T. Fuhrmann. Louisville: Westminster John Knox Press, 1964.

Blank, Rebecca M. "Viewing the Market Economy through the Lens of Faith." In *Is the Market Moral? A Dialogue on Religion, Economics and Justice*, edited by Rebecca M. Blank and William McGurn, 11–56. Washington: Brookings Institution Press, 2004.

Eucken, Rudolf. *Das Lebensproblem in China und Europa*. Leipzig: Quelle, 1922.

Heschel, A. J. *The Insecurity of Freedom*. New York: Schoken Books, 1972.

Mantzaridis, Georgios I. *The Deification of Man*. New York: St Vladimir Press, 1984.

Móu Zōng-sán. *Zhong Guó Zhe Xue Zhī Tè Zhì* [The distinctive character of Chinese philosophy]. Taiwan: Student Press, 2003.

———. *Li Shî Zhé Xué* [Philosophy of history]. Taiwan: Student Press, 1976.

Nelson, Robert H. *Economics as Religion: From Samuelson to Chicago and Beyond*. University Park: Pennsylvania State University Press, 2014.

Posner, Richard A. *Sex and Reason*. Cambridge: Harvard University Press, 1998.

Reich, Robert B. *Supercapitalism: Transformation of Business, Democracy and Everyday Life*. New York: Alfred A. Knopf, 2007.

Slingerland, Edward. *Effortless Action: Wu Wei as Conceptual Metaphor and Spiritual Ideal in Early China*. Oxford: Oxford University Press, 2003.

Soros, George. *The Crisis of Global Capitalism: Open Society Endangered*. London: Little, Brown & Co., 1998.

Táng Jūn Yì. *Zhong Guó Wen Hua Zhî Jing Shén Jiá zhí* [The spiritual values of the Chinese culture]. Taiwan: Student Press, 1951.

Tönnies, Ferdinand. *Community Association*. Translated by C. P. Loomis. London: Routledge & Kegan Paul, 1974.

16

Reconciliation and the Kingdom of God
Reflections from the Middle East

Salim J. Munayer

Musalaha Ministry of Reconciliation

Then He who sat on the throne said, "Behold, I make all things new." (Rev 21:5 NKJV)

Introduction

Middle Eastern Christians have endured historical, political, economic, and religious adversity since the formation of the early church, but for the purposes of this chapter I will focus on the events that have taken place since the early twentieth century. I will highlight how these events along with their challenges have played a major role in shaping the history of the modern Middle East. I will then propose a theological and ethical response for Middle Eastern Christians.

For more than 500 years, most of the Middle East was ruled by the Ottoman Empire, one of the largest and most influential empires in history. Christians under Ottoman control lived as second-class citizens but were granted some freedoms under the millet system. The millet system was a separate court of law applied to non-Muslim minorities, mainly Christians and Jews, who were allowed to rule themselves under their own laws. This gave Christians the freedom to worship according to their own practices and traditions as well as to have their own legal courts to address mainly family and religious issues. The millet system also required non-Muslim inhabitants of the Ottoman Empire to acknowledge the supremacy of Islam and pay several taxes while additional restrictions were imposed upon them. The millet system was challenged as a result of major changes in the Middle East.[1]

Though the Ottomans had a once vibrant and thriving empire, they were unable to match the growing economic, technological, and military organization and power of western European nations. Western imperial powers aimed to exploit the weaknesses of the Ottomans, competing amongst themselves for colonial control of the Middle East due to its strategic location. With control of the Middle East, these European nations would gain access to resources like oil as well as to the major trade routes between Europe and East Asia.[2] At a time when Islam was perceived as weak, European imperial powers believed that the Middle East was ripe for spreading Western Christianity and did so through establishing Christian missions, schools, and churches.[3] They would gain access to the Holy Land for the purpose of finding archaeological evidence for the biblical narrative, and as a place for Christian pilgrimage and devotion.

Among British leaders and politicians were those who embraced a theology (mostly associated with what is known today as Christian Zionism) in which they believed it was the role of Christians to assist the Jewish people in re-establishing the Davidic kingdom within the borders of Palestine.[4] This included rebuilding the temple in hopes of expediting the return of Jesus. Those who propagated this theology saw it as a historical opportunity to influence British politicians, which came in light of Jewish suffering in Eastern Europe and was used as a means for gaining political leverage with America to draw them into the war in Europe.

Western powers ventured to divide the Middle East among themselves through a number of agreements. The first was the McMahon–Hussein Correspondence in which the British agreed to recognize Arab independence in exchange for launching the Arab Revolt against the Ottoman Empire. Britain and France next arbitrarily carved up the Middle East through the secret Sykes–Picot Agreement. The Sykes–Picot map created new political state-lines that divided the Middle East without taking regard for geographical location, tribes, families, or the wishes of the local ethnic peoples of the land, and brought about

---

1. David Thomas, "Arab Christianity," in *The Blackwell Companion to Eastern Christianity*, ed. Ken Parry (Chichester: Blackwell, 2010), 20.

2. Bernard Lewis, *The Middle East: 2000 Years of History from the Rise of Christianity to the Present Day* (London: Phoenix Giant, 1996), 273–285.

3. Lewis, *Middle East*, 323.

4. For further reading on the political implications of this theology, see Stephen Sizer's book *Christian Zionism: Road-Map to Armageddon?* (Downers Grove: IVP Academic, 2006).

instability to the region. Following these events, in the Balfour Declaration Britain announced that they would support and assist the Jewish people in establishing their own homeland in Palestine. This combination of theological, political, economic, and ideological endeavors brought new elements of instability to the Middle East. This culminated in the formation of the State of Israel, the tragedy of the Palestinian people, the Palestinian struggle, and several wars between Israel and the Arab states.[5]

With the end of the Ottoman Empire, the imposition of imperial powers, and broken promises, the Middle East was shadowed by another movement, that of nationalism. As lands were divided into countries, people were identified according to their nation-states rather than their religion. This appealed to Arab Christians as it was seen as a unifying thread by means of which they could no longer be discriminated against by their religion. Arab nationalism freed the Arabs from the Turks and the British and aided in countering imperialism and Zionism. They could join together with others in their country and seek national freedom as "Iraqis" or "Syrians." By the mid-1950s most countries, with the exception of the Palestinian people, were liberated from Western control.[6]

Unfortunately, Arab nationalism, which had begun as a liberating movement, later resulted in military dictatorships. Many of these dictators were unable to meet the needs of the people in the areas of employment, education, and healthcare, or provide them with a good quality of life. Soon there arose great distrust and dissatisfaction, eventually exposing the weaknesses of Arab nationalism and states. The failure was due, ultimately, to two major factors: internal issues and the ongoing external interventions of Western powers in the Middle East.[7]

This paved the way for the competing ideology of the Muslim Brotherhood to gain credibility in the region. The Muslim Brotherhood had emerged around the same time as Arab nationalism in the early 1920s, founded by Hassan al-Banna as an Islamic religious response to social and political injustice. It began as an education and charitable-focused organization but morphed into a political force. This ideological movement also sprang out of dissatisfaction with the dictatorships being unable to catch up with or counter the West. It began in Egypt as a movement to propagate "true Islam." They believed that

---

5. Salim J. Munayer and Lisa Loden, *Through My Enemy's Eyes* (Milton Keynes: Authentic Media, 2013), 1–23.

6. Adeed Dawisha, *Arab Nationalism in the Twentieth Century: From Triumph to Despair* (Princeton: Princeton University Press, 2003), 1–14.

7. Dawisha, *Arab Nationalism*, 252–281.

by going back to the early formation of Islam in its golden age and embracing an Islamic lifestyle according to the *sharia*, they would be able to counter the challenges Middle Eastern Muslims were facing. A major clash between Arab nationalism and the Muslim Brotherhood in Egypt was manifested by the imprisonment and execution of leaders of the Muslim Brotherhood, causing some branches of the Muslim Brotherhood to embrace militant power.[8]

The 1967 military victory of Israel over Egypt, Jordan, and Syria further exposed the weaknesses of Arab nationalism and allowed the Muslim Brotherhood to gain popularity. The Muslim Brotherhood and its different branches took this as their opportunity to show to the masses the inability of Arab nationalism to solve the challenges of Muslim Middle Eastern people, and propagated slogans stating that Islam was the solution. Their power grew following the 1973 war between Israel, Egypt, and Syria with the success of gaining the Suez Canal, and later, during the Iranian Revolution, with the formation of the Islamic Republic of Iran.

For Middle Eastern Christians, the rise of the Muslim Brotherhood created further complications. It brought them back to an era of discrimination based upon their religious identity. There was now a different interpretation of Islam that wanted to impose a lifestyle based on certain interpretations of *sharia* law that was different from what they had previously experienced. This was accompanied by hostility toward Middle Eastern Christians who were looked upon with suspicion and perceived as a vehicle for Western ideology and politics in the Middle East.

In addition to Western imperialism, the Israeli-Palestinian conflict, and the rise of the Muslim Brotherhood, Arab nationalism was further provoked by the US invasion of Iraq, which created chaos and the collapse of the state structure. This chaos and vacuum of law and order made room for more radical and militant Islamic groups to take control and begin creating what later became known as the Islamic State.[9]

The Islamic State has had a devastating impact on Christians and other minority groups primarily in Syria and Iraq. They have committed atrocities against Christians and the Yazidi people, and have demolished some of the oldest existing churches. There has been mass migration of Christians from these areas, with millions fleeing for their lives.

---

8. Ibrahim M. Abu-Rabi, *The Contemporary Arab Reader on Political Islam* (Alberta: University of Alberta Press, 2010), vii–xiv.

9. Jessica Stern and J. M. Berger, *ISIS: The State of Terror* (London: William Collins, 2015), 33–45.

The breakdown of these Arab states and the invasion of Iraq moved young and educated Arabs to take action, prompting a revolution called the Arab Spring. The Arab Spring was a series of anti-government protests and uprisings primarily among the young and educated who used social media and other means to fight against their country's oppressive regimes. It began in Tunisia, moved to Egypt, and then spread into other countries throughout the Middle East. These young people wanted to see major changes in their countries in the areas of democracy, economy, and in addressing corruption. In countries such as Tunisia there were drastic changes, but for others, like Egypt, the people ended up under a military dictatorship. In Syria, the Arab Spring turned into a civil war with devastating impacts on civil society, forcing millions of Syrian refugees to seek asylum in other parts of the world. The disheartening and disappointing failure of the Arab Spring greatly affected Middle Eastern Christians who were hoping to see more freedom, democracy, and equal opportunities.

The shockwaves from all of these events caused many Christians to migrate, primarily to the West, while others closed themselves off from the outside world, embracing a ghetto mentality. The majority of church leaders and Christian institutions or establishments continue to live their lives as they have done for centuries, with little engagement with society and politics. While some are taking an active role in being a voice and advocate in the midst of the Israeli-Palestinian conflict, such as in the organizations Kairos Palestine, Christ at the Checkpoint, and Musalaha, it is not true of the majority.[10] We often see how the evangelical community have adopted a two-citizenship identity, recognizing their earthly citizenship but emphasizing their heavenly citizenship as a means to escape their involvement in the present reality, especially when it comes to the Israeli-Palestinian conflict. They continue to demonize and dehumanize Muslims. This form of thinking is in contradiction to Jesus's teaching for us to be salt and light in society. Therefore, in the rest of this chapter, I will address how the kingdom of God and reconciliation provides a response to those aligning themselves with earthly kingdoms and powers. This will also highlight reconciliation as the vocation of the church in the Middle East.

This chapter addresses two perceived gaps in contemporary theologies of reconciliation. One gap is the widespread neglect of the kingdom of God as a model for reconciliation. The other gap concerns the role that power plays in reconciliation. In particular, in the context of the Israeli-Palestinian

---

10. See Salim J. Munayer, *Palestinian Christian Perspective on Justice* (forthcoming).

conflict, the issue of power, and specifically the power imbalances between the two sides, frequently arises in the reconciliation process. This issue must be addressed from a theological standpoint, but is often not addressed as such. As we consider how Jesus used power and how we are to use power, whether we find ourselves on the more powerful or more powerless side of the conflict, the kingdom approach offers important insights.

In this essay, then, we will first explore the role that power imbalances play in conflict and reconciliation. Second, we will describe a kingdom approach to reconciliation and lay out both its vertical and its horizontal aspects. Along the way, we will discuss the approach to power in Jesus's teaching and the biblical vision of the kingdom of God, and how that approach provides a model for addressing power within the context of reconciliation.

Power, Conflict, and Reconciliation

Any discussion of reconciliation and conflict must address the dynamics of power between conflicting groups. In any given conflict, each side exercises different kinds of power; one side may have more material power at their disposal (such as a larger army, more and better weapons, or simply more money), while the other side may have public opinion to back them up. In some cases, power imbalances can be so extreme that a conflict amounts to a struggle between the powerful and the powerless. It is noteworthy that this distinction does not necessarily have to do with the relative number of people in either category, as structural discrimination and access to resources can often give numerical minorities outsized influence. Moreover, we should note here that to call a group "powerless" in this context does not mean that the members of this group literally possess no power at all. Instead, it indicates that the power differential can be *so great* that, in relative terms, the less powerful can offer no serious opposition to the group in power. Because their status affects their everyday lives in visible, concrete ways, individuals in powerless groups tend to be more aware of their status, while the powerful, as part of the privilege of being powerful, tend not to think about their social position. Due to this perception, once the powerless start to assert themselves and challenge the status quo, the powerful often react negatively because they fear the loss of their position in society and the advantages associated with it.

Powerful–powerless relationships express themselves in a number of ways in a society, including in individual discrimination, institutional discrimination, and behavioral asymmetry. Individual discrimination simply refers to discriminatory actions that affect individual members of the less powerful group (for example, a woman getting passed up for a promotion because of her gender). Institutional discrimination affects more people and is a result of specific decisions made by an institution, such as a government or university (for example, African-Americans being denied the right to vote in the American South). Finally, there is behavioral asymmetry, which refers to submissive behaviors that minorities themselves adopt toward the powerful that signal acceptance of their powerlessness (for example, "Uncle Tom" is a derogatory term used to refer to African-Americans who are perceived as too submissive to the white majority).

Different approaches to addressing conflict can be defined by how or whether they address power imbalances between the powerful and powerless. "Conflict settlement" approaches simply find a way to end the immediate conflict without addressing the underlying imbalances that led to the conflict. "Conflict resolution," in contrast, addresses power imbalances as a part of addressing the basic human needs on both sides. Yet the only power imbalances typically addressed are those explicitly mentioned in the resolution agreement, leaving other imbalances unaddressed. "Conflict reconciliation," in contrast to these first two approaches, addresses power imbalances in all their forms by insisting on complete honesty regarding the historical record and the complete societal transformation required to foster equality and healthy relationships among all members of the population. A kingdom approach to reconciliation describes how Christ demonstrates the proper approach to handling power imbalances.

The Kingdom Approach

At the end of this age Jesus will say these words: "Behold, I make all things new" (Rev 21:5 NKJV). At that time, he will have made a holy and forgiven people who will love him and worship him forever. He will have judged all wrongs and sinners with perfect justice. He will have lifted the curse on creation and restored the whole cosmos to a right relationship with himself. Another way of saying this is that he will have reconciled all things to himself, finally realizing the completion of his mission.

In light of this perspective, it is clear that the Christian vision of reconciliation is expansive. It cannot be limited to our personal salvation, as it must also encompass a believer's personal relationships, and ultimately the reconciliation of all things under God's rule. Jesus is reconciling the world to God so that individuals and groups can experience reconciliation among themselves. Properly understood, reconciliation has two dimensions: vertical and horizontal. These two aspects are closely related and cannot be divorced. Nevertheless, we will address each one in turn. Because, as Robert Schreiter has rightly noted, the "vertical dimension is the foundation of all Christian discourse on reconciliation,"[11] we will start with the vertical dimension of reconciliation (God–humanity), which provides the framework for the second, horizontal reconciliation.

Vertical Reconciliation

The Kingdom of God

We have chosen to call our approach to reconciliation a "kingdom approach" because it focuses on the reality of Jesus's kingship, and, by implication, his kingdom, and contends that reconciliation is central to the kingdom of God.[12] This approach, while contextual and timely in our situation in Israel-Palestine, is applicable to other contexts as well. We focus on Jesus's kingship, the kingdom, and the framework they provide for a theology of reconciliation, especially as it relates to Jesus's understanding and use of power. However, before discussing reconciliation and the kingdom of God it is necessary to understand the background of God's rule announced by Jesus.

The Kingdom of God before Jesus

The kingdom of God is a prominent theme in the New Testament, and more particularly, the Gospels. Anyone who reads the four canonical accounts of Jesus's life will quickly notice that the evangelists considered this to be an essential part of Jesus's proclamation and mission. However, in order to understand the complexity and depth of this concept it is important for the disciples of Jesus to first grasp the narrative that sustains it: the narrative of Israel's history and their relationship with Yahweh, as narrated by the Old Testament authors. The Old Testament also demonstrates key elements of the godly stewardship of power.

---

11. Robert J. Schreiter, "The Emergence of Reconciliation as a Paradigm of Mission: Dimensions, Levels and Characteristics," in *Mission as Ministry of Reconciliation*, eds. Robert J. Schreiter and Knud Jørgensen (Oxford: Regnum, 2013), 13.

12. The authors who inspired this approach are Glen H. Stassen and David P. Gushee, *Kingdom Ethics: Following Jesus in Contemporary Context* (Downers Grove: InterVarsity Press, 2003); Alan Storkey, *Jesus and Politics: Confronting the Powers* (Grand Rapids: Baker Academic, 2005); and N. T. Wright, *How God Became King: Getting to the Heart of the Gospels* (London: SPCK, 2012).

The ultimate act of God's power was creation. With a word, God brought forth everything from nothing. Then God created man and woman to enjoy and flourish within his creation, and invited them to partake of his power by giving them dominion over it. The creation narrative shows key elements of godly power: its creativity, its promotion of human flourishing, and its collaborative nature. Then Adam and Eve sinned by disobeying God and eating of the fruit of the tree of good and evil. In so doing, they distorted the power that God had given them. Instead of creation, there would be destruction. Instead of flourishing, humankind would decay. Instead of collaboration, there would be division and separation.

The stories recounted in Genesis 2–11 illustrate the chaotic situation of humanity guided by its sinful desires and distortions of power. God sends a flood because "every inclination of the thoughts of the human heart was only evil all the time" (Gen 6:5). Even after the flood, we find the descendants of Noah building a tower meant to reach heaven, and God again has to intervene. But then, at last, in chapter 12, the book of Genesis starts to tell the story of God's intervention in the world. Whereas the tower of Babel was meant to reach heaven, in the story of Abraham we see heaven starting to reach the earth, bringing a plan of redemption of humanity. God chooses Abraham in order to bring his blessings into the world through Abraham's descendants.

Nevertheless, the story of Abraham's descendants – the people of Israel – is a story of subjugation under worldly and spiritual powers: foreign rulers who always threaten to subjugate Israel – and sometimes succeed – and Israel's sin, which causes them to repeatedly break the covenant with Yahweh. In many episodes of Israel's story these two are connected: Israel are not obedient to Yahweh, and, as a consequence, God allows them to be conquered by other nations. This is well illustrated by the many episodes of the book of Judges and by the constant skirmishes against the Philistines during the monarchy; but no other episode is more emblematic than the Babylonian exile.

The Old Testament narrates time and time again the clash between the worldly kingdoms and their gods and Yahweh. The story of the exodus – the very beginnings of Israel as a nation – is perhaps the best example of this war. Yahweh shows that his power is greater than, and fundamentally different from, the power of any other god, ruler, or nation. God's power breaks into human history to liberate the oppressed. Jumping ahead to the monarchic period of Israel, we find David expanding and establishing the kingdom of Israel under Yahweh's command, along with God's promise to David that his kingdom and his throne will be established forever. This is exemplary of God's desire to collaborate with his people to bring about his purposes.

The monarchic period and Israel's failure to keep the covenant with Yahweh lead to the Babylonian exile. It is during this dark period in the history of Israel that the hope of a new exodus leading to an everlasting kingdom of which God is the king becomes more developed. The prophets envision the time when God will himself come to free his people from bondage and will rule not only Israel but the entire world. Texts like Isaiah 40–55, the book of Daniel, Ezekiel, and others, show that Israel looked forward to the time of God's intervention to establish his everlasting kingdom.

The exile ended partially when Cyrus allowed the Jews to go back to their land and rebuild it (Ezra 1). However, the marvelous new exodus and the establishment of God's kingdom envisioned by the prophets did not happen. Israel was still under the power of Persia, and then the Greeks. Even when the people of Israel managed to acquire their freedom from the rule of other nations during the Maccabean period, they knew that they were not yet living in the promised kingdom of God. Roman domination soon emerged and once more Israel had to suffer under new rulers. Yet they kept hoping for the day of Yahweh's intervention.

Jesus and the Kingdom of God

> Jesus came into Galilee, proclaiming the gospel of God, and saying, "The time is fulfilled, and the kingdom of God is at hand; repent and believe in the gospel." (Mark 1:14–15 ESV)

The kingdom of God begins with the incarnation of Christ in human flesh. Jesus, as it says in Philippians 2:6–8, "being in very nature God, did not consider equality with God something to be used for his own advantage; rather, he made himself nothing by taking the very nature of a servant, being made in human likeness. And being found in appearance as a man, he humbled himself by becoming obedient to death – even death on a cross!" As these verses demonstrate, Jesus rejected the normal patterns of power. Instead of clinging to his position of privilege, he abdicated it; instead of separating himself from humanity, he engaged with it; instead of ruling over others, he served under them. Furthermore, the impetus behind the incarnation was God's love for humanity (John 3:16). It was only through the incarnation, this giving up of power, that Jesus created the conditions by which we may be reconciled to him. This is not to say that Jesus was never tempted with the power of worldly rulers. In fact, Jesus's temptation in the desert, described in Matthew 4 and Luke 4, concerned exactly that. The devil offered Jesus political, religious, and economic power – in other words, the powers of worldly domination – and Jesus refused each. His path would be the more difficult and costly one to tread. Others, too, wished worldly kingship upon him. Indeed, when Jesus announces in the Gospel of Mark that the kingdom of God is at hand, his audience would have assumed that their liberation from the Romans was at hand and that God was about to become the king of the world through the Messiah! But Jesus actively resisted the trappings of abusive power, going so far as to spend the bulk of his ministry in the geographical margins of power, the Galilee region, as opposed to Jerusalem, the power center of the region.

Jesus's ministry of signs and wonders testified to the inauguration of God's kingdom. Many in Israel started to believe that Jesus was the promised Messiah, the one who would free Israel from every foreign domination and reign forever. However, had they paid attention to Jesus's ministry and teachings, they would have seen something quite different. Far from attacking the dominating powers, Jesus advocated love for one's enemies. In Matthew 5:38–41 he says, "You have heard that it was said, 'Eye for eye, and tooth for tooth.' But I tell you, do not resist an evil person. If anyone slaps you on the right cheek, turn to them the other cheek also. And if anyone wants to sue you and take your shirt, hand over your coat as well. If anyone forces you to go one mile, go with them two miles." Not only are we to love our enemies, we are called to love them creatively, to actively seek ways to love them even as we are suffering under them. This teaching has implications for power dynamics within reconciliation, as we shall see.

God's wisdom has different plans from the world's wisdom, and it is Jesus who discloses the methods and the nature of the kingdom of God. The Gospels show us that Jesus is enthroned by his suffering and crucifixion. In Jeremy Treat's words, "the cross becomes not only the center of redemptive history, but also the fulcrum upon which the logic of the world is turned upside down."[13] The suffering servant of Isaiah 53, the liberator of Israel and the world, goes to the cross and suffers in order to bring redemption and to begin the promised new creation. As N. T. Wright points out, the *tetelastai* ("it is finished") of John 19:30 echoes the *synetelesen* in Genesis 2:2: "and on the seventh day God finished his work that he had done."[14] By his death, Jesus finished the first stage of the new creation and demonstrated that suffering has power, especially when one suffers willingly out of love for another. Through

---

13. Jeremy Treat, "Exaltation in and through Humiliation: Rethinking the States of Christ," in *Christology, Ancient and Modern: Explorations in Constructive Dogmatics*, eds. Oliver D. Crisp and Fred Sanders (Grand Rapids: Zondervan, 2013), 96.

14. Wright, *How God Became King*, 148.

his suffering, Jesus demonstrated his power over death and sin, which are themselves more powerful than any ruler or empire.

Jesus's resurrection and ascension were the proof that he is, indeed, the God-sent Messiah, and proof of the power that God has over death. Furthermore, as it says in Ephesians 1, that same power also resides in us, his followers. But more than that, these events show that Jesus is now King of the world. Daniel 7, a text that is essential in the understanding of God's kingdom, speaks of "one like a son of man" who comes before the Ancient of Days: "He was given authority, glory and sovereign power; all nations and peoples of every language worshiped him. His dominion is an everlasting dominion that will not pass away, and his kingdom is one that will never be destroyed" (Dan 7:13–14).[15] Luke 24:51 and Acts 1:9 both describe the ascension as the moment when the Son of Man was lifted up to the presence of the Ancient of Days to reign over his everlasting kingdom. And this is what the followers of Jesus believed and still believe: Jesus is King of an everlasting kingdom!

The Nature of the Kingdom of God

What kind of king is Jesus? What does it mean for us in the twenty-first century to say that Jesus is King? It is easy for us, as followers of Jesus, to see him as king of our lives in a vague spiritual sense. Yet can we cope with the idea of Jesus as king over all spheres of life and of his rule over this whole world?

While the crucifixion turned the logic of the world upside down, the same is true of Jesus's kingship. Therefore, we have to turn to the Gospels to understand the nature and principles of Jesus's kingship.

A Kingdom of Peace

> Jesus said, "My kingdom is not of this world. If it were, my servants would fight to prevent my arrest by the Jewish leaders. But now my kingdom is from another place." (John 18:36)

The kingdom of God does not come by coercive force, nor do Jesus's followers form a political party as part of following him. Quite the contrary, it is Jesus's lack of coercion, his subversion of the typical markers of power, that marks

---

15. This text has received different interpretations in biblical scholarship. The interpretation provided by verse 15 onward seems to indicate that the "one like a son of man" refers to the "saints," the righteous of Israel. These interpretations, however, are not necessarily mutually exclusive. Further, we have reason to believe that the evangelists, and consequently the primitive church, interpreted this text as referring to the Messiah Jesus.

his kingship as one of peace. As the Gospel of John narrates, when Jesus is questioned by Pilate, he affirms that his kingdom is not of this world – or better, is not *out of* (Greek preposition *ek*) this world. It is a kingdom *for* the world, but its origins are not *from* this world. It is a kingdom that is not established through violence, but through the power of God and the power of love.

A Kingdom of Servants

> Jesus called them together and said, "You know that those who are regarded as rulers of the Gentiles lord it over them, and their high officials exercise authority over them. Not so with you. Instead, whoever wants to become great among you must be your servant, and whoever wants to be first must be slave of all. For even the Son of Man did not come to be served, but to serve, and to give his life as a ransom for many." (Mark 10:42–45)

Jesus is the Servant King. Unlike the Roman emperor and other rulers of the world, Jesus does not exercise tyranny over his subordinates. As it states in Philippians 2, Jesus willingly gave up his status as God in order to become a servant. Once again, the logic is turned upside down. Jesus comes to the world to become the King, but a king who serves his people by giving his life for them. And so his followers should serve one another, even if they have to give up their status and positions of privilege (John 13:1–17).

An Inclusive Kingdom

> Then Jesus came to them and said, "All authority in heaven and on earth has been given to me. Therefore go and make disciples of all nations, baptizing them in the name of the Father and of the Son and of the Holy Spirit, and teaching them to obey everything I have commanded you. And surely I am with you always, to the very end of the age." (Matt 28:18–20)

Whereas some Jews believed in a kingdom exclusively for Jews, who would subjugate the Gentile nations, Jesus proclaimed a kingdom available to and constituted of every race, language, social status, gender, and so on. The world in which Christ lived was marked by a variety of divisions: Jews and Gentiles, men and women, slaves and masters, rich and poor. But in the kingdom of God, where Jesus has all power and authority, these divisions become empty and meaningless. Jesus's power and authority is collaborative, inviting others to participate in what he is doing in history. As Paul writes in Galatians 3:28, "There is neither Jew nor Gentile, neither slave nor free, nor is there male and female, for you are all one in Christ Jesus." When Paul speaks of relationships between men and women in Ephesians 5, he argues that husbands should love their wives sacrificially as Christ loved the church; when he speaks of relationships between slaves and masters, he also encourages equality, going so far as to say of God, "there is no favoritism in him." Paul addresses divisions between the rich and the poor in 1 Corinthians 11, where he chides his audience for fostering class divisions during the Lord's Supper by not sharing with the poor. In sum, no other identity mark could be more important than the mark of the Messiah for those who believe in him, and the mark of the Messiah equalizes the power imbalances that create conflict between peoples, a truly revolutionary concept for the social structures of the first-century world.

A Kingdom above Every Other

> Now is the time for judgment on this world; now the prince of this world will be driven out. And I, when I am lifted up from the earth, will draw all people to myself. (John 12:31–32)

God exalted Jesus above every authority and power. He is the ultimate ruler of this world, and it is to him that our deepest loyalties must be given. As a result, worldly rulers are subjected and accountable to him. Although Jesus's teachings do not contain a political program, they do disclose God's intentions for political power.[16] Moreover, the fact that Jesus is the ultimate ruler sets the limits to worldly politics. As Storkey puts it, "Jesus is . . . anti-totalitarian; he refuses the state or the ruler the possibility of defining the meaning of life."[17]

Furthermore, according to N. T. Wright, rulers are to look to the ultimate *eschaton*, the age to come, and enact in advance the time when God will make all things new.[18] The new creation should be the ultimate model for the governors of this world, whether they believe in Jesus and the kingdom or not. It is the responsibility of the community of believers, whatever cost it might carry, to remind rulers of their task and call them to account.

---

16. Allen Verhey, *The Great Reversal: Ethics and the New Testament* (Grand Rapids: Eerdmans, 1984), 32.

17. Storkey, *Jesus and Politics*, 125.

18. N. T. Wright, "Kingdom Come: The Public Meaning of the Gospels," *Christian Century* 125, no. 12 (2008): 29–34.

Vertical Reconciliation and the Kingdom of God

As has been made clear from what has been said about the kingdom of God so far, conflict is repeatedly in the background of the promises and situations involving God's kingdom. In the Old Testament these promises emerge from the conflict between Israel and other nations. The judgment that brought Jesus to the cross came from every angle: not just from Israel, but also from the Roman Gentiles, from the powers, from the religious and pagan alike. Israel stands with blood on its hands and so do the Gentile rulers, the Romans, who did as much to nail him there. But above every other conflict, it is the conflict between humanity and God that nailed Jesus to the cross. Since Adam and Eve's sin, every generation of humanity has been complicit in rebellion against God. This conflict of creatures against their creator is at the root, and is the essence, of every other human conflict.

The kingdom of God is a kingdom in which conflicts are resolved and power imbalances are righted. In the first place, every human being is invited to submit to Jesus, the King of the world, ending the time of rebellion against God. As with Israel's sin that led the nation into exile, and Adam and Eve's sin that led them away from the garden of Eden, so our sins lead us away from the place where we are supposed to live: under the kingship and guidance of God. Therefore, forgiveness of sins brought about by Jesus takes us back where we belong: under God's rule. Jesus reconciles us to God, leading us to his kingdom. But the only way he could do that was by giving up his position of power and privilege and entering into life with us.

The theme of new creation further expands our understanding of what the coming of the kingdom entails. It is certainly not by accident that the Gospel of John starts with the same words as the book of Genesis, and we have also mentioned the resemblance between Jesus's last words and Genesis 2:2. Paul writes in 2 Corinthians 5:17, "Therefore, if anyone is in Christ, the new creation has come: The old has gone, the new is here." Both John's and Paul's perspectives on the new creation come from the promises of the Old Testament, where God pledges to renew all things: "See, I will create new heavens and a new earth. The former things will not be remembered, nor will they come to mind" (Isa 65:17). For the early community of believers, Jesus's resurrection inaugurated the new creation, in which God, the King, renews the whole creation. Every human being who receives the Messiah is given a new kind of existence in the power of the Holy Spirit, sent by Jesus to continue his work through the community of believers. Thus, God not only reconciles humanity with himself, but also calls human beings to cooperate with him and with each other in his work of reconciling all things to himself.

Horizontal Reconciliation

The Community of the Reconciled Ones

> For he himself is our peace, who has made the two groups one and has destroyed the barrier, the dividing wall of hostility, by setting aside in his flesh the law with its commands and regulations. His purpose was to create in himself one new humanity out of two, thus making peace, and in one body to reconcile both of them to God through the cross, by which he put to death their hostility. (Eph 2:14–16)

One of the consequences of sin was alienation from God – the exile from the garden God planted for humans where they would live under his rule and protection. However, soon enough, sin revealed its consequences regarding human relations as well. The peace of the garden of Eden was replaced with a world full of murder, even between brothers (Gen 4). Conflict among human beings extended throughout creation, to the point that soon in Genesis we find a man, Lamech, boasting about his murderous exploits: "I have killed a man for wounding me, a young man for injuring me" (Gen 4:23). People began to use their power over others in violence and oppression; thus, power imbalances formed. Sin created an almost irreversible breach in human relations that is still felt today.

The early community of believers saw in Jesus and in the establishment of God's kingdom the initiation of the reversal process. Jesus not only brought peace between God and his creation, but through his work he also restored the relationship between human individuals and groups. Jesus created a community of reconciled ones who live in peace because they have a tie uniting them that is stronger than any difference that may separate them; and this tie is the submission to their King and the advancement of the kingdom.

While the powerful and the powerless may have the common tie of the kingdom, the reality is that they live within social systems that maintain the very power imbalances that encourage conflict. These power imbalances must be addressed from a kingdom perspective and using the principles of power that Jesus demonstrated. The powerful will resist this leveling process since they benefit from the status quo and have more to lose. Therefore, the powerful must look to the incarnation and Philippians 2:6–9 as a model for how to address their own power. Just as Jesus gave up his position of power in order to serve humanity, so too those with power ought willingly to give up their position and privilege in order to serve those without power. Just as Jesus engaged with humanity through taking the form of human flesh and moving among them, so too the powerful ought to engage directly with the powerless by going where they are. Just as Jesus took on the role of servant, the lowest rung on the Roman social ladder, so too the powerful ought to be willing to accept losing some of their power. Just as Jesus was obedient to the Father, so too the powerful ought to be obedient to God as they carry out the work of reconciliation. Finally, just as Jesus lowered himself out of his love for the world, so too the powerful ought to lower themselves out of genuine love for the powerless; not guilt or shame or grief – love.

The powerless have their own role to play in reconciliation. The common responses by the powerless to their situation are submission or rebellion: submission internalizes and accepts the status quo, while rebellion pushes back on the status quo with violence. Jesus's Sermon on the Mount offers the paradigm for how the powerless ought to address their condition. Glen Stassen describes Jesus's teachings in the Sermon on the Mount as "transformative initiatives that are the way of deliverance from anger and killing."[19] The status quo of the time was to hate one's enemy and retaliate against him or her. But Jesus preached love of the enemy, which resists evil not through violent means, but through nonviolent love. Nonviolence need not mean simply submitting to the enemy's actions, but includes action that also confronts injustice without recourse to violence. In sum, then, in order for there to be true reconciliation, the powerful must give up their position of privilege, while the powerless must give up recourse to violence.

Perhaps the greatest symbol in the New Testament of the peace brought about by Jesus is the reconciliation of Jews and Gentiles, mentioned in Ephesians 2:14–16. In the temple in Jerusalem there was a wall that prohibited the Gentiles from entering the temple courts. This wall was a symbol of the barrier between Jews and Gentiles: the former were considered pure and privileged and had access to the place of habitation of Yahweh; the latter were impure, separated from God and consequently in a position of inferiority. Without a leveling out of the power imbalances, it is impossible to achieve effective reconciliation. But Jesus inaugurated a kingdom of total equality, where every individual, Jew and Gentile, has unrestricted access to the King and forgiveness of sins. Therefore, there is no longer a wall separating those

---

19. Stassen and Gushee, *Kingdom Ethics*, 135.

from different ethnic origins. Everyone is welcome! And everyone receives a new identity, the identity of a new creation. As Paul boldly affirms in Galatians 6:15, "neither circumcision counts nor uncircumcision means anything; what counts is the new creation."

Therefore, followers of Christ are called to live as the community of the Messiah in peace and reconciliation. This is not to suggest that conflict will disappear inside the community of believers – sin has not been totally eliminated – but every conflict should be dealt with from the perspective that none of our differences is greater than what unites us: our King and his kingdom. Furthermore, as 1 John 2 states, love ought to infuse the entire community of believers; there is no room in the body of Christ for hate or for the inequality hate breeds. Love is the animating factor behind believers reconciling with other believers and addressing power imbalances, whether through the powerful giving up their power, or the powerless responding to their enemies with nonviolence. More than that, we are called through Christ's power to call others to be reconciled to Christ and to be preachers of peace to this world, both in word and deed.

Reconciling the World

> Therefore, if anyone is in Christ, the new creation has come: The old has gone, the new is here! All this is from God, who reconciled us to himself through Christ and gave us the ministry of reconciliation: that God was reconciling the world to himself in Christ, not counting people's sins against them. And he has committed to us the message of reconciliation. We are therefore Christ's ambassadors, as though God were making his appeal through us. We implore you on Christ's behalf: Be reconciled to God. God made him who had no sin to be sin for us, so that in him we might become the righteousness of God. (2 Cor 5:17–21)

We are not only called to experience reconciliation as part of the community of the Messiah, but, according to Paul, we are also called to be ambassadors of Christ, ministers of reconciliation. Although the term "ambassador" in the Roman Empire had a broader use, basically it refers to someone representing his or her country or territory in another country, or sent on a mission to a foreign territory. One of the tasks of Roman ambassadors was to arrange the terms of peace when a place was to become a Roman province.[20] In the same way, we are called to go beyond the limits of the believing community and proclaim peace to all individuals, of all nations, so they might become citizens of the kingdom. We do this in the power of the Holy Spirit, who allows us to be collaborators with Christ in his work of reconciling the world to himself.

We are also called to become peacemakers, to work for peace even outside the boundaries of the kingdom, to those who do not know Jesus. Paul says that Jesus became sin so that we might become the righteousness of God. Morna D. Hooker interprets this in the following manner: "if God's righteousness is a restorative power, bringing life and reconciliation, then those who 'become righteousness' will be the means of manifesting that power in the world."[21] She adds, "what Christ is to us – righteousness, wisdom, sanctification, redemption – followers of Jesus must now be to the world."[22] This is a bold affirmation from Paul. If we are to be the righteousness of God, imitating Jesus's example, we must live lives of sacrifice and abdication to bring peace to the world, just as Jesus did in order to bring peace to us. The ministry of reconciliation will most likely involve suffering, and certainly will demand sacrifice. Jesus's commitment to peacemaking took him all the way to the cross, and so our path in peacemaking may demand profound personal loss. Yet we find strength in Jesus's words: "Blessed are the peacemakers, for they will be called children of God" (Matt 5:9).

As part of our vocation as ambassadors of reconciliation for the kingdom we need to recognize that reconciliation is "first and foremost the work of God."[23] Therefore, as ambassadors we are totally dependent upon God's grace and direction for this task. In Schreiter's words, "our effectiveness as messengers and ministers of reconciliation arises out of our co-operation with God."[24] We must remain faithful to our vocation even if we do not experience success in our mission, and humbly admit that every favorable outcome in this task is an act of God's grace. The work of reconciliation is a cooperative labor between God and us, his ambassadors. Therefore, our spirituality is fundamental for the work of reconciliation. Through spiritual disciplines – prayer, meditation, communion – we exercise our sensitivity to the Holy Spirit, who enables us to be

---

20. Hulitt Gloer, "Ambassadors of Reconciliation: Paul's Genius in Applying the Gospel in a Multi-Cultural World: 2 Corinthians 5:14–21," *Review and Expositor* 104, no. 3 (2007): 589–601.

21. Morna D. Hooker, "On Becoming the Righteousness of God: Another Look at 2 Cor 5:21," *Novum Testamentum* 50, no. 4 (2008): 358–375.

22. Hooker, "Becoming the Righteousness of God," 358–375.

23. Schreiter, "Emergence of Reconciliation," 15.

24. Schreiter, 15.

aligned with God's plans. As Schreiter affirms, "the ministry of reconciliation, then, is more a spirituality than a strategy."[25] Every work of reconciliation is different in its actors, difficulties, and history; for that reason, we need to rely on the Holy Spirit in a close relationship with him.

Finally, we come back to where we started: the end of this age. Although the kingdom of God is already present, bringing reconciliation to this world, the New Testament authors are clear that all things will finally be fully reconciled with God only at the end of this age, when Jesus comes back to definitively establish his kingdom upon the earth. This teaching should fill us with sobriety, because "even in our best efforts at working for reconciliation, we typically find what is achieved is still incomplete."[26] Thus, as writes Schreiter, "we are reminded too that reconciliation is not only a goal or end; it is also a process in which we are called to co-operate."[27] Let us be part of this process, as God's co-workers!

The challenge to live this out has prompted us at Musalaha to develop an approach for peace and reconciliation. Years of trial and error led to the birth of the Six Stages of Reconciliation, a six-stage nonlinear process of reconciliation that has proven successful. Musalaha not only facilitates reconciliation among those who have a common faith in Jesus, but also is taking an active role in peacebuilding in the wider society by forming a network of communities that have compassion, solidarity, and empathy toward people who are otherwise considered enemies. Often there is a temptation to align ourselves with present powers and empires, secularization, materialism, and religious-ethnic ideology. However, just as the early church presented an alternative to the Roman Empire that peace did not come by the sword but through sacrifice, so we also must not align ourselves with the world. It is our King who set the example and calls us to serve others.

References

Abu-Rabi, Ibrahim M. *The Contemporary Arab Reader on Political Islam*. Alberta: University of Alberta Press, 2010.

Dawisha, Adeed. *Arab Nationalism in the Twentieth Century: From Triumph to Despair*. Princeton: Princeton University Press, 2003.

---

25. Schreiter, 15.
26. Schreiter, 18.
27. Schreiter, 18.

Gloer, Hulitt. "Ambassadors of Reconciliation: Paul's Genius in Applying the Gospel in a Multi-Cultural World: 2 Corinthians 5:14–21." *Review and Expositor* 104, no. 3 (2007): 589–601.

Hooker, Morna D. "On Becoming the Righteousness of God: Another Look at 2 Cor 5:21." *Novum Testamentum* 50, no. 4 (2008): 358–375.

Lewis, Bernard. *The Middle East: 2000 Years of History from the Rise of Christianity to the Present Day*. London: Phoenix Giant, 1996.

Munayer, Salim J., and Lisa Loden, eds. *The Land Cries Out*. Eugene, OR: Cascade, 2012.

———. *Through My Enemy's Eyes*. Milton Keynes: Authentic Media, 2013.

Schreiter, Robert J. "The Emergence of Reconciliation as a Paradigm of Mission: Dimensions, Levels and Characteristics." In *Mission as Ministry of Reconciliation*, edited by Robert J. Schreiter and Knud Jørgensen, 9–29. Oxford: Regnum, 2013.

Sizer, Stephen. *Christian Zionism: Road-Map to Armageddon?* Downers Grove: IVP Academic, 2006.

Stassen, Glen H., and David P. Gushee. *Kingdom Ethics: Following Jesus in Contemporary Context*. Downers Grove: InterVarsity Press, 2003.

Stern, Jessica, and J. M. Berger. *ISIS: The State of Terror*. London: William Collins, 2015.

Storkey, Alan. *Jesus and Politics: Confronting the Powers*. Grand Rapids: Baker Academic, 2005.

Thomas, David. "Arab Christianity." In *The Blackwell Companion to Eastern Christianity*, edited by Ken Parry, 1–22. Chichester: Blackwell, 2010.

Treat, Jeremy. "Exaltation in and through Humiliation: Rethinking the States of Christ." In *Christology, Ancient and Modern: Explorations in Constructive Dogmatics*, edited by Oliver D. Crisp and Fred Sanders, 95–114. Grand Rapids: Zondervan, 2013.

Verhey, Allen. *The Great Reversal: Ethics and the New Testament*. Grand Rapids: Eerdmans, 1984.

Wright, N. T. *How God Became King: Getting to the Heart of the Gospels*. London: SPCK, 2012.

———. "Kingdom Come: The Public Meaning of the Gospels." *Christian Century* 125, no. 12 (2008): 29–34.

Contributors

George N. Capaque (PhD, De La Salle University, Manila) is adjunct professor of Theology at Asian Theological Seminary (ATS), Manila. He recently "retired" as Dean (Principal) of Discipleship Training Centre, Singapore. Prior to this he served as Associate Professor of Theology and Dean at ATS. He has also served as pastor of Baptist churches in Canada and in the Philippines and on the staff of InterVarsity Christian Fellowship Philippines. Besides his current part-time teaching, he helps his local church in preaching and together with his wife, Dawn, helps look after their two grandchildren. George has edited one book and contributed essays and articles in various books and journals.

Simon Chan (PhD, Cambridge) was Earnest Lau Professor of Systematic Theology at Trinity Theological College, Singapore. He retired in 2018 but continues to conduct spiritual retreats at TTC. Currently, he is the editor of *Asia Journal of Theology*. He has authored books and articles on spirituality, liturgy, Asian theology and Pentecostal theology. His abiding interest is in the relationship of the liturgy, spirituality, and the church. His most recent essay has been published in *The Oxford Handbook of Ecclesiology* (2018).

Roland Chia (PhD, University of London) is Chew Hock Hin Professor of Christian Doctrine at Trinity Theological College and Theological and Research Advisor of the Ethos Institute for Public Christianity. He is author of numerous articles and books including *Revelation and Theology: The Knowledge of God According to Balthasar and Barth* (Peter Lang, 1999), *The Right to Die? Christian Response to Euthanasia* (National Council of the Churches of Singapore, 2009) and *Hybrids, Cybrids and Chimeras: The Ethics of Interspecies Research* (National Council of the Churches of Singapore, 2011).

Havilah Dharamraj (PhD, University of Durham) serves as the Head of the Department of Old Testament and as the Academic Dean at the South Asia Institute of Advanced Christian Studies in Bangalore, India. One of her research interests is Old Testament narrative. Here, she sees storytelling as a vehicle for developing narrative theology in South Asia. A second research interest is comparative literature, in which biblical texts can be placed into conversation with parallel non-Christian sacred texts. A work-in-progress is a comparative thematic study of the *Song of Songs* and the *Gita Govinda*, a Hindu sacred poem. Besides these, she explores innovative assessment methods in higher theological education and in training for ministry. Her publications include *Altogether Lovely: A Thematic and Intertextual Reading of the Song of Songs* (South Asian Theology) (Fortress, 2018); *Challenging Tradition: Innovation in Advanced Theological Education* (ed.) (Langham, 2018); *South Asia Bible Commentary: A One-Volume Commentary on the Whole Bible* (ed.) (Langham/Zondervan, 2015); and *A Prophet Like Moses?: A Narrative – Theological Reading of the Elijah Stories* (Paternoster, 2011).

Timoteo D. Gener (PhD, Fuller Theological Seminary, PGDip, London School of Theology) is Chancellor and Professor of Theology at the Asian Theological Seminary (ATS), Metro Manila, Philippines. He has been serving in ATS since 2002 teaching systematics and contextual theology. He is a member of the World Evangelical Alliance (WEA) Task Force on Ecumenical Affairs and took part in the International Consultation between the WEA and the Catholic Church on Scripture and Tradition and Salvation in the Church (2009–2016). He is also Moderator of the Theological Commission of the Philippine Council of Evangelical Churches (PCEC) and a member of the Philippine Commission on Higher Education (CHED) Technical Panel on Christian Formation. Tim was co-editor of *The Earth Is the Lord's: Reflections on Stewardship in the Asian Context* (ATS/OMFLit, 2011) and has written essays in various books and journals, most recently "Doing Contextual Systematic Theology in Asia: Challenges and Prospects" in the *Journal of Asian Evangelical Theology* (2018). Tim is married to Caroline, and they are blessed with three children: Mia, Chelsea, and Emil. They are members of Victory Christian Fellowship in Quezon City, Metro Manila.

Ken Gnanakan (PhD, London University) is an Indian educator, environmentalist, musician, and theologian. He is a frequent speaker worldwide at workshops, seminars and conferences. Dr Gnanakan is Chancellor of the ACTS Group of Institutions, which includes primary and secondary schools, colleges and a private university. He also teaches in universities in India and in other parts of the world on varied subjects such as mission, management, environment, education, theology, and philosophies. He is the author of several books on philosophy and theology, including an internationally used textbook in theology, *Kingdom Concerns: A Biblical Exploration Towards a Theology of Mission* (TBT, 1989 and IVP, 1993). Other books like *Proclaiming Christ in a Pluralistic Context* (TBT, 2000), *The Whole Gospel of God* (TBT, 2014) and *Wellness and Wellbeing* (TBT, 2016) are widely read.

Kar Yong Lim (PhD, University of Wales) is Lecturer in New Testament Studies at Seminari Theoloji Malaysia, Seremban. He is also the Director of Postgraduate Studies and the founding Director of the Centre for Bible Engagement at the seminary. An ordained minister with the Anglican Diocese of West Malaysia, he also teaches at various seminaries in Malaysia and throughout the region. His publications include *The Sufferings of Christ Are Abundant in Us* (T&T Clark, 2009); *Jesus the Storyteller* (Armour, 2015); *Metaphors and Social Identity Formation in Paul's Letters to the Corinthians* (Pickwick, 2017), and numerous essays. He is currently working on a major monograph on social identity formation in the Philippians due to be published in 2021.

Wonsuk Ma (PhD, Fuller Theological Seminary) is a Korean Pentecostal scholar in Old Testament studies by training, but also has ongoing research interests in Pentecostalism, Mission, and Global Christianity. He currently serves as Dean and Distinguished Professor of Global Christianity, College of Theology and Ministry, Oral Roberts University in the USA. During his service as a missionary to the Philippines, he worked at Asia Pacific Theological Seminary, Baguio City (1983–2006), helped establish the Asian Pentecostal Society and served as Founding President (1998–2000), and launched two journals: the *Asian Journal of Pentecostal Studies* and the *Journal of Asian Mission*. He previously served as Executive Director and David Yonggi Cho Research Tutor of Global Christianity at Oxford Centre for Mission Studies (2006–2016). He also served as Director of Regnum Books, which has published, among others, the 35-volume Regnum Edinburgh Centenary Series. His publications include *Until the Spirit Comes: The Spirit of God in the Book of Isaiah* (T&T Clark, 1999), and (with Julie C. Ma) *Mission in the Spirit: Towards a Pentecostal/Charismatic Missiology* (Regnum, 2010), and thirteen (co-)edited titles.

Salim J. Munayer (PhD, Oxford Centre for Mission Studies) is a Palestinian-Israeli who is also the Founder and Executive Director of Musalaha Ministry of Reconciliation, an organization that brings together Israelis and Palestinians, facilitates reconciliation encounters, and trains leaders to be agents of peace in society. He is also a Professor at the Bethlehem Bible College and Adjunct Professor at the Hebrew University of Jerusalem. Salim is a regular contributor to theological and academic journals on issues related to reconciliation, justice, theology, and politics in relation to the Israeli-Palestinian conflict. His most recent book (with Lisa Loden), *Through My Enemy's Eyes* (Paternoster, 2014), addresses the universal theological dimension of reconciliation and seeks to pave a way forward.

Lalsangkima Pachuau (PhD, Princeton Theological Seminary) is the John Wesley Beeson Professor of Christian Mission and Dean of Advanced Research Programs at Asbury Theological Seminary, USA. A native of India (Mizoram), Pachuau taught for seven years at the United Theological College, Bangalore, India, before joining Asbury in 2006. He has also served as a visiting professor at a number of institutions in Asia, Africa, and Latin America. Dr Pachuau was the editor of *Mission Studies: Journal of the International Association for Mission Studies* for eight years (2004–2012). Author of *World Christianity: A Historical and Theological Introduction* (Abingdon, 2018), and *Ethnic Identity and Christianity* (Peter Lang, 2002) and numerous articles in academic journals, Pachuau has edited and co-edited several books including *Witnessing to Christ in a Pluralistic Age* (Regnum, 2011). He is an ordained minister of the Presbyterian Church of India and serves in the Transylvania Presbytery (Kentucky) of the PCUSA, where he currently is a member of the Commission for the Preparation of Ministry.

Stephen T. Pardue (PhD, Wheaton College) is Associate Faculty at the International Graduate School of Leadership and Asia Graduate School of Theology, where he teaches theology. He was co-founder of the Theology and Bible in Global Context study group in the Evangelical Theological Society, and has served as co-editor for the six-volume Majority World Theology Series (Langham). He is the author of *The Mind of Christ: Humility in Early Christian Thought* (T&T Clark, 2013) and several journal articles and essays. He is currently working on a forthcoming volume on the subject of evangelical theology and the global church, as well as a monograph on the subject of humility and discipleship. He is married to Teri Pardue, and they keep busy raising their four children Ava, Lucy, Simon, and Ivy.

Aldrin M. Peñamora (PhD, Fuller Theological Seminary) is Executive Director of the Commission on Justice, Peace and Reconciliation of the Philippine Council of Evangelical Churches. He has taught theology and ethics at the Koinonia Theological Seminary in Davao City in the southern Philippines, and is currently a faculty member of the Asia Graduate School of Theology, Philippines and the Asia Theological Seminary. As an advocate for interfaith dialogue and just peacebuilding, especially between Christians and Muslims in the Philippines and Southeast Asia, he is often involved in initiatives aimed at fostering harmonious Christian-Muslim relations, and has published several essays on the subject. He is married to Christine Ching Peñamora.

Ivor Poobalan (PhD, University of Cape Town) has served as the Principal at Colombo Theological Seminary, Sri Lanka, since 1998. His previous ministry was as a youth pastor for Methodist churches in the city of Colombo. In 2018 the Lausanne Movement appointed him as Co-Chair of the Theology Working Group. He is a graduate of the London School of Theology, UK, and Trinity International University, USA. His PhD thesis was on the interpretation of 2 Corinthians 4:4. Ivor teaches in the fields of Biblical Studies, Pastoral Theology and Leadership. He is a contributor to the *South Asia Bible Commentary* (Amos), *NIV God's Justice Bible* (Haggai), and the *NIV Understand the Faith Study Bible*. Ivor is married to Denisa and they are parents to daughters, Anisha Eng, and Serena.

Ivan Satyavrata (PhD, Oxford Centre for Mission Studies) spent several years in Christian leadership training but presently serves as Senior Pastor of the Assembly of God Church in Kolkata, a church with a significant social outreach, providing education and basic nutrition for several thousand children in and around the city of Kolkata. He is a pastor-theologian whose special interests include Christian witness to people of other faiths and the Christian response to social issues. He has authored a number of articles and three books: *Holy Spirit, Lord and Life Giver* (InterVarsity, 2009; Langham, 2012), *God Has Not Left Himself without Witness* (Regnum, 2011), and *Pentecostals and the Poor* (APTS Press, 2017). Ivan's wife Sheila [Elizabeth], and children, Rohan, Rahul, Phengsy (Rahul's wife) and granddaughter, Maia, are the pride and joy of his life.

Kang-San Tan (PhD, University of Aberdeen, DMin, Trinity International University) is General Director of Baptist Missionary Society, or BMS World Mission in the United Kingdom. A Malaysian Chinese, he was formerly Head of Mission Studies at Redcliffe College, UK, and has served with OMF International and the Church Mission Society. His expertise is in Interfaith Theology, Intercultural Theology, Buddhism, and Islam. He has participated in theological consultations of the WEA Mission Commission and Lausanne Theology Group. He has published over forty articles on mission studies and interfaith issues, and co-edited, *Contextualisation and Mission Training: Engaging Asia's Religious Worlds* (Regnum, 2013), and edited *The Soul of Mission: Perspectives on Christian Leadership, Spirituality and Mission in East Asia* (SUFES, 2007).

Juliet Lee Uytanlet (PhD, Asbury Theological Seminary) is the Field Education Director of the Biblical Seminary of the Philippines. She teaches

Cultural Anthropology, Hybridity and Chineseness, Global Missions, and Urban Missions. She also teaches Ethnographic Research Methods at the Asia Graduate School of Theology. She and her husband pastor on weekends at Gerizim Evangelical Church, which is located in the oldest Chinatown in the world. She served as the Lausanne Catalyst on Diasporas for the years 2016–2018. Her dissertation, entitled *The Hybrid Tsinoys: Challenges of Hybridity and Homogeneity as Sociocultural Constructs among the Chinese in the Philippines* was published in the American Society of Missiology Monograph Series (Pickwick, 2016).

Carver T. Yu (DPhil, University of Oxford; DD *honoris causa*, University of Edinburgh) is President Emeritus, and was President and Distinguished Professor of Systematic Theology, of China Graduate School of Theology, Hong Kong. He had also served as Head of Department of Religion and Philosophy at Hong Kong Baptist University. He was elected a Member (Research Fellow) of Center of Theological Inquiry, Princeton. Before his retirement, he had been actively involved in Asia Theological Association (ATA), International Council for Evangelical Theological Education (ICETE) and the Langham Foundation. He was a member of the Theological Commission of the World Evangelical Fellowship. He was a plenary speaker at the Lausanne Congress 2010, Cape Town. He has written ten books including *Being and Relation: A Theological Critique of Western Dualism and Individualism* (Scottish Academic Press, 1987); *Freedom and Commitment: Theological Reflections on Cultural Crisis and Reconstruction* (Chinese Christian Literature Council, 2001); and two volumes in systematic theology, *Listening: The Beginning of Theology* (Campus, 2008) and *The God of Extreme Mercy* (Christian Communication Limited, 2016). He has also written over a hundred articles including more than thirty academic articles published in journals and books. He has been actively engaged in discussions on the Christian critique of both modernity and postmodernity. He is an ordained minister of the Cumberland Presbyterian Church.

Index of Names

A
Aalen, Sverre 251
Amalorpavadass, D. S. 210
Anangguru Yewangoe, Andreas 163
Appasamy, A. J. 209
Askew, Emily 255
Auffhammer, Maximilian 300

B
Barth, Karl 62, 281, 297, 302, 306, 311
Benko, Stephen 150
Bevans, Stephen 153, 212–213
Bhabha, Homi 271, 273
Blank, Rebecca M. 310
Blomberg, Craig L. 50, 53
Bonhoeffer, Deitrich 249
Bourdieu, Pierre 150
Braaten, Carl E. 25
Brueggemann, Walter 252
Brunner, Emil 172, 289
Burnham, Gracia 182

C
Carson, Richard T. 300
Chambon, Michael 124
Chan, Simon 29, 30, 31, 67–68, 74, 92, 96–98, 290–291
Chesterton, G. K. 146
Cicero, 250
Coburn, Thomas B. 48
Coe, Shoki 210
Cohen, Robin 266
Confucius 291, 307
Copeland, Edwin Luther 50
Cortez, Marc 26
Cox, Harvey 122
Crone, Patricia 158

D
David, Randolph 162

D'Costa, Gavin 280–282, 285
Detweiler, Robert 56
Dyrness, William 212, 247

E
Elsdon, Ron 109
Evans, Craig 254

F
Fabella, Virginia 258
Farquhar, J. N. 50
Fernando, Ajith 95
Fielder, Caroline 132,
Flemming, Dean 86
Franke, John R. 20, 62
Fraser, Nancy 257
Frei, Hans 279, 282–286, 294
Friedman, Thomas L. 222

G
Gaventa, Beverly R. 215
Gener, Timoteo D. 245
George, Sam 269
Giddens, Anthony 158
Goodman, David S. G. 162
Griffiths, Bede 110
Gunton, Colin E. 27–28, 78

H
Habermas, Jürgen 250
Haire, James 247
Hanson, Bradley 88–89
Harvey, David 252
Hebblethwaite, Brian 166
Hebden, Keith 256
Hedges, Paul 259
Heschel, Abraham J. 46, 303
Hick, John 94, 224, 281–282
Hooker, Morna D. 333
Hutchinson, John 267

Hwa Yung 3, 122, 248

I
Ibrahim, Azeem 256

J
Jenson, Matt 142, 147
John Paul II 144

K
Kärkkäinen, Veli-Matti 23–24, 48, 61, 71, 74, 120, 281
Kim, Chi Ha 249
Kim, Rebecca Y. 208
Knitter, Paul F. 282
Koyama, Kosuke 90, 211, 248
Küng, Hans 163
Kunin, Seth D. 252, 255
Kvalbein, Hans 251

L
Lane, Dermot A. 170
Larsen, Timothy 5
Lee, Jung Young 70–71, 75, 77
Lim, Ka-Tong 203

M
Maggay, Melba 24, 28, 248
Ma, Julie C. 128
Ma, Lawrence J. C. 266, 270
Ma, Wonsuk 6,
Mao Zedong 167–168
Marcel, Gabriel 158
Marsden, George M. 140–141
McDermott, Gerald R. 141, 286
McDonald, H. D. 17
McGrath, Alister E. 16, 25
McGuire, Meredith B. 271, 273–274
Mohamad, Mahathir 190
Moller, Philip 51
Moltmann, Jürgen 64, 111, 115, 161
Móu Zōng-sán 307
Muck, Terry C. 292
Munayer, Salim J. 8
Myrdall, Gunnar 163

N
Neill, Stephen 210
Nelson, Robert H. 309
Netland, Harold A. 281
Nirmal, Arvind 72–74
Nor, Hilmy 190–191

O
O'Collins, Gerald 78–79
Olson, Roger E. 28
O'Neill, J. C. 252

P
Pachuau, Lalsangkima 7
Pannenberg, Wolfhart 111–112
Phan, Peter C. 223
Pieris, Aloysius 69, 76, 90, 93–94, 246
Polanyi, Michael 151
Posner, Richard A. 310
Pua, Boon Sing 190–191

Q
Quito, Emerito 24

R
Ramachandra, Vinoth 86, 93–95
Richard, H. L. 234
Robison, Richard 162
Rorty, Richard 250
Rule, Paul 168

S
Samartha, Stanley J. 92, 94, 226, 228
Samuel, Vinay 91
Sanders, E. P. 254
Satyavrata, Ivan 7
Schreiter, Robert J. 153, 322, 333–334
Seamands, John T. 202
Sen, K. M. 205
Singh, Sadhu Sundar 95, 209
Smith, Anthony D. 267
Smith, Steven G. 40
Smith, Wilfred Cantwell 39, 45, 289
Smith, Jonathan Z. 24
Song, C. S. 211, 246, 248

Soros, George 309
Stassen, Glen H. 331
Storkey, Alan 328
Stott, John R. W. 4–5, 13, 16, 49, 51
Sugden, Chris 91
Sugirtharajah, R. S. 90–91
Sunquist, Scott W. 185

T
Talmon-Heller, Daniella 48
Tan, Andrew 7–8, 132, 138, 160, 176–177, 270, 277, 279, 295
Tan, Kang-San 7
Tanchanpongs, Natee 74
Tennent, Timothy C. 184–185, 193, 286
Thomas, M. M. 207, 211
Thompson, John 62
Tiessen, Terrance 150, 285
Tilak, L. 233–236
Tinder, Glenn 169–171, 174
Tira, Sadiri Joy 268
Tong, Daniel 290
Tooley, Michelle 248

U
Uytanlet, Juliet Lee 7

V
Vanhoozer, Kevin J. 25, 56
von Rad, Gerhard 103

W
Walls, Andrew F. 4, 216
Walzer, Michael 259
Weerasingha, Tissa 96–97
Wenell, Karen J. 253
Wesley, Luke 123–124
White Jr., Lynn 102
Wickeri, Philip L. 203
Wiesel, Eli 248
Wilfred, Felix 245, 258
Williams, Paul 165
Wink, Walter 258
Winslow, J. C. 233

Wright, N. T. 325, 328

Y
Yeh, Allen 270
Yeo, K. K. 291
Yewangoe, A. A. 163
Yoo, Boo-Woong 135
Yu, Carver T. 8, 213, 216

Z
Zizioulas, John 143

Index of Subjects

A
advaita 71–72, 227–229
ancestor 97–98, 121, 134–136, 150–153, 290
Asia Theological Assoication 1, 5, 14, 16, 28, 31–32, 135, 197
atonement 32, 96, 149

B
baptism 64, 86–87, 93, 142–143, 145, 148
bhakti 209, 227, 232–235
body of Christ 4, 20, 30, 116, 127, 147, 332
Buddhism 67–68, 92, 96, 163–166, 204–206, 223, 227, 280, 283–284, 292, 304–306

C
Canon 6, 40, 42–45, 47–48, 52–54
Cappadocians (Gregory of Nyssa, Basil of Caesarea, Basil the Great, Gregory of Nazianzus) 65–66, 89, 303
caste 73, 96, 183, 202, 205–206, 246, 247, 256
Central Asia 182, 256
charismatic 123–124, 133, 136
China 1, 8, 68, 70, 91, 124, 132, 136, 162, 166–168, 182–183, 200–204, 206, 217, 269–270, 291, 299–301, 305, 309
Chinese 121, 123–124, 126, 135, 148, 151, 183, 190–191, 208, 246, 266, 268–274, 286, 290–291, 299–302, 304, 307–309, 311–312
communion of saints 97, 142, 144, 146, 149–150, 153
communism/communist 166–168, 183, 203, 207, 217, 247, 290, 309

Confucianism 67–68, 204, 206–209, 216, 220–221, 292, 304, 306
contextualization 3, 28–29, 86–87, 203, 210–212, 216–217, 238, 248
creation 6, 19–21, 23–24, 26–27, 62, 68, 88, 101–117, 121, 127, 129–130, 136, 144, 146, 170–171, 174–175, 208, 227–228, 231, 233, 237, 260, 302, 311–312, 321, 323, 325, 328–330, 332
cross/crucified 6, 74, 86, 96–97, 105, 112, 133, 170, 172, 174–175, 186–188, 192–193, 217, 249, 324–326, 329–330, 333

D
Daoism/Dao 204, 206, 304–307
dialogue, interfaith 15, 24, 62, 121, 129, 140, 240, 259, 279, 284, 286–289, 292
docetism 87–89, 148
dukkha 164

E
East Asia 93, 140, 204–205, 316
Ebionitism 87
ecology/ecological 6, 101–102, 105–110, 112–116, 161, 252, 267, 283, 292, 300
economy, divine 51, 62, 65, 130
economy/economic 32, 69, 73, 108, 158–159, 161–163, 176, 245, 247, 252, 254–259, 267, 269–270, 274, 285, 300, 309–312, 315–317, 319, 325
exclusivism 73, 232, 280–282
exile 22, 41, 255, 265, 268, 323–324, 329–330
exodus 22, 323–324

347

F

family 31–32, 71, 74–79, 97–98, 114, 116, 119, 141, 145, 148, 153, 214, 273, 290–291, 310–312, 315
Filipino 15, 24, 75–79, 258, 260, 268, 271–272, 274
fulfillment (of cultural and religious longing) 172, 230–232, 235–240, 284, 308

G

globalization 8, 14, 31, 152, 162, 221, 224, 269–270, 309, 312
gospel (euangellion, evangel) 3–5, 7, 19, 25–26, 31–32, 42, 44, 56, 73, 85–86, 88, 90, 94, 106, 144, 147, 183–184, 186–189, 192–194, 223, 225, 229, 234, 238, 240–241, 271, 284–288, 292–293, 302, 308
  centrality of 5, 15–16, 28–30, 142,
  contextualization of 32, 210–213, 216–217, 236, 298–299

H

harmony 108–109, 168, 206–208, 214, 222, 225–226, 228–230, 239
healing 23, 122–124, 128, 131–136, 257, 288
Hindu/Hinduism 39–40, 43, 45–46, 48, 50, 55, 57, 68, 71, 73, 91, 92, 163–166, 182, 204–206, 214, 216, 227–229, 230–236, 239, 280, 285
homoousios 65, 89
Hong Kong 258, 269–270

I

incarnation 50, 74, 96, 214–216, 230, 232, 236, 302, 311, 324, 330
inclusivism (inclusivist) 232, 241, 280–281, 285
indigenous (indigenizing, indigenization) 123, 132, 201, 203, 208–211
India/Indian 46, 50, 55, 57, 72–74, 85, 92, 95–96, 140, 174, 182, 199, 200–202, 208–211, 226, 231–236, 239, 256, 259, 269
Indonesia 159–161, 182, 259, 284
Islam 43, 45–46, 48–49, 54–55, 67–68, 95, 133, 159–160, 182–183, 189–193, 223, 227, 280, 283–285, 288–289, 290, 316–318

J

Japan 70, 90–91, 200, 206, 209–210, 211, 258
Judaism 40, 42–43, 47, 52–54, 68, 83–85, 104, 136, 188, 204, 222, 230–231, 251, 253, 276, 288–289, 303, 316–317
justice 73, 91, 93, 95, 113–114, 121, 129–130, 143–144, 161, 163, 175, 240, 248, 250, 252, 257–258, 262–263, 283–284, 303, 306, 310, 313, 319, 321
justice (injustice) 122, 175, 193, 240, 248, 274, 317, 331
justification (justify) 18, 27, 63, 114, 308

K

karma 97, 166, 205, 227, 285
kenosis 71
kingdom of God 8, 64, 81, 89, 172, 239, 242, 251–253, 255, 260–262, 264, 285, 288–289, 315, 319–320, 322, 324–327, 329, 334

L

Laos 161, 181, 284
Lausanne Covenant 13, 52, 59

Lausanne Movement 5, 14, 16, 52, 59, 129, 133–134, 137, 212, 268, 277, 341
liberate 249, 323
liberation 62, 69, 73–74, 76, 81, 92–93, 95, 99, 111, 129–130, 135, 160, 165, 204, 206, 211, 214, 224, 226–227, 230, 242, 246, 249, 256, 258, 261, 263, 297, 304–305, 308, 325
  theologies of 13, 95, 102, 294, 319
Lord's supper (Eucharist) 146–148, 154

M

Malaysia 132, 160–161, 181–182, 184, 189–193, 195–197, 280, 284
Marx, Marxist 166–167, 290
Marxism 167, 176
Middle East 48, 59, 181, 204, 315–319, 335
migration 14, 35, 223, 241, 247, 265–270, 274, 277, 291, 318
migration (diaspora) 7, 14, 35, 265–271, 273–277, 286, 291, 295
minjung 95, 130, 135, 211, 246, 256, 262
miracles 123–124, 128, 131–133, 288
miraculous 236
mission 7, 9, 13–16, 18–19, 22–23, 26, 28–30, 32–35, 37, 86, 93–95, 98, 100, 104, 113–114, 117, 120–121, 127–133, 135, 137–138, 141, 143, 145, 147, 181–187, 189–190, 193–198, 208, 217, 219, 223, 225, 228, 239–242, 255, 267–270, 277, 279–281, 284, 286–288, 292–293, 295, 321–322, 332–333, 335
  theology of 7, 13–14, 16–18, 22–23, 25, 32–35, 43, 69, 76, 79–81, 93–94, 99, 102, 105, 109, 128, 139, 144, 147, 154, 181, 184, 195–198, 209, 211–213, 215–217, 219, 225, 242, 246, 251–253, 261–264, 275, 280–283, 285, 288, 294–295, 301–302, 312, 322
missions, missionary 4, 7, 9, 17–18, 50–51, 91–93, 132, 141, 184–186, 192–197, 200, 212, 216–217, 220, 223, 241, 248, 262, 268–269, 277, 280, 286, 292, 295, 301, 316
modalism 65
Mongolia 1, 119, 206
monotheism 87, 288
Muhammad 43, 46, 54
Myanmar 182, 206, 256, 259, 284

N

Nepal 1, 181–182
Nicene Creed 3, 89, 126
nirvana 56, 71, 164–165, 227, 285

P

Pakistan 182–183, 195
Pentecost 143
Pentecostal 120–124, 128–129, 131–132, 134–138, 143, 153, 211, 283, 290, 295
persecuted 7, 134, 181, 203
persecution 131, 181–186, 190–191, 193, 197
Philippines 28, 34–36, 67, 75–77, 80–81, 90–91, 128, 130, 135, 137, 141, 160, 162, 182, 256, 259, 265, 268, 270–274, 277, 295
pluralism 67, 69, 90–91, 94–95, 192–193, 217, 221–241, 279–282
politics (political) 7, 32, 85, 92, 95, 108, 158–161, 182, 193, 201, 203, 211, 222, 239, 245–260, 270, 285, 288–289, 292, 309–310, 315–320, 324, 326, 328
poverty 14, 31, 62, 69, 72, 84, 90–91, 93, 95, 130, 136, 140, 143–144,

161–163, 181, 183, 211, 219, 240, 246–247, 258, 283, 285, 288, 292, 327–328

R
rebirth 148, 164–165, 202, 205–206, 227
reincarnation (reborn) 165–166
reconciliation 8, 23, 49, 99, 104, 111, 113–116, 201, 307–308, 319–322, 325, 331–334
Reformed 121, 129, 283
Revelation 13–32, 45–51, 53–55, 63, 72, 77, 79, 84–85, 98, 113, 129, 133, 147, 170–172, 208, 225–226, 230, 232, 235, 293, 298, 312
   general 8, 21–23, 50, 121–123, 232
   in other religions 16, 22–25, 49–50, 72, 92, 121–123, 127–129, 225–226, 230, 231, 237–238

S
Sabbath rest 108
Sabellius, Sabellianism 88–89
Sacraments/sacramental 27, 48, 57, 141–142, 147–150, 152
samsara 166, 205–206, 227
sanctification 148, 303, 333
sat-cit-ananda 68, 209, 228
Shang Di 68, 167
shirk 68, 227
Sikhism 39, 205, 221–222
Singapore 158–162, 164, 258, 290
South Asia 43, 94, 204, 207
Southeast Asia 45, 158–161, 266–267, 270, 280, 286–289
South Korea 70, 91, 95, 121–122, 130, 135, 206, 208, 246, 256, 258
Sri Lanka 91, 94, 181–182, 206
suffering 6–7, 14, 62, 74, 96, 129–130, 161–165, 168, 170, 206, 256, 304–306, 311, 316, 325–326, 333

Christian response 173–174, 181–194, 247–249, 298, 306

T
Taiwan 210–211, 246, 269–271
technology 108–109, 169
Thailand 90–91, 158, 160, 174, 182, 284
Trinity 15, 31, 50, 61–79, 89, 97, 125–127, 144, 171, 209, 228, 239
   development of 17, 63–67, 126–127

V
Vietnam 162, 200, 284
violence 69, 161, 222, 224, 247–248, 256, 259, 267, 303, 327, 330–331

W
World Council of Churches 30, 114, 122–123, 127–129
World Evangelical Alliance 5, 31

Z
Zoroastrianism 39, 221

Index of Scripture

OLD TESTAMENT

Genesis
1–11 22
2–11 323
2:1 103
2:2 .... 325, 329
4 330
4:23 330
6:5 323
6:18 109
9:11–12 109
9:16 109
12 .... 19, 22, 110
12:3 .... 22, 110
14:17–20 22
16:7 .... 47, 64
20 22
22:11 47
28:10–22 252

Exodus
3:1–5 252
3:2 .... 47, 64
3:2–6 64
3:4–22 64
5:22–6:8 22
16:10 47
19:18 47
24:16–17 47
33:11 52
33:22 47
34:5–6 47
40:35 47

Leviticus
19:2 303
19:18 303
25:1–17 107
25:5 108

25:17 108

Numbers
21:14 52
22–24 22
22:22 47

Deuteronomy
10:14 22
18:21–22 52
26:5 73
28 53

Joshua
10:13 52

1 Samuel
3:10 47

1 Kings
14:29 52
16:34 41
18:38–39 47

2 Kings
19:15 22

2 Chronicles
24:20–22 42

Ezra
1 324

Nehemiah
8:1 41

Psalms
14 52

19:1 .... 21, 84
19:1–6 21
47:7 22
53 52

Proverbs
8 64
30 21
31 22

Isaiah
24:23 251
32:15 130
40–55 324
40:5 52
42:1–4 131
49 .... 19, 187
49:6 .... 19, 187
49:8 187
49:22–23 19
53 .... 73, 325
54:5 22
56:7 256
65:17 329
66:22 113

Jeremiah
7:11 258
29:1–14 23
32:27 22

Ezekiel
36:22–23 22
37 74

Daniel
7 326
7:13–14 326

Joel

2 146
2:28 128

Amos

3:2 22
9:7 22

Zechariah

4:7 251
14:16–17 251

NEW TESTAMENT

Matthew

1:20 .... 19, 77, 87
3:16–17 64
4 324
5:9 333
5:17 230
5:38–41 325
6:28 22
6:30 22
8:10 23
8:11–12 23
10:16–42 186
10:22 161
21:12–13 253
23:35 42
25:13 175
25:31–46 186
28:18–20 .... 19, 327
28:19 .... 64, 131, 269, 276
28:19–20 .... 131, 269, 276

Mark

1:14–15 .... 29, 324
1:15 .... 215, 254
2:5–7 236
3:22–29 253
4:26–34 255
5:1–20 257
7:1–23 253
7:24–8:9 257
8:22–9:29 257
8:31 86
10:32–34 236
10:42–45 327
10:45 96
11–16 86
11:12–14 254
11:15–16 254
11:15–17 246

11:16 257
11:18 259
11:20–21 254
11:27 254
11:28 254
12:35 254
13:5–23 186
16:1–6 236
16:15 217

Luke

1:1–4 44
1:30–38 236
1:33 252
1:35 .... 77, 87
4 .... 29, 324
4:14–21 29
8:13–15 186
9:23 186
10 289
14:25–35 186
18:8 186
19:45–46 253
21:10–19 186
21:28 161
24:44 42
24:51 326

John

1:1 .... 19–20, 88–89,
   106, 216, 236, 240
1:1–14 .... 19–20, 236
1:3 105
1:10 106
1:14 .... 89, 216
2:13–17 253
3:5 .... 77, 130
3:16 .... 269, 324
3:5–8 77

5:17–18 236
5:21–29 236
5:22 236
5:27 236
8:12 50
10:10 276
10:30–33 236
12:31–32 328
13:1–17 327
14:6–10 237
14:11 70
14:12 187
14:20 67
15:18–21 186
16:8 131
17:3 276
17:23 67
18:36 326
19:30 325
20:21 .... 19, 30

Acts

1:1–11 19
1:8 131
1:9 326
2:1–11 19
2:1–41 131
4:1–22 186
4:12 .... 92, 237
4:19–20 240
4:29–31 131
5:12–41 186
6:5 131
6:7 20
6:7–15 186
7:54–8:4 186
7:55 131
8 215
9 215

Index of Scripture

10:1–7 238
10:24–48 238
12:1–18 186
12:11–12 44
12:24 20
12:25 44
13:49–14:7 186
14 .... 22, 186, 231
14:19–20 186
16:16–24 186
16:16–34 186
17 .... 22–23, 237–238
17:1–15 186
17:22–31 237
17:27 238
17:28 238
18:12–17 186
19:20 20
19:23–32 186
19:23–41 186
21:27–36 186
23:12–15 186
27:13–44 186
28:16–31 186

Romans
1 .... 23, 50, 84, 143,
172, 175, 186,
217, 231, 241
1–2 231
1:8 64
1:18–20 50
1:20 84
2–3 23
2:4 276
2:14 21
3:25–26 276
5:9–11 276
7:25 64
8:11 130
8:15 64
8:17 78
8:18–25 20
8:18–30 19
8:22 112

8:24 172
8:26–27 63
8:29 78
9:1–4 188
10:12–15 217
12 .... 143, 186
12:14–21 186
16:27 64

1 Corinthians
1:23–24 192
2:1–5 188
2:2 .... 86, 188
2:10 63
4:9–13 186
8:6 105
11 328
12 .... 123, 143
12:8–10 123
12:11 63
13:12 149
14:33 27
15 .... 44, 64, 85–86,
111
15:3–8 85–86
15:8 44
15:42–43 111
15:57 64

2 Corinthians
1:3–11 186
1:5 .... 187, 189
1:6 187
2:14–15 186
2:14–16 194
2:14–17 186
2:15–16 187
3:18 63
4:7 .... 186, 189
4:7–12 186
4:10 187
4:10–11 187
4:10–12 187
4:12 187
4:16–5:1 275

4:18 276
5:1 .... 92, 99, 116, 188,
329, 332–333, 335
5:6 173
5:14–15 188
5:17 .... 92, 116, 329, 332
5:17–21 332
5:18–20 188
5:19 99
6:1–11 186
6:2 187
6:3 186
6:4–10 186
10:5 217
11:4 .... 189, 193
11:23–12:10 188
11:23–33 186
11:24 188
12:9–10 186
12:10 188
13:4 187–188

Galatians
4:6 64
3:26–29 276
3:28 327
6:15 332
6:17 188

Ephesians
1 .... 65, 77–78,
105, 326
1:3–14 65
1:10 105
1:18 77
1:4–5 78
2:14–16 330–331
2:19 114
3:14–15 75
5 .... 64, 276, 328
5:1–2 276
5:20 64

Philippians
1:12–14 186

2 .... 189, 324, 327, 330
2:1–11 189
2:6–8 324
2:6–9 330
3:7–11 186
3:10 186

Colossians
1:15 .... 19, 27, 47
1:15–20 19
1:16 105
1:17 105
1:19–20 105
1:20 217
1:24 .... 186–187, 189
3:11 217
4:14 44

1 Thessalonians
1:6 186

1 Timothy
4:4 104

2 Timothy
2:3–13 186
3:10–12 186
3:16 .... 21, 49
4:11 44

Philemon
1:24 44

Hebrews
1 .... 19, 23, 47, 92, 105, 276
1–2 92
1:1–2 19
1:1–3 47
1:2 105
1:3 105
4:12–13 20
11:10 276

James
1:2–8 276

1 Peter
1:23 20
1:25 20
1:3–9 276

2 Peter
1:3 56

1 John
1:1–2 240
2 .... 107, 332
2:15 107
4:8 66
4:10–12 276
4:16 76
5:19 107

Revelation
1:17 106
3:14 106
4:8 105
17:12 252
17:14–18 252
21:5 .... 315, 321
22:13 106

Asia Theological Association
54 Scout Madriñan St. Quezon City 1103, Philippines
Email: ataasia@gmail.com Telefax: (632) 410 0312

OUR MISSION

The Asia Theological Association (ATA) is a body of theological institutions, committed to evangelical faith and scholarship, networking together to serve the Church in equipping the people of God for the mission of the Lord Jesus Christ.

OUR COMMITMENT

The ATA is committed to serving its members in the development of evangelical, biblical theology by strengthening interaction, enhancing scholarship, promoting academic excellence, fostering spiritual and ministerial formation and mobilizing resources to fulfill God's global mission within diverse Asian cultures.

OUR TASK

Affirming our mission and commitment, ATA seeks to:

- **Strengthen** interaction through inter-institutional fellowship and programs, regional and continental activities, faculty and student exchange programs.
- **Enhance** scholarship through consultations, workshops, seminars, publications, and research fellowships.
- **Promote** academic excellence through accreditation standards, faculty and curriculum development.
- **Foster** spiritual and ministerial formation by providing mentor models, encouraging the development of ministerial skills and a Christian ethos.
- **Mobilize** resources through library development, information technology and infra-structural development.

To learn more about ATA, visit www.ataasia.com or facebook.com/AsiaTheologicalAssociation

Langham
PARTNERSHIP

Langham Literature and its imprints are a ministry of Langham Partnership.

Langham Partnership is a global fellowship working in pursuit of the vision God entrusted to its founder John Stott –

> *to facilitate the growth of the church in maturity and Christ-likeness through raising the standards of biblical preaching and teaching.*

Our vision is to see churches in the majority world equipped for mission and growing to maturity in Christ through the ministry of pastors and leaders who believe, teach and live by the Word of God.

Our mission is to strengthen the ministry of the Word of God through:
- nurturing national movements for biblical preaching
- fostering the creation and distribution of evangelical literature
- enhancing evangelical theological education

especially in countries where churches are under-resourced.

Our ministry

Langham Preaching partners with national leaders to nurture indigenous biblical preaching movements for pastors and lay preachers all around the world. With the support of a team of trainers from many countries, a multi-level programme of seminars provides practical training, and is followed by a programme for training local facilitators. Local preachers' groups and national and regional networks ensure continuity and ongoing development, seeking to build vigorous movements committed to Bible exposition.

Langham Literature provides majority world preachers, scholars and seminary libraries with evangelical books and electronic resources through publishing and distribution, grants and discounts. The programme also fosters the creation of indigenous evangelical books in many languages, through writer's grants, strengthening local evangelical publishing houses, and investment in major regional literature projects, such as one volume Bible commentaries like *The Africa Bible Commentary* and *The South Asia Bible Commentary*.

Langham Scholars provides financial support for evangelical doctoral students from the majority world so that, when they return home, they may train pastors and other Christian leaders with sound, biblical and theological teaching. This programme equips those who equip others. Langham Scholars also works in partnership with majority world seminaries in strengthening evangelical theological education. A growing number of Langham Scholars study in high quality doctoral programmes in the majority world itself. As well as teaching the next generation of pastors, graduated Langham Scholars exercise significant influence through their writing and leadership.

To learn more about Langham Partnership and the work we do visit **langham.org**